The Physiology and Phenomenology of Action

The Physiology and Phenomenology of Action

Alain Berthoz
Director, Laboratory of Physiology of Perception and Action,
UMR/CNRS, Collège de France, Paris, France

Jean-Luc Petit
Professor of Philosophy, Université de Strasbourg,
Strasbourg, France

translated by

Christopher Macann
Professor of Philosophy

OXFORD
UNIVERSITY PRESS

OXFORD
UNIVERSITY PRESS

Great Clarendon Street, Oxford OX2 6DP

Oxford University Press is a department of the University of Oxford.
It furthers the University's objective of excellence in research, scholarship,
and education by publishing worldwide in

Oxford New York

Auckland Cape Town Dar es Salaam Hong Kong Karachi
Kuala Lumpur Madrid Melbourne Mexico City Nairobi
New Delhi Shanghai Taipei Toronto

With offices in

Argentina Austria Brazil Chile Czech Republic France Greece
Guatemala Hungary Italy Japan Poland Portugal Singapore
South Korea Switzerland Thailand Turkey Ukraine Vietnam

Oxford is a registered trade mark of Oxford University Press
in the UK and in certain other countries

Published in the United States
by Oxford University Press Inc., New York

© Odile Jacob September 2006

The moral rights of the authors have been asserted

Database right Oxford University Press (maker)

First published (French) 2006
First published (English) 2008

British Library Cataloguing in Publication Data

Data available

Library of Congress Cataloging in Publication Data

Data available

Typeset by Cepha Imaging Private Ltd., Bangalore, India
Printed in Great Britain
on acid free paper by
Biddles Ltd., King's Lynn, UK

ISBN 978–0–19–954788–3

10 9 8 7 6 5 4 3 2 1

Preface

This book is intended to make a contribution towards establishing the philosophical foundations for a *physiology of action*. In turn, this requires that we look for a link between certain concepts made use of in philosophy and those operative in a particular field of scientific research, namely, that of a physiology recently transformed by the advent of the neurosciences, on the one hand, and the cognitive sciences, on the other, without forgetting the multiple interconnections between the latter and the social and human sciences.

To try and relate disciplines which tend to be ever more disconnected by virtue of a trend towards specialization has become a particularly important task. For a serious gap has developed between our empirical knowledge of the functioning of the brain, which never ceases to improve, and our still very limited ability to understand (with a view to curing) cognitive dysfunctions. We are already unable to contain major neurological illnesses and psychiatric disorders of the personality. We are therefore likely to remain relatively helpless faced with individual and collective violence, particularly that of fanatics and sectarians of all kinds, if only because the latter cannot be reduced to pure and simple cognitive dysfunctioning, and evoke instead the entire sphere of human relations as well as their history. Even in the field of contemporary science, a rather similar gap has opened up between the remarkable discoveries made in genetics or in molecular biology and the rather slow progress made in the behavioural and social sciences, thereby accentuating the opposition between the local character of our knowledge and the global character of the questions that this knowledge raises. A multi- and inter-disciplinary effort at integrating these different bodies of knowledge has therefore become necessary. If physiology is to remain what Claude Bernard said it was when he called it the 'study of the coordination of the parts with the whole', it will be called upon to play an important role in this integrative process.

Faced with this serious challenge, cooperation between philosophers and physiologists is called for. The fact that in France the medical profession has always maintained a humanist orientation, thereby promoting dialogue between philosophers and physiologists, makes our task easier! Nevertheless, the outcome has proved to be more difficult than anticipated, and for the following reason. For several decades, philosophers in the two principal schools of thought, analytical philosophy on the one side, and phenomenology or hermeneutics on the other, have each adopted a procedure which, however appropriate it might have been for the conceptual analysis of arguments, in the first case, and for the interpretation of works of philosophy from Plato to the present day, in the second, has led them to thematize concepts rather than to interacting intensively with physiology or the neurosciences.

For their part, physiologists employ concepts as pragmatic resources, as tools, as vehicles or symbols, and rarely as objects of sufficient interest to deserve theoretical investigation.[1] Let us take the concept of the brain as our example. The word concept will be employed here in the same epistemological sense as that in which Georges Canguilhem talked of 'the concept of the reflex'.[2] For the physiologist, the brain is a complex unity of anatomical structures, and of connections between these same structures, which regroups them simultaneously or alternatively in a multitude of interconnected circuits, where these structures play the role of relay stations within larger systems devoted to processing brain functions. What interests us here is the *use made by the physiologist* of the word brain when he refers to this brain every time he deals with this or that anatomical structure, or physiological function, as cerebral structures or functions.

For many philosophers the brain only has to be taken account of as a concept, a concept which is no doubt necessary to understand what physiologists are saying. But philosophers are still very far from being ready to admit that the lived experiences and beliefs of human beings have biological correlates. At the very least, the meaning of the word correlate appears to them much less evident than is generally supposed in popular scientific works. 'My brain,' the phenomenologist will say, 'does not enter into my experience of my body. It is only an object for scientific investigation.' In so saying they are simply claiming that no reference to the functioning of the brain is required to carry through a complete phenomenological description of meaningful acts of consciousness; and this because we have no experience of the brain.[3]

---

[1] This observation is not solely aimed at today's researcher, the victim of a pitiless competitive pressure. It is also aimed at a biologist, like Claude Bernard, working at the juncture between Lavoisier and Pasteur. On the vicissitudes surrounding the transition from his concept of 'oxygenation-oxidation' and Pasteur's concept of 'respiration-fermentation', see F. Dagognet (1967) *Méthodes et doctrine dans l'œuvre de Pasteur*, Paris, PUF, pp. 245–250.

[2] G. Canguilhem (1955) *La formation du concept de réflexe aux XVIIe et XVIIIe siècles*, Paris, PUF.

[3] See P. Ricœur (1998) in J.-P. Changeux and P. Ricœur (eds), *Ce qui nous fait penser. La nature et la règle*, Odile Jacob, Paris, p. 64; see also J.-L. Petit (2006) Sur la parole de Ricœur: "Le cerveau ne pense pas. Je pense.", *RHPR* 86(1), 97–109.

In analytical philosophy, one encounters the same kind of reservations concerning the possibility of establishing a direct correlation between statements or concepts and states of the brain.[4] For example, the few references to the brain that arise in conversation, like the one habitually employed to talk about what goes on 'in my head', have been analysed as replacements for non-referential statements. And this in the name of the principle: 'Don't always look for a substance behind a substantive!' In other words, there are expressions employed by the speaker that are used not to say something about something but rather to signal his own position with regard to the utterance of a sentence in a given context of discourse.

Some even choose the extreme position, which consists of denying that there can be any relation between two ontological regions as radically distinct as mind and brain. Happily, and largely thanks to cooperative work inspired by the development of the cognitive sciences in Paris,[5] but also in London, in Italy, in the USA and elsewhere, these doubts and denials are becoming increasingly untenable the more the relevant disciplines interact with each other.

For its own part, physiology has little respect for the concepts of the philosophers, concepts that seem to deal with purely abstract, even *semantic*, and so therefore useless, issues, for the obvious reason that our choice of words

---

4 See L. Wittgenstein (1967) *Zettel*, Basil Blackwell, Oxford; L. Wittgenstein (1980) *Bemerkungen über die Philosophie der Psychologie* I-II, Basil Blackwell, Oxford. On Wittgenstein's position, see S.A. Kripke (1982) *Wittgenstein on rules and private language*, Basil Blackwell, Oxford and also J.-L. Petit (1999) Le langage est-il dans le cerveau? *Intellectica* 2(29), pp. 101–130. See too P.F. Strawson (1959) *Individuals*, Methuen, London; G.E.M. Anscombe (1979) *Intentions*, Basil Blackwell, Oxford; D. Davidson (1980) *Essays on Actions and events*, Clarendon Press, Oxford; H. Putnam (1981) *Reason, Truth and History*, Cambridge University Press, Cambridge; F. Dretske (1995) *Naturalizing the Mind*, MIT Press, Cambridge, MA (to mention only the most important references). The presence at the heart of that school of philosophy called Philosophy of Mind of other tendencies better disposed towards the cognitive sciences does not affect our argument.

5 These interactions were stimulated in France by the crucial colloquium 'Prospects for the Sciences of Cognition' launched in 1991 by the minister Hubert Curien, and whose chairman, at the initiative of the biologist Jean-Pierre Changeux, was Alain Berthoz. These interactions were deeply influenced by a comprehensive overview produced by the neurophysiologist Michel Imbert, in the framework of a European report. In Paris the efforts of a community of philosophers, neurophysiologists, psychologists, mathematicians, computer scientists, linguists, and neuropsychologists, brought together by Michel Imbert from 1980 to 1990 in the DEA of the Cognitive Sciences co-piloted by the EHESS, the University Paris VI, and the Ecole Polytechnique, have brought into being a new generation of researchers and teachers operating at the frontiers of these disciplines. This intellectual movement is currently supported by a master's degree in cognitive science, inspired by Daniel Andler and Emmanuel Dupoux.

changes nothing in the nature of things themselves. Quite spontaneously in fact, the physiologist will say that concepts are useful to him simply as 'tools to describe the reality of facts arising from experimentation or operations employing theoretical models.'

However, when one does get back to these same concepts or theoretical models, no longer just to make use of them simply as 'tools with which to grasp realities' but by treating them as mental frameworks presupposed by the procedure of investigations, they are transformed into analytical grids, organizing schema, *a priori* structures for which the role of language becomes once again quite critical. Conferring this kind of importance upon language in science in turn raises serious questions. In addition to their value as leading to new discoveries, might not these frames of thoughts also exercise a disturbing, even systematically misleading, influence upon the attempt to determine the objects of knowledge? No wonder the scientist hesitates to throw himself into an adventure whose risks he has assessed in advance.[6]

We should not underestimate the difficulty of making this kind of conversion. For the positivist scientist, it calls for an almost violent abrogation of his utopian confidence in the possibility of seeing right through our linguistic expressions to the reality of things and their properties. It requires that we become conscious of the pitfalls language sets for us, of our imprisonment in language. A physiologist asked to raise serious questions with regard to the language of physiology is in rather the same position as Orpheus: turning around brings with it the penalty of losing your Eurydice.

This book cannot therefore pretend to offer a completely worked out theory. At the very most it is a manifesto, a working proposal, an experience for those interested in the questions we find ourselves confronted with. This is why it is important to clarify the way in which this book came about.

The principal aim of this book is to confront the kinaesthetic theory developed by the philosopher Edmund Husserl (as per his published work but also his still unpublished manuscript material) with recent theories and discoveries in the field of the physiology of perception and of action.

The approach we adopted was the following: Jean-Luc Petit, a specialist in the philosophy of Husserl and who wanted to put phenomenology to work as a tool for examining the presuppositions underlying the work of the empirical researcher, wrote out a number of texts which he then presented to the physiologist, Alain Berthoz, for critical review. Our discussions took place in a series of

---

[6] Certain of our colleagues, like J.-P. Changeux and P. Ricœur (see above), or again M. Jeannerod and P. Jacob (*Ways of Seeing*, Oxford, Oxford University Press, 2003), have become involved in this development through cooperative publications.

meetings from September 2000 to August 2003, over a three-year period through which Jean-Luc Petit was transferred from the Marc-Bloch University in Strasbourg to the Laboratory of the Physiology of Perception and Action (LPPA) at the Collège de France, a transfer authorized by the French government research center (CNRS). They were recorded, transcribed, and rewritten in a ceaseless shuttle between us, an exchange further prolonged into the English version by Dr Christopher McCann. So the book really emerged out of the drafts produced by a philosopher. But these drafts were themselves developed out of a collaboration going back some ten years (first at the University of Strasbourg where, from 1993, J.-L. Petit organized an interdisciplinary workshop on the Philosophy of Action[7] and then later at LPPA-Collège de France), a collaboration which resulted in seminars, articles[8] (some co-authored),[9] theoretical debates, scientific workshops for students and researchers in the cognitive sciences, etc.

This confrontation should have resulted in a book presented in the classic form of a dialogue. We decided to try and bring together the two facets of its construction into one text, at the risk of covering over the disagreements and the debates that have gone on between us. Not that, in our view, the divergences are that negligible, but because it has seemed to us more important to try and capture what emerged in the most fruitful moments of our dialogue as the shared intuition of a *physiology of action capable of drawing its basic notions from phenomenology* rather than the predictable communication of this or that 'ideological position'. But the pedagogical benefits of a continuous text will not have to be paid for at the cost of a deliberate concealment of the difference between our respective positions, because our respective enquires have never failed to make known our differences.

Obviously, the physiologist has not become a philosopher and vice versa. But we shall both be at fault if the reader is not able to grasp nor to appreciate either the philosophical or the physiological aspects of the problems addressed! Our aim is therefore to make it possible for any reader who has the patience to follow the analyses step by step to clearly comprehend the importance of the kinaesthetic theory of action. We hope that our book will provide such a reader with new and nourishing food for thought.[10]

....

7 See the summaries of the presentations at these workshops at www.chez.com/jlpetit.

8 See J-L Petit's website (www.chez.com/jlpetit) for a bibliography and articles that can be downloaded.

9 A. Berthoz and J.-L. Petit (2003) Nouvelles propositions pour une physiologie de l'action, in J.-L. Petit (ed.), *Repenser le corps, l'action et la cognition avec les neurosciences*, *Intellectica* 1–2(36–37), 367–372; reproduced in J.-M. Barbier and M. Durand (eds) (2006) *Sujets, activités, environnements. Approches transverses*, PUF, Paris, pp. 253–259.

10 J.-P. Changeux and A. Connes (1989) *Matière à pensée*, Odile Jacob, Paris.

Contents

Chapter 1

Representation versus action

Act and action

Today we are witnessing a breakdown of our scientific discourse on mind and brain into a multitude of disciplines, a plurality of models and levels of approach or explanations. No wonder the plural has been adopted to describe this situation: 'the cognitive sciences' or 'the sciences of cognition'. The same holds at the level of the leading ideas for the cognitive sciences. We are going to claim that the brain is essentially an organ for action, whereas others hold that, on the contrary, the brain is an organ of representation. Many have concluded that the basic division is between those who hold the view of representation for action, and those who hold the contrary view, of action for representation.

We shall first define what we mean by action. Underlying the concept of action there is an even more essential concept: that of the act. 'An act, in the true sense of the word, is a spontaneous creation which initiates a sequence through which behaviour is qualitatively modified' (Merleau-Ponty[1]). When the mathematician Poincaré[2] said: 'imagining a point in space is imagining the movement that is needed to attain it', he was not just defining a point in terms of a displacement. He was referring to a complete act, an act brought about by someone equipped with muscles whenever this same individual intends to reach this point and realizes his intention with the effort required to attain his goal. He also wanted to take account of the displacement of attention from the point where I am to the point that has become my goal. And when Einstein wrote: 'Poincaré was right, the foundations of geometry are to be found in sensible experience', he meant by this word *experience* the totality of relations between the world and the subject who acts and perceives. The primacy of the act over language was also mentioned by Goethe when he has Faustus say: 'In the beginning was not the verb, nor the force, but the act'. What we want to

---

[1] M. Merleau-Ponty (1942/2002) *La structure du comportement*, PUF, Paris, p. 105.

[2] H. Poincaré (1902) *La Science et l'Hypothèse*, Flammarion, Paris, Chap. IV; H. Poincaré (1905) *La Valeur de la Science*, Flammarion, Paris, Chap. III; H. Poincaré (1908) *Science et Méthode*, Flammarion, Paris.

uphold are the intuitions of the aforementioned great mathematicians, who were perfectly capable of highly abstract formal thought. In *Krisis*, Husserl tied down to phenomenological evidence what the words of the poet left in a mythical religious nimbus: 'The true beginning is the act itself, it alone is capable of revealing the possibility at work within reality'.[3] In a related context it has been shown recently that reason does not function without emotion; for, as Ribot noted, it too is 'motion', that is, yet again, an act.

All these references can be arranged along a single axis relating the *act*, in Aristotle's sense, to the *act* in Husserl's sense. In order to resolve some of the difficulties Greek thought encountered in dealing with movement, Aristotle introduced his triple distinction between the subject qua 'substance' (ὑποκεί-μενον), its 'potential' (δύναμις), and its actual being, that is, its being 'in act' (ἐνέργεια -ἐντελέχεια). Thanks to this distinction, it was no longer necessary to kill Clinias,[4] a young ignorant student who wanted to follow the master's teaching, in order to have him pass from being ignorant (which he was initially) to becoming knowledgeable (which he was not at that time). It was enough that this same Clinias (as permanent subject) should be potentially (as a rational being) what he was not actually: namely knowledgeable.[5]

Husserl introduced the notion of *intentional act* to resolve difficulties with regard to the double status of mental abilities, both biologically implemented in the head and nevertheless standing in relation to objects existing in the world. Perception is not just a mental state (not even a vector of the 'representational content' of such a mental state). For perception bears within it an as-yet-empty but already fully articulated claim. The articulation of this perceptual claim is conferred upon the intentional act by the fact that it is a directed act (*noesis*), an act directed towards an object which is the aim of the act (*noema*). This is what is known in phenomenology as the noetic-noematic correlation. As the target of what is aimed at, the direction of the intentional aim is prescribed in advance by the perceived object. This perceived object is

---

[3] E. Husserl (1976) *Ideen zu einer reinen Phänomenologie und phänomenologischen Philosophie, Erstes Buch: Allgemeine Einführung in die reine Phänomenologie*, Hrsg. v. K. Schuhmann, Martinus Nijhoff, Husserliana III/1, LVI–LVII.

[4] Socrates offers this ironic suggestion in Plato's dialogue, *Euthydemus* (283 d) with reference to the naive young man who wanted to follow the teaching of a sophist.

[5] See P. Aubenque (1966) *Le Problème de l'être chez Aristote*, PUF, Paris, pp. 412–484 and also J.-L. Petit (2005) Quelques apories (anciennes et modernes) du mouvement dans les neurosciences, in E. Végléris (ed.), *Cosmos et Psychè. Mélanges offerts à Jean Frère*, Georg Olms, Hildesheim, pp. 355–377.

then as much 'in the head' (where it features as a component of the perceptual act: its *noema*) as it is 'in the world' (where it features as an element emerging within the horizon of the perceived world).[6]

In his recent book on Spinoza, the neurologist Damasio,[7] who has greatly contributed to the reintroduction of the role of emotion and bodily action into cognitive functions, saw in Spinoza a precursor of such modern theories as those that now take account of the fundamental role of the body in higher cognitive operations. However, he failed to do justice to Spinoza's conception of the body as a capacity for action: a capacity which can increase or diminish but which, within the limits it sets itself, is that of a being who ceaselessly tries to 'persevere in its being'[8] (to ensure its preservation). For all that, 'the body in act' is not an expression employed by Spinoza, even though one does come across the expression 'idea of the body existing in act'[9] (that is the *actually* existing body). This is a definition that has little to do with the dynamic aspect of the body inasmuch as it is oriented towards action.[10]

Action was, for Spinoza, an 'affection' of our body and such that we are ourselves the sole cause of this affection.[11] Affections that stem from other causes he called passions. Despite the limitations of this traditional conception, his concept of the body is certainly not the sort of passive body Descartes had in mind when he talked of the body as an extended thing. As a result of failing to appreciate the significance of this concept of the body, Damasio is led to restrict the role of emotion to the maintenance of an equilibrium, a homeostasis of the body, whereas in fact emotion is a tool developed in the course of evolution to enable us to prepare the future, to organize action as a function of past experience.[12]

---

[6] A paradox the theory of constitution will be able to resolve: see Chapters 5 and 6 in this volume.

[7] A.R. Damasio (2003) *Spinoza avait raison*, Odile Jacob, Paris.

[8] B. Spinoza (1954) Ethique, II, Propositions VI and VII, *Œuvres Complètes de Spinoza*, Gallimard, Paris.

[9] B. Spinoza (1954) Ethique, II, Proposition XI, *Œuvres Complètes de Spinoza*, Gallimard, Paris.

[10] For the metaphysics of classical rationalism, 'act' evokes much less action as the perfection of an actuality that has exhausted all its latent possibilities by realizing them in states of affairs effectively produced. And which in consequence no longer harbours that dynamic element stemming from a virtuality still awaiting realization. We have lost sight of such a concept of the act.

[11] More exactly, the adequate cause; that is, a cause such that we can have a clear and distinct idea of the effect produced by us, and which is precisely not usually the case in human action (*Ethics*, III, Definitions I, II, III).

[12] A. Berthoz (2004) *La décision*, Odile Jacob, Paris.

A logician might argue that what is described as action could, without any objection on his part, be re-described as representation, since these two concepts are not contradictory in themselves, even if propositions expressed by means of statements constructed on the basis of these concepts turn out to be contradictory. In addition, the empirical task of implanting micro-electrodes in neurons or the construction of a histogram of action potentials would not be greatly altered by this change of terminology. But this would not change our basic conviction because the choice between a physiology of action and a physiology of representation is a philosophical and not a technical choice. We want to get away from the metaphor of the brain as a representational or calculating machine. We want to get back to the age-old intuition of the living as act, and we want to demonstrate the fruitfulness of such a notion with empirical and theoretical suggestions.

The cogito of the physiologist and mimetic pragmatics

Even if it might be taken as a caricature, the behaviour of one of us (A.B.), who is a physiologist, could be cited as an example of the importance of the act of live thinking. When explaining facts and theories, he gets up from his chair and, in order to explain locomotion, orientation, change of point of view, etc., makes himself understood by acting. It is as if he feels that in remaining seated and inviting his audience to take account of objects of purely theoretical import he would be instilling in himself, and in his auditors, forgetfulness of their common *posture*. At one stroke, by moving his body, he becomes once again the agent he never should have stopped being, the agent who moves and who, in moving, moves himself and also his audience, an audience composed of agents just like himself.

We should not underestimate the philosophical bearing of the *behaviour* adopted by the physiologist. In fact he is recreating the Socratic method, which obliges the disciple to become his own master by putting himself to the test, or even the pre-Socratic method: that of the sage who said nothing but who restricted himself to simply wagging the tip of his finger and so, by the simple exhibition of this movement, refuted all the logical sophisms constructed to deny its existence. The wisdom and the power of the gesture reminds us of the *kathakali* theatre of Kerala![13]

The physiologist is not in fact satisfied with constructing mathematical models, as if the objects of his research were some kind of a physical system.

---

[13] A. Berthoz (1997) *Le sens du mouvement*, Odile Jacob, Paris; published in English as A. Berthoz (2000) *The Brain's Sense of Movement*, Harvard University Press, Cambridge, MA, p. 205.

He regards his task as incomplete just as long as he has not raised the level of all this model building to that of the '*cogito* of the physiologist'. How does the *cogito* get into all this? The Descartes of the *Philosophical Meditations* sought in his reader a subject capable of constituting itself as a thinking being by the very fact of carrying through, for him or herself, the 'I think'. For, as analytical philosophy finally concluded (without however going back over its traditional anti-Cartesianism), the cogito is an act that each of us actually carries through in the course of uttering it: a performative utterance.[14]

In the same way, the physiologist invites the reader to carry through for him or herself the *corporeal cogito*, a cogito that activates, in his brain, the relevant networks of action and the relevant *mental simulation of movement*; that is, the simulation of the movement one wants to make (or refrain from doing), that one is prepared to carry out or that one observes someone else carrying out. Such a reminder is not just relevant for philosophy and the cognitive sciences. For even in the world of theatre the primacy of the word has depleted the power of the body, a body whose emotions are expressed in actions. Only recently was the importance of bodily expressions of the dramas and joys of life, fundamental in the work of the great Russian stage leaders like Meyerhold[15] and the Asian tradition of Kabuki, No, or Katakali, recognized in the teaching of someone like Jacques Lecoq[16] in his school, and the same holds for Grotowski[17] and Ariane Mnouchkine,[18] over and beyond the *commèdia dell'arte*.

Harking back to the advice offered by the theoreticians of rhetoric and the gestural tradition, the orator-professor-actor practises this gestural thinking.

---

14 J.L. Austin (1955/1962) *How To Do Things With Words*, Oxford University Press, Oxford; J.R. Searle (1969) *Speech Acts*, Cambridge University Press, Cambridge.

15 B. Picon-Vallin (1990) *Meyerhold. Les voies de la création théâtrale*, vol. XVII, Eds du CNRS, Paris.

16 Jacques Lecoq started an acting school in Paris which trained a number of very great actors on an international scale. This school continues its work under the direction of Fay Lecoq. Some aspects of the teaching of Fay Lecoq can be found in *Le Corps Poétique – Un enseignement de la création théâtrale* (1997), in collaboration with J.-G. Carasso and J.-C. Lallias, Arles, Actes Sud; *Le Théâtre du Geste, mimes et acteurs, ouvrage collectif sous la direction de J. Lecoq* (1987), Bordas, Paris; see also M. Bourhis (1999) J. Lecoq, Les lois de mouvement, *Registres* no. 4.

17 Grotowski was a director who pleaded for a 'poor theatre' where bodily expression would play a major part. He created the first chair of theatre at the Collège de France. J. Grotowski (1971) *Vers un théâtre pauvre*, L'âge d'homme, Lausanne.

18 Ariane Mnouchkine is director of Théâtre du Soleil in Paris. Her work in stage setting is founded on integrating into the actor's performing skill certain oriental traditions which recognize the importance of the sensible body over and above the vocalizing of the text. A. Mnouchkine (2005) *L'Art du Présent. Entretiens avec Fabienne Pascaud*, Plon, Paris.

Why? Because he thinks that only the production of this personal effort could give to the totality of the mechanisms involved in moving (and not just in movement but also in perception and cognition) the meaning of a reality lived out from within. The putting into practice of these mechanisms derives its meaning from the personal situation of someone confronted with circumstances and with his own biographical context.

As a result of this invitation to reproduce the process by which the incarnate subject constitutes himself, each exercise of this physiology of everyday life is a new occasion. The same physiologist, when he wants to explain the brain mechanisms involved in spatial memory and, for example, those which allow us to memorize our journeys, demands of those present at the lecture: 'reproduce in thought the route you take to get to your home from your office'. This is not a matter of adopting complicated protocols of measurement nor of assigning artificially impoverished tasks making possible the recording and control of significant variables in the laboratory. What is at stake is of philosophical, more exactly, *hermeneutical*, interest. All that matters, for a correct interpretation of the facts, is that each subject should be capable of carrying through the action and that, in so doing, be able to freely recruit the brain structures whose activation conditions the realization (actual or virtual) of the behaviour in question.

To prevent these examples from appearing trivial, it is worth mentioning the commentary of the geometrician, Bernard Tessier, during a conference at the Collège de France on the cognitive foundations of geometry. He conceded that sometimes a simple gesture on the blackboard made it easier for him to explain a concept to a mathematical colleague, a concept the mathematical symbol was unable to illustrate. All the same, having made this important concession, he then went on to downplay its importance by commenting: '*my* primate brain explained the concept with a gesture to *his* primate brain'. He was ready to admit the usefulness of the gesture, but only on condition that it was reduced to an affair of his primate brain and not his mathematical brain!

He did however write: 'Poincaré said that our perception of a point in space was our perception of the gesture needed to attain it . . . .. I propose that the mathematical line be treated as the result of an identification of the visual line with the vestibular line, and by way of what I am going to call the Poincaré–Berthoz isomorphism. This isomorphism says that we can represent our walking by a movement along the visual line, and reciprocally, we can imagine ourselves walking along a visual line to get from one point to another (what Einstein always claimed was one of the basic principles of intuition)'.[19]

[19] B. Teissier (2005) Protomathematics. Perception and the meaning of mathematical objects, in P. Grialou, G. Longo and M. Okada (eds), *Images and Reasoning*, Keio University Press, Tokyo, p. 137.

The logician Giuseppe Longo has this to say about the anchoring of concepts, even the most sophisticated concepts, in action: 'In sum, it could well be that the first conceptual invariants arose as developments (complex developments constituted across procedures of human communication) from original gestures which were fundamental for space and action in space.'[20]

To react against the excessive intellectualism that has put the cognitive sciences at a distance from the spirit of physiology is also to promote the revival of a *philosophy of experience*. In order to enable the notion of the act to replace that of representation in our conception of the mental world, it is important to reintroduce the idea of lived experience. To illustrate what we mean by lived experience, we encourage the reader to recall mentally some lived experiences. For instance, the well-known ambiguity of perception induced when we touch one hand with the other: 'with one hand I touch my other hand which, from being passively touched can in turn become a touching hand.' Or also 'I live through the movements of the acrobat's body on his wire not as a distant spectacle but as if I was myself in his body.' Or this remarkable extension of our perceived body: 'I grab a hammer and in place of the tactile sensation of the palm of my hand in contact with the handle, I experience the prolongation of my own body through the instrument.' Another example of this kind of extension: 'I climb into my car and as soon as I start driving I feel myself incorporated into it.' Or again, this nightmare of a city dweller seized by panic in the corridor of a metro in which he has lost his way: 'Oh to be outside with the earth under my feet, the blue sky above me, looking across an empty space framed by mountains or by the sea!' The reader can complete the list. These are some of the favourite examples of Husserl, popularized by Merleau-Ponty, of Theodor Lipps, popularized by Max Scheler, or even of Heidegger.

Philosophy of experience or philosophy of language?

That today we have to make a special effort to get back to the apparently simple and evident idea that *thinking is rooted in experience* is most probably a symptom of the venerable age of the profession of philosophy. For too many of our colleagues, the task of the philosopher is an exclusively theoretical task, one bearing solely upon theoretical elements, one which starts out from a theory and remains within a theory: in a word, a purely *intra-theoretical* task. In this sense it is obvious that philosophy remains poles apart from physiology.

---

[20] G. Longo (2005) The cognitive foundations of mathematics: human gestures in proof and mathematical incompleteness of formalisms, in P. Grialou, G. Longo and M. Okada (eds), *Images and Reasoning*, Keio University Press, Tokyo, p. 130. See also G. Chatelet (1993), *Les enjeux du mobile*, Seuil, Paris.

We have to get back to the spirit of a *philosophy of experience*. In so doing we will be struck by the affinities between philosophy and physiology. Our behaviour is quite different from that of analytical philosophy which basically, and despite the genuine interest it has shown recently for the neurosciences, often remains enclosed within the frontiers of language and logic. Although it is true that many different schools have modified the initial ideas of analytical philosophy, many authors still condemn as sheer naivety the belief we support that *philosophical theory can only be justified in the light of a more primordial experience which is not itself a theoretical matter*. Remember that Einstein himself said we had forgotten that the axioms of geometry are based on 'sensible *experience*'. This ultimate reference to experience is said, by some, to be pointless, because any experience is already saturated with ineliminable theoretical elements.

According to this interpretation, which takes the place of common sense, Descartes is definitely dead and buried. However he, Descartes, did not envisage the cogito as an incomplete syllogistic formula (an enthymeme) nor as a linguistic statement. He carried it out and wanted it to be carried out as an act unfolding in the context of a complete experience of thinking, an experience that cannot be communicated nor even described. For what would be the point of describing it to someone who ('at least once in his life,' Descartes insists) had not experienced the need to carry through this act for himself?

This philosophical approach remains imprisoned in the domain of concepts without being able to appropriate the act in question. And we must insist upon the fact that we are not talking about a simple sensori-motor mechanism but about a complete act, with its intentional directedness, as defined hereafter.

The philosophy that physiology needs is the very opposite of the above: that is, a philosophy that has rid itself of the constraints of linguistic analysis, freed itself from the referential *impedimenta* of the history of texts and which has re-discovered the meaning of an originary thinking. Experience is not meaningful simply because it is composed of elements corresponding to the propositions or propositional attitudes employed to give expression to it. Propositional attitudes, the attitudes a mind can adopt towards the proposition expressed by a statement p – 'I think that p', 'I want p' – do not encompass all the mental activities represented in human experience.

In analytical philosophy, it is often taken for granted[21] that any state of mind is either a desire or a belief or a combination of the two (although perhaps for an exception that certain philosophers[22] have timidly proposed recently,

---

[21] See D. Davidson (1980) *Actions and Events*, Clarendon Press, Oxford.

[22] A.R. Mele (1992) *Springs of Action*, Oxford University Press, Oxford. See also A.R. Mele (1995) *Autonomous Agents. From Self-control to Agency*, Oxford University Press, Oxford.

and which bears upon *expressions of intentions* which cannot be treated either as desires or as beliefs). For all that, our experience is meaningful in virtue of the complexity of its pre-linguistic organization. To this already complex initial organization, the linguistic organization only serves to add another layer, without which it would never have been possible to pass from experience to expression and the objectification of meaning in a form of words, which of course then facilitates its conscious recovery through thematic reflection, etc.[23]

Making language the unifying factor in the organization of 'perceptual modules' may have some relevance when it comes to a certain class of cognitive processes of a highly advanced level. When visiting Venice, one of us found himself completely disoriented in front of a huge painting covering an entire wall upon which horses, persons, boats, etc. were mixed together in an inextricable tangle. The dispersion of the attention of the spectator about these diverse juxtaposed fragments had the effect of disorganizing his thinking. However, it was enough to read the legend of the painting giving the general meaning of the scene (a famous battle) to induce an immediate coherence in the perception. So language certainly can be useful in organizing perception, just as we can use memory to help us retrace our steps to our hotel in an unfamiliar town. So we are not denying the place of language in the organization of thinking, which would be to expose oneself to ridicule.

On the other hand, to pretend that language is the only tool capable of ensuring the coherence of perception[24] is an absurdity. The monkey does not speak; but that does not prevent it from organizing its perceptions, without which it could not leap from branch to branch. We will come back to the role of non-verbal communicative processes in Chapter 8 on inter-subjectivity. In particular, we will make use of the recent discovery by Jacqueline Nadel, of the ability of autistic children to communicate by way of shared action.

What we want to insist upon is that our perceptual grasp of the world is *originally* anchored in action. And from there it is indeed tempting to conclude that language itself must be anchored in action. This idea was developed elegantly by Lashley[25] and his theory has been put back on the table recently.[26]

....

[23] E. Husserl (1913/1968), *Logische Untersuchungen*, I. Ausdruck und Bedeutung, Max Niemeyer, Tübingen.

[24] As has been proposed by E. Spelke (2003) What make us smart? Core knowledge and natural language, in D. Gentner and S. Goldin-Meadow (eds), *Language and Mind: Advances in the Study of Language and Thought*, MIT Press, Cambridge, MA, pp. 277–311.

[25] K.S. Lashley (1951) The problem of serial order in behavior, in L.A. Jeffress (ed.), *Cerebral Mechanisms in Behavior*, Wiley, New York, pp. 112–146.

[26] G. Rizzolatti and M. Arbib (1998), Language in our grasp, *Trends Neurosci* 21(5), 188–194.

Analytical philosophy of action, which has committed itself to describing action exclusively from the standpoint of what can be said about it, seems to us to underestimate this underlying complexity by concentrating upon the level of the grammatical (or semantic) organization of meaning. But let us now get back to the link between philosophy and physiology, with a view to reaching the solid ground of experience, the ground upon which William James, Bergson, Husserl, and Merleau-Ponty never failed to take their stand.[27]

False representational models

We are still living in the aftermath of peripheralism,[28] which, in certain respects, proved to be very fruitful in establishing the foundations of experimental psychology. James' theory reintroduced the sensible body as the origin of emotive feeling. He claimed for example that being afraid was a matter of running away and was the result of experiencing the physiological and vegetative reactions to the fearful situation and not the contrary. Hence the famous short expression: 'I am afraid because I run away'. Lately these ideas have been brilliantly taken up again and developed by Damasio.[29] This on-going influence combines with that of analytical behaviourism,[30] the doctrine initially embraced by the analysis of

---

[27] From an experiential standpoint one might be tempted to say that the most direct solution for the philosopher would be to reject any intellectualist restriction upon thought, and to rejoin the physiologist on the empirical field which is his professional preoccupation. But the question is more complicated. It is not just that calling a model-bound and computational science like contemporary neurophysiology 'empirical' is already an abuse of language, a part of its experience depends on the calculation time of computers which rely upon dynamic models for simulating neuronal networks. It is not a matter of changing professions but of inducing in this profession a new awareness. The philosopher of today seems to us too ready to accept a pale substitute for experience. Leaving physical experience to the empirical sciences we have fallen back upon the kind of 'thought experiments' in which armchair philosophy likes to indulge, incorrectly convinced that nothing is lost just as long as we keep what is essential, the noblest part, the experience of a Galileo with his continuous frictionless planes and of an Einstein with his virtual elevators. This situation could only satisfy those who, from the first, have reduced their requirements to the minimum. Pointing out these inadequacies should be enough to bring us back to the more substantial experience of the thinkers we have mentioned.

[28] Peripheralism: a conception of behaviour according to which the organism has no information about the realization of motor action except that coming to it through the sensation of the movement of its limbs. The opposite conception (centralism) admits the possibility of the organism having direct access to its own motor initiatives.

[29] A. Damasio (1994) *Descartes' Error. Emotion, Reason and the Human Brain*, A. Grosset/Putnam Books, New York.

[30] Analytical behaviourism, the philosophical analysis of concepts of action, was developed in the 1970s and 1980s by authors influenced by the philosopher W.V.O. Quine, who

concepts of action within the horizon of analytical philosophy. These approaches nevertheless leave unanswered the question concerning the projective, the intentional or the *top-down* character (as the neurophysiologists are used to saying) of action itself, with its anchorage in the sensible body.

When the so-called cognitive revolution taught us that sentences and propositions did not float in the air but were carried by mental representations in our heads, a discovery which happily lent credence to the recuperation by cognitive psychology of the propositional analysis undertaken by analytical philosophers, nothing changed. For certain representationalists, actions are only environmental or corporeal events corresponding to these actions. Cognition consists of forming a representation of these events in our minds. And why should we form such internal representations? Because we are cognitive systems coupled to rational agents and because, in consequence, our only objective is to explain things and events, and above all actions. With regard to non-human physical events, we develop representations which are nothing less than the laws of Nature. With regard to human actions, what we develop in our minds are maxims of conduct, personal preferences or universal values, which furnish practical reason with premises from which it is able to deduce what to do.

Other representationalists, annoyed at having to get rid of what cannot be reduced to movement plus representation, want to hold on to what remains unformed prior to movement, what is inarticulate prior to expression,[31] by trying to make room for certain 'motor representations'[32] alongside corporeal movements and verbal representations. But they failed to convince. Their efforts proved unconvincing because, so far from preceding movement, these representations succeeded the movement they were supposed to represent, and which had to have already taken place in order to be represented. One of the difficulties facing physiology and the philosophy of anticipation is that of accounting for both what precedes and what succeeds action. The concept

....

thought that the only truly scientific psychology was that which limited itself to the study of the external aspects of behaviour, in the manner of B.F. Skinner.

[31] Verbs that express the beginning of an action are called inchoate: to leave means to take one's leave.

[32] 'By virtue of the constitution of our nervous system, we are beings whose present impressions are prolonged into appropriate movements', said Bergson (who himself referred to Ribot) in *Matter and Memory*. Wanting, no doubt, to reinsert this dynamism into the mental representations of cognitive psychology, M. Jeannerod fused the concepts of representation and action: 'we consider representation and action as one and the same thing in the sense that action is a modality of representation and inversely, representation a modality of action' (M. Jeannerod (2002) *La nature de l'esprit*, Odile Jacob, Paris, p. 84).

of simulation (or emulation)[33] was introduced to deal with this difficulty without ever really solving the problem.

A curious impression of over-exposed photography followed from this constraint imposed upon action to make it fit into the category of 'representation'. For some, a representation only covers what can be described in the propositional content of a sentence, and which must therefore be a fact or a state of affairs, the eventual content of a state of mind. For others, representation and action have to be brought together, not only made compatible with each other but even fused together, so to speak, and this by taking account of the non-verbal and dynamic character of action.

By applying this representational filter, everything in the external as well as in the internal world appears frozen, fixed, and stabilized by the projection of the propositional form, which implicitly structures representation. Everything that comes to mind is a mental state that only exists as a representation. Without deviating from the same ideal of objectivity, the cognitive theoretician treats mental states as the physicist treats physical systems, even though his theories lack the compelling power of the dynamic theories of modern physics.

Getting back to the inchoate

The basic idea behind this chapter—let us insist on this in case we have not already made it clear enough—is a critique of the general prejudice (one that has extended its sway from the natural sciences right up to the sciences of cognition) in favour of 'actuality'; that is, of the conclusive phase of complete realization, the phase in which all the potentialities of an act have been exhausted: the act as fact. If we really want to take account of the act as such in the physiology of action, we will have to move on from a science of the stabilized state of affairs, of what has been done, to a science of process, of what is being done. In other words, a shift from the perfect tense expressing a completed action: the fact, to the gerundive expressing what has still to be done. This theme is certainly familiar to philosophers (since James, Bergson, Whitehead, Husserl, Merleau-Ponty, etc.). But it has not, for all that, lost its importance for common sense and positive science. What we are trying to do is to solicit this theme in connection with the sciences of cognition. This is what is at stake in a physiology of action that tries to adopt a new approach to the living: to promote an alternative to the actualist dogma in science. And this by according to the inactual the place it merits in an act as an initial and essential component of the act.

---

[33] A. Berthoz (2000) *The Brain's Sense of Movement*, Harvard University Press, Cambridge, MA; M. Jeannerod, etc.

One of the major difficulties for a theory of action that seeks to appropriate experience is that action is possible only if everything is *not already actual*. So we have to look for 'the inchoate'; that is, the precursory and incipient phase of each and every act of action or of perception, and treat it as being of no less importance than the fully-fledged realization of that act. Here is a simple example that can be described easily, even if it is limited to motor anticipation and so falls short of the generality of the concept of inchoation: when I take hold of a cup of coffee, there is a phase which necessarily precedes this act. In that phase, many essential aspects of the action are gathered together and put into place. So, the action is already there, despite the fact that nothing has yet been done. One of the challenges confronting the physiology of action is therefore that of getting back to the meaning of the inchoate. In order to do that, what is needed is a philosophy of anticipation, something for which the practice of the physical sciences[34] has hardly prepared us. Today it is in the field of robotics and artificial intelligence that the greatest effort is being made in this direction.

The fact that the sciences of physical matter would prefer a world dispossessed of potentialities and reduced to mere actualities is all the more understandable the more we stick to classical (or even relativistic) mechanics

---

[34] It is impossible to place an action, for example, in the space-time of Einstein's theory of relativity. In fact, this system of representation is conceived to represent exhaustively, and in an a-temporal fashion, every event: those that are linked by causal influences (whose limit transmission is the speed of light) as well as those which neither exert nor are subject to any causal influence. For each given 'event' (each instantaneous point) P in this space a double cone of light centred on P contains in an a-temporal way: (1) all events related among themselves by virtue of the fact that they exert a causal influence on P and (2) all the events related among themselves by virtue of the fact that P exerts a causal influence on them. Outside this light cone there still remain those events that have no causal relationship with P. However, these events, in turn, are to be found at the centre of a double cone of light of all those events in a causal relationship with them. And so on. In order to be able to include all events in this system of representation it was necessary to recur to a speculative fiction, which consists of imagining these events as all being actualized in the same way in advance. A fiction of this kind—presupposing the framework of the Cartesian reduction of being to the being-extended of physical matter—eliminates the entire potential aspect of concrete experience. This does not present a problem for physics as a particular scientific discipline, for the theory of relativity was conceived to resolve precise physical problems. It was never intended to be a theory of everything. It would also, for precisely this reason, be pointless to try and introduce action into such a universe. For actions, in so far as they imply anticipation, preparation, and effort are precisely not instantaneous event points but unfold across a certain duration and a certain spatial extension. For a fairly accessible account, see H. Reichenbach (1958) *The Philosophy of Space and Time*, Dover, New York, Chap. III, pp. 151–228; see also R. Penrose (1994) *Shadows of the Mind. A Search for the Missing Science of Consciousness*, Oxford University Press, Oxford.

as the paradigm for our scientific view of the world. But the same prejudice straddles the physical–cognitive divide. Thus, on the logical, and therefore no longer physical, plane, although in an analogous way, in his *Tractatus Logico-philosophicus* Wittgenstein has the transcendental subject see all the facts but without doing anything himself. Since all the facts cannot be but already out there in the world, no space is left for an action, with the depressing consequence that the subject of cognition is totally powerless to act. And this for the sole reason—a purely logical reason founded in the constraints of exact determination of the 'truth-bearers' of meaningful propositional discourse—that he cannot add one single fact to 'what is the case'; that is, to the closed totality of the facts corresponding to the truth of all the propositions of science.[35] From such a logically frozen world of facts to the cognitively frozen mind of mental representations, there is only one step: the subject of the *Tractatus* is a mind inhabited by the representations so dear to certain theoreticians of cognition, a mind turned in on itself. Rather than fixing its gaze on the facts of the world, the subject is focused on mere representations. All mental states are already there, peacefully juxtaposed along the one and only homogeneous plane of 'Mind'. Nothing inchoate: no action.

What escapes such a view of things is experience, lived out as the shock of the world appearing in its overwhelming plenitude of potentialities. To illustrate the inchoative character of perception, let us imagine that we are standing in front of the window at dawn. The sun-lit landscape can hardly be described as being there already complete in itself and waiting for us to represent it in our minds, any more than we ourselves can be described as having a representation of it. Rather, it actively *presents* itself, is *given* for the first time. And in contemplating it we participate in that activity, in so far as we actively contribute to deploying, detailing and ordering the scenery. In so doing we also constitute it for ourselves for the first time, so to speak, and this by bringing into play the resources of our organs of perception and of our bodily movements. One of the central theses of phenomenology is to be found in this affirmation of the active contribution of the perceiver to the very sense of being of the world perceived, an affirmation that physiology has been confirming through experimentation.

What is underestimated by theoreticians who interpret perception as the introjection of what is external or the projection upon the external of internal representations is the fundamental unity of perception-and-action, a unity responsible for the centrality of inchoation in the cognition of an acting subject.

---

[35] For an analysis of this logical powerlessness of the will and the role it has been able to play as a motivating factor in the analytical theory of action, see J.-L. Petit (1991) *L'action dans la philosophie analytique*, PUF, Paris, pp. 25–43.

In consequence, they tend to import into the unitary character of perception what might be called a crypto-dualism:

- dualism and repetition in space: there are physical things outside of us, mental representations inside;
- dualism and repetition in time: the retinal stimulus comes first and then comes the percept, or first the (memory) image and then the (really perceived) thing;
- dualism and repetition in the causal order: first comes the cause (a physical event or state of the brain) and then comes the effect (the visual representation).

We know that the problem is difficult and that it must not be over-simplified. We don't want to deny that in dreams the world is experienced without the brain being in contact with the external world. This is a case where all the elements of a world–mind dualism are still present. For it is tempting to call representation the mnemonic traces that make dreams possible. A simulating and emulating brain might in fact be able to construct the world through an internal experience. But it is our hunch that, even in dreams, the dreamer does not engage in a dialogue between an acting brain and a representation of the physical world but that what happens is an emulation of the traces of action in the world, traces that are lived out again. The highly serious physiologist Michel Jouvet has noted that when they dream men sometimes have an erection, and he infers from this that dolphins are also capable of dreaming! The basic difference between dream and the reality of perceived experience is still beyond us. Perhaps it is a matter of two different modes of functioning. Schopenhauer drew the conclusion that perception is nothing other than a waking dream and the phenomenal world a vast illusion. This is not our point of view.

The notion of representation can be likened to that of the illusion undergone by the sceptical onlooker who, on seeing the artist in front of his canvas, says: 'Now I know what he's up to. He must have got into his head an image just like the one he gets us to see, and so has simply copied what he is actually looking at in his head.' All the models habitually employed to account for 'creation' in art conspire to plant this illusion in us. The brush employed to depict the wondrous landscape of childhood dreams in the first sequences of *Peter Pan* seems to be simply washing clean an opaque medium hiding from our eyes an already prepared set.

Even better, look at the way Cézanne paints the Lauves landscape.[36] For there can be no better way of getting back to perceived phenomena, no better

---

[36] See J. Gasquet (1921/2002) *Cézanne*, Encre marine, Fougères.

lesson in perceptual physiology. Just like any perceiving subject, he does not get caught up in contingent detail, still less in a pre-established programme. Rather, he frees up an open circulation between the local and the global. With his painterly hand he intervenes everywhere at once, moving himself in a practical field which is neither physical nor mental, though certainly corporeal, a field made up of a multitude of variously exploitable sketches, a swarm of inchoate gestures which hit their mark in full flight or mere suggestions indicative of further extensions. Cézanne paintings show that for thè perceiving organism, reality is nothing if it is not nourished by potentialities, and that the non-actual is something which could always make sense, provided only that it is inscribed in a still-to-be-completed, as-yet-disjointed, contour, or in a fragile harmony that has constantly to be restored.

Continuing on the same track, the success of Munch's painting *The Scream*[37] would be incomprehensible were it not for the fact that the viewer is captivated by the picture. When we are standing in front of it, we can suppose that a brain structure called the amygdala,[38] essential in emotional reactions, is so activated by the directness of the look that our mouth wants to scream. This is what psychologists call emotional contagion.[39] For those familiar with the frustrations and the tormented life of Munch, this picture, the summit of his art, or so they say, enables us to share the dramatic experience of his inability to transmit his despair. It expresses the powerlessness of language to disclose the complete experience. For the complex play of the movement of the lines, of the expression, and the colours does not pretend to represent this experience but has us live it out as immediately and completely as if we were, for a moment, Munch himself.[40]

Later, in Chapter 8, we will get back to this mental functioning known as mirroring, whose neural basis is the system of mirror neurons discovered by Rizzolatti. For they can be held responsible for provoking, in part, this resonance and the affective contagion symptomatic of this unity between the world and our perception, our experience.

---

[37] A good example of the ideal unity of the artistic thing—despite its material plurality—*The Scream* by the Norwegian painter Edward Munch (1863–1944) exists in four versions: one at the Oslo National Gallery, two others in the Munch Museum in the same town (one of which was stolen in a spectacular holdup on 22 August 2004 and only recovered on 31 August 2006), and one in a private collection.

[38] The amygdala is a brain centre belonging to the limbic system, which is the principal station for the processing of information relating to emotions.

[39] E. Hartfield *et al.* (1994) *Emotional Contagion*, Cambridge University Press, Cambridge.

[40] For a psychiatric reading of Munch's work, see: J. Thuillier (2003) *La Folie. Histoire et dictionnaire*, Robert Laffont, Paris. Of interest is also the work by J. Thuiller (2003)*Histoire générale de l'histoire de l'art*, Odile Jacob, Paris, in which he proposes a return to the 'phenomenological reduction'.

Representation or projection?

It seems obvious that the human brain contains representations of external things. We see the tables and chairs around us. We dream at night. The truth of this trivial claim does not seem to be altered when one reformulates it as follows: our mind contains visual representations of tables and chairs standing around us and a part of this stock of mental representations gets reproduced when we dream at night. Perception therefore comes down to nothing more than the construction of a visual, tactile representation, or again, a multi-modal representation, or even a supra-modal representation in the mind of the perceiving subject.

In fact, however, the passage from tables and chairs to their representations in our mind is not the innocent operation of simply transposing from without to within that it might appear to be. The theoreticians of the causal theory of perception never stop repeating: 'the object of my percept of the chair is the real chair, whose introduction into my field of vision causes the formation of the percept in my visual centres'. However, the entire problem is there, as the physiologists of perception know only too well. Replacing the immediate presence of the thing to the perceiving subject with this supposed transfer from an external reality into an internal representation sets in motion a series of complex analyses and syntheses to which there appears to be no end.

The notion of representation exerts a quite peculiar fascination precisely because it is two-sided. On the one side, a representation can be treated as a mental thing. On the other, something is represented in it and by means of it; which is then reformulated in such a way as to allow one to believe that one is talking about the same thing: a representation has a content. From there one is tempted to add that the thingly aspect constitutes its 'form', which functions as the receptacle for the content aspect. But this does not make these two aspects any more alike. As a thing, a representation is either a phase of psychic activity or a phase of the corresponding neural state of the brain.

All attempts to reduce this duality to the unity of a thing normally constituted at the heart of Nature, where things are supposed to be eternally fixed in themselves, have failed. To cite only one attempt among others: supplementing ordinary physical properties with non-physical properties, called 'semantic'.[41]

....

41 See F. Dretske (1988) *Explaining behavior: Reasons in a world of causes*, MIT Press, Cambridge, MA. From this standpoint, the fact of referring to something, of supporting such a meaning by being the bearer of an objective reference, could be made to look as if it could be assimilated to a purely 'thingly' property. It was enough to accept that, in addition to occupying our minds for a certain period of time, our representations also had the 'property' (as if such a property could feature at the same level) of being representations of things represented.

The problem is that this unification through the relation thing-property requires us to admit an unavoidably heterogeneous class of properties, in other words, a class that is not a single class at all. It is not difficult to time the occurrence and the period over which a representation occupies the mind. However, trying to take into account what it represents does not increase the stock of information at one's disposal. The change is systemic, a category change or a change in the language game. As Hegel realized, it is not enough to interpose an 'and also' to obtain a homogeneity when it does not exist. It might appear more convenient to keep quiet about the seriousness of this difficulty and to pretend that the physical/semantic property difference could be brought down to a simple additive difference. There are many for whom this fiction has never ceased to be convincing.

All these theories presuppose, in general, that the activity of the brain is dependent upon a stimulus, is limited to the faithful reproduction of the thing as it was, and is in consequence oriented towards the past. Against these prejudices we can only keep on repeating: the functioning of the brain is projective. It constructs hypotheses and predictions. This claim is based on important observations that have been made over some considerable time in experimental psychology.

To take visual illusions first; it turns out that, in situations where perception is ambiguous, the brain takes decisions (a current shortcut expression in neurophysiology) depending upon its rules for interpreting the world, rules which in turn are moulded by the material constraints the agent experiences in its interaction with the world, and rules which, in the course of evolution, have optimized the treatment of its sensory input and have contributed to the ontogenesis of the species through the organization of the neuronal networks of the brain. For the moment we are only in possession of a limited number of these laws of perception, but at least we do know that the brain 'prefers' symmetrical objects or spaces, that 'it chooses' its frames of reference so as to resolve ambiguities in visual perception, and that 'it assumes' that certain visual forms are rigid. These rules are not representations; they probably consist of modes of functioning of neuronal networks which serve the purpose of optimizing the processing of data, so diminishing the complexity of the neuronal computation.

An example will show how these hypotheses can be put into practice. A subject is presented with a hemisphere drawn on paper. Half of the surface of the hemisphere is darkened as if a shadow was on it and in such a way that the hemisphere can be perceived as either convex or concave. The brain has to make a choice between these two possibilities. But why does the brain opt in favour of a perception of the form corresponding to a light shining from above?[42] This is most probably as a result of the natural ecology of perception. Given that the perceiving subject lives on Earth, its familiarity with the orientation of the light of the Sun intervenes right from the start to arbitrate the perception in the case of an ambiguous form.

Many examples of such perceptual decisions could be cited, all of which depend upon *a priori* functions that are partly innate and partly acquired. Their ecological anchorage is a safeguard against the temptation of a current tendency to think of the brain as a demiurge. That the brain functions in a projective fashion does not mean that there is, in our brains, a busy little scientist tirelessly constructing theories about the world.

In Nature, where everything is expected to conform to rules, an apparent exception simply requires that we look for a deeper regularity. Hence the bold hypothesis that any organism equipped with a brain proceeds at all times by anticipating, at the centre, whatever information is received in the peripheral sensory receptors. *The brain is a predictor*, the physiologist willingly asserts. And right away we find ourselves confronted with a striking revision of the classical paradigm, a revision according to which anticipation, instead of being an exception, proves to be the rule for any intelligent behaviour.[43]

Any organism equipped with a brain already possesses all the resources necessary for what it is no longer appropriate to describe as a perceptual processing of sensory information derived from without but which should more properly be described as a continual affection of its self by itself on the part of a being who both acts spontaneously and is sensible to the effects upon itself of its own action. For the organism both experiences these effects in its body and objectifies them in its environment, an environment it projects in advance and, in so doing, both discovers and appropriates at the same time. Theories of the passive impregnation of the organism by an information coming to it from without therefore have to be replaced by a theory of the constitution of (an internal model of) the world by the organism itself. An organism which, therefore, takes possession of the world just as, by the same token, it also takes possession of its own mind and body by appropriating them and developing internal models of them.

From the standpoint of the philosophy underlying physiology, what all this means is that we shall now have to take account of Husserl and the transcendental

---

[42] A. Berthoz and R. Recht (2005) *Les espaces de l'homme*, Odile Jacob, Paris. Jean Petitot reminds us of the *shape from shading* phenomenon: an assumption implicit in visual perception, that light comes from above, permitting us to distinguish convex from concave forms.

[43] In particular, this thesis has been upheld by Alain Berthoz in *The Brain's Sense of Movement* and by Rodolpho Llinás in *I of the Vortex*, MIT Press, Cambridge, MA, 2001.

tradition (Kant), with a view to substituting the former for Locke and the empiricists—or at least supplementing the latter with the former. For despite its fruitfulness, empiricism has only offered a partial description of a complete process that transcendental philosophy shows us how to recover, even while leaving the field open.

Speaking generally, the organism deals with objects it has itself actively 'constituted' as such. It only has to interact with those natural events that satisfy (or fail to satisfy) its provisional expectations, or at least to verify or modify the style of such expectations, other organisms being apprehended, from the first, as like or unlike itself, etc. What under normal circumstances this organism is never confronted with is the pure stimulus, free from all interpretation, with data never before subsumed under any perceptual, cognitive, or practical categories.

The philosophical leap of faith: refusing the concept of representation

Part of the prestige of theories of internal representation is due to their apparent naturalness. We have no difficulty in understanding the construction of internal representations of external things because we rely on habits, widespread in our iconophagic societies, of always separating and comparing two things: (1) the ideal object represented by the image and (2) the material object this image really is.

In fact it is generally supposed that the mind is some kind of a portrait gallery and that, in consequence, it is always possible to distinguish the thing that is a mental representation, or a state of the brain, from the thing that exists outside the head or the mind. In addition there is a split between two kinds of objectivity: the material objectivity, whether psychic or neuronal, which is an internal representation, and the specifically representational objectivity, in as much as it carries a represented content.

It follows that the link between the representing and the represented, the link in virtue of which 'this' is designated as a thing in the world whereas 'that' is designated as a representation in the mind, is itself folded back upon itself and, as it were, packed together under the head of a third object to which the epistemic subject (always carefully kept hidden away in the background) stands in relation. Hence the strange notion of representational content, as different from the material container which sustains it in the flux of psychic life or the metabolism of the brain as it is different from the external thing represented.

What we are suggesting is that the cognitive sciences need to take full account of the act of being directed towards something according to a certain type of behaviour, whether through perception, memory, imagination, desire, etc.

Faced with this irrepressible need for representation, one cannot accord much confidence to the supposedly neutral uses of the word representation in the neurosciences: neuronal representation, mnemonic representation, visual representation, spatial representation, motor representation, and so on. Those who use these terms should be wary of the imperceptible shifts in meaning! From 'the circulation of information about X in a network or a projection pathway' (let's not get into the question of the neutrality of the term information) it is so easy to pass over to 'the circulation, in the same network or projection pathway, of *representations of X.*'

We are only too well aware that any interdisciplinary dialogue between specialists in the cognitive sciences is infested with representational vocabulary. Is this to be regarded as the inoffensive result of the use of pidgin English, where appropriate terminology is desperately wanting, or is it not rather an embarrassing witness to the indestructible character of the prejudice that the brain, no matter what might be learned about its functioning, *must* serve to represent the external world? Let's just say that many authors, Varela, Edelman, Llínas, and others,[44] have tried to avoid the temptation to employ the language of representations by insisting on the dynamic, anticipatory character of cerebral functioning, rooted as it is in action.

The example of coding

It might be as well to consider an example of the kind of presupposition that is not affected by the transition from pre-theoretical prejudices to the theoretical conception. Our example is taken from a certain uncritical use of the concept of coding in the neurosciences. Without getting into the history of science, the idea can be traced back to the analogy between the cognitive functioning of the central nervous system and a processor whose operations can be accounted for by Information Theory.

Interpreting the activity of a nerve cell as coded information carried by a sensory signal, the neurobiologist could be compared with an engineer in telecommunications who observes the messages exchanged within the network with the same ideally objective eye as the physicist observes his material system.

----

[44] This diagnosis only concerns the dominant ideology in the cognitive sciences, itself always dependent upon the representational conception of mind common to both common sense and the philosophical tradition from Locke to Fodor. For alternative views see R. Llínas (2001) *I of the Vortex*, MIT Press, Cambridge, MA; G.M. Edelman (1989) *The Remembered Present. A Biological Theory of Consciousness*, Basic Books, New York; F.J. Varela (1989) *Autonomie et connaissance. Essai sur le vivant*, Seuil, Paris. This appeal for a conceptual renewal is still topical.

There can be no doubt that the concept of coding is useful as a working hypothesis, serving as an intellectual and scientific tool with which to examine the brain. Since the 1950s when specialists in the processing of signals, like Perkel and Gerstein,[45] noted that the brain makes use of a number of codes, cooperation between physicists, mathematicians and computer scientists has given rise to several proposals concerning the coding of messages processed by the brain: examples include frequential coding, coding by *population*,[46] temporal coding,[47] the *Bayesian* coding,[48] theory of spins,[49] synfire chain coding,[50] and oscillation phase coding.[51] As a result, neuronal coding has become a focus of attention. Some authors hope that there might be only one form of coding and that a single solution, as for the genetic code, will one day come to encompass all the rest, whereas others think that the brain will be shown to make use of all of these codes, or a good many of them, a solution which seems to us more likely. But in all such cases, the deciphering of the code will not lead to an understanding of the essential features of our lived experience even if, in the end, it turns out that there is nothing more to it than neuronal activity.

[45] D.H. Perkel, G.L. Gerstein, and G.P. Moore (1967) Neuronal spike trains and stochastic point processes, *Biophys. J.* 7, 391–448.

[46] A.P. Georgopoulos *et al.* (1986) Neuronal population coding of movement direction, *Science* 233, 1416–1419.

[47] C. von der Malsburg and W. Singer (1988) Principles of cortical network organization, in P. Rakiç and W. Singer (eds), *The Neurobiology of Neocortex*, Dahlem Konferenzen, Wiley, New York, pp. 69–99; E. Bienenstock (1996) Composition, in Ad. Aertsen and V. Braitenberg (eds), *Biological and Computational Theory of Vision*, Elsevier, Amsterdam, pp. 269–300.

[48] A. Pouget and T.J. Sejnowski (2001) Simulating a lesion in a basis function model of spatial representation. Comparison with hemineglect, *Psychol. Rev.* 108, 653–673; R.S. Zemel, P. Dayan, and A. Pouget (1998) Probabilistic interpretation of population code, *Neural Comput.* 10, 403–430.

[49] J.-P. Nadal, G. Toulouse, J.-P. Changeux, and S. Dehaene (1986) *Biophys. Lett.* 1(10), 535–542.

[50] A synfire chain is a synchronous discharge of groups of neurons which induces a chain of synchronous disharges of other groups of neurons; M. Abeles *et al.* (1993) Dynamics of neuronal interactions in the frontal cortex of behaving monkeys, *Concepts Neurosci.* 4, 131–158.

[51] N. Burgess, M. Recce, and J. O'Keefe (1994) A model of hippocampal function, *Neural Networks* 7(6–7), 1065–1081.

An eidetics of physiology?

The very idea that an eidetics of physiology might be necessary cannot but appear repugnant to many epistemologists. For it implies a theory of ideas in physiology, capable of founding the epistemological decisions made by this science at the very highest level. A foundation which consists essentially of basing such decisions on the intuitions that the researcher gains from his special relationship with the special ontology of the living (in as much as it differs in principle from the general ontology of inert physical matter). Chapter 6 will be devoted to a more detailed examination of this question.

Under the weight of these philosophical formulae, the genuine meaning of the originality of the living by comparison with inert matter has been grasped. This is what motivates the physiologist to intervene, every time that he sees, that he feels, that the point has not been appreciated: here, in the construction of a non-biological mathematical model, there in the construction of a non-biomimetic robot, elsewhere again, in the parameters of an equation that fails to capture the essence of natural movement, etc.

At this new level of responsibility, under the weight of commitments so consciously entertained, a solution has to be found to decide between the two rival claims: the brain exists basically for representation, and the brain exists basically for action. How are we to arrive at a rational justification for such a decision? The approach we have adopted in this book is to go backwards and forwards across the range of theoretical options available to us, over the different sources of intuitive evidence and of those exemplary discoveries that open the way down unexplored paths. To what aspects of the living are we capable of becoming aware, attentive, attuned by virtue of the simple fact of posing the act at the origin and not just sensori-motor mechanisms? And are these aspects not the very aspects that would necessarily be overlooked were we to remain under the hold of the metaphor of the brain as a calculating machine operating on the basis of internal representations?

Perhaps we shall be drawn to the conclusion that the singular use of the term the brain is an abusive simplification, and that we should recognize that this wonderful biological machine encompasses such a quantity of subtle mechanisms that it would be better to talk of brains in the plural, just as one talks today of memories in the plural (implicit, explicit, episodic, visual, motor, etc.), each corresponding to a mechanism at once both autonomous and in interaction with the rest. It will also be necessary to take account of what evolution either produced or revealed (depending upon whether one thinks that everything existed in advance or that the slow process of natural selection was responsible for bringing into being these new mechanisms).

The risks of our venture

In raising these questions it might seem that we run the risk of getting locked into what will remain an epistemological quest limited to the future of the physiology of action. So, curiously enough, meeting this challenge might finish up locking us into an epistemological provincialism far removed from the philosophical tradition from Aristotle on, and which consists of remaining open to science, not to this or that particular branch of science but to science in general.

To avoid this danger of provincialism, we are going to place the debate between representational models and the potential models of a physiology yet to be developed in the framework of the tradition of a philosophy of action and of the living as act. In so doing we do of course run the risk of merely displacing the ambiguity that reigns in cognitive science. The indecisiveness to which we referred will simply be recovered over again at a higher stage, at the level of philosophical doctrines and traditions. But the tradition going back from Fodor and Chomsky to Locke and Descartes, and upon which a part at least of the cognitive sciences of today largely depend, is certainly no less respectable than that which goes back from Hubert Dreyfus to Husserl and Kant.

We will have failed to make ourselves understood if we are taken to be engaged in the dubious project of transposing over into philosophy the controversies of science, at the risk of making of the latter the squabbles of dogmatists, or conversely, of transposing over into the positive sciences the age-old dialectical oppositions internal to philosophical Reason.

It could well be that, for the researcher in the cognitive sciences, phenomenology harbours still largely unexploited key ideas which we need to recover. This means no longer deriving these ideas from secondary sources by rummaging around in the field of a linguistic analysis that remains a late-comer to the semantics of action, and which is in any case still very far from representing a philosophy of lived experience.

Of course, we have already identified the traps that await us in our attempt, as also the limits of the usefulness of a phenomenology which, after all, is itself also founded on the manipulation of language and not just on life itself: how could it possibly be otherwise? In addition, we are only too aware that one of the great, one of the unavoidable, limitations of phenomenology is to place excessive emphasis upon conscious experience, whereas the functioning of the brain is essentially unconscious. Some take this for a knock-down argument. It is their right to do so!

We are not claiming that phenomenology will settle all the difficult questions with which we are confronted. It is a fact that, of the two of us, the philosopher is seriously committed to phenomenology (those who think that philosophy requires no commitment from its practitioner will no doubt hold this against him). But if the physiologist has not, for his part, sworn allegiance so to speak, nevertheless, for him too, the phenomenological approach provides a means of reflecting upon the best way of working out a physiology of action and perception. Hence the need to test the fruitfulness and the limits of such an approach.

Chapter 2

Getting past the traditional concepts

In this chapter we are going to try and develop a theoretical posture for the physiology of action. The reader may wonder why we use an expression paradoxically associating posture with theory. Posture does not just describe the relative position of the parts of our body. The Russian physiologist Bernstein[1] wrote that posture is a 'preparation for action'. Posture is an expression of emotions and a reflection of intentions; it is influenced by our culture and by our social training. The fact is that physiologists do not always have the time, or the need, to formulate and legitimate the concepts and procedures employed in their empirical science, even if in fact their hypotheses are driven by an implicit epistemology. Scientific procedures adopted in physiology are in fact determined by an entire range of theories, bodies of knowledge, hypotheses, techniques, ways of cooperating, animal models, fashions, or even social pressures.

Another reason is that research always has a point of departure and the researcher, like the sprinter, starts out from his blocks. He is always already committed at the ideological level, that of his preferences (and his reticence) with regard to possible ways of tackling the objects of his investigations. To the extent that physiology, as Claude Bernard used to say, is the study of the 'coordination of parts within a whole' every experiment in physiology rests upon an implicit theory that invokes 'the whole'. If philosophy can be of any help it is in formulating general hypotheses. Our colleague Ideo Sakata in Japan, who discovered the neurons of the parietal cortex responsible for coding the form of objects, told us that he had been inspired by certain texts by Merleau-Ponty on the subject of perception. On the other hand, even if the interest in phenomenology shown by Giacomo Rizzolatti and Vittorio Gallese contributed little to their discovery of mirror neurons (made haphazardly in the course of an experiment), it did much for their *interpretation* of the nature of

[1] N.A. Bernstein (1967) *The Coordination and Regulation of Movement*, Pergamon Press, New York.

these neurons,[2] neurons responsible for coding the gestures of the experimenter just as much as those of the monkey itself (see Chapter 8 in this volume).

By posing action or the act (and not representation) at the origin of cognition, a genuine theoretical decision has been taken. A decision which might (let's risk the prognosis) soon help to restore an epistemological dignity to the holistic aspect of behaviour and contribute to the integrative and cognitive status of the neurosciences. The latter are presently caught in a bind between a genomic and molecular approach and an equally exclusive concentration, on the part of some psychologists, upon the external aspects of behaviour.

We should also make it clear that our position is different from (or to be more precise includes but attempts to go beyond) that of one theoretical approach presently attempted and which consists of anchoring cognition in sensori-motor mechanisms. It is just as well that psychologists and philosophers should have rediscovered, as did Poincaré before them, the need to bring movement back into the picture as the foundation of our ability to extract invariants in the world. For this is precisely what Piaget also appealed to in his constructivist theory. But however interesting it might prove to be to base the extraction of perceptual invariants upon action and interaction, the use of the expression sensori-motor tends to diminish the interest of these theories, if only because both of the terms employed in the expression remain overly mechanistic. With a view to rehabilitating the sensori-motor approach, O'Regan and Noe have opted for the concept of 'sensori-motor contingencies'. In their reshuffled version, an implicit knowledge of the influence of the future movements of the perceiving organism upon what is given in sense replaces any suggestion of movement coming before sensation.[3]

In our view, what might prove to be still more valuable would be a theory in which action came first, and in such a way that it is this action which defines and decides about the relevant sensory contents and which modulates the activity of the latter through attention. Of such a theory it could be said that it is projective, thereby conferring upon the theory the full force of the word project. It is a case of being thrown towards the future no matter what the circumstances, and even if they are very far from being fortuitous.

The theory we hope to outline here might even be capable of changing our conception of the cognitive sciences, a conception which, for the moment, is derived from what Husserl used to call the 'natural attitude', an attitude common

---

[2] G. Rizzolatti and C. Sinigaglia (2006) *So quel chef ai. Il cervello che agisce e i neuroni specchio*, Raffaello Cortina Ed., Milan; V. Gallese (2005) Embodied simulation: from neurons to phenomenal experience, *Phenomenology Cog. Sci.* 4, 23–48.

[3] J.K. O'Regan and A. Noe (2001) A sensori-motor account of vision and visual consciousness, *Behav. Brain Sci.* 24(5), 939–1011.

to both science and common sense. What is presupposed, basically, in this attitude, in this theoretical posture? Above and before all else it is that there *is* an external reality, objective, independent of us, even 'absolute'. Only after these assumptions have been made does the question of human knowledge arise, with its necessary phases, presented classically in the following order:

the supposedly passive contact of the external object with the surface of one's own body or with a sensor (sensation);

the formation of a representation (or image) of this object in the mind, together with a reflection on this representation dominated by language, etc.;

and finally, a judgement concerning the question of whether this representation is objectively true; that is, corresponds to the external objects it is supposed to represent.

Of course, in modern psychology, the notion of top-down influences has been promoted by prestigious authors such as Stephen Kosslyn and many others, and the idea that a peripheral analysis of the world operates under the influence of attentional mechanisms is nowadays explored systematically. We have no doubt that a great change in perspective is on the way and the last 5 years have witnessed a drastic revision of this traditional point of view. Those who persist in interpreting the action as a 'motor output' resulting from the transduction of data made available by a 'sensorial input' are now rare.[4] But we believe that an even more drastic change should be made, if only because these approaches actually make little difference to the fundamental hypothesis about the relation of the brain to the world. They add new mechanisms without changing the initial hypothesis. We shall discuss this point further later on.

We also want to make it clear that we are perfectly aware that representational theorists interested in action have never wanted to deny the importance of action in perception nor the importance of anticipatory processes. In this connection, the classical works by Marc Jeannerod should be mentioned, and more recently the work done in common by this author and the philosopher Pierre Jacob.[5] In the light of recent developments in neuropsychology, in which Jeannerod is an expert, these two have undertaken projects similar to our own, but on the basis

....

[4] For an author who, all the same, still holds this view, and whose influence in cognitive science has not diminished, see: J. Fodor (1983/1989) *The Modularity of Mind*, MIT Press, Cambridge, MA: 'Since, in the general case, transducer outputs underdetermine perceptual analyses (p. 68). That is, perceptual categories are not, in general, *definable* in terms of transducer outputs; phenomenalists, operationalists, Gibsonians, and procedural semanticists to the contrary notwithstanding (note 22)'.

[5] M. Jeannerod and P. Jacob (2005) Visual cognition: a new look at the two-visual system model, *Neuropsychologia* 42(2), 301–312; M. Jeannerod and P. Jacob (2005) The motor theory of social cognition, a critique, *Trends Cog. Sci.* 9(1), 21–25.

of the presuppositions of the theory of action in analytical philosophy. Here it is convenient that we open up some lateral perspectives on work published after the discussions that served as the basis for this book. It would indeed have been surprising if, given the discussions registered at that time (2000–2003), no one had had the idea of writing about action, or about phenomenology from the standpoint of action, or even to engage in a dialogue between phenomenology and the neurosciences. Thus there are a number of books that have come out recently that take up many of the topics found in this book, but not in exactly the same way, or not with the precise focus that this one has, in so far as they are primarily books on an embodied approach combining phenomenology with empirical science.[6] With regard to the latter literature our position remains original, no one yet having ventured to even attempt to justify empirically the Husserlian theory of kinaesthetic constitution in its radical transcendentality (a word that still arouses suspicion in cognitive circles). This becomes even clearer if one takes these authors separately and individually. For then one sees that they pursue a path divergent from our own, because they follow Francisco Varela, whose positions we hereafter take into consideration and criticize (Alva Noë), or because they remain within a strictly phenomenological frame of reference or at least an intra-philosophical frame of reference (Dan Zahavi), or because their interest in empirical research is focused on a particular problem common to phenomenology and neuroscience, for example the body scheme (Shaun Gallagher), or again because they maintain an unbridgeable 'Wittgensteinian' gap between philosophy and the neurosciences (J. Bennett and P.M.S. Hacker),[7] or because they have openly chosen to follow a non-phenomenological path (Jeannerod and Jacob).

To put it in a nutshell, we maintain that few authors have, for instance, conceived of movement as a way of perceiving in Poincaré's sense. For Poincaré argued that if an object appeared to have changed its form, the only way of knowing whether it had really changed its form or whether this apparent change was simply due to our movement was to resolve the ambiguity by actively reproducing the movement. As far as we are concerned, the expression 'sensory

---

6 M. Sheets-Johnstone (1999) *The Primacy of Movement*, John Benjamins, Amsterdam; E. Thompson (2007) *Mind in Life*, Harvard University Press, Cambridge, MA; S. Gallagher (2005) *How the Body Shapes the Mind*, Oxford University Press, Oxford; A. Noe (2004) *Action in Perception*, MIT Press, Cambridge, MA; D. Zahavi (2006) *Subjectivity and Selfhood. Investigating the First-Person Perspective*, MIT Press, Cambridge, MA; S. Gallagher and D. Zahavi (2007) *The Phenomenological Mind: an Introduction to Philosophy of Mind and the Cognitive Science*, Routledge, London.

7 J. Bennett and P.M.S. Hacker (2003) *Philosophical Foundations of Neuroscience*, Blackwell, Oxford.

receptivity' is itself a misnomer, because sensing is fundamentally proactive while perceiving is itself a form of movement. Poincaré went further than this since he even attributed the genesis of space to movement, for example, in a passage where he writes:

> 'When a frog is decapitated and a drop of acid is placed on a point of its skin, it tries to wipe away the acid with its nearest paw, and if this paw has been amputated, it will wipe the acid away with the other paw. Here we find ourselves confronted with a double parry [...] making it possible to cure an evil with a second remedy if the first is inoperative. And it is this very multiplicity of parrying gestures, together with the coordination that result therefrom, which *is space*.'[8]

Theory of mind

What concerns the perception of objects is also true for a higher cognitive function like the perception of the ideas and intentions of others in social interactions. Psychologists have given the name theory of mind to the fact that we can guess at the intentions and knowledge or 'theories' present in the brains of others. The conceptualization of this, in theoretical terms, leads to the idea that we can construct a meta-theory;[9] that is, a theory bearing upon the theory of the other subject. The classical example is given by the following experiment. A subject is shown two boxes, B1 and B2. A person P puts an object in one of the boxes and leaves the room. Without the subject's knowledge, the experimenter takes the object and puts it in the other box. Then he brings back person P and the subject is asked to say what P is going to do to find the object. The subject may or may not think that P thinks that the object is in the box B1. In the first case he will designate B1. The psychologists explain this by saying that he has a theory about what is going on in P's mind. To describe just such a capacity to infer the thoughts of another subject, these psychologists have developed an entire battery of tests. A considerable literature has been devoted to this cognitive function, whose absence is then going to serve as an explanation for some of the cognitive deficits of autism, for example. It was even held

---

8 H. Poincaré (1908) *Science et Méthode*, Flammarion, Paris, p. 108.

9 Meta-theory: in a context which is not, as in psychology, that of ordinary language (which bears on things just as much as it does on linguistic expressions bearing on things) but that of a strict hierarchy of levels in formalized languages, where a first theory whose statements deal exclusively with things and their properties is distinguished from a collection of statements expressing the semantic properties of such expressions, the latter theory (containing the truth conditions of the former) will be the meta-theory of the former. It should be noted that the concept of meta- is only valid within such a formalist frame of reference and so has no bearing on any psychological theory of mind! See A. Tarski (1939/1972) Le concept de vérité dans les langages formalisés, in *Logique, sémantique, métamathématique* 1923–1944, tome 1, Armand Colin, Paris, pp. 157–269.

that a particular area of the pre-frontal cortex was responsible for this, up until the day when a patient with an important lesion in this area proved capable of succeeding in all these tests, or almost all!

This notion of a theory of mind was also supposed to render intelligible the intentional character of action, to the extent that the latter bears upon the beliefs and intentions of the other subject, beliefs and intentions that are usually brought under the category of representations. This must not be overlooked. Indeed, it is all the more necessary to keep coming back to it because phenomenological philosophy has never ceased to protest that this conception of an intentionality based upon mental representations in a mind and of theories understood as inferred ensembles of such mental representations in a mind, 'theories of a theory of mind', and so on, rests upon the presupposition of the cognitive primacy of representation, the very presupposition that has made it necessary for us to write this manifesto.

Towards a physiology of interaction

If we want to go beyond the current views about brain/object relations we have to consider a number of questions. How, for example, does one know that the internal representation conforms to the external object if it represents not the object itself but the interaction of the subject with this object? The inevitable and inevitably naïve answer to this question—that it is enough to carefully compare the two—rests on a double error, or so it seems to us.

Either the person (the scientist) responsible for judging the matter is supposed to be exterior to the knowing subject, in which case the interiority of the mind of the knowing subject is closed to him. Here, brain imagery has obviously not helped to solve the problem, given the huge amount of statistical manipulation based on hypotheses that are often counter-intuitive, such as that of a cerebral rest implied by so-called snapshots of the acting brain. In fact, the recent interest of researchers for the so-called default activities of the brain, and their growing acknowledgement of the continuity of cerebral activity (the brain correlate of a wandering mind or of day-dreaming in the absence of any stimulus-driven task) calls for a radical reconsideration of brain imagery, and this because subtracting the images of a brain at rest from those composing the brain of subjects performing a specified task ceases to be an acceptable procedure.[10]

---

[10] D. Mantini et al. (2007) Electrophysiological signatures of resting state networks in the human brain, *Proc. Natl. Acad. Sci. USA* 104(32), 13170–13175; H. Laufs et al. (2003) Electroencephalographic signatures of attentional and cognitive default modes in spontaneous brain activity fluctuations at rest, *Proc. Natl. Acad. Sci. USA* 100(19), 11053–11058;

Or, alternatively, the knowing subject is himself regarded as the person responsible for judging, which means that he must already have been accorded, alongside his ordinary cognitive faculties limited to the informational channels of his sensors, an extra-ordinary, direct access (as Gibson[11] supposed) to the very things situated in surrounding space, one that does not require intermediary mental representations.

In order to get out of these contradictions, we shall have to unearth their hidden presuppositions. To such an attempt to determine, by dint of reflection, the structure of the epistemological space in which the scientist moves, it might be objected that any science worthy of the name must restrict itself to the intrinsic structure of its object and that, in consequence, any attempt to take into consideration the relation between this science itself (*sub specie subjecti*) and these objects is to be avoided, unless it is a matter of anticipating difficulties that might arise later on as a result of not being clear about this relationship. The point of view from which such a critique is directed is the following: cognition is nothing other than (should not be anything else than) the study of the bipolar relationship between an entirely self-contained object and another object equally, even symmetrically, self-contained, which is the brain.

Our response is to point out that if we look into the matter a little more carefully, we can see that the situation is more complicated. There is a reciprocal inclusion of the brain in the world and of the world in the brain and so on. The new physiology of action therefore has to be a physiology of interaction, *one that goes beyond the simple fact of constructing invariants.*

....

van de Ven VG *et al.* (2004) Functional connectivity as revealed by spatial independent component analysis of fMRI measurements during rest, *Hum. Brain Mapp.* 22(3), 165–178; T. Jiang, Y. He, Y. Zang, and X. Weng (2004) Modulation of functional connectivity during the resting state and the motor task, *Hum. Brain Mapp.* 1, 63–71; M. De Luca *et al.* (2006) fMRI resting state networks define distinct modes of long-distance interactions in the human brain, *Neuroimage* 29(4), 1359–1367; M. De Luca *et al.* (2005) Blood oxygenation level dependent contrast resting state networks are relevant to functional activity in the neocortical sensorimotor system, *Exp. Brain Res.* 167(4), 587–594; M.D. Fox *et al.* (2005) The human brain is intrinsically organized into dynamic, anticorrelated functional networks, *Proc. Natl Acad. Sci. USA* 102(27), 9673–9678; M.E. Raichle (2006) The brain's dark energy, *Science* 314, 1249–1250; M.F. Mason *et al.* (2007) Wandering minds: the default network and stimulus-independent thought, *Science* 315, 393–395.

11 J.J. Gibson (1950) *The Perception of the Visual World*, Houghton Mifflin Co., Boston, MA: 'in a special sense, the outer world *does* get into the eye. It implies that a least the surfaces, slopes, and edges of the world have correlates in the retinal image specifically related to their objective counterparts by a lawful transformation (9). [...] The characteristic of perception is that the result is not so much spontaneous as it is faithful to the thing perceived. [...] If the total stimulation contains all that is needed to account for visual perception, the hypothesis of sensory organization is unnecessary (25).'

The difficulty the scientist has with his own naturalized epistemology

The study of the relationship between representation and action-based theories is complicated by the fact that the debate is also dependent upon the position of the scientist, someone who is both the observer and the subject of the problem.

The situation can be reproduced schematically in two points:

1 Current theories make implicit reference to an epistemic subject, the idealized double of the scientist who remains detached from his investigations and this despite the naturalization of epistemology that has been attempted in the cognitive sciences.

2 In addition, one notes the persistence, in the epistemology of a part of the cognitive sciences, of a non-biological concept of an *absolute reality* existing in itself,[12] a reality envisaged just as it is and without any subjective interference on the part of this same epistemic subject, due to his contemplating the scene from his privileged position.

Our critique will be directed primarily against these two presuppositions, that of a detached subject, on the one hand, and a reality in itself, on the other. The subject engaged in science (the epistemic subject) may very well think of himself as a little omniscient God by comparison with the brain he studies. In fact he is omniscient; because he knows, for his part, that there is an objective world in front of him. But the brain knows nothing of this. He also knows that there is a brain in the midst of the world. And about that, the brain again knows nothing.

World and brain: everyone agrees that these are the terminal poles of cognition. A cognitive science has to have access to signals emitted in the world just as much as to data-processing systems lodged in the brain. Not being enclosed within a cranium (like the brain) the epistemic subject thinks he enjoys a ubiquitous omniscience. Everywhere present without being situated anywhere, he abstracts his own cognition from the cognitive relation between brain and world, the very relation he wants to observe impartially.

On the other hand, inasmuch as the functioning of the brain is an indispensable condition of this cognitive relation and the latter remains precisely *cognitive*, that is, concerned with the truth (or, what amount to the same thing, subject to the possibility of error and error correction) the operations of this brain are also themselves necessarily oriented towards the truth. Truth, the object *par excellence* of science, is situated within the horizon of perception, so much so that the operations of the brain display a curious affinity with the epistemic subject itself in its investigation of cognition.

---

12 The *in itself* and the *for itself*: reality conceived in the absolute or as it appears to a subject.

Initially, the brain's capacity for *objectivation*—at the root of the subject's capacity of accessing independent things in the world—might have seemed constrained by the well-known limits of the sensory receptors and the brain's functional systems (small receptive fields, long time of nervous conduction, etc.). But the brain's capacity turns out to be more or less equivalent to the virtually limitless capacity of the epistemic subject responsible for scientific knowledge. By allowing the brain to include such a duplicate of itself,[13] this epistemic subject has then managed to create a discrete little place for itself in the picture of the world where—officially—it should not appear, and this with a view to saving the objectivity of its science. One cannot fail to note the ambiguity of this game on both planes: that of the opacity of an actual cognition in its structural and functional constraints; that of the transparence of the physical world, assumed to be accessible to the epistemic subject in all its localized systems, even those (the brain's) that are of a cognitive kind.

Only someone placed upon the plane of reality as it is in itself, and therefore able to say in advance what it represents, would be capable of deciding about the relevant conformity of representation and world. And this is what very easily passes unperceived in the presuppositions of the cognitive sciences. To make true statements one has to be able to compare the mental representation with reality. And for that, one necessarily has to be situated on the ontological plane of this reality in itself and not be caught up in mere representations. But who could pretend to be situated at this level? Certainly not the scientist himself as someone working in conjunction with other members of the scientific community. For him, reality cannot so easily be detached from his laborious means of access to it. But if he persists in trying to incarnate the epistemic subject, and in repressing any question about his own relationship to his subject matter, the temptation to introduce, into the brain, a double of his idealized self will remain.

The independence and the objective character of Nature

While we are on the subject of the obstacles confronting a physiology of action, we should also mention one that gives rise to the idea that there is a perfectly objective reality independent of the knowing subject and which we call Nature. Merleau-Ponty, in his lectures at the Collège de France entitled 'Nature', suggested that the seemingly unavoidable *objective reality* in fact stems from the disassociation of a more fundamental phenomenon, namely the *link binding humanity to the Earth*. Referring to an objection Husserl brought against himself

---

[13] On the subject of the double, see the chapter devoted to it in A. Berthoz (2004) *La décision*, Odile Jacob, Paris, pp. 143–173.

he wrote: 'Inasmuch as we refer the universe to our body and to our humanity, have we not forgotten that life might disappear? If this reference to a life that might disappear implies that all life is subject to contingencies, are we not obliged to suppose that over and beyond all that there must be "pure things"?'[14]

It seems perfectly clear for us that it is indeed possible to posit the existence of a Nature independent of the perceiving subject. If we are prepared to concede that the dinosaurs had a 'certain conception' of what Nature is, this Nature has remained while the dinosaurs have disappeared. Are we not entitled to infer from this that objects are what they are in themselves, quite independent of the existence of a knowing subject? At Kamchatka, for example, bacteria have been found that were apparently generated in the original lava. So they were there before there were knowing subjects. One can go there and see the same bacteria that were there before us. Indeed, these bacteria existed even before there were people to know that they were bacteria. In the same way, if the human race were to disappear today, Nature would go on as before. Does this not mean that we should try to avoid the sort of anthropomorphism that implies that humans (or life or an organism equipped with a brain) create a Nature of their own, an Umvelt as proposed by Von Uexküll?[15]

In this kind of situation the researcher is tempted to reduce the problem to the minimum, or to avoid it altogether, by making a basic distinction between what exists (or does not exist) in the absolute, on the one hand, and the knowing process, as an act of the living subject, on the other. The advantage of this tactic is that it is no longer the existence of things that is modified by the knowing subject doing the experiments. It is simply the description of the way in which things exist that is modified. But we should nevertheless be aware of the fact that this distinction itself relies upon the unassailable validity of the distinction between the object described and its description by a subject. But this is precisely what is in question.

Is the concept of the Umwelt a solution?

The above-mentioned distinction between description and existence looks like a superficial solution to a profound problem. It is a problem encountered at the two ends of the chain of knowledge; on the one hand, by the most serious

---

[14] M. Merleau-Ponty (1994) *La Nature*, Seuil, Paris. In reply to this argument relating to the possible disappearance of humanity, he evoked Husserl's demurrer based on the fact that 'nothing can diminish the evidence of references' because he assumed, along with Husserl 'the apparent paradox of a physical reality based upon the human body (111)'.

[15] J. von Uexküll (1956) *Streifzüge durch die Umwelten von Tieren und Menschen*, Bedeutungslehre. Rohwohlt, Hamburg.

candidate for the status of a fundamental science, sub-atomic physics, and, on the other, by those sciences for which the act of knowing turns back upon itself to become knowledge of the knowing subject, the cognitive sciences.

Physics has already reached the limit of our capacity for scientific objectification and has come to the conclusion that it is impossible to maintain the classic myth of an entire Nature brought together under the contemplative gaze of an epistemic subject who is not itself involved with this same Nature.

As for physiology, it is worth bearing in mind what Von Uexküll had to say when he insisted that there was no such thing as a universal Nature embracing all phenomena, including the phenomena of life, and which relates them systematically among themselves by laws that remain homogeneous with those that prevail at the level of the most basic physical interactions. Or if such a thing does exist, it could only appear to us as a chaos we could not even represent coherently. On the other hand, what does exist for living subjects, in particular human subjects capable of knowing and therefore of acting intelligently, are the worlds of perception and action: the Umwelt that belongs to each subject or community of subjects. These are worlds that he compares with a bubble surrounding each active subject and enabling the subject to confer upon external objects those perceptual and actional characteristics which they only possess as a function of these vital activities.[16]

Uexküll does not hesitate to compare the Umwelts of the tick, the sea urchin, and the hermit crab with the environment (in the ontological sense of a domain of objects) of the astronomer, the deep-sea explorer, the chemist, or the physicist dealing with electro-magnetism. Is that shocking? Not if we pay attention to what the interpreters of quantum physics[17] tell us when they call on their colleagues in the cognitive sciences to bring their physics up to date. Will they be listened to?

----

16 We should not cry irrationality when alluding to Benjamin Lee Whorf's incommensurability thesis. If the objects are just as real despite the different worlds in which they are to be found, it is because they are only to be differentiated on the grounds of their having to be referred back to the subjects which inhabit these worlds or intervene in them. With the exception of primitive animals, the subjects of these different worlds can participate in each other's worlds. Our human worlds intersect, and dogs participate in the world of their masters. With regard to the constitutive operations by means of which the agent projects upon its objects properties corresponding to its interests and to the instruments it employs to make use of them, Nature only exists as an all-encompassing but constantly retreating horizon. It certainly does not contain the 'things' pertaining to these different worlds in the manner of a reservoir.

17 See M. Bitbol (2003) La physique et la primauté de l'action, in J.-L. Petit (éd.), *Repenser le corps, l'action et la cognition avec les neurosciences*, *Intellectica* no. 36–37, pp. 271–291; G. Auletta (2003) Some lessons of quantum mechanics for cognitive science: intentionality and representation, in J.-L. Petit (éd.), *Repenser le corps, l'action et la cognition avec les*

For example, classical physicists thought they really were referring to something completely determined when they talked about particles pursuing a trajectory and possessing at each instant a position and a momentum (mass × speed). A field was defined by determining for each point in space the property associated with it (its intensity as manifested in the deflection of a magnetized needle).

In quantum physics, on the other hand, and even if states are currently defined for one particle, two particles, etc., it has nevertheless become almost paradoxical to talk of *the* particles, to the extent that their enumeration is in any case quite impossible. Even if one knows that a radioactive material has a half-life of a certain period, one still cannot predict the atom that will be affected by this decline at a given instant. In place of a trajectory, one finds a cloud of points whose position cannot be determined, since any determination concerning the moment will have to be compensated by some uncertainty concerning the position and vice versa. A quantum field will at best only include 'observables' which are not (contrary to a conventional interpretation of the expression) objects of some possible observation and to which properties can be ascribed. All that can be associated with such a field is a certain potentiality for these properties to be observed through the use of specific measuring instruments.[18] Preferring to calculate probabilities accurately rather than to apply a deterministic law (false at this microscopic level) to the description of objects or movements, quantum physics admits explicitly that all it can do is describe our possible knowledge of these objects or movements. Such is the novelty of the present epistemological situation.

Let's admit it. The modesty and the openness of mind of physicists is not something that is found in all currents of the cognitive sciences today. Nature still often figures there as a system of independent objects between which there prevail mechanical causal laws. Take the recent case of the celebrated John Searle who claimed with his usual self-confidence: 'This is the backbone

---

neurosciences, *Intellectica* no. 36–37, pp. 297–317. These authors make us aware of an epistemological revolution. For what was only valid of position and speed in Heisenberg's Uncertainty Principle is now extended to cover all the concepts of quantum physics. If the Uncertainty Principle initially had little to do with the intervention of the observer save for the latter entailing the emission of at least one photon, the generalization of this principle brings with it the recognition of the dependence of any ontology upon human practice.

[18] On this subject it is worth reading the commentaries of Bitbol: 'conceptual instrument, of use in partial synthesizing of whatever might manifest itself at our own scale, in our own *Umwelt* in von Uexküll's sense, in an experimental framework which has been set up by a human praxis in view of expectations of paramount humanity [...], such as means, goals or environment of actions'. M. Bitbol (2003) La physique et la primauté de l'action, in J.-L. Petit (éd.), *Repenser le corps, l'action et la cognition avec les neurosciences*, *Intellectica* no. 36–37, p. 280.

of our ontology. *We live in a world* entirely made up of particles caught up in fields of force, etc.'[19] It is not just the phenomenologist with his eyes fixed on the correlation between the living organism and the lived world who rejects this naïve dogmatism but also the contemporary physicist.

The need for a new theoretical posture

A new posture demands that the physiologist stop trying to investigate a pre-constituted world independent of the actively living subject, at least for the time being. This means recognizing the limits of his own situation, as also of the situation of each incarnate and situated agent and, moreover, recognizing the *act of a living being* as the *common source of both cognition and science*. Finally, he is also called upon to take account of the interaction between the physical world 'existing independent of himself' and his brain, the *brain of an intentional subject who acts and projects*.

In the framework of such rigorously decisionist and interactionist pragmatism (a provisional description that anticipates the philosophical position developed in Chapter 3), one that rejects the legacy of a naïve ontology, the terms in which the question of cognition have been posed traditionally are, henceforward, transposed radically.

Together with the pretension of omniscience, the insurmountable dualism of opposed objective poles also disappears: the opposed poles of a hypostatized objective world in itself outside the knowing subject and this same subject itself, also and equivalently objectified under the form of the being in itself of its brain, a brain existing to produce an internal representation of the external world. At the same time, the whole problem of this representation also disappears, a representation which had hitherto always been projected upon the description of these internal activities, despite the fact that these activities prove to be more essentially pro-active than reactive (or to speak in more phenomenologically appropriate language: more originally meaning-giving than secondarily representational).

Knowledge re-thought in terms of an effective act of knowing, and no longer as a reflection in an internal mirror, now finds itself reinvested with a new positional efficacy and a new ontological creativity, which means that for each knowing subject there now exists a world: his Umwelt, or surrounding world. Moreover, such a world can, properly speaking, only exist in the context of an interaction between this knowing subject and its objects of interest and

---

[19] J. Searle (1995) *The Construction of Social Reality*, Penguin Press, London, p. 7 (our emphasis).

goals of action[20] (no matter what might be the case in the field of sciences other than those dealing with life).

By appealing to innate dispositions inherent in action, and rendered intelligible through reflection and an elaboration of his intuition of the living, the physiologist obtains access, in an original way, to properties which cannot be grasped by a derivative theory of mind representing an objective world or the feelings of others as objects in the world. Here too we are of course conscious of the objections that can be brought against us. We are going back to ideas like those of the mathematicians of the so-called intuitionist school of the twentieth century (Brouwer's alleged slogan: 'Mathematics is an act rather than a theory!'), for example, and in so doing run the risk of both overlooking unconscious processes and underestimating our power of abstract thought, a power that enables us to escape the flux of lived experience with a view to inventing new solutions. But this is precisely the challenge this book attempts to meet by at least posing the problem, if not furnishing the solution.

The real world, perceived and lived: Euclidian or affine?

So the 'real world' is not the perceived world operative on the plane of an experience that is actually lived out. The real world is that virtual reference theoreticians construct in order to be able to distinguish what is 'true' from what is 'false' in the perceptual experience of living beings. Immediately one comes up against the following question: if things are not as they were believed to be, if one is the victim of a perceptual illusion, of an error of interpretation and imagination, of a hallucination perhaps, is one not then forced to turn away from this supposedly 'perceived world' and to turn back to the true world, the real world, the physical world which actually exists as a matter of fact? Yes, no doubt. But never forget that the world of the corrected error, the world to which one reverts as being the 'true' world will once again be a world perceived through instruments, very much as the stars and galaxies are

---

[20] With social animals like humans, we could expect the emergence of an unusual mode of community between one knower and the other knowers existing in the frame of one and the same life world, a world which is itself shared in common. According to Husserl in *Krisis*, under certain historical and institutional conditions (e.g. the Renaissance) their mutual interaction would be a basis for the procedure of idealization of an objective world common to the universal virtual community formed by researchers of all times. And this operation would in turn be publicly (intersubjectively) knowable and directly validated by each to the extent that it simply requires the realization of what we all know how to do: our innate and universal vital praxis, our kinaesthetic system, the repertory of possible actions written into our genetic heritage, both ontogenetic and historical, both personal and communitarian.

perceived through long-distance waves of energy. What else could it possibly be? Nobody can get back to the physical world as it is in itself. The only world capable of reconciling the local dissonance that we call error or illusion, and which in integrating this dissonance constantly manages to weave it back into the seamless fabric of daily life, is the world of our hopes and our fears.

Every time we are deceived by the perceived world we appeal to the real world[21] we inhabit. However, this perceived world is completely real for the living organism to the extent that it actually carries through the operations by means of which it is projected. It acquires a contour to the extent that the living organism configures it. It is made of matter that resists to the extent that forces of contact, pressure, and slippage are constantly exerted against it. This 'real being' is therefore 'real *for*', just as consciousness is 'consciousness *of*'. Does this mean that it lacks any foundation, aside from the purely internal foundation of the act by which it is posited?

A question like this gives expression to the need to develop in physiology (and not just in philosophy, where it already exists thanks to the efforts of phenomenologists) a theory of the world of lived experience. Hence the title of the course of lectures given by Alain Berthoz at the Collège de France in 2003: 'Perceived world, Lived world, Conceived world'.

It is not our intention in this book to hark back to this difference between the perceived world and the physical world. The phenomenal aspect of the perceived world has been described superbly using the resources of natural language (aided by literary talent) in a number of works.[22] Let's just get rid of a dictum that might prove discouraging for students of the cognitive sciences: *Phenomenologicae sunt, non leguntur!* As for the purely mathematical description of its specific formal properties, a good deal of progress has been made since 1923 and Oscar Becker's essay[23] on the formalization, in non-Euclidian

----

21 For the contribution made by Galileo to the determination of this movement of thought as a procedure characteristic of modern science, see Husserl's *Krisis* (E. Husserl (1976) *Die Krisis der Europäischen Wissenschaften und die Transzendentale Phänomenologie*, Hrsg. W. Biemel, Martinus Nijhoff, The Hague; *Crisis of European Sciences and Transcendental Phenomenology* (1970) trans. D. Carr, Northwestern University Press, Evanston, IL).

22 M. Merleau-Ponty (1945) *Phénoménologie de la Perception*, Gallimard, Paris, trans. C. Smith (1962) *Phenomenology of Perception*, Routledge, London; E. Husserl (1973) *Ding und Raum. Vorlesungen 1907*, Husserliana XVI, Martinus Nijhoff, Den Haag, and also E. Husserl (1989) *La Terre ne se meut pas*, Minuit, Paris; M. Heidegger (1962) *Sein und Zeit*, trans. J. Macquarie and E. Robinson (1962) *Being and Time*, Harper & Row, New York; P. Kaufmann (1967) *L'expérience émotionnelle de l'espace*, Vrin, Paris; J.-P. Sartre (1943) *L'être et le néant*, Gallimard, Paris.

23 O. Becker (1923/1963) *Beiträge zur phänomenologischen Begründung der Geometrie und ihrer physikalischen Anwendung*, Max Niemeyer, Tübingen.

geometry, of the Husserlian intuition into the possibility of a morphology or 'material eidetics' of the vague forms of the phenomenal world. Recently, the non-Euclidean character of perceived or motor space has been the object of works by Koenderink and his school[24] for visual perception, by Pollick and Sapiro,[25] and Flash and Hanzel,[26] and more recently also Tabareau *et al.*,[27] for the generation of movement. Whereas, for hundreds of years, it was thought that the geometry of the brain was Euclidian, it is now thought that the brain may use affine geometries and even more complex geometries. Poincaré was aware of this possibility when he wrote that the use of Euclidian space could be explained as being the space that has proved to be 'most useful' on Earth.

Examples of 'interpretations' of the physical world by the brain are numerous. We now know that the contours of an object are not delineated by a continuous black line clinging to the bumps and hollows of the object, and which the brain would simply have to re-copy in order to have the form of the object. The contour of the object does not have a physical existence. It is determined by the ability of the neurons of the visual cortex to undertake an analysis of form, one that relies primarily upon contrast. One might as well say that it has to be invented as the brain invents the Kanizsa forms.[28] Nobody knows better than the caricaturists that the contour also depends upon the point of view of the perceiving subject. And the same goes for each of the so-called physical properties of objects. They keep on being referred back to someone who projects his own capacity for movement upon the object.

The fact that the perceived world is a construction of the brain is illustrated by the existence of multiple systems of interpretation of sense data in the brain. For example, whenever we want to grasp an object, an image of this object is processed along two paths:[29] the first, dorsal path makes its way

....

[24] J. J. Koenderink (1984) The structure of images, *Biol. Cybernetics* 50, 363–370. See also O. Faugeras *et al.* (2001) *The Geometry of Multiple Images of a Scene and Some of their Applications*, MIT Press, Cambridge, MA.

[25] F.E. Pollick and G. Sapiro (1997) Constant affine velocity predicts the 1/3 power law of planar motion perception and generation, *Vision Res.* 37(3), 347–353.

[26] T. Flash and A.A. Handzel (2007) Affine differential geometry analysis of human arm movements, *Biol. Cybernetics* 96(6), 577–601.

[27] N. Tabareau, D. Bennequin, A. Berthoz, J.-J. Slotine, and B. Girard (2007) Geometry of the superior colliculus mapping and efficient oculomotor computation, *Biol. Cybernetics* 97(4), 279–292.

[28] G. Kanizsa (1979) *Organization in Vision: Essays in Gestalt Perception*, Praeger Press, New York.

[29] Milner and Goodale have shown that patients with a lesion of the parietal cortex belonging to the dorsal stream of processing of visual data are unable to position a thin object to make it fit into a slot, whereas patients with a temporal lesion can position the hand correctly but

through the parietal cortex to rejoin the pre-frontal cortex and is concerned with space and action; the other, ventral path rejoins the temporal cortex to make 'identification' possible. The data processed along these two pathways are combined with information processed in the limbic system, the brain of the emotions, which attributes an affective value to the object. From there, all this information is in turn referred to the pre-frontal cortex, which is then able to arbitrate, 'take decisions', and, in turn, influence the way in which information is obtained at the source. The unity of the perceived world depends upon this extraordinary capacity of the brain which, in the first instance, breaks up the world into multiple components. The world of our lived experience is then the result of a synthesis of the activity of all these stations, plus all those which are the object of investigation in the neurosciences today. The central hypothesis of this book is that the *act* is an indispensable feature of this unity. Without the notion of the *act*, it would be impossible to account for this fundamental unity.

The difference between a perceived world and a physical world has become clearly formulated as a subject of study, even if no definitive theory has yet been agreed upon. But there is a big difference between agreeing upon the formulation of the question and the development of the new physiological and philosophical theory of action needed to cope with it. The very possibility of a new theory of action calls for the rejection of a number of concepts we would like to call myths and this is for two reasons. On the one hand, they are based upon beliefs and not upon well-founded hypotheses; on the other, they stand in the way of any improvement in our understanding of the functioning of the brain, just as the hypothesis of *chronaxia*[30] very nearly blocked the development of neurophysiology in France.

The myth of the bottom-up process

As mentioned above, the idea of a bottom-up process is certainly one of the foundations of the classical analysis of perception. Cognition is willingly represented as a staircase which starts out from a bottom level, that of the sensorial receptors: the retinae, the tactile cutaneous receptors, the cochlea,

---

cannot describe the slope of the slot. In this connection a disassociation has been established between a dorsal path for action in space and a ventral path for the identification of objects. (A.D. Milner and M.A. Goodale (1993) Visual pathways to perception and action, *Prog. Brain Res.* 95, 317–337).

[30] Chronaxia: a measure of the excitability of the nerves or muscles, the smallest period of effective electrical stimulation, whose intensity is half that required for the stimulus. This kind of approach to the functioning of the nervous system, more electrical than physiological, could have constituted an epistemological obstacle.

the olfactive epithelium, etc., and which continues to the top level of the asso-
ciative areas of the cortex specializing in perceptual interpretation and
conceptual categorization, to finish up with the pre-frontal cortex where decisions are taken.[31] From up there, top–bottom mechanisms intervene to
modulate and influence the sensorial systems and to select actions. One still
finds this double approach today in all the main chapters of the study of cognitive functions in the neurosciences (as well as in the analysis of attention,
memory, etc.). The tendency to generalize this model, a tendency reinforced
by the successful decoding of the organization of the visual paths or the sensori-
motor mechanisms, has to be questioned. The evidence suggests in fact, and
in a fairly clear way, the existence of an order of regular progression from one
nervous centre to another, in virtue of which the receptor field of the cells of
these centres (the part of the visual field where a light-source stimulus provokes
a selective reaction from these cells) gets bigger as one moves up from the retinal
ganglions to the lateral geniculate bodies of the thalamus to the striated regions
of the occipital cortex (V1), and from there to the ventro-lateral and orbital
regions of the occipital cortex. This progressive embedding of the cellular receptor fields is coupled with a transition, from the simple to the complex, of those
characteristics of the object, or of the visual scene, which are pertinent for cellular activation. Starting from simple differences of local luminosity associated
with an edge or an angle detected by the V1 cells, this progressive complexity
can be followed right up to the inferior temporal cortex, responsible for the
recognition of faces which could, according to certain authors,[32] have the 'purely
cognitive' value of a recognition of individual identity.

The same applies to the progressive elaboration of the motor commands on
the basis of sensorial information. In the visual cortex one would find purely
visual information. Then in the parietal cortex this information would
be combined with data concerning the body; finally, in the pre-motor cortex
then the motor cortex, one would find a mixture of action and perception
leading to a 'motor' activity at the level of the motor cortex. Recent models
of attention serve to confirm this functional schema. A series of spatial filters
is interposed successively along the path upon which visual information is
processed by producing a selection of forms.[33]

---

[31] Hence the expressions bottom-up and top-down.

[32] G.C. Baylis, E.T. Rolls, and C.M. Leonard (1985) Selectivity between faces in the
responses of a population of neurons in the cortex in the superior temporal sulcus of the
monkey, *Brain Res.* 342, 91–102.

[33] M.I. Posner and S. Dehaene (1994) Attentional networks, *Trends Neurosci.* 17(2), 75–79.

Can this order be generalized to all the sensory modalities, and does the same rule apply to the entire system of cerebral functioning? Probably not. Just as the history of mathematics began with Euclidean geometry, which proved to be so restricted a branch of mathematics that this science was obliged to free itself from the model that had given rise to it, so, in neuro-science, the time has probably come to shake ourselves free of the authority of the sensori-motor model.

All the more so since this schema, a schema we have attacked on several occa-sions, no longer holds up in the face of the discoveries of the neurosciences. The idea of a descending influence (top-down) of the dispositions, expectations, beliefs, or knowledge of the subject in advance of its analysis of the sensory evidence now has to be admitted. Today this hypothesis can no longer be dis-missed casually, as was done by Jerry Fodor,[34] by attributing it to a sentimental attachment, in the community of the cognitive sciences, to the New Look move-ment of Jerome Bruner[35] going back to the 1970s (This professor of psychology at Harvard, then Oxford, popularized Piaget's developmental psychology in the English-speaking world. The New Look movement emphasized the fact that perception is modified by the individual values of the child).

The neuropsychologist Luria[36] also emphasized the role of contextual and even social influences in Russia by showing to what an extent the perception of an object was linked to the habits and knowledge of the community. For example, a form was interpreted as a vase or a bucket depending on the origin, town, or country, of the subjects. With the psychologist Vygotski[37] one finds similar remarks on the importance of the use made of an object on its percep-tion. For instance, a pencil can be used to draw but also as a pointer or to prevent a door from closing; or again, it can be used as a drumstick to play on a drum. Each time the perception will change. Vygotski insisted that social interactions were also important in specifying percepts. This question opens up an area where anthropologists and specialists of the cognitive sciences are able to cooperate.

In fact, even if we restrict ourselves to the visual mode, it is enough to intro-duce the movement of the eye, inseparable from its behavioural use in the exploration of the world, to discover that the visual cells do not serve simply to

[34] J. Fodor (1983/1989) *The Modularity of Mind*, MIT Press, Cambridge, MA, p. 66.

[35] J.S. Bruner, On perceptual readiness, *Psychol. Rev.* 64, 123–152.

[36] A.R. Luria (1966), *The Higher Cortical Functions in Man*, Basic Books, New York; A.R. Luria (1973), *The Working Brain*, Basic Books, New York.

[37] L. Vygotski (1997) *Pensée et langage*, Éditions La Dispute, Paris; L. Vygotski (1998) *Théorie des émotions*, L'Harmattan, Paris; Y. Clot (1999) *Avec Vygotski*, La Dispute, Paris.

make possible a passive and cumulative coding of the properties of the stimulus. Indeed, in the dorsal visual path, at a relay centre between the occipital visual areas and the frontal eye fields where the ocular movements are planned, the cells of the intra-parietal sulcus displace their retinal receptor field just before an ocular saccade, and in such a way that the object looked at will fall precisely into this receptor field.[38] The active character of the ocular saccade, at the convergence of the sensorial analysis and the intentions of movement, makes of it an excellent model for cerebral functioning. We suggest that it should replace the system of inputs centred exclusively upon the detection of objects of perception in the retinal stimuli.

The local and the global

We are happy to apply to the brain the formula attributed to Nicholas of Cusa:[39] 'the centre is everywhere, the periphery, nowhere'. Let us stop talking about primary areas and secondary areas. Colin Blakemore, one of the best physiologists of vision, said that there are as many, or even more, pathways that are projected upon the primary visual area as pathways that leave it. As early as 1977, Alain Berthoz and Robert Baker[40] showed, for the first time, that motor signals modulated the neurons of the vestibular nuclei, the first vestibular information relays starting from the inertial receptors of the internal ear. This conferred a completely new status upon these neurons which, instead of being simple sensorial relays, acquired an integrative role in perception and action. It offered a neurophysiological proof of the fact that action influences perception at its very source.

The division of labour in the research devoted to mechanisms regulating cognitive activity has today become a real epistemological obstacle to any physiological understanding of cerebral functions and their interactions. We find the same thing in medicine, where doctors who have specialized in the treatment of specific organs tend to forget the unity of the organism. For example, for years the otorhinolaryngologists treated, at the level of the throat, disturbances due in fact to a reflux of liquid acid in the stomach through the oesophagian channel. Many troubles suffered by persons with

---

[38] J.R. Duhamel et al. (1992) The updating of the representation of visual space in parietal cortex by intended eye movements, *Science* 255, 90–92.

[39] Nicholas of Cusa (1401–1464), born at Treves, bishop of Brixen (Tirol), philosopher, mathematician, theologian of the Renaissance, precursor of Copernicus (*De docta ignorantia*, 1440).

[40] R. Baker and A. Berthoz (1977) *Control of Gaze by Brain Stem Neurons*, Elsevier, Amsterdam.

crano-facial asymmetries,[41] and which are treated separately by a whole series of specialists, share a common cause in a distortion of the body scheme, which exercises a disturbing influence on numerous functions.

In the same way, the researcher in the cognitive sciences is tempted to extract, from the general problem of cognition, those questions which appear to be better circumscribed and which he thinks lend themselves more directly to scientific treatment. As a result of this he tends to postpone indefinitely the general problem of tackling the way in which perception is guided by an intention to act in a global context. The local takes precedence over the global and the interactions between the two are ignored. The psychology of form and psychoanalysis have attempted to come to terms with this interaction between the local and the global but their theories now have to be revised in the light of the evidence of the neurosciences. There is no other way of proceeding.

How do we move from the unconscious functioning of cerebral mechanisms to full consciousness of the operations of the mind? At present nobody is in a position to answer this question. But if you want to know how we recognize a sentence (or a melody) against the surrounding noise, how we identify an object against the general distribution of light signals in the visual field, or a face in the series of aspects made available to us from varying points of view, for all these partial questions explanations are presently available. And in a misleading way they incite us to think that the more we succeed in breaking up the general question of cognition into sub-questions of this kind the more we are likely to solve even the most difficult of them, like that concerning access to consciousness. How can the multiple representations produced by the different modular systems at the interface with external reality be integrated into one unique consciousness? Today this question is taken seriously by modern cognitive neuroscience.[42]

---

[41] A. Berthoz and A. Rousié (2001) Physiopathology of otolith-dependent vertigo. Control of the cerebral cortex and consequences of cranio-facial asymmetries, *Adv. Otorhinolaryngol.* 58, 48–67.

[42] Numerous attempts are presently being made to resolve the problem of the unity of the field of consciousness. Thus, Edelman and Tononi have shown a synchronization of cerebral activity on the appearance of a conscious percept by using ambiguous figures (G. Edelman and G. Tononi (2000) *Comment la matière devient consciente*, Odile Jacob, Paris). Dehaene *et al.*, following Baars (B.J. Baars (1998) *A Cognitive Theory of Consciousness*, Cambridge University Press, Cambridge), have developed the hypothesis of a network of cortical neurons, with long axons that relate the different centres implied in the processing of information relative to an object. The emergence of this long network is supposed to lie at the root of the appearance of a conscious percept (S. Dehaene, M. Kerzberg, and J.-P. Changeux (1998) A neuronal model of a global workspace in effortful cognitive tasks, *Proc. Natl. Acad. Sci. USA* 95, 14529–14534).

In *The Brain's Sense of Movement*,[43] the problem of the unity of perception and of its coherence was addressed. But we can take the analysis a step further. In isolating visual perception, auditory perception, tactile perception, the perception of language, etc., from the rest of cognition, as so many independent mechanisms, one also isolates—though in another sense and as an irreducible residue—this same cognition as a global phenomenon.

If one follows the course of the development of a sensory signal of whatever kind, one finds that one passes insensibly from peripheral systems to central systems. And this without being able to say at any one moment: here the signal has left the system for the analysis of visual forms (for example), there it has entered the system for the interpretation of the meanings of things, meanings responsible for the fact that they appear to us in this or that fashion. This is all the more so as the 'motor' signals linked to action profoundly modify the activity of the first sensorial relays. Surprising devices operate over here to ensure the voluntary control of the sensitivity of the stretch receptors in the neuromuscular spindles of the motor muscles by an innervation (γ) parallel to that of motor command (α). While over there, other devices make possible a modification of the acuteness of the cutaneous sensory discrimination of the hand, due to the fact that its expert use induces receptor fields of neurons, in the somato-sensory cortical regions of representation, to migrate towards the skin areas being used; or again, close attention to the instrument in the early stages of learning and the intensive use of the musical instrument[44] later on bring about a modification of the sensitivity of the ear to the pitch of a sound. For those who want to stick with the centre/periphery distinction: the centre would have to be located in the legs of the walker, in the hands of the artisan, in the ear of the musician!

The pure sensation, a sensation uncontaminated by central influences, devoid of projective interpretation or voluntary control but which is supposed to faithfully reproduce the impact of the physical energies surrounding the organism, does not exist. What do exist are nerve cells with multiple receptor fields in multiple modalities; for example, a particular neuron activated by a visual stimulus in the space close to the animal might be activated in the same way when one touches its arm.[45] And these neurons are influenced by the action projected. In order to minimize the difficulty of explaining the

---

[43] A. Berthoz (1997) *Le sens du mouvement*, Odile Jacob, Paris, Chap. 3, pp. 75–105.

[44] For example, the violin demands more careful manipulation than the piano to get the right notes and the right pitch on the strings.

[45] S.A. Graziano *et al.* (1994) Coding of visual space by premotor neurons, *Science* 266, 1054–1057; A.J. Mistlin and D.I. Perrett (1990) Visual and somatosensory processing in the macaque temporal cortex: the role of 'expectation', *Exp. Brain Res.* 82, 437–450.

integration of different sensorial modalities, the existence of supramodal representations has been proposed. But it has not been proved that such a type of coding exists. On the other hand, we are finding more and more cases of neurons that code entire types of behaviour: defence, attack, etc.[46] Once again, it is the act that matters.

A 'multi-sensorial' forum under the aegis of a psychologist like John Driver and his disciples recently brought together researchers concerned with the problem of multi-sensoriality.[47] But once again, we have to be on our guard. The problem is not one of deciding how we move from a division of the senses to their cooperation (or competition). The brain performs projective comparisons. Recent collaboration between physiologists and decision-making theorists might help us to make progress in this area.

The theory of perception in act

We have just pointed out the impossibility of establishing a frontier between sensation and motricity, because action is already to be found in perception.[48] The reader may remember that just such an identification of the perceptual categories with those of action had been condemned in advance as a 'theoretical aberration'.[49] Fodor, again, thought that his modular theory could only be applied to entry systems and so not to motor systems whose role was, for him, limited to 'the motor integration of behaviour'.[50]

We know that the functioning of the first relays of the visual pathways is modulated by attention. But what psychologists of attention have perhaps not sufficiently underlined is that it is not just any part of the visual field that attracts our attention. As if attention was a totally indifferent cognitive faculty engaged in a haphazard exploration of all the regions of surrounding space! In fact, the region of interest towards which the gaze is directed is

---

[46] D.F. Cooke and M.S. Graziano (2004) Super-flinchers and nerves of steel: defensive movements altered by chemical manipulation of a cortical motor area, *Neuron* 43(4), 585–593; D.F. Cooke and M.S. Graziano (2004) Sensori-motor integration in the precentral gyrus: polysensory neurons and defensive movements, *J. Neurophysiol.* 91(4), 1648–1660.

[47] A. Maravita, C. Spence, and J. Driver (2003) Multisensory integration and the body schema: close to hand and within reach, *Curr. Biol.* 13(13), R531–539; E. Macaluso and J. Driver (2005) Multisensory spatial interaction: a window onto functional integration in the human brain, *Trends Neurosci.* 28(5), 264–271.

[48] A. Berthoz (1997) *Le sens du mouvement*, Odile Jacob, Paris; A. Berthoz (2003) *La décision*, Odile Jacob, Paris.

[49] By J. Fodor (1983/1989) *The Modularity of Mind*, MIT Press, Cambridge, MA, p. 40.

[50] J. Fodor (1983/1989) *The Modularity of Mind*, MIT Press, Cambridge, MA, p. 42.

specified in advance by an intention to act which never fails to accompany this gaze. Rizzolatti and Gallese offered a clear formulation of this position under the heading of a 'pre-motor theory of attention',[51] and a hierarchic mechanism based on inhibition has been conceived by our team to elucidate its neuronal foundations.[52]

The psychologists of cognition have pursued their old dispute with behaviourism without having appreciated that the neurosciences, in between times, had already accommodated action as a category irreducible to that of movement and representation. In the new situation that has arisen, action as such has ceased to be a holistic notion qualifying behaviour in a way which remained global and so non-specific because we have since learned that it rests on precise neural foundations. It is time to get rid of our former suspicion of physiology as the intuitive description of corporeal movements directed towards hygienic or therapeutic ends (in functional re-education, among other things). Perhaps the term motor makes one think too much of muscles, and it would have been better to designate the theory in question as *theory of perception in act*.

An evaluation of the new epistemological situation that has arisen in the neurosciences needs to be offered by the philosopher. For he will be able to relate the tendency towards a physiology of action to the distinction drawn by Aristotle between 'being in act' and 'being in potency'.[53] And he will be able to confirm that this distinction did not initially (as became the case in the later interpretation offered by the so-called medieval scholastic, according to philosophy encyclopaedias) disjoin the two terms as having nothing to do with each other: a being possessing a non-actualized potency and an actual or effective being that has exhausted its potentiality. Originally this distinction was intended to grasp intuitively a tension essential to all living beings, a tension between an already fairly precisely, though inchoately,[54] determined potentiality and the actuality of a form still wholly animated by the power it actualizes in being.

---

[51] G. Rizzolatti and V. Gallese (1998) Mechanisms and theories of spatial neglect, in F. Boller and J. Grafman (eds), *Handbook of Neuropsychology*, vol. 1, Elsevier, Amsterdam, pp. 223–246.

[52] A. Berthoz (1996) The role of inhibition in the hierarchical gating of executed and imagined movements, *Cog. Brain Res.* 3(2), 101–113.

[53] Respectively, *entelecheia* and *dunamis*.

[54] The inchoate: what lies in general at the origin, the start of an action, or the beginning of a change.

Perception for action

Elsewhere we have argued that perception is simulated action,[55] and that perception is decision.[56] Many have seen in this a serious infringement of *functionalism*,[57] an ideology held in the greatest respect in the cognitive sciences for some time. It seemed as though we were going back upon a major advance in modern scientific thinking. Functionalism[58] based its difference from teleology (and also its victory over it) on the principle that the function determines nothing with regard to the nature of the mechanism upon which its realization depends. It is not because perception can eventually serve the interests of action that one needs to conclude that perception exists for action. For a long time this objection was made against any motor theory of perception. Its ability to convince rested on the fact that, in their most familiar versions (like those of Gibson, Piaget, or Lieberman),[59] these theories were situated in the field of a psychology of behaviour reluctant to delve into the underlying mechanisms. This has no force today against a neurophysiology of action, which has adopted the slogan 'perception for action', since the latter is now based on a detailed knowledge of the neural foundations of behaviour. The engineers of motor control will no doubt insist that there are in principle innumerable ways of connecting a mechanical arm to a camera in the construction of a robot and that therefore there is no reason, *a priori*, to make the movements (or even the optics) of this camera depend upon the movement of the arm. This argument may perhaps be decisive for robots, and retains a certain value for understanding the originality of perception in the case of the animal, to the extent that the latter obeys laws

---

55 A. Berthoz (1997) *Le sens du mouvement*, Odile Jacob, Paris, p. 15.

56 A. Berthoz (2004) *La décision*, Odile Jacob, Paris, p. 177.

57 Functionalism: a less restrictive reformulation of the physicalist ideology identifying mental with brain states and which consists of identifying these same mental states with abstract functional descriptions of the cognitive system, without any particular commitment regarding the way in which these described configurations are actually realized (therefore not necessarily in a brain but also possibly in a computer).

58 With reference to the substitution in modern biological thinking of the anthropomorphic notion of goal with the (supposedly non-anthropomorphic) notion of function. The latter notion is the theme of a historical and epistemological study in the framework of the ACI (Action Concertée Incitative, a programme funded by the French ministry of scientific research), 'La notion de fonction dans les sciences humaines, biologiques et médicales', led by Jean Gayon, Institut d'Histoire et Philosophie des Sciences et des Techniques, Paris.

59 J.J. Gibson (1996) *The Senses Considered as Perceptual Systems*, Houghton Mifflin, Boston, MA; J. Piaget and B. Inhelder (1948) *La représentation de l'espace chez l'enfant*, PUF, Paris; P. Liberman (1984) *The Biology and Evolution of Language*, Harvard University Press, Cambridge, MA.

which simplify the neuro-computation in the recognition of the biological movement.[60] But the function of perceived movement cannot be reduced to this.

Observed movements, like walking, turning the head, holding out a hand, and leaning forward, particularly when they are directed towards a goal and imply interaction with an object, result in the activation of visual neurons in the superior temporal sulcus in monkeys.[61] In addition the manual actions which belong to the repertoire of the observer are directly recognized without any preliminary analysis of the movement of the limbs individually brought into play, or any appeal to the mental states of the agent. Grasping an object with the whole hand or between finger and thumb, manipulating it, twisting and tearing it, carrying it to the mouth, all these actions possess the property of activating a visual-motor family of cells in the frontal pre-motor area 5 (Rizzolatti's mirror neurons).[62] With humans too, imagery by functional magnetic resonance has made it possible to establish that observed actions activate a network (superior temporal sulcus, parietal cortex, pre-motor cortex) now known by the name of mirror system.[63] We shall come back to this question in Chapter 8. The new concepts that have grown out of the debate aroused by the discovery of these mirror neurons have today contributed much to the enrichment of these notions. This modality of being in act goes much further than the local translation of the limbs responsible for movements in physical space.[64] The psychology of enaction in particular owes much to Varela,[65] whose recent death was a great loss.

....

60 P. Viviani and N. Stucchi (1992) Biological movements look uniform: evidence of motor-perceptual interactions, *J. Exp. Psychol. Hum Perception Performance* 18(3), 603–623; P. Viviani and T. Flash (1995) Minimum jerk, two third power law and isochrony. Converging approaches to movement planning, *J. Exp. Psychol. Hum Perception Performance* 21, 32–53.

61 D.I. Perrett *et al.* (1989) Frameworks of analysis for the neural representation of animate objects and actions, *J. Exp. Biol.* 146, 87–113.

62 G. di Pellegrino *et al.* (1992) Understanding motor events: a neurophysiological study, *Exp. Brain Res.* 91, 176–180.

63 G. Buccino *et al.* (2001) Action observation activates premotor and parietal areas in a somatotopic manner: an FMRI study, *Eur. J. Neurosci.* 13, 400–404.

64 The mathematician will also remind us of the intellectual victory represented by the conquest of the concept of infinity '*in actu*', not just for infinitesimal calculus but also for classical metaphysics (Giordano Bruno, Spinoza, Leibniz). It would also certainly represent a major step in our thinking to learn how to grasp all the properties locally distributed on the trajectory of a variable function in its infinite variations as paradoxically united in one point. But, even if (on a cloudless night) the stars all cast light on the Earth, the gathering of any and every context of the expression 'in act' will not necessarily be enlightening for the physiologist.

65 Enaction: the circular relationship by virtue of which the schemas of interaction between an embodied agent and its environment produce the cognitive structures through which

The identity between the somatotopic organization of the patterns of neural activations correlated in the brain with accomplished actions and with observed actions[66] suggests that the comprehension of actions brings into play a mechanism through which the circuits of perception and action enter into resonance. This mechanism enables the observer to use his own motor repertory to grasp the sense of the movements of others without going through processes of analysis, construction, representation, or even inferential reasoning. Reciprocally, the loss of motor capacities (hemiplegia associated with aphasia following a stroke) can make perceived actions incomprehensible.[67] The ability to do is a direct knowledge or, as Zajonc says, 'knowledge without inference'.[68] On the other hand, all representational theories of the mind in cognitive science postulate just such processes as indispensable intermediaries.

The discovery of mirror neurons has given rise to an extended reflection on the origin of language. In fact the cerebral area which, with humans, is activated by the observation of the actions of others is Broca's area, which is also one of the areas implied in language. This leads Rizzolatti and Arbib to trace the origin of language[69] back to an elementary form of imitation and communication linked to action. Arbib, in a recent reformulation of his thesis (still, however, dependent upon Fodor's modularism) was forced to concede that in any case language required the participation of other 'modules'. According to him, the qualitative leap forward would have been the acquisition of the ability to abstract the meaning of a gesture and so to extract a metaphor from it.[70] For example, we can imitate the flight of a bird with our hands, as is done in the

this agent interprets this environment, and orients its action therein. See F. Varela *et al.* (1993) *L'Inscription corporelle de l'esprit. Sciences cognitives et expérience humaine*, Seuil, Paris, Chap. 8, pp. 207–248.

[66] Somatotopy: topographical correspondence between sensorially stimulated (or recruited in action) regions of the body and certain areas or centres of the brain that receive signals (or from which signals are emitted) coming from (or having as their goal) these same regions of the body. See Chapter 8 on our discussion of the work of Rizzolatti, Fadiga, Decéty, Grèzes, etc.

[67] Luciano Fadiga, at the University of Ferrara, has brought to light the difficulty aphasics suffering from a lesion of Broca's area have in ordering the successive views of simple motor action (ongoing research).

[68] R.B. Zajonc (1985) Emotion and facial efference: a theory reclaimed, *Science* 228(4695), 15–21; W.R. Kunst-Wilson and R.B. Zajonc (1980) Affective discrimination of stimuli that cannot be recognized, *Science* 207(4430), 557–558.

[69] As K.S. Lashley assumed: G. Rizzolatti and M.A. Arbib (1998) Language within our grasp, *Trends Neurosci.* 21(5), 188–194.

[70] This connects with the theories of the linguist G. Lakoff: see V. Gallese and G. Lakoff (2005) The brains concepts: the role of the sensory-motor system in conceptual knowledge, *Cog. Neuropsychol.* 21, 1–25.

language of deaf-mutes. Mirror neurons can contribute to the production of the gesture just as well as to the perception of someone else's gesture. But the ability to recognize that this gesture signifies metaphorically the flight of a bird requires a new level of abstraction. This theory is based on the idea that Broca's area is crucial for imitation. However this has recently been criticized on the basis of work with a more precise cerebral imagery which made it possible to disassociate several parts in the pre-motor cortex.[71] One of the problems physiologists confront is the lack of precision in the measurements permitted by imagery. There is a tendency to impute a function to a given zone of the brain just as soon as it appears to be activated. But the greater part of the areas of the cerebral cortex are made up of a multitude of sub-zones that can be implicated in different circuits, which means that a superficial examination of the evidence can easily lead to a confusion of roles. This idea has called into question the entire theory of the relationship between the pre-motor area, where the mirror neurons are found, and Broca's area.

This is where the issue becomes fundamental. Any new theory for a physiology of action will have to be capable of doing justice to the evolution of this symbolizing function. How did the human brain acquire the capacity for symbolization? Our view is that the abstraction of action has been made possible by new ways of processing cerebral information and not by specific modules which appeared all of a sudden and which would be peculiar, for example, to language. So far from diminishing the significance of language, anchoring the latter in action, in inter-animation, and in actional exchange, is the only way of understanding how language arose.[72]

The rehabilitation of the notion of an act

Rather than subordinating sensation to perception and perception to action, the priority has to be accorded to the act, that act which remains identical in feeling, perceiving, and acting, or even to the *conatus*, as defined by Spinoza: 'The effort with which each thing seeks to preserve its existence is nothing other than the actual essence of this thing'.[73] The act too is the pure product of this persistence in being, this maintenance of what has been acquired, this

---

[71] M. Makuuchi *et al.* (2005) Is Broca's area crucial for imitation? *Cerebral Cortex* 15, 563–570.

[72] The recent reflections of mathematicians like Bernard Tessier and Guiseppe Longo are relevant here: G. Longo (éd.) (2003) Géométrie et Cognition, *Revue de Synthèse*, 5e série, tome 24.

[73] B. Spinoza (1954) Ethique, III, Proposition VII., *Œuvres Complètes de Spinoza*, Gallimard, Paris, p. 421.

updating of memory, a constantly renewed actualization and re-actualization. With regard to whatever is alive, these properties are more essential than obtaining information about external events, the latter, as we now know, being intermittent rather than continuous.

Contemplation or intervention? This apparent alternative is not really one at all. Organisms that have developed a complex brain have secured a margin of liberty with regard to the immediate constraints of their needs and the satisfaction of these needs. Dreams, day-dreaming, mental experience, the conception of intentions, the development of projects, thought, and even creativity: we have to restore to all these activities the central role that belongs to them in the life of the organism, especially the human organism.

The very first survival value, which is also the very first value, is the *act* through which a living being maintains itself in being and thereby brings into the sphere of the appearing (that is, drags out of the nothingness of insignificance) each and every object of interest to it, each goal of possible action, everyone with whom the individual has to cooperate in order to realize this action. A minimal condition for anything whatever to be endowed with the value of being the substrate of an *act* is the presence of an instantaneous neural activation pattern in an anatomical brain circuit.

But this pattern cannot be only a localized state of activation in a certain region of the brain (the presumed support of a mental representation). On the contrary, its importance stems from its insertion in a functional 'loop' (or an interconnected set of functional loops involving both structures mainly involved on the side of perception in conjunction with structures mainly involved on the side of action)[74] and the contribution that this instantaneous activation pattern makes to the total meaning of the behaviour that this loop upholds. In its very geometrical distribution, the spatial configuration of the pattern records whatever experience has been acquired. Building up a reservoir of memories, aptitudes, habits, hedonistic shadings, etc., it brings to the total meaning of the action an unpredictable modulation, due to the composition of the temporarily recruited cell population, to the extent that the latter differs from all the neighbouring cell populations engaged at the same time in other operations. It is also in this way that the configuration in question actually acquires a spatial presence. It is the instantaneous actualization of an individual history concentrated at that point, or rather, to employ the words we just used, which is *spatialized* in this way.

....

[74] J.M. Fuster (2000) Executive frontal functions, *Exp Brain Res.* 133(1), 66–70; J.M. Fuster (2005) The cortical substrate of general intelligence, *Cortex* 41(2), 228–229; J.M. Fuster (2006) The cognit: a network model of cortical representation, *Int. J. Psychophysiol.* 60(2), 125–132.

Dynamic reconfiguration and internal loops

The discovery of the *operational closure*[75] of the cortico–sub-cortical functional loops[76] has made it necessary for us to reform our point of view on the brain. The non-professional reader needs to be reminded that the brain contains neuronal circuits in loops which, for example, rejoin the thalamus, through which all sensory information comes into the brain, the cortex, and then go on to the basal ganglia (responsible for the selection of action) only to come back again towards the thalamus. The basic thalamus–cortex–ganglia loops set up in this way function in an autonomous manner, five parallel loops (at least) controlling the movements of the limbs and eyes, and memory and emotions. Lately, other systems of loops connecting the cortex to the cerebellum have been discovered. They have similar specializations to that of the basal thalamus–cortex–ganglia loops. So, we should think of the brain as constituting these systems of loops coordinated among themselves in a dynamic way. It is in this sense that we can say that the operations in the brain are closed (thereby making dream possible) and not sensori-motor.

What is it, in fact, that gets developed and passed on from relay to relay across the pathways of the nerve impulses in and through these loops? Let us exercise the utmost care in looking for the right words. If one really wants to think seriously in terms of closed circuits, concepts deriving from a conception of the nervous system as an open linkage have to be rejected. To say that they are mental representations in one sense and motor orders in another is simply not tolerable. Mental representations assume an external object that has to be represented internally, and are therefore a way from this interiority towards that exteriority. Motor orders assume a movement to be accomplished with the body in surrounding space, and therefore require that all internal activity find a motor outlet.

....

[75] Operational closure: a functional system (not to be confused with the nervous tissues it recruits) is operationally (and not physically) closed if its activity contributes to the preservation of the material conditions necessary for its unitary existence, if not for its autonomy as a system. A closed system in this sense has neither an input nor an output, nor an environment, and so calls for a massive revision of physiology, traditionally described in terms of sensorial inputs, motor output, and causal influence from or on its environment. See F.J. Varela (1989) *Autonomie et Connaissance*, Seuil, Paris, p. 86.

[76] E. Hoshi, L. Tremblay, J. Feger, P.L. Carras, and P.L. Strick (2005) The cerebellum communicates with the basal ganglia, *Nat. Neurosci.* 8(11), 1491–1493; D.M. Clower, R.P. Dum, and P.L. Strick (2005) Basal ganglia and cerebellar inputs to 'AIP', *Cerebral Cortex* 15(7), 913–920; R.M. Kelly and P.L. Strick (2003) Cerebellar loops with motor cortex and prefrontal cortex of a nonhuman primate, *J. Neurosci.* 23(23), 8432–8444.

One characteristic of functional loops is that of being able to function *independently* of any reception of information through sensorial receptors and of any motor efferences towards the limbs responsible for effecting movements. So we have to get back to bilateral concepts that bring together what should never henceforward be allowed to fall apart: the motor and the sensory aspects. However, simply associating these two aspects in one sensori-motor arc would bring us back to the pre-cognitive theory of the reflex. Another way of getting back to the sensori-motor arc is needed. For this reversion would not be complete without the revival of the traditions of Wundt's innervation feeling (*Innervationsgefühl*)[77] and James' kinaesthesia[78] (*kinesis—esthesis*, kinaesthesia), traditions that have been neglected unjustly.

But it should be possible to go further still by advancing boldly along the track of a physiological 'decisionism' capable of doing justice to the direct influence of motor activity over sensory data processing. Or, reciprocally, along the track of the generalization of a kinaesthetic theory of feeling oneself acting to any type of behaviour. For the former has been unnecessarily restricted to an oculo-motor theory of efference copy[79] or corollary discharge. That is, to a copying of the motor command sent from the motor areas towards the sensory areas, the automatic subtraction of which from visual afference is supposed to hold the visual scene stable over an ocular saccade.

The theoretical and experimental evidence of the neurosciences opens up still more interesting avenues than efference copy. For example, the idea of a functional re-configuration of neuronal networks: rapid changes in the nature of the activation patterns of a group of neurons is supposed to intervene from one phase to another of the flux of activity in the neural networks. Brain imagery is beginning to discriminate such events in their passage across the differentiated regions but is still incapable of apprehending them in their changing functional value. To illustrate this phenomenon of one mode of functioning switching into another,

---

[77] W. Wundt (1874–1810) *Grundzüge der Physiologischen Psychologie*, Leipzig, Engelman; trans. into French by E. Rouvier (1886), *Éléments de Psychologie Physiologique*, Paris, Alcan. See H.E. Ross and K. Bischof (1981) Wundt's views on sensations of innervation: a reevaluation, *Perception* 10, 319–329.

[78] W. James (1980) *The Principles of Psychology*, 2 vols, Dover, New York.

[79] Efference copy is a concept developed in the 1950s by Von Holst and Mittelstaedt in Germany. The idea is that, at the same time that the brain produces a motor command, a copy of this command is sent to the perceptual centres in order to anticipate the consequences of action. So the brain does not have to wait for sensory information to know the results following upon the realization of this action. This is the equivalent of what the roboticians call feed-forward in contrast to feedback. The neural foundations of this efference copy are known today, in particular for the system of vision control.

qualitatively different, mode, we can cite the proposal advanced by Christopher von der Malsburg,[80] for whom neural networks can be re-configured. The idea is that when a neuron belongs to several neural networks connected to different brain centres, extremely rapid molecular mechanisms make it possible for the neurons to be re-configured in such a way that one and the same neuron, in a certain sense, belongs to different networks, a bit like persons in their social interactions. We belong to the society of the neurosciences; but we may also be members of a political party or a religious sect. In our daily lives we are constantly changing hats; that is, changing our social status.

One and the same neuron might turn out to be capable of effecting a change of functional status along analogical lines. If (metaphorically) the neuron changes its point of view, this is because, in belonging by turns to distinct networks, it is at all times placed in a particular point of view. Llínas and Sotelo once propounded the view that the Purkinje cell of the cerebellum, this magnificent neuron, could entirely change its 'functional form' and therefore its physiology, depending on whether it is activated by the entry of mossy fibres or by climbing fibres. It is as if a transistor in an electronic apparatus might have two completely different functions, depending on the band through which it was receiving information.[81]

All the same, von der Malsburg's theories are very difficult to verify today because electrodes have to be implanted in ten different spots at once and because, in consequence, we are running up against the limits of our instrumental finesse. And the same holds of the recent theories of Edelman and Tononi, who have established models of cooperation between entire collections of neurons in which thousands (or more) of neurons, distributed in several areas of the brain, form groups that change from one moment to the next.[82]

To observe these mechanisms at work in the living individual organism, it is going to be necessary to develop news ways of recording large populations of neurons in several places in the brain at one and the same time, and this with the new methods of analysis that may be made available through the cooperation of physicists, roboticians, and information theorists. A huge field is presently being opened up with the recording of the cerebral activity of epileptic patients carrying electrodes chronically implanted in their brains.[83]

---

[80] C. von der Malsburg (1985) Nervous structures with dynamical links, *Berichte d. Bünsengesellschaft f. Physikalische Chemie* 89, 703–710.

[81] R. Llínas and C. Sotelo (1992) *The Cerebellum Revisited*, Springer, New York.

[82] G.M. Edelman and G. Tononi (2000) *Comment la matière devient consciente*, Odile Jacob, Paris.

[83] J. Lachaux, D. Rudrauf, and P. Kahane (2003) Intracranial EEG and human brain mapping, *J. Physiol. Paris* 97(4–6), 613–628.

Autonomy, hierarchy, heterarchy

One of the present preoccupations of our colleagues in robotics is to make their robots 'autonomous' in order that they should get as close as possible to living organisms characterized by just such an autonomy. But the use of this term is fraught with a dangerous ambiguity. It is possible to pick out certain modular functional systems which seem to merit the term 'autonomous', but only in the sense in which the different functional circuits of a car may be called autonomous. And if they are so, it is because automotive mechanisms cannot be confused with those of emotion or even of vision. By holding to this particular conception of autonomy, the description of cognitive functioning has led to a functional phrenology, by analogy with the traditional anatomic phrenology.[84]

To deal with just such a multiplication of locally autonomous systems, it is going to be necessary to re-combine these systems, understand their collective organization so as to be able to save the global unity of the living organism. Let us think a little bit about this concept of autonomy.

It is possible to distinguish: (a) a local autonomy like, for example, that of the peripheral and encapsulated modular systems (*à la* Fodor); (b) a global autonomy through *autopoeitic*[85] operational closure of the nervous system (*à la* Varela); (c) an autonomy stemming from the self-starting character of the dynamic of the cortico–baso–thalamo–cortical functional loops (*à la* Edelman or Llínas);[86] and (d) an *ad hoc* autonomy that changes from one moment to the next as a result of the regrouping of the agents in the brain contributing to a particular function, in rather the same way that experts with different types of expertise can be regrouped around a specific project: constructing a dam, sending a man to Mars, or fighting cancer or bird flu.

Perhaps we shall have to go through a similar four-term dialectical sequence if we are going to arrive at a solution to the problem of getting past the traditional

---

[84] 'Phrenology' or organology, a theory according to which the cerebral circonvolutions (assumed to be reproduced in the bumps of the cranium accessible to palpation: cranioscopy) feature as the locus of organs differentiated in the brain, and whose function corresponds to different mental functions. See F.J. Gall and G. Spurzheim (1809), *Recherches sur le Système Nerveux en général et sur celui du Cerveau en particulier*, Schoell et Nicolle, Paris.

[85] Autopoeisis: from the Greek *autos-poiein*, a process by means of which a system produces both its own components and their organizational unity, even while resisting the disturbances to which it is subjected by its environment. This intuition into the manner in which life is typically organized is explained in F.R. Varela (1989) *Autonomie et Connaissance. Essai sur le Vivant*, Seuil, Paris, Chaps II and III, pp. 37–91.

[86] A. Berthoz (2004) *La décision*, Odile Jacob, Paris, the fountains *intermezzo*.

oppositions in the formulation of our intuitions on living organisms, even while conserving what has been acquired by the neurosciences in the way of the differentiation and specialization of the anatomo-physiological cerebral correlations.

The adoption of a circular conception of cerebral functioning through major functional loops underlying each type of behaviour will require of us that we replace the Cartesian or Newtonian schema of a successive (sensori-motor) causal ordering with a schema more like that employed by Leibniz (or rather Husserl),[87] and we are still struggling to adapt our current concepts to just such a schema – synchronization, de-synchronization, resonance, dissonance, simulation, emulation, expansion—retraction of transitory vortex-type[88] disturbances.

And as we already suggested, it will also be necessary to re-insert the whole problem into the general context of evolution, more particularly that of the hierarchization of functions in the brain. We have suggested elsewhere that this somewhat too compelling notion of hierarchy needs to be toned down in such a way as to render intelligible the functioning of systems in a heterarchic[89] fashion. Our intuition is that these new ways of conceiving of the functioning of the brain are going to call in question current conceptions of *causality*, and that our reference to the notion of the *act* in these first two chapters will prove to be decisive for the reconciliation of the local and the global. Finally all of this will have to be related to the notion of the Umwelt,[90] a notion which has proved to be both extraordinarily fruitful and flexible. This will be our next challenge.

---

[87] 'Everything conspires', 'everything symbolizes' in Leibniz' Monadology. See also the generalization of this view in Husserl's theory of intersubjectivity. For Husserl, the transcendental constitution of the meaning of being of the world traverses all the dissonances of the flux of lived experience in the direction of their resolution.

[88] R. Llínas (2001) *I of the Vortex*, MIT Press, Cambridge, MA.

[89] A. Berthoz (2004) *La décision*, Odile Jacob, Paris.

[90] J. von Uexküll (1956) *Streifzüge durch die Umwelten von Tieren und Menschen, Bedeutungslehre*. Rohwohlt, Hamburg. A notion adopted by the phenomenology of the life-world (*Lebenswelt*), which confers upon it a strict operational status in the context of the description of the constitution of the structures of human experience.

Chapter 3

Anticipation and prediction

Life depends upon anticipation.

Husserl.[1]

In the preceding chapter we tried to justify our feelings about the need for a new philosophy of action designed to make possible a new physiology of action. At the very centre of this new concept we place anticipation and prediction. In fact, the projective dimension, widely recognized in the neurosciences today as essential to the functioning of the brain in living organisms, depends upon the existence of a multitude of *anticipatory mechanisms*. But this is not enough. For, having been discovered one after the other in the course of the history of physiology, these mechanisms have to be put back together again in a coherent vision, in the absence of which they would appear as so many pragmatic solutions to particular problems. And without even noticing it, one would overlook what is probably a fundamental property of the nervous system and, no doubt, of all mental (not to mention cultural) activity in humans.

The idea of anticipation is certainly not entirely new in the history of our science. As far back as the 1950s, a bio-electrical activity had been discovered: the negative contingent wave, a preparatory potential (*Bereitschaftspotential*) preceding the issue of the motor command, one that can be recorded on the surface of the scalp, more exactly in the supplementary motor area about one second before the movement.[2]

The difference between this notion and the notion of anticipation, as we would like to define it, comes down to the way in which the role of activities preparatory to action were understood at this pioneer epoch. It was thought then that there was a sort of progressive accumulation of neuronal activity

---

1 E. Husserl (1970) *The Crisis of European Sciences and Transcendental Phenomenology*, trans. D. Carr, Northwestern University Press, Evanston, IL, Part II, §9.

2 H.H. Kornhuber and L. Deecke (1965) Hirnpotential bei Willkürbewegungen und passiven Bewegungen des Menschen: Bereitschaftspotential und reafferente Potentiale, *Pflügers Arch. Ges. Physiol.* 284, 1–17.

which, bit by bit, somehow put together an action. The action itself was not supposed to occur until it was actually executed, its execution being released by the successive fitting together of the relevant pieces in this game of Lego. The action as a whole, its meaning, its sense, only appeared with the motor command. The idea of a simple and progressive accumulation of 'evidence', which ends up with a decision, is not without merit, for it is to be found even today in the analysis of the neuronal mechanisms responsible for decision. A decision is taken when the activity of a neuron reaches a certain threshold under the influence, whether supportive or opposed, of the excitatory or inhibitory influences of the other neurons converging upon it.[3]

What interests us about anticipation today, on the other hand, and notably across the concept of the brain as a simulator, is that during this period of preparation there is already a genuine simulation of action and perhaps a veritable emulation of the world. Extremely important elements belonging to the complete meaning of the action are put into place even before the motor command is released. What is brought into play in the preliminary phases of the micro-genesis of the action is not just an accumulation of energy awaiting the moment of release but rather the formation of an intention before the occurrence of the movement; that is, of a sense content that would make of this movement something more than simply a movement: a motor behaviour, but precisely an 'action' directed towards a goal.

The same speculations preoccupy the minds of those contemporary physiologists who have appreciated the need to borrow the concept of decision from mathematical economists and analytical theorists of action with a view to giving it a new use. In fact those researchers who are working on the motor preparation of sensory analysis have shown that real decisions take place in this phase of anticipation, which implies the frontal cortex but also the pre-frontal cortex.[4]

....

[3] A. Berthoz (2003) *La décision*, Odile Jacob, Paris. This aspect has been developed in the English translation of the book: A. Berthoz (2006) *Emotion and Reason, the Cognitive Foundations of Decision Making*, Oxford University Press, Oxford. See also D. Milea (2007) Prefrontal cortex is involved in internal decision of forthcoming saccades, *Neuroreport* 18(12), 1221–1224; D. Lee, M.F. Rushworth, M.E. Walton, M. Watanabe, and M. Sakagami (2007) Functional specialization of the primate frontal cortex during decision making, *J. Neurosci.* 27(31), 8170–8173.

[4] M.N. Shadlen and W.T. Newsome (2001) Neural basis of a perceptual decision in the parietal cortex (area LIP) of the Rhesus monkey, *J. Neurophysiol.* 86, 1916–1936; J.L. Gold and M.N. Shadlen (2007) The neural basis of decision making, *Annu. Rev. Neurosci.* 30, 535–574; T. Yang and M.N. Shadlen (2007) Probabilistic reasoning by neurons, *Nature* 447(7148), 1075–1080; R. Kiani, T.D. Hanks, and M.N. Shadlen (2006) When is enough enough? *Nat. Neurosci.* 9(7), 861–863; A.C. Huk and M.N. Shadlen (2005) Neural activity in macaque parietal cortex reflects temporal integration of visual motion signals during perceptual decision making, *J. Neurosci.* 25(45), 10420–10436; M.E. Mazurek, J.D. Roitman,

All the same, the brain during this same period selects those elements from the motor repertory that have the greatest relevance for the action, all of which implies that the goal of the action is in a certain sense already present (without which it would be difficult to talk of a decision), since it is the latter that is going to direct the process of selection. The brain also selects the relevant reference frames in which the movement will be coded,[5] and even the relevant geometry of its future trajectory.[6] So it is not just a matter of an increasing intensity of activity but of an entire series of processes that call for comparison. Norman and Shallice[7] advanced the hypothesis that the brain disposed of a supervisory module responsible for this arbitration. But today these hypotheses have to be reformulated to allow for discoveries in the neurosciences concerning the processes of re-configuration, dynamic loops, synchronization, multiple coding, etc.

The diversity of the cerebral mechanisms of anticipation

A few examples will give the reader an idea of the extraordinary diversity of the mechanisms of anticipation and prediction.

The sensory receptors themselves are equipped with anticipatory mechanisms. Examples of anticipation in the processes linked to vision are legion, and we referred to some of them in the preceding remarks. Bear in mind that everything happens as if the brain interpreted the visual world in terms of its 'hypotheses'. Hence the numerous illusions resulting from the fact that the brain seems to prefer symmetrical forms, that it decides between ambiguous forms or movements by choosing the solution that offers the greatest stability and, in so doing, assumes that objects are rigid,[8] etc. From the above, it should be clear to the reader why it is that, for us, anticipation is near to expectation.

J. Ditterich, and M.N. Shadlen (2003) A role for neural integrators in perceptual decision making, *Cereb. Cortex* 11, 1257–1269; J.L. Gold and M.N. Shadlen (2001) Neural computations that underlie decisions about sensory stimuli, *Trends Cog. Sci.* 1, 10–16; J.L. Gold and M.N. Shadlen (2000) Representation of a perceptual decision in developing oculomotor commands, *Nature* 404(6776), 390–394.

[5] A. Berthoz (1991) Reference frames for the perception and control of movement, in J. Paillard (ed.) *Brain and Space*, Oxford University Press, Oxford, pp. 81–111.

[6] T. Flash and A.A. Handzel (2007) Affine differential geometry analysis of human arm movements, *Biol. Cybernetics* 96(6), 577–601.

[7] D.A. Norman and T. Shallice (1986) Attention to action: willed and automatic control of behavior, in R.J. Davidson *et al.* (eds), *Consciousness and Self-regulation: Advances in Research and Theory*, vol. 4, Plenum, New York, pp. 1–18.

[8] M. Wexler *et al.* (2001) The stationarity hypothesis: an allocentric criterion in visual perception, *Vision Res.* 41(23), 3023–3037; M. Wexler *et al.* (2001) Self-motion and the perception of stationary objects, *Nature* 409(6816), 85–88.

In addition there are mechano-receptors that measure the derivatives of quantities of movement (speed, acceleration, jerk, etc.) and so make it possible to anticipate the future position of the body. Neuro-muscular spindles measure the speed of muscular stretch and these dynamic properties can be modulated by central actions. In fact they are themselves equipped with little motor mechanisms activated by so-called gamma motoneurons that amplify the dynamic response of the spindle, and in such a way that, when we are about to make a movement, the response of the spindle can be regulated by an anticipation of the movement itself. In the same way the vestibular receptors are sensitive to the angular and linear acceleration of the head. So perception is itself fundamentally anticipatory.

Another example is the question of what physiological mechanism corresponds to our 'sense of effort' when, for example, we manipulate a heavy object. It seems that it is derived not just from sensorial information provided by the force receptors situated in the tendons and muscles but also from the motor commands that the brain sends to the muscles. The perception of effort experienced by the one who makes the effort derives as much from an anticipation of the force to be deployed as from any sensorial feedback from the movement accomplished.[9]

The inhibition of sensorial information by an active movement and its re-establishment by passive simulations in the course of exploration is another example of anticipation. For example, we know for a fact that we cannot tickle ourselves. This is because the brain inhibits the activation of certain neurons of the temporal cortex (superior temporal sulcus) when we touch ourselves, these neurons being important for tactile perception.[10] Further investigation into the mechanisms responsible for this inhibition has led to the discovery that the cortical areas called somatic (SI and SII) are not just sensorial relays. Neurons are activated there by 'descending' influences which prepare sensibility for the influxes coming from the periphery.[11] It seems that even certain parts of the sensorial thalamus participate in this anticipatory activity, which

[9] G. Westling and R.S. Johansson (1984) Factors influencing the force control during precision grip, *Exp. Brain Res.* 53(2), 277–284; V.G. Macefield and R.S. Johansson (1996) Control of grip force during restraint of an object held between finger and thumb: responses of muscle and joint afferents from the digits, *Exp. Brain Res.* 108(1), 172–184; J.R. Flanagan, M.K. Bursted, and R.S. Johansson (1999) Control of fingertip forces in multidigit manipulation, *J Neurophysiol.* 4, 1706–1717; R.S. Johansson and I. Birznieks (2004) First spikes in ensembles of human tactile afferents code complex spatial fingertip events, *Nat. Neurosci.* 7(2), 170–177.

[10] S.-J. Blakemore *et al.* (2005) Somatosensory activations during the observation of touch and a case of vision-touch synaesthesia, *Brain* 128, 1571–1583.

[11] D.M. Santucci *et al.* (2005) Frontal and parietal cortical ensembles predict single trial muscle activity during reaching movements in primates, *Eur. J. Neurosci.* 22(6), 1529–1540.

implies that it is also at this highly preliminary stage that sense data are sorted and modified, before being processed at the cortical level.

The anticipatory character of perception is completed by the fact that the perceptual centres are informed about the actions in progress thanks to the corollary discharge; that is, the fact that the brain sends a copy of the motor command in advance to the perceptual centres, permitting them to stabilize the perceived world thanks to an anticipation of the movement. It is for example due to this mechanism that we do not perceive any displacement of the world when our eye makes a saccadic movement that displaces the image of the environment on our retina. This stabilization is in part due to the anticipatory displacement of the frames of reference and the receptor fields of the neurons of the parietal cortex before the occular saccade.[12]

Anticipation is also at work in the perception of distances. On many occasions when we need to move somewhere or when an object approaches us, it would be too complicated to calculate the distances. Instead, the brain is able to infer directly 'the time to contact'[13] with an object that is approaching and that we want to avoid. Such an inference is direct in the sense that it simply requires that the relation between the apparent surface of the object and its speed of expansion be evaluated. It is this kind of inference that makes it possible for a bird, for example, to plunge into the sea to catch a fish and to fold back its wings in time so as not to break them when making contact with the water.

The theory of time to contact is only a special case of a more general theory making it possible for the brain to extract from the surrounding world the information relevant to action. Psychologists did not have to wait for the discovery of mirror neurons to set up perception in a relation of correspondence with action situated in the world. That perception is structured by the interaction of an agent with the world is the theme of ecological theories, one of whose best-known promoters is Gibson. According to such theories, the evaluation of the height of a step on a staircase by the brain of someone wanting to climb up it is not done by measuring the height in centimetres. How could the brain possibly know anything about the standard metre! The evaluation in question is undertaken by relating the perceived height of the step and the perceived height of the subject's own step (his action of raising his foot). It was

---

[12] We will come back to this mechanism in Chapter 6.

[13] D.N. Lee (1978) On the functions of vision, in H. Pick and E. Saltzman (eds), *Modes of Perceiving and Processing of Information*, Erlbaum, Hillsdale, NJ, pp. 159–170; D.N. Lee and P.E. Reddish (1981) Plummeting gannets: a paradigm of ecological optics, *Nature* 293, 293–294; D.N. Lee and D.S. Young (1996) Visual timing in interceptive actions, in D.J. Ingle, M. Jeannerod, and D.N. Lee (eds), *Brain Mechanisms Spatial Vision*, Martinus Nijhoff, Dordrecht, pp. 1–30.

Turvey[14] who introduced this perspective, and in this context it is worth also mentioning Gibson's affordances or 'do-ability' theory.[15] Gibson noted that, regarding the visual objects that surround us, we perceive primarily what has a practical bearing on our action. He considered these practical resources as perceptual invariants anticipating our possible actions on them, or those that we might be able to accomplish by employing the objects as instruments. To perceive is to anticipate the affordance of a gesture or an action.

Before grasping an object with the hand, we first have to 'grasp' our target visually with our eyes.[16] Each time that we set out to get hold of an object, our eyes focus first on the object in order to guide our hand towards it. Anticipation is a fundamental property of the neuronal control of vision. When we try to catch an object in movement with an ocular saccade, the eye is no longer directed to where the moving object actually is, but it gets ahead of its target to compensate for any delays in the execution of the motor command. When the lizard projects its tongue to where the fly it wants to catch will be, it releases in its brain a mechanism of this kind, a mechanism involving the upper colliculus, a sub-cortical structure. This unconscious anticipation came before all the conscious mechanisms developed in our cortex, and constitutes one of the foundations of the very possibility of action.

Anticipation can also be found in another element of the motor repertory of vision and which only appeared towards the end of evolutionary development: ocular pursuit. This is what makes it possible to retain the image of an object in movement on the fovea. This rather slow mechanism is remarkably accurate in its predictions. If we move a finger to and fro in front of our eye, at the end of two or three trips the eye will get ahead of the finger. Similarly, if the finger passes behind a screen the eye will continue to move as if it were still there.[17]

Visual anticipation is also evident in more complex perceptive tasks, like driving a car. When a car is driven along a zigzagging road, the eye focuses on

[14] M.T. Turvey (1977) Preliminaries to a theory of action with reference to vision, in R.E. Shaw and J. Bransford (eds), *Perceiving, Acting and Knowing: Toward an Ecological Psychology*, Erlbaum, Hillsdale, NJ, pp. 211–265.

[15] J.J. Gibson (1977) The theory of affordances, in R.E. Shaw and J. Bransford (eds), *Perceiving, Acting and Knowing: Toward an Ecological Psychology*, Erlbaum, Hillsdale, NJ, pp. 67–82.

[16] R.S. Johansson *et al.* (2001) Eye-hand coordination in object manipulation, *J. Neurosci.* 21(7), 6917–6932.

[17] This remarkable property is due to the fact that, in an area of the medio-temporal cortex (MST), an 'extra-retinal' signal, no doubt a corollary discharge resulting from an eye movement, gets added to the retinal signal and can even replace it for a short time. Here too, motricity and sensation are combined!

the tangent to each turn in order to be able to better predict the curve on the basis of the optic flow.

Even posture is a preparation for movement. Bernstein insisted upon this. Posture is not just a matter of maintaining one's equilibrium; it is also a matter of preparing to act.[18] Babinski's synergies are an illustration of this. This great French neurologist, a pupil of Charcot, identified a backward movement of the body (a synergy) that precedes its voluntary inclination.[19] This movement is necessary in order that, when we lean, the projection of the centre of gravity should not fall outside the polygon enclosed by our feet, which might result in our falling. Patients suffering from disturbances of the cerebellum don't have this anticipatory posture, and so they fall. This posture is even maintained in space where it is useless since there is no force of gravity that could make it possible for the astronaut to fall. Maintaining one's equilibrium always requires the anticipation of the consequences of action, which, in this particular context, are no longer habitual consequences.

Finally, over and beyond the particular systems that make looking and postural control possible, we find anticipations even in complex motor tasks, like the control of locomotive trajectories. For example, when we move our eyes and our head anticipates the trajectory of our body.[20] This is no doubt due to the fact that the generation of a locomotive trajectory is controlled in a 'cognitive' fashion (that is not directly motoric) by an internal simulation of this trajectory which guides our eyes, which in turn guides our head, then our body. We go wherever we are looking.

We could continue in this vein by talking about 'internal models' which are in themselves powerful mechanisms of anticipation. But we will come back to this later.[21]

Could 'reality' be an anticipation?

This selection of cases of anticipation could certainly be explained away as an evolutionary tinkering, our species having been endowed with a tool box of

[18] N.A. Bernstein (1967) *The Coordination and Regulation of Movement*, Pergamon Press, New York.

[19] J. Babinski (1899) De l'asynergie cérébelleuse, *Revue Neurologie*, 7, 806–816.

[20] R. Grasso *et al.* (1998) Eye-head coordination for the steering of locomotion in humans: an anticipatory synergy, *Neurosci. Lett.* 253(2), 115–118; R.M. Wilkie and J.P. Wann (2005) The role of visual and nonvisual information in the control of locomotion, *J. Exp. Psycho. Hum. Percept. Perform.* 31(5), 901–911; J.P. Wann and D.K. Swapp (2000) Why you should look where you are going, *Nat. Neurosci.* 3(7), 647–648.

[21] See Chapter 7.

anticipatory mechanisms whose purely contingent convergence in the human organism has maximized its chances of survival.

What better testimony to the strategic importance of the initial time lapse could one wish for than the 100-metre sprint, one of the most renowned of Olympic events? Those responsible for drawing up the rules had to come to terms with the plasticity of the (badly named) reaction time of sprinters. A normal reaction time to the firing of the pistol would be of the order of 150 milliseconds. If a runner starts before this lapse has elapsed he is penalized. But faced with the large number of false starts (anticipated starts) the normal time has had to be brought down from 150 to 100 milliseconds, for runners were being penalized for false starts due not to an intention to cheat but to the training of their natural capacity for anticipation.

Today, anticipation is no less necessary in an area, symbolizing the modern form of survival in the twenty-first century: the trading stations of the great banks where pitiless economic warfare is conducted are the modern equivalent of the law of the jungle. These young persons whom one sees frantically gesticulating in the stock markets have one, two, perhaps five seconds at the most, to decide whether or not to buy the shares of some company and an error can cost them, if not their life, at least 50 million dollars! This game has replaced the struggle for existence since we are no longer eaten by lions, nor do we have to try to catch elusive fish. But we can be eaten by IBM and we do have to try and catch a good price for Microsoft shares. A few seconds' hesitation can cost millions. One might find this analogy rather naïve and ask oneself whether imagery is really needed for all this. But it is precisely cerebral imagery that is used today to study risk-taking and decision-making in financial affairs. A new and fascinating cooperation is taking place between neurophysiologists and economists. We are witnessing the birth of neuroeconomics.[22]

---

[22] K. McCabe *et al.* (2001) A functional imaging study of cooperation in two person reciprocal exchange, *Proc. Natl. Acad. Sci. USA* 98(20), 11832–11835; J.H. Kagel and A.E. Roth (eds) (1995) *Handbook of Experimental Economics*, Princeton University Press, Princeton, NJ; T. Takahashi, H. Oono, and M.H. Radford (2007) Comparison of probabilistic choice models in humans, *Behav. Brain Funct.* 3, 20; V. Stuphorn (2006) Neuroeconomics: cardinal utility in the orbitofrontal cortex? *Curr. Biol.* 16(15), R591–R593; P.W. Glimcher, M.C. Doris, and M.C. Bayer (2005) Physiological utility theory and the neuroeconomics of choice, *Games Econ. Behav.* 52(2), 213–256; O. Oullier and J.A. Kelso (2006) Neuroeconomics and the metastable brain, *Trends Cog. Sci.* 10(8), 353–354; N. Lee, A.J. Broderick, and L. Chamberlain (2007) What is 'neuromarketing'? A discussion and agenda for future research, *Int. J. Psychophysiol.* 63(2), 199–204; D. Lee (2006) Neuroeconomics: best to go with what you know? *Nature* 441(7095), 822–823; T. Takahashi (2006) A mathematical framework for probabilistic choice based on information theory and psychophysics, *Med. Hypotheses* 67(1),

Anticipation also helps us to understand what action is. This second aspect of anticipation needs to be distinguished carefully from the evolutionary considerations with which it often tends to be confused. For the question: what is action, its nature, its very being, is a question for science as much as it is for common sense. No one would be satisfied with an answer that simply traced its evolutionary history, however interesting and instructive the genesis (in the sense of onto- or phylogenesis) of human kind might be.

We all know that a certain conventionally causal thinking clings to the reality of the (physical) event as to a life-saver. That the event might be preceded by something by which it is prepared is an idea that bothers this kind of thinking almost as much as if one were to reintroduce Aristotelian teleology into science. Anticipation, an implicatory[23] mode of being that gets ahead of what is, that posits what is to be in advance of its arrival, testifies to the mysterious ability of an agent—an entirely real, though paradoxical ability—to precede the event by executing a simulation (or an 'emulation').

Whatever sophisticated forms (as described above) anticipation may take, the concept and its biological implementation is not reducible to mustering up an inventory of neuronal mechanisms still mostly unelucidated, and this on the basis of a simple mentalist metaphor. Anticipation is a property of the animal and human organism, one that belongs to it by right. Such a property could never have been acquired in the context of that naïve ontology of an 'external reality', a flawless 'absolute' reality where anticipation is a 'non-being', given the absence of an objective referent, given that no movement has as yet been accomplished! It can only be assigned in the context of a completely different ontology, which is that of the mutually formative interaction of this organism with its life world.

So what, in the final analysis, does it mean to say that anticipation is not limited to a few curious and isolated cases but represents a fundamental aptitude possessed by all living beings? It amounts to saying that the brief lapse of time in which it takes place is no less significant for biological ontology than are light years for cosmological ontology. If the decisive events for our metabolism, for behaviour, for survival and therefore for everyday life, take place in the few dozen milliseconds preceding action or a perceptual interpretation,

---

183–186; K. Inukai and T. Takahashi (2006) Distinct neuropsychological processes may mediate decision-making under uncertainty with known and unknown probability in gain and loss frames, *Med. Hypotheses* 67(2), 283–286; A.G. Sanfey, G. Loewenstein, S.M. McClure, and J.D. Cohen (2006) Neuroeconomics: cross-currents in research on decision-making, *Trends Cog. Sci.* 10(3), 108–116.

[23] Implication: the inverse of explication, the process of becoming explicit, the realization of differences in natural cognition and scientific explanation.

and if the framework of lived experience is made up of a multitude of such acts of anticipation carried out in the same lapse of time, this is because *'reality' for the perceiving subject, reality itself, is a vast anticipative construction*, or to use more phenomenologically appropriate language: *it is protentional by constitution.*[24] In this perspective, dream and hallucination are only aspects (pathological, in the case of hallucination) of this fundamental property of the brain, that, namely, of being able to construct its own reality. Contrary to what is currently supposed, it has not always already been there, outside us, without us and before us. This reality in which we intervene through action and which we take account of in cognition, gets constituted (perhaps not *in itself* but at least *for us*) in and through the acts of subjects engaged in a process of reciprocal interaction in a common world, the latter of which is brought into being and maintained in being by this very interaction.

Anticipate or predict: does one have to choose?

Having reached this point we might be tempted to leave the reader to draw his own conclusions from this key idea, that reality is constructed by anticipation, since we already do have enough supporting evidence in physiology, upon which we could therefore rely to find in philosophy an eventual echo or premonition of a truth already well established on the empirical plane. But however solid the intuition we have defended, it nevertheless still has to be expressed in language, the language of a certain community, and so it is important to determine right away whether we are talking the same language. However, in physiological literature the words anticipate and predict are often employed interchangeably. Where one researcher talks in terms of prediction another talks in terms of anticipation, without there being any confusion in their communication. On the other hand, if the sphere of communication is extended to take in the philosophical community, the absence of such a distinction would not pass unnoticed, since physiologists tend to confuse what philosophers insist upon distinguishing. This is enough in itself to justify the distinction between a language of the physiology of action and a language of the philosophy of action. So, in order to be in a position to establish a common language we now have to take account of those conceptual analyses of action (more pronounced in analytical philosophy but not absent from phenomenology) which mark a deeply entrenched distinction between the contexts in which the two words anticipate and predict are employed. Anticipate refers to

---

[24] See E. Husserl (1964) *The Phenomenology of Internal Time Consciousness*, M. Heidegger (ed.), trans. J. Churchill, Indiana University Press, Indianapolis, IN.

human action and the will of the agent, predict to natural events independent of our will.

Anticipating, in a sense readily comprehensible without any special explanation, is a matter of getting ahead of an event or an action, and this by going through the action oneself before the scheduled moment. It is in this sense that one can pay back a bank loan by anticipation, that is by paying back the capital, in one sum, ahead of the schedule set up for the remaining monthly payments. Or again, before obligatory military service was abolished, a young man could enlist by anticipating his call-up, that is, without waiting for the conscription date fixed by law for a person of his age.

But these highly conventional actions are not apparently typical examples of what the physiologist means by action. For they refer to social contexts of practices and norms implying speech acts with their institutional conditions of validity or invalidity, conditions whose bearers cannot but be ideal objectivities pertaining to a system of law.[25] At this level, physiology has nothing to teach us. But alongside actions such as these, one also talks of anticipation for purely 'natural' events.

Of a natural event taking place by itself independent of human volition, and sometimes in virtue of a fatality,[26] one often says that it can be predicted. But does it make any sense to say of such a natural event that it can be anticipated? Let's take a closer look at what might serve to distinguish anticipation from prediction. For example, it is well known in the Chamonix valley that on 15 August towards 5 o'clock in the afternoon there is often a storm due to the particular climatic conditions that prevail at that time of year. This storm can be predicted; but it can also be anticipated, as when one takes precautions: by carrying an umbrella.

Wittgenstein[27] claimed that 'one could not predict what one could anticipate nor anticipate what one could predict'. For even if it is obvious that one can anticipate what one can do or what one cannot do (take an umbrella in case ...)

---

[25] On the eventual naturalization of social acts through 'a social neuroscience' see J.-L. Petit (2005/2006) Les systémes résonnants: bases de cognition sociale? I & II, *PSN – Psychiatrie, Sciences Humaines, Neurosciences* III, 15 (2005), 240–247; IV, 16 (2006), 16–22.

[26] It can be predicted either by means of an obscure presentiment, or by means of a more rational inductive inference, or again on the basis of a nomological recurrence registered in the experiential data of a laboratory experiment, etc.

[27] L. Wittgenstein (1958) *The Blue and Brown Books*, Oxford University Press, Oxford; G.E.M. Anscombe (1979) *Intention*, Basil Blackwell, Oxford. For a discussion from a phenomenological viewpoint, see P. Ricœur and the Centre de Phénoménologie (1977) *La Sémantique de l'action*, Eds du CNRS, Paris and also J.-L. Petit (1991) *L'Action dans la Philosophie Analytique*, PUF, Paris.

this does not in itself decide the question of knowing whether one can do likewise—and in the same sense—with regard to events over which the will of the human agent has no control (the storm).[28]

Wittgenstein's observation suggests the existence of a difference in the rules implicit in the use of the words governing the intelligibility of our expressions in everyday discourse: on the one hand, a preference for the concept of prediction in contexts where physical events are described or explained without relation to human action; on the other, an affinity between the concept of anticipation and contexts relative to human or animal actions, the latter of which cannot, in consequence, be understood as purely physical events.

In the philosophical literature on action this difference has tended to be driven home to the point of a complete separation between the two meanings: a lexicon or language of action (including expressions for anticipation) and a lexicon or language of events (including expressions for prediction). This disjunction serves the purposes of a certain positivist empiricism that wants to save scientific induction from any *a priori* contamination. Following up on an intuition we shall try to develop here, the importance of anticipation consists of the fact that its admission as an essential property of the brain implies nothing less than an *a priori* rehabilitation in the traditional epistemology of the empirical sciences.

Whether it is a matter of reintroducing into the scientific conception of human nature an agent's ability to anticipate its actions or a knowing subject's ability to anticipate what is going to happen with a predictive judgment (by consulting the ephemeris or by doing a rain dance to provoke rain or by holding up a brand to the Sun to stop an eclipse), the cause to be defended is not, in the end, so different. In any case, the transcendental philosophical tradition[29] (the one Wittgenstein wanted to demolish on the grounds that its representatives would have ignored these distinctions) did not think so either. For the latter always sought to link the conditions of the possibility of anticipation and of its generalization to new cases in judgments bearing on experience (prediction) with practical anticipation (anticipation properly so called) as a capacity to initiate a causal chain of events through a free act of will.

Whenever one commits oneself to acting one gets involved in a process of which only one phase (not necessarily the first) is realized: the fiat of the decision. But this does not prevent our plan of action also covering all the

---

[28] The existence of anticipations, in addition to predictions, concerning events that take place not because they were willed but because they were predicted: these creative predictions, well known to economists, are not of such a kind as to sort out questions of this kind.

[29] Kant, Fichte, Schelling, the neo-Kantians, and Husserl.

preliminary and the ulterior phases of the motivation (it should not come as a surprise to find that we are obliged to regress back to the bedrock of a pulsional intentionality: not just Freud but also Husserl[30] agree here), as also of the concept of an intention directed up to the realization of the goal in view.

On the basis of this minimal agreement between physiology and transcendental philosophy, let us then accept that an event can be said to be predictable when one anticipates it just as well as when one predicts it.

---

[30] See N.-I. Lee (1993) *Edmund Husserls Phänomenologie der Instinkte*, Kluwer, Dordrecht.

Chapter 4

Who's afraid of the transcendental subject?

The objectivity of knowledge

From now on we shall be comparing two problems, a classical philosophical problem and a problem in the cognitive sciences of today. The classical philosophical problem is the problem of knowledge, of how we gain access to an object that does not belong to the subject, an external object. We are going to try and compare this philosophical problem with a problem in the cognitive sciences, which is that of determining how a brain, with its own anatomy, can develop within itself the mechanisms needed for objective knowledge. Hence the question: how does an internally active brain, which is, in a certain sense, enclosed within itself since it only has very limited contact with the external world[1] through the sensorial zones of the body, actually acquire knowledge of an object external to itself? By internally active we mean that the brain can create, for instance during dreaming, a completely 'real world' with objects in it that seem real, and in the last chapter a novel thesis was proposed to the effect that this creation might be linked to the anticipation of action. A beautiful example of this autonomy and closedness of the brain is the fact that it is very active during sleep when, for instance, it is supposed to be transferring short-term memories into long-term memories through interactions between the hippocampus and the cerebral cortex, reproducing the lived experiences of the day,[2] etc. We also find

---

[1] This closure has not been called into question by the discovery of 'resonant systems' like mirror neurons, activated in the same way both by the subject carrying through certain actions and by the same subject watching the corresponding actions being performed by others. In fact, if the latter are treated as 'complex stimuli', the supposed opening can be reduced to the sum of visual interface + sensory-motor associations.

[2] G.R. Sutherland and B. McNaughton (2000) Memory trace reactivation in hippocampal and neocortical neuronal ensembles, *Curr. Opin. Neurobiol.* 10(2), 180–186; C.M. Pennartz, H.B. Uylings, C.A. Barnes, and B.L. McNaughton (2002) Memory reactivation and consolidation during sleep: from cellular mechanisms to human performance, *Prog. Brain Res.* 138, 143–166; A. Takashima *et al.* (2006) Declarative memory consolidation in humans: a prospective functional magnetic resonance imaging study, *Proc. Natl. Acad. Sci. USA* 103(3), 756–761.

an on-going activity in the loops linking the thalamus to the cortex and to the basal ganglia involved in action selection, etc. We have explained in the preceding chapters why the fact that during a dream the brain can have a perception of objects should not be interpreted as meaning that it has a representation of these objects.

Henceforth there exists a very interesting parallel between a philosophical position about the problem of objective knowledge and the neurophysiological position about the problem of knowing what are the neural correlates of the recognition of a permanent and independent object; an object which is independent of that other object, our brain. How can the brain make it possible for us to identify objects existing in a world independent of its own body, and so of the self, and how is it that the multitude of sensorial data by which the senses are bombarded can be identified as belonging to an object that really exists in the external world?

There is a story that recurs in philosophy, arising first with Descartes, and which then finds an echo in the thinking of Kant and also more recently in that of Hilary Putnam. It is the story of the evil genius. Instead of being able to rely on a good and all-powerful God, the God of traditional theology, who arranged things for us so that our impressions really do correspond with what is to be found in the external world, there might have been an evil genius who arranges for us to be deceived each time that we think we have grasped the truth of the matter. Each time that we think we have identified an object, we are the victims of a hallucination caused by an all-powerful evil being who is in total control of the information coming to us from the external world and who systematically falsifies everything we take to be true. Kant has another version: if we had not had those *a priori* principles of knowledge that make it possible for us to order and frame the flux of sensorial data and to unify it, and this by enabling the subject to impose upon the manifold of sensations its own subjective unity,[3] we would not have been able to make judgements based upon an organized experience, thereby making of such an experience an object of knowledge.

---

[3] 'If cinnabar (mercury sulphate, the vermillion of painters and already used by medieval illuminators: a lively and saturated red which can however alter by blackening) were sometimes red, sometimes black, sometimes light, sometimes heavy, if a man changed sometimes into this sometimes into that animal form [...] my empirical imagination would never find opportunity when representing red colour to bring to mind heavy cinnabar.' 'In the absence of a precise rule to which phenomena are already subject in and of themselves there could be no empirical synthesis of reproduction.' (I. Kant (1781/1782) *Critique of Pure Reason*, A100, B123).

Closer to us, Putnam[4] tells the story of a brain in a vat. He imagines all our actual appearances of things being preserved, except of course that we would have been reduced to a brain extracted from our cranium by wicked scientists and maintained in existence by being placed in a vat filled with nutritive fluids and connected to the external world by artificial neural networks equivalent to those that function normally. (Not too far from the scenario of the film *The Matrix*.) As a result it would be impossible for this brain, that is, from the activity internal to it, to know that it is in the situation described rather than functioning normally. It follows that nothing it took to be true (to the extent that any such belief could be attributed to it), namely that its brain was located in the body of a person living out their life's experience in a world, would actually be true.

In support of this argument, Putnam was ready to appeal to the transcendental approach of Kant,[5] who was also concerned with the conditions of the possibility of thoughts in the mind (or brain) being referred to external things (as being *true* or *false* of these things). The impossibility that the being in question (ultimately reduced to its brain) finds in trying to decide between two outcomes—'I am an ordinary person in an ordinary situation' and 'I am no more than a brain in a vat'—is presented by Putnam as an objection to the representational conception dominant in the philosophy of mind and in the cognitive sciences. In advancing this objection he hoped to discredit their prejudice in favour of a 'magical' conception of reference according to which mental (cerebral) representations would be necessarily endowed with the power to refer to things. In fact, however, our ability to refer to things is a power we confer not upon mental representations in our head but upon linguistic expressions drawn from ordinary language, and which we employ in a referential way. That said, Putnam shares with other analytical philosophers a distorted conception of phenomenology as reducible to a simple introspective psychology, which is why he thinks he has already included the former in his critique. And that's where he goes wrong. For it makes no sense to say of intentionality, as an active orientation on the part of the perceiving agent vis-à-vis some thing (and so not as the property of a mental representation), that it either is or is not 'in the head' of the agent.

There is a continuity to be found throughout this philosophical tradition. For in both cases it puts us in a situation where we are completely deceived about the objectivity of our knowledge. In all such cases there would be an

---

[4] H. Putnam (1981) *Reason, Truth and History*, Cambridge University Press, Cambridge, Chap. 1.

[5] H. Putnam (1981) *Reason, Truth and History*, Cambridge University Press, Cambridge, p. 16.

appearance of knowledge which, in fact, corresponded to nothing at all. This is another way of posing the transcendental question of the conditions of the possibility of knowledge.

This question of the reality of the external world is equally central for the physiology of perception. All the same, the problem is not that simple. Much of pathology is rooted in the difficulty of recognizing one's own body or objects. Such deficiencies make up the long list of so-called agnosiae.[6] In addition, certain patients with cerebral lesions suffer from a cognitive deficit known as somatoparaphrenia. They either deny that certain parts of their body belong to them or are incapable of identifying them. They think that it is someone else who actually moves their limbs. A patient used to say: 'This arm is not mine, it belongs to my mother.' This disturbance has a cognitive origin. But it is rooted in the perception of the body, since it suffices to inject a little hot water in the ear (thereby stimulating the vestibular receptors), or to effect a tactile stimulation of the skin of the neck, for the deficit to disappear, at least temporarily, leaving the patient with the feeling of having regained consciousness, or possession, of his arm.[7]

Psychiatrists and psychologists like Christopher Frith[8] have developed theories to account for the difficulty certain patients have with the reality of an external world. Schizophrenics, in particular, suffer from hallucinations, which make it difficult for them to distinguish objective events from the products of their imagination, which in turn makes it difficult for them not to confer an objective character upon their hallucinations. They also tend to think that other people manipulate their senses, their thinking, and their actions (influence syndrome). This dysfunction of the neural system affects the attribution to oneself of the actions of which one is the author, and is described in the literature of the cognitive sciences as an agentivity disturbance; that is, a disturbance in the feeling (not just a belief but a lived experience) an agent normally has with regard to the fact that he is the author of his actions. It is an ingenious and fruitful hypothesis, even though the existence of alternative explanations makes it debatable.[9]

------

[6] Many examples can be found in treatises of neuropsychology. But the book by Grüsser and Landis deserves special attention: O.J. Grüsser and T. Landis (1991) *Visual Agnosias and Related Disorders, Vision and Visual Dysfunction*, J. Cronly-Dillon (ed.), MacMillan, London.

[7] G. Vallard *et al.* (2003) Anosognosia for left-sided motor and sensory deficits, motor neglect, and sensory hemiinattention: is there a relationship? *Prog. Brain Res.* 142, 289–301.

[8] C. Frith (1996) The role of the prefrontal cortex in self-consciousness: the case of auditory hallucinations, *Phil. Trans. R. Soc. Lond. Ser. B Biol. Sci.* 351, 1505–1512.

[9] It is debatable in the light of studies imputing the 'voices' of schizophrenics to a localized disturbance of the neural system of speech perception (normally devoted to the voices of others) rather than to a more general cognitive disturbance concerning attention to the

Still more curious is the difficulty certain patients experience in recognizing and designating the body parts of others. Discovered by Jean Denis Degos, this disturbance is a designation disturbance.[10] Patients cannot, for example, designate the ears of the doctor in front of them. They point at their own ears as being those of the doctor! They are unable to objectify the doctor's ear as external to their own body.

This problem acquires a philosophical dimension from the fact that it is common to perception—I perceive objects external to myself, not just the impression objects make on me—and to knowledge in general, including scientific knowledge. For it is the pretension of scientific knowledge to be objective, that is to know the world just as it is, and not as we would like it to be, not even as the organization of our mental structure makes us believe it is.

The immanent, the transcendent, and the transcendental

Transcendental philosophy is the examination of the conditions that make it possible for us to be torn away from our psychic interiority and to have access to a common object through experience. Modern physiology is also founded on just such an experience, an experience to which Claude Bernard and his successors accorded great importance. Furthermore, contrary to what used to be the dominant paradigm of the middle and end of the twentieth century (which emphasized the study of anaesthetized 'preparations' or brain sections), the contemporary tendency is to register cerebral activity with humans and animals that are active; that is, involved in an act responsible for establishing a relation to an object in the world and not just in a stimulus–response process.

The same word, experience, is then employed as an instrument of objective knowledge both by scientists (for whom it remains the principal research tool) and by philosophers, at least certain philosophers, those who are working to

....

external world: R.E. Hoffman *et al.* (1999) Selective speech perception alterations in schizophrenic patients reporting hallucinated 'voices', *Am. J. Psychiatry* 156, 393–399. It is complemented by other studies examining the incidence of schizophrenia on the adaptation of motor behaviour to the circumstances of action: Y. Delevoye-Turrell *et al.* (2003) Abnormal sequencing of motor actions in patients with schizophrenia: evidence from grip force adjustments during object manipulation, *Am. J. Psychiatry* 160(1), 134–141; Y. Delevoye-Turrell *et al.* (2002) A deficit in the adjustment of grip force responses in schizophrenia, *Neuroreport* 13(12), 1537–1539.

10   On this subject it is worth looking at the chapter by Bachoud-Levi in *L'Empathie*: A.C. Bachoud-Levi and J.-D. Degos (2004) Désignation et rapport à autrui, in A. Berthoz and G. Jorland (eds), *L'Empathie*, Odile Jacob, Paris, pp. 89–119.

restore to this experience the eminent role it enjoyed in a long tradition presently regarded with suspicion. We have to say 'certain philosophers' because, outside phenomenology, there exists another tradition (running from Wittgenstein to Austin and beyond) which puts language first, on the pretext that whatever follows from experience ought to be handed over to relevant departments of scientific research while the philosopher has to be content with a logical analysis of language and the conditions of meaningful expression. If the connection between science and philosophy is to be re-established today, a philosophy of experience will have to be invoked, one that makes it possible to justify the assumption of objective being. The authors of this manifesto share the view[11] that we have to get beyond a formalist thinking which requires of language that it be structured in logical propositions whose whole rationale consists of making human knowledge possible. For human cognition cannot be reduced to language.

It would obviously have been absurd to want to conjoin a positive science—physiology—with a branch of philosophy like phenomenology. So the reader will appreciate our attempt to relieve any possible anxiety with an invitation to join us on an excursion along the frontier of these two domains. For the latter can be envisaged as running between the two terms transcendent and transcendental. Let us begin our explanation with the threefold distinction between immanent, transcendent and transcendental.

What is *immanent* is whatever pertains to the subject. I am presently looking at a table. My perception of the table, the visual or tactile impressions I derive from it, are immanent. This is not the case for the table itself as 'a thing in itself', a thing that is out there in the world. This table, if conceived as an independent object in the world, is said to be *transcendent*. That is, it exists outside of me, separated from me and from whatever belongs to me. If you prefer, it owes nothing to me. And the fact that I see it makes no difference to it.

All the same I can hardly say anything about this table without immediately relieving it of its superb indifference. Because anything I might want to say about it would have to be connected with a possible use I make of it, an action that I have the intention to perform: as a table to write at, on which to stand a projector, on which to place documents, etc. Janet wrote that the perception of an armchair was, for instance, driven by the intention to sit on it.[12] So it is

---

[11] See A. Berthoz (1997) *Le sens du mouvement*, Odile Jacob, Paris; and J.-L. Petit (2003) La spatialité originaire du corps propre. Phénoménologie et neurosciences, in Géométrie et cognition, *Revue de Synthèse*, 5th series 124, 139–171.

[12] See A. Berthoz (2000) *The Brain's Sense of Movement*, Harvard University Press, Cambridge, MA, p. 10.

possible to distinguish the table in itself (referred to above) from this meaning of the table, the meaning that it has for us. A meaning always has to be referred back to a subject. Just as the table itself owes nothing to us, so its meaning of being owes us everything. Another way of saying this is that each subject *constitutes* the table by the use he makes of it and, more generally, by the types of relation he entertains with the table, again not the table in itself, but the meaning of being a table, a meaning that is relative to the subject. Let us spend a bit of time with this distinction and, keeping in mind the notion of the table as a thing in itself, try and make do with the table as constituted in its sense of being by our subjective activities.

Immanence is about the internal world of the knowing subject. Its states, physiological states,[13] mental states,[14] all that is immanent to me. What is transcendent is distinguished from what is immanent by its opposition to the latter. What is transcendent is what is independent of us, autonomous in relation to us, and whatever owes nothing to us.

In the light of this distinction between the immanent and the transcendent, what is called *transcendental* appears intermediary. Suppose that I am familiar with an object, my leather spectacles case. If I am totally naïve and am not thinking philosophically, I might say 'this spectacles case is there, outside of me', 'it has its own properties', or 'it is brown'. Certainly, we know perfectly well that our perception of brown is the outcome of a process that begins with a modification of the visual cells of our retina and which ends up with a modification in the V4 area of the visual cortex subject to many contextual influences. Modifications of this kind are not the passive effect of luminous stimulation but are the result of an interpretation whose origin has to be traced back a long way to the neural circuits of the occipital visual areas of our brain. The activation patterns of these circuits are the substrates of our experience of the coloured world and, notably, of the 'permanent colour of objects'. So what in effect happens is that I *perceive* the object as brown, I *attribute to it* the property of being brown.

....

[13] In a more restrictive sense of internal which relates to psychic interiority, physiological states are treated as transcendent in the same way as external objects. In this more restrictive sense, pain, for example, remains a lived experience immanent to the subject. And this despite the fact that it is conditioned by precise physiological factors that can be controlled.

[14] This notion of the mental can have surprising consequences since one can say of stones, rivers, and mountains, elements of the external world, that there is something mental about them too, to the extent that they make up my environment, the environment of a mental subject, and since I can always get interested in them and, in so doing, include them in my mental life. On the other hand, would stones, rivers, and mountains ever have been isolated in this way from the continuum of physical existence were it not for the fact that we throw stones, cross rivers, and climb mountains?

Having a *transcendental* point of view on this perception of the object means that I am attentive to the conditions which make it possible for me to see brown. I then have to say that this object is the support, unknown in itself, of properties familiar to me. This is the transcendental point of view, at least as a first approximation, because we are for the moment only walking in the steps of the physiologist engaged in analysing vision.

But we have already made a good deal of progress. For if we were enclosed in immanence we would be living in a perpetual dream. Nothing would be true. There would be no objects. There would be no science. There would be nothing but opinions. But our science thinks that there are objects. We think that there is a difference between what is true and what is false. Where does all this come from? What is the objectivity of knowledge? It's a fact, or so we are told, that certain internal states—that is, beliefs—have an objective referent. Let us not get too involved with the details of this definition, since it suffices for all practical purposes. In particular, it already allows us to get out of the sphere of immanence. By falling back upon internal events, we are able to indicate the existence of objects, of events, of states outside of us about which we can say a great many things that are true without falling back into the naïvety of one who thinks that things are there outside of us, totally independent of us and that we grasp them just as they are in themselves.

Here the reader who has made the effort to follow us along these dangerous philosophical pathways will perhaps be tempted to protest: you introduced the notion of the transcendent, a notion we thought we have understood, then you went on to talk about the transcendental, and without waiting to see if we accepted it, you then went back to the transcendent. The result is, you have lost us! Instead of digging a ditch between the transcendent and the transcendental, a ditch which might in the end become an insurmountable obstacle, why not make life easier for us by admitting that there are certain processes in our brains that make it possible for us to link thoughts in our heads (immanence) with physical things in the world around us?

We understand perfectly well the disquiet the reader might experience when faced with notions that we say are fundamental but which appear utterly foreign to daily life, but we are obliged, nevertheless, to draw attention to the fact that this proposal only makes the difficulties worse. For how are we to describe this process that he thinks is going to resolve the difficulty? If it is a scientific hypothesis bearing on the way in which things in the physical world (and among them our brains) are organized in themselves, then this process itself belongs to what is transcendent. If on the other hand, we take this process, whatever it might be, to be something belonging to us, to our mental states or to their cerebral correlates, then, just like any other element brought under the head of the mental, this process remains immanent. There is only one way out, to appeal to those still unknown conditions which make it possible for us knowing subjects (epistemological and not merely psychological subjects) to posit things as existing and to attribute the right properties to them; in which case, this process has then to be classified as transcendental (or empirical-transcendental).

Let us take an example drawn from something I might find on my desk: my spectacles case again. If I am in the natural attitude, there is an object there. It can be taken away and won't be there any more. It is shiny and reflects light. It has a certain colour, a certain resistance, etc. But what is this resistance? It is the fact that I can put my finger on it and feel its presence. If I take away everything that is linked to me, what remains of the object? It is difficult to say, except that it is what exists independently of me. Everything I say about it—any property I attribute to this X—refers back to me. Only I cannot reduce it to a bundle (Hume's word) of impressions because, if it were nothing but a collection of my impressions, it would be an illusion. So what are transcendent are not the properties themselves but their unknown support, the absolute, physical support of properties all of which refer back to me because they feature as elements in my acts of knowing.

It turns out that the greater part, if not all, of the phases, moments or elements of our experience refer to objects that are transcendent with regard to this experience. When I see the table, my percept, as a visual sensation, refers to the table in front of me, not to me. All thinking (as Descartes used to say) refers to its object rather than to the thinking subject. In order to focus on the thinking of this thinking subject a special discipline is needed, one which is little encouraged today. This discipline is called reflection. Even the sceptical Hume, who would only admit impressions, could not help talking about impressions *of* trees, stones, etc. So there must be something in the immanence of the subject of experience, certain conditions which make it possible for this subject to have an experience of things which, outside these same conditions, remain transcendent to it.

Anticipation and the transcendental

In the tradition from Kant to Husserl, passing across Fichte, it was at first thought that the ability to link *immanence* and *transcendence* was due to *a priori* knowledge of the world and its constraints. *A priori* means (a provisional definition) knowledge not acquired in the course of experience (inductive knowledge). Today we might be tempted to talk of the genetic origin of certain categories of perception as, for example, the fact that a snake releases an almost irresistible fear when it is analysed by the amygdala in the brain of the subject who experiences this fear.[15] In any case, the *a priori* was posited by Kant as the formally abstract framework of possible experience, a framework in which something not only actually presents itself but can present itself to me, and this whether or not it does actually presents itself.

This *a priori* was then re-thought, in particular by Husserl,[16] as an entirely concrete constitutive operation whose effectuation cannot even be distinguished from the flux of the experience of the subject. Husserl took Kant's frame of explanation to be too formal, almost virtual, and sought to re-anchor it in operations such as exploring an environment by carrying through ocular displacements, movements of the head and of the whole body, such as walking; or again, by running over a surface with the palm of the hand or the tip of the fingers, in other words by relying upon kinaesthetic sensations. Thanks to operations such as these, objects emerge for us in our environment. Husserl sought the (transcendental) link between what takes place in the perceiving subject and the objects as they exist in themselves in their transcendence, in the action of exploration. He got there by conferring upon perceptual activities a responsibility for the subjective construction (or rather: constitution) of what is.

Our intuition, the one we would like to share with our readers, is that this whole tradition remains highly relevant to the development of a physiology of anticipation. What we now have to do is show how *the passage from the immanent* (in which I am enclosed) *and the transcendent* (which is external to me) *to the transcendental* (the condition of possibility of bridging the gap in-between) *is presupposed in the fact that I anticipate the worldly properties of things.* The difficulty is perfectly understandable. For the transcendental still has no place in the cognitive sciences. On the other hand, countless works on anticipation are to be found. And who is going to devote their precious time to the philosophical history of a concept once it has been established that this concept is useful in science and it becomes important to harvest the maximum of results? The thing or the fact that the words anticipate or predict so conveniently designate and describe is sufficient, we think, to justify the use of these words.

....

[15] Many works have been recently devoted to the amygdala. On the responses of amygdala to aversive stimuli, see: in the monkey, M.K. Sanghera, E.T. Rolls, and A. Roper-Hall (1979) Visual responses in the dorsolateral amygdala of the alert monkey, *Exp. Neurol.* 63, 610–626; and in humans, J.S. Morris *et al.* (1996) A differential neural response in the human amygdala to fearful and happy facial expressions, *Nature* 383, 812–815.

[16] E. Husserl (1907/1973) *Ding und Raum. Vorlesungen 1907*, U. Claesges (ed.), Martinus Nijhoff, La Haye; E. Husserl (1913) Ideen zu einer Reinen Phänomenologie und Phänomenologischen Philosophie, in *Jahrbuch für Philosophie und Phänomenologische Forschung*, t. I, Max Niemeyer, Halle.

For, as real natives of today's science, our scientific training has made it difficult for us to admit too great a distance between words and things.[17]

In an evolutionary perspective, where one is concerned exclusively with the performance of the adaptive devices of the living organism, the formation of anticipation appears easy to explain by the need to simplify the otherwise excessively complex analysis of the world and so to gain time. On the other hand, recurring to anticipation to try and establish a link between the immanent and the transcendent must appear shocking, if only on account of its seeming arbitrariness and its philosophical jargon.

And yet the success of the word 'anticipate' in contemporary physiology is not unrelated to a philosophical project: that of bringing back to the field of concrete experience this transcendental, which was at first simply described as a formal framework in an abstract space. For, concretely speaking, any object or event which might manifest itself in the flux of our experience is susceptible to being formed in advance by the act and rendered possible by this actional formation, which act is nothing but the act of anticipating. And the importance of this particular act for the experience of a living organism comes down to the fact that the act exercises a (implicitly) transcendental function. In other words action links the object in the mind and the object in the world.

Constitution of the perceived world

Let us now take the liberty of generalizing further. In the course of my perception of the world I constitute it actively through my anticipations, or *protentions*. So I am thrown ahead of myself and at the same time I retain (without it being possible to talk of memory, since everything still takes place in the present) what I am doing (*retention*). Protention and retention are two fundamental concepts of transcendental phenomenology which we have just managed to introduce into the discussion.

These anticipations are not completely indeterminate: we expect to be dealing with types or prototypes of objects.[18] In the particular context represented by a discussion among researchers in a laboratory, for example, certain objects

---

[17] '*Eu gosto de meu pais, onde* cavallo *ê cavallo mesmo!*' (popular Portuguese saying): 'I love my country where the word "horse" really means a horse!' proudly exclaims the worthy peasant of Alentejo in his pre-Saussurian innocence.

[18] See Biederman's theory of 'geons': the fact that certain neurons of the parietal cortex are sensitive to the forms of particular objects, the fact that mirror neurons are sensitive to a given repertory of behaviour, etc.; I. Biederman and P. Kaloczat (1997) Neurocomputational bases of object and face recognition, *Phil. Trans. R. Soc. Lond. Ser. B Biol. Sci.* 352, 1203–1219.

will be tables or note books, others more technical objects like a projector or a computer, while others again will be human beings. And all these different types of object are endowed with a fully-fledged existence, but only in so far as they respond to certain expectations. Any and every perception has just such a typifying or normative character. Once I have the requisite general types, I can modify them and determine them. My kinaesthesia carries through the (more or less typical) sketches of the objects given to me through my sensory fields. These successive series of sketches do not give me the thing directly but only a certain diversity, a manifold of appearances that can be concordant or discordant.

The proof that we sometimes anticipate can easily be provided by analysing our errors of perception or of judgment. As in the fable by La Fontaine, *Le chameau et les bâtons flottants*, where the ship seen from afar proves only to be a simple piece of wood (or like Descartes viewing passers-by from his window and reflecting on the fact that he can only see hats and coats which might cover 'ghosts or dummies only moved by clockwork')[19] what I take to be a man may in fact only be a mechanical puppet, a delusion, or a perceptual illusion. But in order to be deceived there has to be an anticipation that makes this error possible. If no project is advanced, one cannot make a mistake, only get impregnated with sensations like a sponge.

As essential as it is to our cognitive capacities, anticipation is (according to Kant and Husserl[20] but also the physiologists of today) of such a nature that it always applies at all times and at all points in space. Understood in this sense, it only displays a remote resemblance to what is called 'anticipation' in everyday life; that is, to processes which are always local and also severely restricted in their scope. Of course, if one is a world chess champion and therefore tends to conceive of the entire world as a chess board, as does the Russian champion Victor Kramnik, it is true that every possible situation has to be anticipated in order to be confronted. But why would philosophy and physiology subscribe to such a generalization of the human capacity for anticipation?

The unpredictable, the unexpected, the probable, and the uncertain

Have we not overlooked something important? If we say (without further qualification) that our brain anticipates—that is to say, that the functional architecture

[19] R. Descartes (1953) Méditation seconde, in *Œuvres et Lettres de Descartes*, Gallimard, Paris, p. 281.

[20] 'All of life depends upon anticipation', claims Husserl in his last work: E. Husserl (1970) *The Crisis of European Sciences and Transcendental Phenomenology*, trans. D. Carr, Northwestern University Press, Evanston, IL, Part II, §9.

of its networks is such that we have the ability to anticipate the presence of objects—surely we also need to allow for cases when objects appear suddenly, or we meet people unexpectedly. For example, we can be taken by surprise by something we did not anticipate, and which can even provoke laughter. So, strictly speaking, it is wrong to say that we construct the perceived world exclusively on the basis of our anticipations.

We often find ourselves faced with unexpected objects or events, so that our brain must also be organized in such a way as to allow for novel associations. No doubt, this is what lies at the root of artistic creation, even scientific discoveries, which necessarily imply the development of new concepts. For certain neuropsychologists, this is the responsibility of the right brain,[21] for the latter is better adapted to creating associations between words, concepts, and images. It would be the right brain that is responsible for 'magical thinking', the thinking that leads to dancing to induce rain, for example. Some structures like the anterior cingulate cortex or the orbito-frontal cortex seem to be involved in evaluation of the difference between expected and actual outcomes of an action, etc.

Physiology offers a concrete basis for such general considerations as these. In fact, for some time now, physiologists know that the brain is equipped with devices capable of analysing the unexpected. In the Russia of the 1950s, Vinogradova and Sokolov suggested that the hippocampus might be a novelty detector.[22] More recently, we have discovered the role played by dopamine,[23] a neuromodulator, in the evaluation of the difference between the reward obtained and that expected. Finally, and in order to keep our examples to the minimum, it is clear that the anterior cingular cortex is implied in mechanisms of evaluation of the difference between expectations and results,[24] in association with an entire network of areas (orbito-frontal cortex, ventro-medial cortex, upper temporal sulcus, amygdala, etc.) belonging to the limbic system, the brain of the emotions. This network is activated, for example, in activities involving financial games,[25]

---

[21] K. Taylor, P. Zäsch, and P. Brugger (2002) Why is magical ideation related to leftward deviation in implicit line bissection task? *Cortex* 38, 247–252.

[22] See E.N. Sokolov and O.S. Vinogradova (1975) *Neuronal Mechanisms of the Orienting Reflex*, Erlbaum, Hillsdale, NJ.

[23] See W. Shultz and A. Dickinson (2000) Neuronal coding of prediction errors, *Annu. Rev. Neurosci.* 23, 473–500.

[24] See H. Gemba, K. Sasaki, and V.B. Brooks (1986) 'Error' potentials in limbic cortex (anterior cingulate area 24) of monkeys during motor learning, *Neurosci. Lett.* 70, 223–227; P. Luu, T. Flaish, and D.M. Tucker (2000) Medial frontal cortex in action monitoring, *J. Neurosci.* 20, 464–469.

[25] See R. Elliott, K. Friston, and R. Dolan (2000) Dissociable neural responses in human reward systems, *J. Neurosci.* 20, 6159–6165.

as well as when the subject expresses regret[26] (which presupposes a disappointed anticipation), or even in *counterfactual* tasks[27] involving choice; that is to say, tasks in which the subject is inclined to choose a solution despite the fact that this decision is quite like one already taken in the past and which is therefore more likely to lead to a set-back than to a reward.

Henceforward, the problem is knowing whether, faced with an unexpected object or event, we are going to be able to apply already constructed schemas, or whether we are going to have to invent new 'types' to deal with the unpredictable and not just the improbable.[28]

While conceding this point, it should be borne in mind that (without being paradoxical) the unexpected never stops belonging to the expected. For a human being deprived of all capacity for anticipation no occurrence could be detached from the flux of experience in such a way as to create a surprise. Why? Because no occurrence would stand out (positively or negatively) with regard to expectations which can be satisfied or not satisfied (as the phenomenologists say). When we say that the *brain constantly compares* (something Bernstein said a long time ago), this implies that it makes predictions and anticipations with a view to comparing them with the results of action.

With these observations we have managed to cover, in a cavalier fashion, the entire range of operations actively involved in what we call perception. These operations make it possible for us to deal with a world endowed with meaning for me. But with this everything has still not been said. We now need to introduce (though this is not the place to do it) the notion of intersubjectivity.

---

26 G. Coricelli *et al.* (2005) Regret and its avoidance: a neuroimaging study of choice behavior, *Nat. Neurosci.* 8(9), 1255–1262; N. Camille *et al.* (2004) The involvement of the orbitofrontal cortex in the experience of regret, *Science* 304(5674), 1167–1170; T. Zalla *et al.* (2000) Differential amygdala responses to winning and losing: a functional magnetic resonance imaging study in humans, *Eur. J. Neurosci.* 12(5), 1764–1770.

27 See G. Coricelli *et al.* (2005) Regret and its avoidance: a neuroimaging study of choice behavior, *Nat. Neurosci.* 8(9), 1255–1262.

28 This ability to take account of the unexpected and the unlikely is no doubt responsible for the construction by the human mind of a remarkable tool: the calculus of probabilities. Today the Bayesian calculus, a method of describing probabilistic processes which use a formula invented by the Reverend Bayes, is very much in fashion, for it makes possible the prediction of the probability of an event as a function of the probabilities of its occurring in the past, together with a certain number of constraints. So it makes it possible to relate past, present, and future, to realize the union of protention and retention, of memory and prediction. But nothing obliges us to say that the brain is a Bayesian processor in the strict sense. For if this model has the advantage of taking account of the fact that the brain always operates in a situation of uncertainty, it might well be that only certain of the properties of the functioning of the brain could be described by it.

For if up till now we only talked of a subject, we were nevertheless always aware that a subject does not exist by itself, and that the interconnection of our respective anticipations is what makes it possible for us to have a world equally valid for all. Acts and interactions now become what one might call in philosophical terms the ontological foundation of being for us. Now, not merely is there being in itself and being for me, but, in addition, being *for us*, this common world put into place by several subjects through the interconnection, at the same level, of our activities of exploration and perception. What we have described is the living threshold of that form of actualization through which all that claims to be is first required to appear in order to be for someone, who can be, but is not necessarily, me (see Chapter 8).

The transcendental or how to get rid of it

When one tries to find an appropriate form of words for difficult thoughts one keeps coming up against presuppositions; that is, principles which are uncritically regarded as being 'true' by their very nature, and this holds in particular of the epistemological (and in this very sense ideological) commitments of the one for whom, and with whom, one engages in one's explanations. Even if what was said above is quite clear, what the physiologist still has difficulty in understanding is how it is that the focus of what we are trying to say seems to keep on shifting from the transcendent to the transcendental.

On the one hand, the term transcendent, defined as that which, in its very existence, owes nothing to me, corresponds to the realm of the physical, the external object, out there, in the world, and which remains utterly indifferent to me, and to my knowledge of it.

Transcendental is almost the same word except that, in this way of using it, the physiologist might suspect a surreptitious reintroduction of subjectivity. We have no objection, he might admit, to the concept of transcendence implying, as it does, objects existing by themselves in the physical world. And we have no objection to the concept of immanence, comprehending everything I perceive when I construct things through my active exploration of this world. All that is quite simple and clear. And we are even ready to concede the need to understand the relation between the two. But why use the word transcendental to designate this process of interaction? A word used first to designate the existence of a being independent of the observer and of the constructive activity of the brain is then re-employed to designate this activity itself. In other words, the word for what is independent is then employed again and in such a way as to imply dependence. To the extent that one defines the transcendental as the domain of possible experience, but only in so far as this experience is constituted by the activity of subjects, one comes back around again to the definition of immanence. Would it not be better to look for another word?[29]

The scientific (even sympathetic) interlocutor will no doubt take it as a provocation, a challenge to be met, that philosophers have deliberately decided to take up again the very term employed to designate what is independent of any construction by the subject, and then to turn it around in order to bring it closer to what is said to be constructed by the subject. And this because the whole point was to move into this zone of exchange between the subject and the object and to show in what sense this was a valid field of investigation. So what he might ask is the following: Don't you have another way of doing justice to the dimension of immanent activity in its formative character which is not exclusively preoccupied with internal states but seeks to penetrate beyond such states towards something which does not belong to them? Is there not some way of accomplishing this move, a way that does not bring with it a perversion (legitimate or illegitimate) of the transcendent?

A substitute solution can certainly always be envisaged: to retain the concept of transcendence, a concept representative (in this philosophical terminology) of the external, physical world 'just as it is', even while enriching the definition of immanence. And this by constructing a physiology of interaction. This is what Piaget tried as a psychologist,[30] and what we should be trying today as neurophysiologists, to show that the brain was not created by a God who gave humans a mind or brain, independent of the physical world, and in so doing to show that living organisms form part of this physical world. The true (physico-chemico-mathematical) 'miracle' which took place was that which made

---

[29] This deviation of the transcendent in the direction of the transcendental was undertaken very deliberately and very explicitly by Kant (and the tradition) to underline the fact that it is not enough to simply separate what is immanent from what is transcendent. Not just because, even within the sphere of immanence, a part is directed towards the transcendent but especially because the transcendent is never posited in and of itself. It is only within the immanence of the subject that the question of transcendence ever arises. Any introduction of the transcendent which failed to mention the subject in relation to which the latter features as the objective correlate of acts of knowledge simply loses the essential. Without wanting to split philological hairs regarding an adjective which modifies a substantive which itself modifies a verbal root expressive of action, we have to conclude that adding the suffix -al brings with it an important conceptual contribution. It functions as a form of expression apt to designate the quality of what transcends, that on the basis of which one has the right to talk of a transcendent thing.

[30] We have known that this interactionism is still not enough to make of the worldly relation that which confers its orientation and meaning upon the activities of the perceiving subject ever since Piaget's *Sagesse et Illusion de la Philosophie*. This refusal of phenomenology, directed above all against Merleau-Ponty's work, indicates that Piaget failed to appreciate the pertinence of the latter from a cognitive standpoint.

possible the appearance of this particular activity: life in interaction with the world. An approach of this kind will tend to develop the concept of immanence on the basis of what we know about embryogenesis, about ontogenesis (nurture), then about evolution; that is to say, about the interaction of life with the physical world. To the physiologist such a solution will always appear preferable to that of misusing a term which originally designated the physical world. If there has to be a detour, it might be preferable that it should be in this sense.

Immanence then stops being an internal state of a brain constructed in the course of evolution without any relation to the physical world, but a state which includes the laws of this physical world or rather the constraints of the environment in which the organism lives, those elements of the world which makes it possible for it to perpetuate its life.[31]

Having to choose between holding on to the term transcendental and replacing the transcendental with the term interaction opens up a minimal basis for an *entente cordiale*. The concepts philosophers have employed to come to terms with the basic problem have often been developed in an immanental context, the context of a perceptual consciousness that is conscious of the conditions by which it is regulated, and deployed from the point of view of the subject alone. What is interesting is that, after a long period over which their knowledge has increased immensely, many scientists too have finally arrived at the conclusion that it might be better not to try and describe the world exclusively from the standpoint of its being in itself 'from the point of view of Sirius', but to rejoin the above-mentioned philosophers, even while remaining on the terrain familiar to them, that of transcendent being. This is assuming of course (and this modification is by no means negligible) that a certain dynamism is introduced into nature, a certain evolutionism, a certain autopoïesis,[32] and that—thanks to this enrichment of naturalism[33]—we come to understand better how complexity emerges in nature in such a way as to make possible a capacity for knowledge. So, starting out from two different premises, a juncture can be envisaged.[34]

---

[31] This reference to the living serves to correct the physicalism of this conception of the world by appealing to von Uexküll's reminder that a living creature does not have to deal with the 'world of the physicists' but with its own surrounding life-world, a world invested with subjective values referring back to this creature.

[32] For the definition of autopoïesis see F.J. Varela (1989) *Autonomie et connaissance*, Seuil, Paris, p. 45.

[33] H. Maturana and F.J. Varela (1987) *The Tree of Knowledge: The Biological Roots of Human Understanding*, New Science Library, Boston, MA.

[34] See J. Petitot *et al.* (eds) (1999) *Naturalizing Phenomenology: Issues in Contemporary Phenomenology and Cognitive Science*, Stanford University Press, Stanford, CA.

But we still cannot avoid indulging in some conceptual sleight of hand with a view to explaining how it is that *immanence can be pointed towards the transcendent*, in the first case, and the *transcendent turned back upon itself to yield immanence*, in the second. And even this way of expressing the difficulty might arouse the suspicions of the physiologist who might very well suspect the new formulation of concealing a trap. For how can the transcendent possibly be turned back upon itself if it has been defined (and that is the whole problem!) as the fact that the existence or non-existence of life has no bearing upon the existence of the world? To return to an argument we employed earlier (Chapter 2) but whose brutal simplicity never fails to fascinate, if humanity were to disappear one day, if life on Earth were to cease, there would still be a physical world.

From the cogito to kinaesthesia

From the preceding arguments we may conclude that the point of departure is then not an absolute reality, the naïve postulate of common sense, but the knowing subject, or rather the agent of the act of thinking, of feeling, of perceiving, of believing, and which is also the one who decides and who acts. Already with Descartes (who only had in mind mathematical knowledge), clear and distinct ideas were in themselves a sufficient criterion of objectivity. For Kant the subjective *a priori* conditions of all possible knowledge were at the same time the conditions of the objectivity of this knowledge. Moreover, Kant also thought we were capable of reflectively apprehending these conditions by taking account of the knowledge effectively produced by means of them (which for Kant meant Newtonian mechanics). So the satisfaction of these conditions was enough to procure for this knowledge an empirical object as correlate.

The whole point of the Kantian programme was to disclose the complete (and hence fixed) set of *a priori* conditions upon which the legitimacy of the mathematical and other sciences depended, and this through a reflection upon a body of already acquired knowledge. Even if we are prepared to grant Kant the legitimacy of his project, we do not think he succeeded in bringing to light the principles responsible for the anticipation at work in perception and human action, and this at a level of natural cognition where science is still not operative: a pre-predicative level.[35] The *transcendental theory of perception and of judgement* bearing on experience is precisely the programme Husserl laid

---

[35] A notion drawn from Husserl's vocabulary and adapted to the French language by Merleau-Ponty.

out for phenomenology but which the contingencies of history made it impossible for him to carry through.

In saying this we should however take care not to create an artificial break between Kantian and Husserlian transcendentalism. The emphasis placed upon perception in the *Critique of Pure Reason* (in the *Fundamental Principles of the Metaphysics of Nature* the emphasis is displaced in the direction of mathematical physics) also opens up interesting perspectives for a phenomenology of corporeal experience, however absent such an experience might have been from the thinking of Kant. For example, he held that the exclusively temporal character of the flux of internal states renders it unrepresentable, since the flux of internal states is only a pure succession without any element of permanence. In consequence, the only way of representing internal experience was to make use of the schema of the line, a schema derived from space, the form of our external intuition. This notion of a schema[36] ought to arouse interest in the physiologist because it can be taken to refer to the line not as a basic axiomatic element in abstract Euclidean space but as something that can actually be traced out by producing a succession of points over time in a continuous movement of one's hand, an idea that has been taken up again in recent research suggesting that the brain actually employs affine geometry:[37]

This was what Kant had in mind when he wrote: 'We cannot think a line without drawing it in thought, or a circle without describing it [...] Even time itself we cannot represent, save in so far as we attend, in the drawing of a straight line (which has to serve as the outer figurative representation of time), merely to the act of synthesis of the manifold whereby we successively determine inner sense, and in so doing attend to the succession of this determination in inner sense [...] Motion, as an act of the subject [...], first produces the concept of succession [...]. *Motion, however, considered as the describing of a space, is a pure act of the successive synthesis of the manifold in outer intuition in general by means of the productive imagination and belongs not only to geometry, but even to transcendental philosophy.*'[38]

---

36 For the ambiguity of the schema in relation to its source in the imagination, see what follows.

37 See T. Flash and A.A. Handzel (2007) Affine differential geometry analysis of human arm movements, *Biol. Cybernetics* 96(6), 577–601; N. Tabareau, D. Bennequin, A. Berthoz, J.-J. Slotine, and B. Girard (2007) Geometry of the superior colliculus mapping and efficient oculomotor computation, *Biol. Cybernetics*, 97(4), 279–292 and also G. Chatelet (1993), *Les enjeux du mobile*, Seuil, Paris.

38 I. Kant (1977) *Werkausgabe*, Bd III, Kritik der reinen Vernunft I, Hrsg. v. Wilhelm Weischedel, Frankfurt am Main, Suhrkamp, trans. N. Kemp Smith (2003) *Critique of Pure Reason*, Palgrave Macmillan, Basingstoke, §24, B154–B156; see also §6, B50.

The objects of sensation have to be deployed in an extension in order to be perceptible. This suggests that the extension in question has to be accompanied by a continuous movement on the part of the perceiver; that is, by a gesture, rather like the hunter who follows the target he is aiming at with his eyes. In accompanying the object with the movement of his eyes, the perceiver is actually producing the continuity of the perceived object. To perceive a geometrical form is to project this form in such a way that it can be materialized by the gazing movements, which can also be simulated mentally. Cerebral imagery has brought to light the fact that when one looks at a static visual form (a drawing, a sculpture, a monument) the curvature of this form can activate the MT area of the brain; an area specialized in the processing of the movement of visual forms.[39] This impression of the movement induced by a static visual form no doubt lies at the root of the pleasure of movement evoked by contemplating natural forms such as flowers, trees, or the human body.

The difference should be obvious. With Descartes, the body (what we know about it through the simple use of our measuring instruments) is quite simply an extended thing, and it is so by axiomatic fiat. With Kant, the laying out of a world of bodies already begins to lose this abruptly axiomatic character since it appeals to an active contribution on the part of the subject. In fact when Kant appears to be following Descartes with his principle 'Every intuition has to have an extensive magnitude', it is the subjective experience of moving that remains his guide.[40] His (only too rare) examples are often more instructive than his theoretical pronouncements. In particular, when he observes that however small a line might be, it still has to be traced out in order to be a line. All of this points in another direction than that of the pre-defined structural schemas for which he is regularly (and not unreasonably) criticized.

The role of kinaesthetic sensations in the perception of the form of objects

What can be attributed to Kant, as least as a premonition—because we will have to turn to Husserl and his theory of kinaesthetic sensations to go further—is that he saw the need for spatial deployment, even if only in a measurable and so already Euclidean space, and therefore along the same lines as Descartes. More important still, he saw the need for us to be able to *deploy the different parts of an object in the very act of perceiving this object*. In order that this object should be

---

[39] S. Zeki (1993) *A Vision of the Brain*, Blackwell Publishing, Oxford.

[40] I. Kant (1977) *Werkausgabe*, Bd III, Kritik der reinen Vernunft I, Hrsg. v. Wilhelm Weischedel, Frankfurt am Main, Suhrkamp, trans. N. Kemp Smith (2003) *Critique of Pure Reason*, Palgrave Macmillan, Basingstoke, §6, §24, B154.

there for me, I have to move my body and to feel myself moving my body (a feeling conveyed to me by kinaesthetic sensations), and this with a view to producing the different parts (for instance, its different sides) of the object. So, deploying in this sense does not mean that extension has to be there in advance in order for it to be possible to produce the elements of figures. For in order to perceive the object I have to first dynamically elaborate its form.

Of course, it is always possible to fix Kant's doctrine in a sort of geometric dogmatism by arbitrarily deciding that all he wanted to say was that perception is given as Euclidean from the first, which happens to be false from both a psychological and a physiological point of view. But nothing prevents us from offering a speculative interpretation of his examples by falling back on his idea of an active transcendental schematism. By coming back down from the sterile and frozen summits of Kant's theory of the *a priori*, we can, in fact, choose between two possible ways of accounting for the genesis of individual form.

Those obsessed by the creative power of the word have accounted for the perception of the form of objects by appealing to the resources of a theory of the interpretation (hermeneutics) of poetic language. Reacting against Kant (who almost entirely ignored the cognitive role of language) with a view to restoring to language its ontological dignity, the philologist Johann Gottfried von Herder and the Romantics sought in the *Bible*, the *Edda*, and in Homer proof that the world peculiar to each nation emerged from a collective experience whose unconscious expression is to be found in these great works.

But another line of thought emerged which did not come out of language (except by analogy). In his early writing,[41] the same von Herder discussed the appreciation of classical sculpture, by Lessing and Winckelmann,[42] and sketched out a *phenomenology of the body capable of accounting for the emergence of the individual form of the thing in and through the act of manual prehension*; that is, through touch alone. The painter Hogarth contrasted the classical ideal of symmetry and uniformity with the 'line of grace and beauty' that the pencil of the artist brings to light by subtly and flexibly enfolding them in the beautiful forms of nature.[43] Taking up this idea,

[41] J.G. von Herder (1778) *Plastik. Einige Wahrnehmungen über Form und Gestalt aus Pygmalions Bildenden Traume*, L.A. Schneider (ed) (1969) Jacob Hegner, Cologne; trans. J. Gaiger (ed.) (2002) *Sculpture: some observations on shape and form from Pygmalion's creative dream*, University of Chicago Press, Chicago, IL.

[42] G.E. Lessing (1766) *Laokoön: oder über die Grenzen der Malerei und Poesie*, Berlin; J.J. Winckelmann (1755) *Gedanken über die Nachahmung der griechischen Werke in der Malerei und Bildhauerkunst*, trans. E. Heyer and R.C. Norton (1987) *Reflections on the Imitation of Greek Works in Painting and Sculpture*, Open Court, La Salle, IL.

[43] W. Hogarth (1753) *The Analysis of Beauty*, R. Paulson (ed) (1997) Yale University Press, New Haven, CT.

von Herder promotes a change in emphasis as between the visible and the tangible. The line traced out by the living hand evokes the hand that touches more than it does the detached vision of the eye. And so it is the former that is primarily responsible for generating the physical form of the object:

> 'The beautiful line constantly altering its course without either brutal interruption or distortion traces out the shape of the body in all its beauty and its splendour. Never at rest, always in progress, it confers fluidity and plenitude to this corporality whose marvellous softness and suppleness surpasses surfaces, angles and corners.'[44]

Or again:

> 'The eye is only the initial guide, the hand's reason. It is the hand alone that reveals the forms of things, their concepts, what they mean, what lies concealed in them. [...]What then are we to say of Hogarth's line of beauty? This line of beauty, together with all that follows from it, teaches us nothing if it does not appear on forms and, in so doing, does not then rejoin the sense of touch.'[45]

At an aesthetic level, this interpretation anticipates the novel point of view accomplished by Husserl in his *Krisis*. There, Husserl asked whether, in giving the name 'Axioms of Intuition' to those principles which could retain no more of this formative dynamism of perception than spatial extension, Kant might have confused the constitutive process with the end result. Even though he thought he was founding the application of Euclidean geometry to perceptual space, what he actually did was to cover over the lived space which precedes the construction of Euclidean space with an ideal construction. But this lived space is actually endowed with a structure that we will now have to come to terms with (see Chapters 6 and 7).

How are we to understand the naturally mathematical functioning of human thought, a functioning which, nevertheless, is so very different from the purely formal games of pure thought (which have no bearing on anything) that it is capable of giving rise to regulative schemas that embrace the entire domain of our experience of nature ? This seeming mystery of perception begins to clear up once one starts paying attention to what might appear to be a trivial circumstance: that the *function of our sense organs is to execute movements and to form the world rather than to capture sensations.*

Right away we are faced with a question, the question whether, in line with his figurative and non-calculatory conception of geometry, Kant himself might not have opened up a perspective on *intentional movement* as the incarnation

----

[44] J.G. von Herder (1778) *Sculpture: some observations on shape and form from Pygmalion's creative dream*, trans. J. Gaiger (ed.) (2002), University of Chicago Press, Chicago, IL, p. 40.

[45] J.G. von Herder (1778) *Sculpture: some observations on shape and form from Pygmalion's creative dream*, trans. J. Gaiger (ed.) (2002), University of Chicago Press, Chicago, IL, p. 64.

of consciousness in an animate body. For, if so, he could then be regarded as having anticipated, in a remarkable way, a phenomenological evidence of the first importance: subjectivity is manifest to itself in the gesture, whether natural or expert (that of the artist, the designer, the dancer, or the craftsman) through which it gets *objectified*. From this one might conclude that Kant's change of perspective—his Copernican Revolution, to employ the term taken up again by Husserl—had not been sufficiently radical, or if you prefer, that Kant had not carried through to its logical conclusion the very programme he set for himself. Not only did Kant want to get beyond the naïve conception of a knowing subject for which things enjoy an absolutely independent reality and so impose themselves upon an essentially passive subject, he also wanted to open the way to a truly transcendental conception of the being of human being, one in the context of which an essentially active subject determines *a priori* its own possible objects of knowledge. These objects are not just those that fall within the field of sense experience but also include those he is capable of giving himself by *actively producing them.*

The programme Kant failed to complete can in fact be traced back to that outlined by Descartes on the basis of the *cogito*. The critique that can be made of Kant's thinking is the following: he failed to distinguish between what one might call simple perception (that is, the natural activity of perceiving) and the natural science of his epoch (that is, the mathematical reconstruction of nature accomplished by Newton in his *Mechanics*). The failure to draw this distinction brought with it a short-circuiting of the description of subjective activities. For these activities are in fact put to work by the subject who perceives at every level. And this even before the result of such activities find intellectual expression in judgement. But why talk about a short-circuit? In the sense in which his thinking might have led to descriptions he never actually carried through as a result of the excessively reflective method he employed. He reflected, as is the wont of the philosopher. But in reflecting he only succeeded in abstracting science from its context, thereby tacitly assuming Newton's presuppositions. Instead of engaging in a description of the way our senses actually function in perception, he introduced into transcendental thinking a highly elaborated science, the product of an abstract procedure of intellectual reasoning.

The sensible body as a transcendental experience

So, among the activities of the perceiving subject, we have to look for operations—acts—of such a kind that the subject actually carries them out effectively. This implies two things which at first sight might appear incompatible. On the one hand, these activities must of course be integrated into the life of the subject, and in such a way that they can be referred to as experienced events. But, at the same time, and in order to preserve the idea of *a priori* conditions of possible experience, these operations cannot be confused with mental states that appear and disappear, purely contingent states, carried along by the flux of this subjective life.

Trying to do justice to this double requirement creates a problem: on the one hand, we have to deal with processes, with a mental flux, so with the conditioned (the material informed by categories of the mind). On the other hand, the epistemological distinction between the conditioning and the conditioned has to be preserved or we will fall back into naïve empiricism. At best, we will simply have gone back to a Humean position.[46] In a sense, this reversion was already accomplished by Husserl, since phenomenology represents a return to things themselves, but only in a sense, for perceived things are not simple sense data. How are we going to resolve this contradiction?

Perhaps the solution is to be found along the lines of what was discussed above. It has already been established that the subject of knowledge determines its own object rather than simply being passively determined. But what about the formative structure of this subject, the determinate capacity of this subject to determine its objects? For his part, Kant abstracted it from the domain of the experience it conditions. The 'I think' as an act unifying a diversity of sense material in one object of knowledge remains a pure thought, and so can provide no content for intuition. We cannot grasp this principle of unity responsible for any intellectual synthesis directly by itself and without applying it in particular cases to the knowledge of this or that object. For that we would need a still higher faculty not to be found in human nature. For we can only experience what is given to us in sense. We have nothing like an intellectual intuition.[47] This at any rate is the doctrine to be found in the published works.

---

[46] D. Hume (1740) *A Treatise of Human Nature*, L.A. Selby-Bridge (ed.) (1888), Oxford University Press, Oxford.

[47] Intellectual intuition: against Kant, Fichte claimed that the transcendental subject is not just the purely formal unity that accompanies all my representations. It is accessible in itself through reflection upon internal experience, thanks to a special, non-sensible intuition. In refusing such an intuition Kant had allowed himself to be enclosed within the limits of common experience, which the philosopher can transcend by paying full and perfect attention to the concepts themselves through which objects are known and so procuring an intellectual intuition of them. This speculative path is not of such a kind as to encourage a dialogue between transcendental philosophy and physiology. We mention it only because it has the merit of disclosing in a radical way the essence of the cognitive process, a process through which the subject is in the end only sensitive to that which acquires meaning through his own thinking as auto-affection. Knowledge is the free determination by the I (or the we) of a power of being affected which essentially

On the other hand, in the *Opus Postumum*, we find a theory of the self-positing[48] (*Selbstsetzung*) of the subject as object of experience, which is worth taking a look at despite its fragmentary nature. For we can see in it an indication that, from the very start, transcendental philosophy recognized the need for its own naturalization. All knowledge in general is accompanied by an 'I think', which is the act unifying the diversity of this experience in the unity of an object. And we even have a certain experience of this act itself. But what kind of experience could we possibly have of an act which takes the form of a simple function of unity, whether logical, formal, or analytical, the unity unifying any sensory diversity whatsoever? This is the point at which we *realize that the unity of the subject cannot be reduced to a purely formal pole and that the synthesis it makes possible has to be grasped as a concrete act.*

But what could possibly be meant by 'concrete act of synthesis'? It is an act such that in executing it a subject actually realizes the conditions of our experience of material objects in the physical world. But the most general characteristic of material objects (in the universe of classical mechanics) is that they are localized in space and that they exert forces of action and reaction one upon the other.[49] So the subject could not posit itself as an object if it did not apprehend itself as a body in space, the source of movements by means of which it intervenes in the world as a force,[50] brought into play through its own initiative (since it is nothing other than its voluntary action)

....

does not differ from itself, which comes down to granting the I (or the we) a power to posit itself. This bold vision of the autonomy of cognition reminds us of Maturana and Varela's theory of autopoïèse and as such has been recalled by Livet in: P. Livet (1987) Intersubjectivité, réflexivité et récursivité chez Fichte, *Arch. Phil.* 50, 4.

[48] The role of the body in Kant's last incomplete philosophical project has come to light as a result of the fine work of translation and editing devoted to the *Nachlass* by F. Marty: I. Kant, *Opus Postumum*, trans. F. Marty (ed.) (1986), PUF, Paris; *Kant's gesammelte Schriften*, Ed. Preussischen Akademie der Wissenschaften, XXI–XXII, III *Handschriftlicher Nachlass*, VIII–IX *Opus postumum*, G. Lehmann und A. Buchenau, Berlin, Leipzig, 1936–1938.

[49] See A. Koyré (1962) *Du Monde clos à l'Univers infini*, PUF, Paris, Chap. VII.

[50] On the physiological aspects of this capacity see D.I. Perrett *et al.* (1985) Visual analysis of body movements by neurons in the temporal cortex of the macaque monkey, *Behav. Brain Res.* 16, 153–170; S.-J. Blakemore and C. Frith (2005) The role of motor contagion in the prediction of action, *Neuropsychologia* 43, 260–267; Nicolelis M.A. (2005) Computing with thalamocortical ensembles during different behavioural states, *J. Physiol.* 566(1), 37–47; Nicolelis M.A. and Shuler M. (2001) Thalamocortical and corticocortical interactions in the somatosensory system, *Prog. Brain Res.* 130, 90–110; Ghazanfar A.A. and Nicolelis M.A. (2001) Feature article: the structure and function of dynamic cortical and thalamic receptive fields, *Cerebral Cortex* 11(3), 183–193.

and which is nevertheless inserted into the general field of all those forces which physical bodies in space exert upon each other.

What has just been said is enough to provide an unequivocal solution to our problem. The transcendental experience we are looking for is the following: our awareness of our body, of its localization, of its movements, and of the forces actively released and passively undergone in all its movements, in a word, our kinaesthesia. This is the experience we have of ourselves as actively engaged in the world through our bodies and not as the simple support of 'mental states in our head', the phrase used by those theoreticians of cognition who have not gone through their own Copernican revolution! As transcendental subjects we are already agents carrying through acts of synthesis making it possible for us to gain access to a physical world and to those other bodies which inhabit this physical world. And from this point on, the reflective theory of the *a priori* conditions of the possibility of an empirical object of knowledge brings us to the threshold of a theory of transcendental constitution: the constitution of objects of knowledge in subjective acts conferring upon the knowledge in question the meaning it has for the community of cognitive subjects as well as for the subject itself.

This self-positing of the knowing subject in the cognitive process has been divested of its apparently abstract and speculative character by Husserl.[51] With him, the pure act of an I that posits itself in the midst of the world described by physical science becomes voluntary intentionality. The auto-affection that consists in my being intimately affected by the very movements I transmit to my limbs becomes kinaesthesia, my own sense of myself as a self-moving being. As a result the *a priori* conditions of the possibility of knowledge are brought down to the plane of concrete events experienced by an incarnate subject. Time, space, causality, and the categories of perception and empirical judgment no longer have to be postulated as abstract conditions in the mind in order that an empirical knowledge of objects be possible for beings such as ourselves.

In Chapter 5, and along the lines developed above, we hold that space, causality, and the other categories do not exist in some heaven of pure formal

---

[51] The connection we have established between Husserl (his kinaesthetic theory of transcendental constitution) and the Kant of the *Opus Postumum* (his theory of the self-positing of the transcendental subject) would no doubt be challenged by Eckart Förster (*Kant's Final Synthesis. An Essay on the Opus Postumum*, 2000, Harvard University Press, Boston, MA), whose interpretation we have nevertheless exploited. But in our view his challenge would be misplaced. In fact he expressly rejects the assimilation to a 'phenomenology of incarnation' (which he inadvertently imputes to Heidegger and not just to Merleau-Ponty) of what he describes in Kant as a theory of the auto-constitution of the subject as object of experience. But in so doing, without meaning to, he characterizes this theory in terms which are strictly applicable to Husserl's theory (p. 195).

possibilities but that they are engendered through regulated operations in the frame of a system whose architecture one can try to understand. As genuine motor capacities, these operations are brought into play by appropriate corporeal movements (which can also be inhibited and internally simulated movements). In the course of its development, the agent engages in a learning process, makes use of its brain and its body, and so becomes a knowing subject. And the execution of these operations has to proceed regularly and uninterruptedly if this being is to gain access to things in the world.

Is it possible to naturalize the *a priori*? Time is of the essence

The physiology of cognition is looking for an epistemology which is not that of a propositional logic poorly naturalized as a psychology of mental representations, itself still looking to be naturalized. One suspects that the dependence of this psychology on this logic is a tribute paid to the anti-psychologism of the founder of naturalized epistemology (Quine).[52] There can be no refuge for a science of the mental outside the proposition! Hence the fiction of representations in the mind transposed over from propositions into this new context. For aside from the fear of letting go of the framework established by the logician, why should the format of mental representations—assuming that there are such things and that they are illustrated by percepts—have been modelled on that of predicative judgment? As soon as one stops projecting elementary logic upon the perceived and starts using more sophisticated formal instruments for the mathematical schematization of this phenomenology, the eidetics that emerges is anything but predicative.[53] Husserl's thought was guided by an intuition into the essential difference between morphology and logic.[54]

What cognitive physiology needs is an epistemology that takes temporality and the material character of sensible experience seriously. This epistemology

---

[52] See W.V.O. Quine (1969/1977) How to naturalize epistemology, in *Relativité de l'ontologie et autres* essais, trans. into French by J. Largeault Aubier Montaigne, Paris, pp. 83–105. For example, his suggestion to treat percepts as perceptual norms: 'It is quite likely that outside language too there exists an alphabet of perceptual norms, in accordance with which we tend unconsciously to rectify our perceptions, If we could identify them experimentally these norms could be taken as building blocks for epistemological constructions, or as modules of experience' (p. 104).

[53] See J. Petitot (1999) Morphological eidetics for a phenomenology of perception, in J. Petitot *et al.* (eds), *Naturalizing Phenomenology: Issues in Contemporary Phenomenology and Cognitive Science*, Stanford University Press, Stanford, CA, pp. 330–371.

[54] See his eidetic morphology, a general theory of the conditions of the independence of objects and of the division of wholes: E. Husserl (1901/1972) *Logical Investigations*, 2. 2. Investigation III, Humanities Press, New York.

already exists, at least 'in concept' (as the philosophers used to say). A first step in the right direction was taken by Kant's transcendental psychology (a second, by Husserl's intentional psychology). Nowhere else in philosophical literature does one find a theory of knowledge that confers so central a place upon time: 'All increase in empirical knowledge is a progression in time'.[55] To take this assertion by Kant in the trivial sense of a knowing process that unfolds through successive phases does not bring very much. Here it will be understood in the radical sense in which knowledge is our spontaneous way of determining the temporal form of all experience.

More simply, *knowing is nothing other than determining the form of time*. Having an experience, experiencing something, perceiving an object is a sort of manipulation of time. Time is associated with the subject as its own subjective dimension, a mode of existence of the knowing organism. It is this frame of reference that makes knowledge possible. Time is what makes it so that we can only know successive events. And this condition is subjective relative to our being. We know nothing about what time is in itself, absolutely, in things themselves. And that's the Copernican Revolution: before this we thought that it was the objective world that turned, but ever since we have recognized that it is the subject itself (or its earthly support) that turns. One attributes to the subject what was formerly attributed to objects, and this is how time gets attributed to the subject as the form of its own experience. Time does not pertain to the external world and to objects; time and space are not properties of a stable and immobile universe outside us.

In this context, Kant made use of an embarrassing phrase that Husserl was ready to take over from him: the *a priori*. There are *a priori* principles of possible knowledge. Principles inherent in us and not extracted from experience. For the temporal and spatial character of the object, what makes it possible for me to experience it, has not been extracted from experience. We are already in possession of principles of knowledge that we bring with us to the world. Knowing consists of imposing upon the sensory diversity furnished by our spatial and temporal intuitions a synthetic unity that makes it possible for us to grasp this diversity in one act of consciousness. And which, at the same time, makes it possible for us to free this diversity from the singularity and the contingency of the sensory impact by conferring upon it the epistemological dignity of an objective knowledge; that is, knowledge of something existing outside of us. So by enquiring back from the materials made available to us by scientific

---

[55] I. Kant (1977) *Werkausgabe*, Bd III, Kritik der reinen Vernunft I, Hrsg. v. Wilhelm Weischedel, Frankfurt am Main, Suhrkamp, trans. N. Kemp Smith (2003) *Critique of Pure Reason*, Palgrave Macmillan, Basingstoke, B255, A210.

knowledge, we ought to be able to bring to light (or so Kant thought) certain cognitive principles of synthesis which do not come to us from experience.

Of course, one can always argue that these *a priori* principles of possible experience are not *a priori* at all. Kant took them over from Newton, who had already come up with the ideas of the permanence of the object, of universal causality, and of 'community'; that is, the belonging together of all objects in one and the same space where they are contained simultaneously. He simply put all this together and declared that from now on they were to be regarded as the *a priori* structures of perception. But even if we concede the legitimacy of this criticism of his procedure (which should be left to the historians of science) it should still be admitted that by approaching matters in this way, he intuitively stumbled across the possibility of perceiving and knowing subjects interiorizing, and so anticipating, the general constraints of the environment (and of their organism).

Today, we would say either that these principles are genetically programmed or that they are extracted from experience by the recognition of 'invariants' in the world, and this from the very first years of life. We project these pre-perceptions upon the world. For the scientist who adopts an evolutionary approach, these *a priori* principles are the results of successful interactions with the world.[56] So, for him, the formalist illusion consists of our having taken these principles to be formal rules disconnected from experience, even though they are in fact the result of three million years of interaction with the world. But the question of the *a priori* cannot be so easily dismissed as a formalist illusion.

Such interiorized constraints as these amount to an intuitive and practical knowledge of the physics of the body and of the environment. They are even better anchored in the real than this 'popular physics'[57] that the philosophers of mind and other theorists of cognition have conceded as belonging to our

---

[56] For fundamental research into naive physics see J. Piaget (1926) *La représentation du monde chez l'enfant*, Gallimard, Paris, and J. Piaget (1937) *La construction du réel chez l'enfant*, Delachaux & Nestlé, Paris, as well as A. Michotte (1963) *La Perception de la causalité*, Methuen, London. Currrent works: R. Baillargeon *et al.* (1985) Objects permanence in five-month-old infants, *Cognition* 20, 191–208; A.M. Leslie and S. Keeble (1987) Do six-month-old infants perceive causality? *Cognition* 25, 265–287; M. McCloskey *et al.* (1980) Curvilinear motion in the absence of external forces: naive beliefs about the motion of objects, *Science* 210, 1139–1141; E.S. Spelke (1991) Physical knowledge in infancy: reflections on Piaget's theory, in S. Carey and R. Gelman (eds), *The Epigenesis of Mind: Studies in Biology and Cognition*, Erlbaum, Hillsdale, NJ. pp. 133–169; E.S. Spelke *et al.* (1992) Origins of knowledge, *Psychol. Rev.* 99, 605–632.

[57] J.A. Fodor (1987) *Psychosemantics. The Problem of Meaning in the Philosophy of Mind*, MIT Press, Cambridge, MA; F. Dretske (1988) *Explaining Behavior. Reasons in a World of Causes*, MIT Press, Cambridge, MA.

theory of mind, and which makes of them simple mental furniture with no objective value. Hence our interest in Husserl's version of the *a priori*. For he succeeded in getting rid of the remnants of the formal frame of classical science and set about investigating the *a priori* principles effectively brought into play in our experience. His research looks for *operations* rather than principles, and so marks a significant departure from Kant.

This new, clearly operational *a priori* can be much better connected with the concepts developed by psychology or psychophysics than the former, formal *a priori*, especially in what concerns the hypotheses the brain makes about the world when it has to resolve what the theorists of probability and the engineers call the inverse problem: for example, that of reconstituting objects in three dimensions on the basis of two-dimensional images. Indeed, it has been shown that this problem cannot be resolved without recurring to the *a priori*.[58]

For example, in what concerns visual perception it is said that the brain develops hypotheses regarding visual objects, hypotheses of rigidity, of symmetry, of stability.[59] Projecting *a priori* hypotheses upon the world, the brain makes use of the latter as a way of interpreting sensorial material. The simplest and oldest experiment is that of Ames' room. A subject is presented with a room into which he can only look through a small hole, which makes of him a voyeur. This room is not in fact cubical or symmetric but trapezoidal, as if the roof of the room in which the reader sits sloped, with non-rectangular walls. If two people of the same size are placed in this room our 'voyeur' is the victim of a remarkable illusion: he sees the room as symmetrical but the two persons as being one a giant and the other a dwarf. This is due to the fact that the brain cannot stand seeing non-symmetrical forms and that it exercises a veritable tyranny over its environment, to the point of deforming the objects or persons situated in this world.

So the brain disposes of interpretive grids which it projects upon the world. To the extent that these grids can be treated as a concept of the *a priori*, the result is a certain 'naturalization' of this concept of the *a priori*. Nothing prevents us from accounting for the availability of these *a priori* tools by treating them as the result of three million years of experience and of the process of natural evolution, or even of laws governing the functioning of the brain. These are laws which, in themselves, are derived from correspondingly general

---

58 See A. Berthoz (2003) *La décision*, Odile Jacob, Paris.

59 M. Wexler, I. Lamouret, and J. Droulez (2001) The stationary hypothesis: an allocentric criterion in visual perception, *Vision Res.* 41(3), 3023–3037; M. Wexler, F. Panerai, I. Lamouret, and J. Droulez (2001) Self-motion and the perception of stationary objects, *Nature* 409(6816), 85–88.

laws of nature, a derivation whose logic still eludes us, over and beyond such facile generalities as that a penchant for symmetry offers many adaptive advantages and that a good many organisms have become equipped with such symmetric structures in consequence. Only those species have survived the evolutionary process that disposed of such interpretive *a priori* grids, for the simple reason that they simplify neurocomputation by diminishing the range of movements that have to be controlled; even more important, they make it possible to obtain a rapid response to a threat or to the presence of prey.

The use of philosophical words such as substance, substrate, and properties might suggest that what is said does not apply to everyday life. The exact opposite is the case: we are surrounded by objects that shine. The copper pot was the pride of the household that kept it shining; the gleaming coachwork of sports cars and the reflecting glass of the office buildings give back to man a magnified image of himself. It is worth bearing in mind that the source of this fascination is the phenomenon of lustre in our visual experience; that is, the coloured fragmentation of a smooth and continuous surface over which light gets reflected,[60] a phenomenon that intrigued Husserl (not to mention the impressionist painters, who were practical phenomenologists). Depending upon the way in which the perceiving subject manipulates a smooth object, depending upon the point from which he looks at it, he sees differently coloured aspects. These coloured aspects can be absolutely distinct from one spot on the surface to the next. From one angle what appears will be the colour of the material of which it is made, from another the blue sky; that is, if a blue sky is indeed reflected in the window. In the absolute, the perceiving subject might be tempted to associate such very different aspects with quite distinct objects, which however he does not do. And the result is that we have a visual experience of the lustre of the surface of a (unique) object.

And this, yet again, because we are organized in such a way that there is perception, there is objective knowledge only because we always relate the succession of our perceptual states to one and the same substance as its underlying support. Never forget that this support cannot be known since we can only know those perceptual states which manifest themselves to us. Changes in experience can only be seen as changes of one and the same object that changes and so becomes constantly other. (In psychology, the term *invariant* is used.) I only perceive changes if I suppose *a priori* a permanent object remaining the same through these changes which thereby become its 'modes of existence in time'.

---

60 See J. Ninio (1998) *La science des illusions*, Odile Jacob, Paris.

This is an absolutely universal condition. There can only be for me, in my lived experience, mental states referred to external things that succeed in time if I associate them with this or that thing and so always to a permanent object. I am convinced that there are such permanent objects, though in fact I have only projected this idea on the world. Piaget's developmental psychology reminds us that, with the child, the permanence of the object is constructed in the course of the first year, and this presents no problem for our *a priori* conception. For what is constructed are the conditions without which we should not have a normal adult knowledge. That we only got to this point gradually, why would anyone want to deny that? For the *a priori* in question is not presented in the form of a logical rule, of an epistemological principle or an innate knowledge inscribed in the mind independent of action. It is an *a priori* of experience not of logic, all of whose laws are indisputably *a priori*. It is not a formal *a priori* in the strict sense of that word but rather in the sense in which one might say metaphorically of time and space that they are the form of our experience. Being in possession of these *a prioris* makes it possible for us to anticipate. Since we know something in advance about every object and every event, we can use these *a priori* principles to determine the form of time in advance.

Is the internal model a neural implementation of the *a priori*?

Biologists and roboticists who work on the control of movement often make use of the concept of the *internal model*. For example, when we catch a ball, the brain does not wait until the ball touches the hand to produce a muscular contraction. The contraction, produced at the moment the ball touches the hand, exactly counterbalances the forces produced by the ball. This led some to think that the brain disposed of an internal model of the laws of gravity in the form of a neural network capable of simulating the physical laws of interaction between bodies and the hand.[61]

In the same way, the fact that one can construct a pretty drawing with one's finger despite the distortions due to a stiff or flimsy support give rise to the thought that the cerebellum contains an internal model of the dynamics of the limbs, and that the physical properties of the limbs, their muscles, and geometrical and dynamic properties, are written into the nervous structures of the cerebellum. This is what makes it possible for the cerebellum to anticipate

---

[61] J. McIntyre, M. Zago, A. Berthoz, and F. Lacquaniti (2001) Does the brain model Newton's laws? *Nat. Neurosci.* 4(7), 693–694.

movement by producing it, somehow, on an internal model of the arm.[62] Time intervenes here in the transition, for it takes time to simulate the movement in the neural network.

Since the internal model consists of a certain functional architecture of the neural network, the geometry of the model can get ahead of time, for the dynamic geometry of the network infiltrates the mechanical movement.[63] This functional architecture makes it possible to simulate the properties of the physical world. Anticipation would then come down to the brain being able to send an informant down to this structure, a structure resembling the physical world, and to read off from it what would happen if …, thereby being able to warn the brain: watch out! If the movement is carried out in this way, the following result will follow. The control of movement then comes down to a sort of comparison between prediction and realization. The brain therefore functions as a sort of detector of differences (the psychologists say 'error') between its own predictions and the movement being made.

This internal model theory enjoys a fairly wide consensus today in the neurosciences of movement, and is frequently employed in robotics. But it contains an implicit hypothesis which has not caught the attention of the specialists. The internal model in question functions with an *a priori* about the physical world.

Static models or a genetic dynamic?

How is the dimension of time presupposed by this inscription of the properties of the physical world into the functional architecture of the brain? Already, it has to be admitted that a certain form of precedence is implied by anticipation to the extent that the physical schema is activated just before the

---

[62] D.M. Wolpert and Z. Ghahramani (2000) Computational principles of movement neuroscience, *Nat. Neurosci.* 3, 1212–1217; D.M. Wolpert, R.C. Miall, and M. Kawato (1998) Internal models in the cerebellum, *Trends Cog. Sci.* 2(9), 338–347; R.C. Miall and D.M. Wolpert (1996) Forward models for physiological motor control, *Neural Networks* 9(8), 1265–1279; D.M. Wolpert, Z. Ghahramani, and M.I. Jordan (1995) An internal model for sensorimotor integration, *Science* 269, 1880–1882; M. Kawato, K. Furukawa, and R. Suzuki (1987) A hierarchical neural network model for control and learning of voluntary movement, *Biol. Cybernetics* 57, 169–186.

[63] A. Pellionisz and R. Llinás (1985) Tensor network theory of the metaorganization of functional geometries in the central nervous system, *Neuroscience* 16(2), 245–273; A. Pellionisz and R. Llinás (1982) Space-time representation in the brain. The cerebellum as a predictive space-time metric tensor, *Neuroscience* 7(12), 2949–2970; A. Pellionisz and R. Llinás (1980) Tensorial approach to the geometry of brain function: cerebellar coordination via a metric tensor, *Neuroscience* 5(7), 1125–1138.

effectuation of the relevant acts of perception and action. Perception and action precede themselves, so to speak, thanks to this anticipation based on an internal model. And in such a way that any experience that unfolds over time will inevitably be affected by the constraints of this internal dynamics. So we certainly are dealing with something like a structuring of time.

But this activation of the internal model in the phases of anticipation of a movement is not itself inscribed in time (objective time); rather, it is constitutive of (subjective) time. Time is what one is obliged to simulate before movement. Of course this definition has to be explained, for we are not going to claim that it is acceptable in its present form. In order to get such an explanation going let us say that time is the entire field of that projection which, in perceptual experience, is made up of our internal models about the world. At the very least it is an essential component of such a process. Or perhaps it is only one of the components of the whole structure enveloping the environment of the subject, another component of which would be the geometry of the neurons making up its brain.

In fact, two aspects have to be taken into account. On the one hand, bringing this internal model into play through neural activity obviously takes time, a very short lapse of time (a few tens of milliseconds) before the movement occurs.[64] On the other hand, if we have an internal model of our organic physics and of the physical properties of the environment, we should not (under normal circumstances) have any experience of something that fails to fall under the rules of this internal physics. All the same, we now know that the networks of neurons in the cerebral cortex which are activated by tactile sensations of movements can be radically modified by experience. And the same most probably holds of these hypothetical internal models whose structures certainly make up one of its components.[65]

....

[64] The discussion of the classic results of Benjamin Libet's cerebral chronometry bore on the question of deciding whether the deflection of the curve of electrical activity registered at the level of the motor areas or the somato-sensorial areas 500 milliseconds before a voluntary movement of the finger or cutaneous sensation could resolve the difference between those who impute action to the initiative of the agent or who date sensation from the moment that it gains access to consciousness (thesis of freedom) versus those who attribute it to a prior increase in nervous excitation (determinist thesis). B. Libet (1985) Unconscious cerebral initiative and the role of conscious will in voluntary action, *Behav. Brain Sci* 8, 529–566; B. Libet *et al.* (1979) Subjective referral of the timing for a conscious sensory experience. A functional role for the somatosensory specific projection system in man, *Brain* 102, 193–224.

[65] Representational plasticity of the adult brain, the discovery of which should be credited primarily to the work of Michael Merzenich and his team: M.M. Merzenich *et al.* (1987) Variability in hand surface representations in areas 3b and 1 in adult owl and squirrel monkeys, *J. Comp. Neurol.* 258, 281–296. This was brought to light through the amputation

Reformulating this problem of the *a priori* of cognitive synthesis in terms of the neurosciences, we know today that the brain disposes of such *a priori* structures, as for example, the hypotheses of rigidity and symmetry. We know that when subjects are presented with objects of perception there is a tendency for this perception to be organized according to a certain number of rules, rules presupposed in all possible experience. In the same way, in the first relays of the visual cortex, the processing of information gives rise to a decomposition of the real into elementary geometric forms. The neurons of the visual cortex are activated in such a way as to respond to certain characteristics of the external world, angles and so on, as a function of principles of continuity, of connection, of neighbourhood. These are principles echoing the Analogies of Experience in Kant's *Critique of Pure Reason*, but solely on the basis of the evidence of modern neurophysiology.

At a primary level the brain decomposes or analyses the world with the help of transformational operators which realize what those neurophysiologists who have had a mathematical training call a 'spatial filtering'. One can imagine these operators written into the structure of the neural networks. But at this level, the perceptual analysis remains passive.

At a second and more interesting level, one that has recently been brought to light by physiology in apes or by psychophysics in humans, one finds action influencing perception in that perceptual analysis is oriented by the act of looking, grasping, avoiding, fleeing, and capturing. So action is unfolded not just in an ecological but also in a reflective frame of reference. Thinking about the world is also an act and one that can be modified by attention, itself in turn subordinated to intention. The point is important. A radical modification of the 'analysis of objects', of the 'analysis of the world' (expressions which turn out to be somewhat inadequate), takes place in each perception as a function, precisely, of the intention inherent in the action.

But there is a third level, the existence of which reinforces this idea of the *a priori* and introduces the dimension of time, over and above the grids of analysis

---

of the fingers of monkeys, this plasticity of the functional substrate of the experience of the body has since proved to be normal with humans and, in the long run, a condition for remembering how to perform manual tasks (F. Spengler *et al.* (1997) Learning transfer and neuronal plasticity in humans trained in tactile discrimination, *Neurosci. Lett.* 232, 151–154; A. Karni *et al.* (1995) fMRI evidence for adult motor cortex plasticity during motor skill learning, *Nature* 377, 155–158; A. Pascual-Leone and F. Torres (1993) Plasticity of the sensorimotor cortex representation of the reading finger in Braille readers, *Brain* 116, 39–52). In the short term it features as a trace of the influence of attention on tactile perception (H. Hämäläinen, J. Hiltunen, and I. Titievskaja (2002) Activation of somatosensory cortical areas varies with attentional state: an fMRI study, *Behav. Brain Res.* 135, 159–165).

materialized in the structure of the nervous system and which select certain types of forms, over and above the role of action, of attention, of perception as having an aim, which also, and in its own way, pre-forms theses analyses ... there is also memory. Thanks to memory, these analyses are also conducted as a function of past experience, as a function of the analyses already conducted in the past and of their consequences. For memory does not just happen as a sort of projection of the past on the current situation; it retains the consequences of what has already happened at a higher level of complexity.

This insight into physiological correlates makes it possible for us to appreciate the structural, one might even say structuralist, side of Kant's transcendental psychology. Even though his thinking had the merit of recognizing the universally embracing role of time in all experience, he made of it a frame of this same experience. He drew up atemporal tables of categories to frame the principles of possible knowledge. This is also what makes it possible for us to distinguish Kant's approach from that of Husserl. Kant thought out everything in a static and global manner, Husserl attempted to rethink along genetic lines.

On the basis of an experience reduced (we are talking here of the transcendental reduction)[66] to the present here—now, with I myself accomplishing acts that are directly under my conscious control[67] —Husserl asks: how can I get back to the vast world of perceptual and scientific experience? His question is 'genetic' in the constructive sense, or more exactly, in the sense of an analysis of the sense-giving operations that the agent itself carries through. He brings us back to action, even though the actions in question are not to be understood in the vulgar sense of those displacements of my limbs needed to accomplish a task.

Introducing any such vulgar sense of action—by definition *a posteriori*—into a foundational analysis would jeopardize its transcendental character, since an action is by definition *a posteriori*. This is why we keep insisting on the notion of an act which is at one and the same time past, future, and present. In the final analysis, the act is resolved into an action. The action is the concrete expression of the act. But this expression of the act results in its losing that richness which consists of its being both prospective and

---

[66] A reduction which takes up again in a more systematic way Descartes' method of doubt (*Méditations métaphysiques*).

[67] Without forgetting that consciousness does not control everything: alongside synthetic acts, room has to be made for 'passive syntheses' (E. Husserl (1966) *Analysen zur passiven Synthesis*, Husserliana XI, Hrsg. v. M. Fleischer, Martinus Nijhoff, Den Haag).

retroactive at one and the same time (Husserl said it better: its constitution is *protentional-retentional*). In recent articles in neurophysiology a new approach to the functioning of the thalamus (a relay connecting all sensory information from receptors) can be found that insists upon the prospective character of the activity of its neurons. But the most crucial notion of action is the one that is going to be developed in the chapters that follow in proportion as the reader gets clearer about the notion of constitution and the constituting activity of the subject. For this problem of the role of action in the active structuring of experience, the way in which action contributes to an identification of the external object as being in the world, is a question that can be traced back right down to its physiological roots.

And so it is that a new approach to the naturalization of epistemology is opened up. For what, with Kant, is true of perception is true by extension for scientific knowledge. His entire theory of *a priori* conditions was in fact supposed to hold not only of the perception of an object as being external to the perceiving subject but also for the knowledge of a world which he took to be that of the physical science of his day. For he assumed (as an optimistic rationalist)[68] a continuity between perception and scientific knowledge. In so doing he entirely overlooked that 'epistemological break'[69] that cuts scientific thinking off from its basis in human action and through which humanity acquires this marvellous facility of free movement in the pure ether of the concept. Look at it this way: once the cognitive neurosciences have become sufficiently clear about the relation between the activity of the brain of the perceiving subject and its perceptual identification of the object, these same sciences could not be prevented from raising the question of whether the latter might not serve as a model for the more general problem of the constitution of science itself. This is a very important (and dangerous) subject that we will have to get to back later. For all the questions we are presently addressing are being raised from within a scientific frame of reference, from within a context where one already admits the principle of objectivity.

....

[68] Optimistic in opposition to the tragic rationalism of a Husserl. For the latter called it a 'crisis' that the modern scientific researcher should have ceased to take account of the concrete things of everyday life in favour of a universe of mathematical formulae which only serve to determine the values of just a few of its parameters. But by way of a reversal comparable to that of René Thom when he transformed 'catastrophe' into a rigorous concept, this 'crisis' is what renders intelligible the idealizing transformation responsible for natural science.

[69] A concept familiar to our generation brought up on Bachelard, Canguilhem, and Althusser.

Image or schema? Imagination and understanding

Kant called the imagination, the faculty of images, 'an art concealed in the depths of the soul'.[70] He distinguished two types, a reproductive imagination, responsible for the persistence of consecutive visual images, for the construction of new forms on the basis of the traces of former perceptions, and a productive imagination. It was to the latter that he attributed our power to organize experience by relying on sources of knowledge contained in the subject itself. For him 'the source of knowledge is the imagination.' Kant also attributed knowledge to the understanding, a faculty thanks to which we are able to impose rules for the organization of experience, to bring our judgments under logical rules, even to conduct ourselves in accordance with moral rules.

To this doctrine of the imagination as an 'art hidden in the depths of the soul', which might suggest (following a somewhat reductive interpretation, to be sure) that in the depths of the soul there might only be the visual cortex and the visual areas, one is tempted to object that there must also be in the depths of the soul, and so also in the understanding, mechanisms bearing on action. It is the neuronal basis of this primordial activity that we are trying to bring to light.

To avoid leaving the reader without an example, let us go back to one already cited: remembering the journey we have to make to get to work every day. And this not in the form of an image of the geographic map but as the lived sequence of our movements, of our points of reference, and even of associated events. We call this ability to recall a route memory, a memory whose kinaesthetic and egocentric character contrasts sharply with map memory, which turns out to be allocentric and topographic.[71] The image can no doubt

---

[70] I. Kant (1977) *Werkausgabe*, Bd III, Kritik der reinen Vernunft I, Hrsg. v. Wilhelm Weischedel, Frankfurt am Main, Suhrkamp, trans. N. Kemp Smith (2003) *Critique of Pure Reason*, Palgrave Macmillan, Basingstoke, A141, B180.

[71] A. Berthoz (2001) Bases neurales de l'orientation spatiale et de la mémoire des trajets: mémoire topo-graphique ou mémoire topo-kinesthésique? *Revue Neurologique* 157(8–9), 779–789; A. Berthoz (1998) Hippocampal and parietal contribution to topo-kinetic and topographic memory, in N. Burgess, K.J. Jeffrey, and J. O'Keefe (eds), *The Hippocampal and Parietal Foundations of Spatial Cognition*, Oxford University Press, Oxford, pp. 381–399; A. Berthoz (1997) Parietal and hippocampal contribution to topo-kinetic and topographic memory, *Phil. Trans. R. Soc. Lond. Ser. B Biol. Sci.* 352, 1437–1448; G. Committeri *et al.* (2004) Reference frames for spatial cognition: different brain aerea are involved in viewer-, object-, and landmark-centered judgements about object location, *J. Cogn. Neusoci.* 16(9), 1517–1535; M. Vidal *et al.* (2004) Navigating in a virtual three-dimensional maze: how do egocentric and allocentric frames interact? *Cog. Brain Res.* 19, 244–258; S. Lambrey *et al.* (2003) Reference frames and cognitive strategies during navigation: is the left hippocampal formation involved in the sequential aspects of route memory? *Int. Congress Ser.* 1250, 261–274; A. Berthoz *et al.* (2002)

also play a role here, but only on condition that it is written into the flux of our lived experience of the action. Neuropsychology has underestimated this route memory. Contrary to what one might think, it is not a matter of a purely sensori-motor memory but the (non-iconographic) memory of a lived experience written into a time already structured by the fact of our having to actively move oneself in a certain direction. This is so much so that a physiology of action would have considerable difficulty with the term imagination, to the extent that the term appeals to the idea of an image. Certainly it is not easy to refuse the use of the term image, a term one finds in all the psychological literature, all the more so since the greater part of the modern theory of perception concerns vision. Nevertheless, this distinction between imagination and understanding might well appear to introduce a specious dichotomy. Let us take advantage of this to explain our objection to the term image.

We are emerging from a century in which the image was king. Just as the sciences of cognition became dominated by notions linked to language so also they became dominated by the image in all its forms. For vision was the most widely investigated sense. We talk of 'mental imagery', of the 'imaginary', of 'cerebral imagery'. We say of some that they are good or bad at 'imaging'. And you will not find a company, a town, or a country that is not concerned about 'its image'. Following the example of the little kings of Ur, twentieth century man saw himself as endowed with huge eyes with which he devoured the world.

This universally admitted importance accorded to the image has to be linked with the extraordinary development of the visual system in humans and other primates; there are thirteen to fifteen visual areas in the brain of the monkey. It is true that vision is the privileged tool of knowledge for human beings. At least a dozen areas of the brain are taken up with it even if many of these areas are multi-modal. Since the greater part of the information yielded by a visual representation of the world by means of images is conscious, we suffer from the illusion of a parallelism between knowledge and the image, which might well be the origin of our epistemological move in the direction of formalism. The preference for a formalist analysis of knowledge has undoubtedly much to do with (alongside and independently of the role of language) the massive development of the visual cortex with humans, which, contrary to

Spatial memory during navigation: what is being stored, maps or movements? in A.M. Galaburda, S.M. Kosslyn, and Y. Christen (eds), *The Languages of the Brain*, Harvard University Press, Cambridge, MA, pp. 288–306; E. Mellet *et al.* (2000) Neural correlates of topographic mental exploration: The impact of route versus survey perspective learning, *NeuroImage* 12, 588–600; G. Galati *et al.* (2000) The neural basis of egocentric and allocentric coding of space in humans: a functional magnetic resonance study, *Exp. Brain Res.* 133, 156–164.

hearing or the kinaesthetic sense, can work in parallel, and which consequently benefits from all those systems of analysis, of pre-perception, of preparation, etc., that we have already discussed.

Yates and Carruthers[72] used to say that the art of memory was based upon a walk around mental palaces the contents of which, it seemed hardly worth adding, were represented by images. Space is described by means of geometric images. Alain Connes, describing mathematical objects, talks of a 'landscape'. In the same way, judgements depend upon a 'point of view'; a person whose thoughts are oriented towards the future has a 'vision'. We should also remember that neurophysiologists have called our memory of our movements in the world topographical, as if we only had a cartographic (that is imagistic) representation of our displacements. It should also be noted that 98% of the tests on perception, on knowledge, and on the brain make use of paper, not because one draws on paper with the hand but because the latter furnishes images. So even in science we encounter an iconolatry which would be a topic worthy of investigation by the historian of ideas. Humanity has known its iconophobe periods,[73] religious movements, and iconoclastic cultures, but we are living in a civilization that worships images.

To the extent that the notion of the imagination seems to refer to the fact of having under one's eyes little pictures that one can contemplate, it might seem reasonable to be suspicious of any attempt to attribute an epistemological function to the (transcendental) imagination. The concept of an image of … presupposes, in fact, that there already is something there, something constituted in advance and outside us, without us, something that we then have to interiorize and eventually to copy, and this by bringing into play a mental process that makes of this representation an adequate model.

Physis and mimesis

But is it indeed the case that the entire Western tradition rests on the prejudice of the model and the copy? As much as this has been claimed, except that if one goes back to Aristotle, to whom this prejudice is often attributed as a sort of original sin, one finds an obfuscating ambiguity coupled with a recurrent debate

[72] F.A. Yates (1984) *The Art of Memory*, University of Chicago Press, Chicago, IL; M. Carruthers (2002) *Machina Memorialis. Méditation rhétorique et fabrication des images au Moyen Âge*, Gallimard, Paris; M. Carruthers (2002) *Le Livre de la Mémoire. Une étude de la mémoire dans la culture médiévale*, Macula, Thorigny-sur-Creuse.

[73] The exhibition at the Musée des Beaux Arts in Strasbourg in summer 2001 was dedicated to this theme, so paradoxical for an exhibition of artwork: 'Iconoclasm: The life and death of the medieval image in protestant Europe'.

rather than a unique and unequivocal heritage. From Aristotle's *Poetics* the scholarly tradition has retained the idea fixed in the conventional formula: '*ut pictura poesis*', or 'poetry is like painting', which clearly means in being made up of images. And of course painting had to be representative of something already there, something existing in nature before it was represented 'in a picture'. But this interpretation, one that persists obstinately in the minds of the public and of historians of art, is no longer taken seriously by the translators and commentators of Aristotle, nor by historians of philosophy. For the meaning of *mimesis* has been subjected to careful re-examination. This has led to a revision of the relation between *physis*, already badly translated as 'nature', and *mimesis*, which is even more poorly translated as 'imitation'. As is often the case, it was realized that the traditional interpretation rested on an error in the translation.

In the name of *mimesis*, Aristotle sought to link poetry, and more generally art, to nature, in particular human nature and the nature of human action. In so doing he had no intention of subordinating art and poetry to the real, at least not in the ordinary sense of the real. Quite the contrary, what mattered to him was to found art in a mode of being human by firmly connecting it with what it accomplished most effectively, not just a passive submission to the real but active creation, the productive power of nature itself. This is what we find in Ricœur's *La métaphore vive*.[74] 'Art imitates nature' not because it makes copies of things already produced in and by nature but because it freely produces works; that is to say, organized and complete beings in as much as they have a beginning, a middle, and an end, all this in accordance with a teleological principle[75] which, for Aristotle, was that of nature itself.

As a result, for him, 'poetry is more philosophical than history'. There is nothing paradoxical about this since history, as a collection of anecdotes (as in Herodotus), is notorious for retaining the insignificant details alongside the important actions. While in poetry or tragedy, Ricœur emphasizes, 'mimesis is the restoration of the human not just in terms of what is essential but in terms of what is greatest and noblest.' This is no doubt an echo of the 'noble simplicity and calm grandeur' characteristic of ancient Greek sculpture according to Winkelmann's famous formula. From this root there stems the tradition of the genius that flourished with the romantics. Poetry is free creation. Imagining is producing by drawing upon one's own resources. The creative imagination is a

---

[74] P. Ricœur (1975) Première étude. Entre rhétorique et poétique: Aristotle, in *La métaphore vive*, Seuil, Paris, pp. 13–61.

[75] Teleology without any supernatural reference and which consists in an orientation of every natural being towards the full realization of all the potentialities inherent in its nature.

capacity to create things anew, the capacity to create 'things that do not exist and that no one has ever seen', the capacity to project into a future which is still to come (the 'singing tomorrows' of revolutionary utopianism), the capacity to advance ideas for the first time, goals, projects for humanity. A demi-God himself, the inspired poet rivals the Gods.

It is with this tradition that Kant has to be associated since, for him, the imagination is less the faculty of images than the art of schematism, an art (notice the practical connotation) that means that we do not just have in us *a priori* forms of a logical type, abstract forms disengaged from all sensory experience; Kant's 'waffle moulds' as Schelling ironically called them. It is an art that means that we can structure our experience in an autonomous fashion, even if it is bound to contain a sensory element entirely appropriate for our receptivity. Minds exhibit just such a productive (and not just reproductive) capacity, which has nothing to do with being fascinated by images.

Certainly, one keeps coming back to the word imagination as if, yet again, we were the victims of the tyranny of language. Even though in German things are not so crassly evident: *Einbildungskraft, Bildungskraft, bildende Kraft*, the faculty, the power, even the formative power, of construction, of free creation. We shall be told that in *Bildung* there is *Bild*, and that *Bild* means 'image'. But *Bildung* also means formation, education, culture, for instance, the *Bildungsroman* through which the reader accompanies the young and naïve child through his childhood until he becomes an adult, full of science and also of disillusionment, of life experience. Here we find something that is much more than (and which in addition does not necessarily imply) the image. The heroes of these novels are rarely 'as wise as images'! In *Einbildungskraft*, one can therefore very well imagine that a native German does not hear the word image in the same way that we hear it in imagination. But this fastening upon the *word* is itself naïve. Since Saussure, Wittgenstein, and modern linguistics, everybody knows that a language is not a collection of words, but a usage in context, a creative use of words. Without allowing ourselves to be constricted by the previous history of words, we can re-deploy them in a creative fashion as a function of the context.

Here we touch upon a problem of terminology that is not unimportant. Today, those neurophysiologists who have shown that when one imagines a movement the same areas are activated as when one actually executes it[76] employ the term imagine in the very way we have been calling in question, and

[76] See S.C. Grafton, M.A. Arbib, L. Fadiga, and G. Rizzolatti (1996) Localization of grasp representations in humans by PET. 2. Observation compared with imagination, *Exp. Brain Res.* 112, 103–111.

this without seeming to see the difficulty. But for us, imagining the movement is not, as it appears to be for these authors, making an imaged representation of it, but to actually live in it. And in the same way, it is interesting to note that in the context of so-called virtual reality (at the very least a paradoxical expression), when one shows a subject a movement and one inspects (vision again) the cerebral areas using brain imagery, the only activated areas are the visual areas. In any case, when one shows the same subject a video film sequence, for example, a sequence showing a person whose face or neck is caressed by someone else's hand, the somato-sensory areas of the brain processing the maps of the hand and the face (SI and SII) are activated in the same way as if the subject were themself caressed on the face or neck, testifying to the fact that this subject does not have a purely visual perception but also apperceives something of the tactile experience of the person seen in the video image.[77]

With a view to stressing this pluri-modality of visual perception Merleau-Ponty said: 'vision is touching with the eyes.' If one asks the subject to simulate the movement mentally (internal simulation) he activates the same motor areas.[78] So again action has to be reintroduced here, since relying upon the imagination is not enough. Besides, it has been shown[79] that the speed of the mental rotation of an object, something that had been attributed exclusively to the visual cortical areas, is increased when one associates a movement of the hand with this mental activity, which again demonstrates the rootedness of this supposed motor imagery in the schemas of action.

This brings us back once again to the term employed by Kant: 'schema', a concept popularized by Bergson and taken up again later in psychology (schemas of action) and in neurology (corporeal schema),[80] but little used today. In any case, once again one comes up against an ambiguity, since there are two concepts to which this schematic procedure might lead: on the one hand, the schema (*schema*), an image which implies vision, on the other, the schemata (*scheme*), a powerful concept in psychology and which implies action, movement, the body. We shall not be appealing to Kant in a misleading way if we take imagination to mean a faculty of schemata. And the schematism

[77] S.J. Blakemore *et al.* (2005) Somatosensory activations during the observation of touch and a case of vision-touch synaesthesia, *Brain* 128, 1571–1583.

[78] M. Wexler, S.M. Kosslyn, and A. Berthoz. (1998) Motor processes in mental rotation, *Cognition* 68(1), 77–94.

[79] M. Wexler, S.M. Kosslyn, and A. Berthoz. (1998) Motor processes in mental rotation, *Cognition* 68(1), 77–94.

[80] H. Head and G. Holmes (1911) Sensory disturbances from cerebral lesions, *Brain* 34, 102–254.

as a power to modulate the frame of our experience, for example by modulating time, modulating space, and figuring things.

This has nothing to do with the naïve and false idea of copying images. The object, properly thought through as what is projected ahead of ourselves thanks to our projective cerebral systems, is, in a certain sense, the product of an actively productive process carried out in perception. We have to get rid of this specious conception according to which there would first of all be the object serving as a model, more or less faithful copies of which would then have to be made so that the latter could then be confronted (we don't even know how) with the former to determine how close they came to the original.[81] For our own part, we are very careful (perhaps more so than is customary in cognitive theory) not to attribute to the pure, objectifiable form (whether logical or geometric) whatever concretely organizes our experience. For what organizes our experience proceeds from the perceiving subject's own activity. We constantly schematize experience: this is the key idea underlying Kant's schematism.

An intellectualist theory of knowledge would attribute all the structural aspects of the imagination to 'reason', an abstract referent operating without any corporeal situation. This is precisely not what Kant did. Like Poincaré and even Einstein, though from a completely different point of view, he worked for a reversal of the primacy exerted over knowledge by an essentially formal type of analytical intelligence, abstract, totally removed from our fleshly condition, a rationality whose most technically sophisticated formulation is to be found in the use analytical philosophy has made of mathematical logic for the transcription of the sentences of natural language, imagining thereby that they had succeeded in formally capturing the basic concepts of all natural thinking.

....

81 In *Kant and the Problem of Metaphysics* Heidegger rightly reversed the tendency of Kant commentators (Marburg school) to downplay the transcendental function of the imagination by subordinating it to judgement. According to these commentators, the imagination could contribute no more than the schema which, lacking both the singularity of intuition and the generality of the concept, could itself only be used to subsume the diversity of intuition under the unity of the concept. Taking a different line from this reading, Heidegger showed that the whole *Critique of Pure Reason* could be read out of the transcendental imagination as the power of connection and unification, a power with a double responsibility. On the one hand, it ensures that the sense data of intuition are subject to the rule of the concept. On the other hand, it ensures that the understanding applies the formal unity of the concept to the apprehension and formalization of the sense content supplied by the receptivity of sense. Henceforward, the transcendental imagination becomes this power available to the knower to project in advance a horizon of not-yet-determined but already determinable possibilities, one of which will be realized at the expense of the others by the object just as soon as the latter is developed across the operations of perception and judgement.

To bring to an end this ruinous dichotomy and to interpose between an analytical logic, void of all experiential content, and an experience reduced to what we encounter in the flux of sensations, Kant introduced a new type of *a priori*: the *a priori* synthetic.[82]

This *a priori* synthetic is not just the trace, the mark or the expression of a purely logical reason, nor is it a derivative of experience taken just as it comes. It is a condition located within ourselves and which is not to be reduced to the simple distribution of sensorial impacts upon our receptive nerve terminals but which makes possible the knowledge of an object outside us, independent of us. Nor is it even a rational core which ought to be extracted from the conditions of empirical receptivity. And this because the empirical already possesses a structure. But what to call it? If one calls it a rational structure, one falls back on pure logic. If one calls it an empirical structure, one falls back on the pure sensorial content. For want of anything better, he attributed this structure either to the imagination or else to the understanding, claiming that, to the extent that it proceeds from our spontaneity, it consists of a *natural poetics*. We impose our own organizational rule not so much upon Nature but upon the flux of an experience which, in itself, might just as well be chaotic. The problem then becomes one of trying to understand what might be the mechanisms implied in what he called imagination or understanding, words inherited from the tradition and which also testify to an ignorance of the mechanisms in question.

As we bring this chapter to a close, we can see that it is not going to be at all easy to effect a reconciliation between a physiology of action (or rather of interaction) and transcendental philosophy, and that the attempt to grasp the link that connects the action and perception of a subject (and so the functioning of the brain that subtends this connection), and in such a way that a transcendent world emerges therefrom, is a challenge that neither the physiologist nor the philosopher can afford to neglect. But the challenge can only be met if the physiologist allows himself to raise questions which he is only too inclined to dismiss as too general and if the philosopher stops simply interpreting (or even re-writing) the history of philosophy and starts trying to renew his conceptual network in the light of the discoveries of science.

----

82 *A priori* synthetic: a feature of judgements, that is, of acts of predication where the predicate is not contained in the concept of the subject and so cannot be developed out of it through a procedure of analysis but rather extends beyond it or adds something to this concept. An example of an *a priori* synthetic judgement is that 'everything that happens has a cause' (formally A=B). An example of an analytic judgement is that 'every body is extended' (A=A). See I. Kant (1977) *Werkausgabe*, Bd III, Kritik der reinen Vernunft I, Hrsg. v. Wilhelm Weischedel, Frankfurt am Main, Suhrkamp, trans. N. Kemp Smith (2003) *Critique of Pure Reason*, Palgrave Macmillan, Basingstoke, Introduction IV.

Chapter 5

Prolegomena to a theory of constitution

Any reader who upholds clear-cut distinctions will no doubt to ask whether we are not confusing what we propose under the heading of 'new ideas in the field of the physiology of action' with a retrospective commentary on the history of philosophy of the kind of 'a little-known aspect of transcendental philosophy from Kant to Husserl'. Our basic idea is, however, quite simple and can possibly be expressed in such a way as to preclude any ambiguity. We find, in the philosophical tradition, a kinaesthetic theory that is still (to our knowledge) largely unknown, and so little exploited, in spite of the contribution it can be shown to make to the cognitive sciences. This theory can be taken as far as the constitution of so-called external objects of perception, which means that, on the basis of this theory, we can account for everything that exists for a subject with the meaning of being 'a thing'. This is what we are going to show in this and the following chapter. It can also be taken as a theory of the perceiving and acting subject's own experience of its bodily being. This will be the theme of Chapter 7. Finally, a theory of intersubjectivity can perhaps also be derived from an extension of this kinaesthetic theory (see Chapter 8).

We are interested here in Husserl's kinaesthetic theory. This choice will assume the strategic role of a rehabilitation because after a brilliant initial development this theory was provisionally laid aside by Husserl (who was himself the first to have detached such a concept of the kinaesthesia from its psycho-physiological sources), and this because he could see no way of bridging the gulf between the transcendental and the naturalism of empirical psychology. So, he missed the opportunity of putting his theory to work in empirical research.

Moreover, this theory has not attracted much attention from other representatives of the phenomenological school, whether or not they were favourably disposed towards psychology. Heidegger was totally opposed to a phenomenology of the body. He preferred to orient his thinking around an interpretation of the ontological structure of the existence of human beings in the world, emphasizing that existence could not be confused with the simple subsistence of a thing within a world. His fear that the meaning of being human might simply become absorbed into thinghood kept him away from any description of corporeal experience. The latter seemed to him to depend upon the Cartesian distinction of mind and body. And this applied to any psychology including the phenomenological, forming for this very reason the principal target of his battle with what he called 'metaphysics'.[1]

Although he was familiar with the posthumous work of Husserl, Merleau-Ponty failed to note the originality of the kinaesthetic theory as well as the transcendental, and so constitutive, status that Husserl accorded to kinaesthesia, because he was too accustomed to the use made by psychologists of so-called kinaesthetic sensations referring exclusively to the internal sensations of the body (*proprioception*).[2] Finally, in his *Philosophy of the Will*, Ricœur was concerned to defend the autonomy of the voluntary act against Ribot, who identified the origin of the will in the ideo-motor reflex. Caught up in his anti-reflexological polemic he only saw in 'kinaesthetic images' representations of movement which as such would be incapable of engendering movement.[3]

As for the opposite tradition, the analytical, Wittgenstein, who also introduced the theme of action into analytical philosophy, cast a negative light on the notion of kinaesthesia by developing, against the use James had made of it, a devastating critique attributing to 'language games'[4] everything the latter attributed to internal sensation.[5] According to Wittgenstein, kinaesthesia featured as a sort of hybrid made up of sensations and movements and which, as such, could never amount to more than a fiction cooked up by abstract theoreticians incapable of noticing that we do not talk about the one in the same terms as those we use to talk about the other. In failing to grasp the fact that the peculiarity of this usage is derived from rules one can not violate with impunity, the introduction of the concept of kinaesthesia could not, he thought, but obscure the meaning of our expressions bearing on the mental.

....

[1] M. Heidegger (1962) *Sein und Zeit*, trans. J. Macquarie and E. Robinson (1962) *Being and Time*, Harper & Row, New York, pp. 69–77.

[2] M. Merleau-Ponty (1945) *Phénoménologie de la Perception*, Gallimard, Paris, trans. C. Smith (1962) *Phenomenology of Perception*, Routledge, London.

[3] P. Ricœur (1950) *Philosophy of the Will I, Freedom and Nature: The Voluntary and the Involuntary*, trans. E. Kohak, Northwestern University Press, Evanston, IL.

[4] Language game (*Sprachspiel*): any system of communication as it is effectively employed by persons interacting with one another in the context of their daily practical tasks (e.g. a mason and his apprentice constructing a wall).

[5] L. Wittgenstein (1980) *Remarks on the Philosophy of Psychology*, G.E.M. Anscombe and G.H. von Wright, Basil Blackwell, Oxford; for an interpretation: J.-L. Petit (1991) *L'action dans la philosophie analytique*, PUF, Paris, and also J.-L. Petit (1996) *Solipsisme et Intersubjectivité. Quinze leçons sur Husserl et Wittgenstein*, Cerf, Paris.

Most of the theories presently being developed within the field of the cognitive sciences after the behaviourist interlude are engaged in a rediscovery of the mental domain as the place where Locke's (not to mention Descartes') mental representations were located. For all that, they have not attempted to revoke the behaviourist condemnation of kinaesthesia aimed at bringing to an end an introspective psychology that no one would want to relaunch. As a result, reverting to the traditional theory of the mind has not proved sufficient to make possible a recuperation of the genuine interiority of a body animated by motor intentions and so furnishing the mind with the sensation of motor innervation.[6]

This is the debate which needs to be reopened,[7] because we hold that the prevailing situation in the cognitive sciences, along with the motor role that the physiology of action is called upon to play, calls for a kinaesthetic theory connected up with a conception of the projective brain, a theory which would not simply be 'sensori-motor' but which would bring back into physiology the idea of lived experience. Having said that, in and of itself kinaesthesia does not provide an adequate point of departure. We first have to set our sights on a theory of perception that firmly upholds a cognitive orientation towards the perceived thing (or towards the other), and so not towards the perceiving subject. Only on this basis will it prove possible to specify the contribution made by kinaesthesia to our understanding of the way perception enables us to gain access to the thing. In the absence of the foregoing step, one runs the risk of falling into the trap of a theory of the sensations of movement experienced by a subject without an object.

Stimulated by those who have tried to naturalize phenomenology[8] or by physiologists promoting the idea of a brain whose functioning would be founded in action,[9] for several years now attempts have been made to promote a theory that anchors cognition in action. A good many philosophers, physiologists, and psychologists have wanted to contribute to a re-orientation of the

---

[6] After having been rejected on the basis of anatomical arguments, Wundt's innervation feeling (*Innervationsgefühl*) was reconsidered in the light of the introduction, by von Holst and Mittelstædt, of their *Reafferenzprinzip* in the psychology of visual perception and of locomotion: E. von Holst and H. Mittelstædt (1950) Das Reafferenzprinzip. Wechselwirkung zwischen Zentralnervensystem und Peripherie, *Naturwissenschaften* 37, 464–476.

[7] That the time has come is evident from several recent attempts to establish an 'incarnate' (Varela) or sensori-motor (O'Regan) cognitive science.

[8] J. Petitot *et al.* (eds) (1999) *Naturalizing Phenomenology: Issues in Contemporary Phenomenology and Cognitive Science*, Stanford University Press, Stanford, CA.

[9] See A. Berthoz (2000) *The Brain's Sense of Movement*, Harvard University Press, Cambridge, MA; A. Berthoz (2003) *La décision*, Odile Jacob, Paris.

cognitive sciences.[10] If we want these efforts to result in a new philosophical physiology of action we will have to prepare the ground in a more systematic way.

Intentionality first: the promise of the perceived object

For us, mind, mental acts, experiences capable of contributing to knowledge, can only exist as a function of intentionality; that is, in relation to an object and to the use one makes of the object. This use can be real (sitting down in an armchair) or virtual (a thought). Sartre (together with every phenomenologist since Brentano) insisted on this: we are always conscious *of* something. We should add: of something we want to make use of either physically or mentally.

As a result, only those psychic activities are relevant to a theory of experience[11] that carry with them the dimension of intentionality, or of a relation to an object and which contribute to the meaning of things for the subject. We should bear in mind that the intentional relation to an object consists of the fact that the targeted object (the aim) of my attention, of my desire, has a *meaning* for me; that is, already possesses an intelligible content that can be intuitively apprehended and eventually expressed by means of a verbal statement. For example, a cup of tea towards which our hand reaches out has the meaning of a receptacle containing a liquid we want to drink. As we have just seen, this meaning can be expressed verbally. But it should also be understood that it is written into the biomechanical structure of the gesture of prehension whose characteristic outline the gesture regulates as a natural movement oriented towards a goal. It is the goal of action that organizes the perception.

But it should also be noted that there is a radical difference between mental activities, mental states, internal processes, dispositions, etc., all of which belong to the subject, and the object of perception. The thing we perceive is not in us, but everything we perceive in regard to it does belong to us (immanence). We stand in *relation* to something that is not itself mental (it is transcendent). In consequence, intentionality can be seen as the capacity of consciousness to

---

[10] J.-L. Petit (éd.) (1997) *Les neurosciences et la philosophie de l'action*, Vrin, Paris; J.-L. Petit (ed.) (2003) Repenser le corps, l'action et la cognition avec les neurosciences, *Intellectica* 1–2, 36–37; R. Sock and B. Vaxelaire (eds) (2004) *L'anticipation à l'horizon du présent*, Pierre Mardaga, Paris; H. De Preester and V. Knockaert (eds) (2005) *Body Image and Body Schema*, John Benjamins, Amsterdam; S. Gallagher (2005) *How the Body Shapes the Mind*, Oxford University Press, Oxford. For more, see the websites of *Intellectica* (www.intellectica.org) and *Phenomenology and the Cognitive Sciences* (www.kluweronline.nl).

[11] We are not simply talking about the transcendental theory referred to above but about a new theory that further develops this transcendental theory in the light of neurophysiological evidence.

enter into relation with something which is not, however, given in itself, except of course in perceptual experience, where it becomes true to say of the thing that it is 'given in flesh and blood' and so is not merely across a mental representation. Recognizing the impossibility of grasping things other than through the desire to attain them, human intelligence has given expression to this perplexity by inventing myths: the quest for the Holy Grail and so on.

This is what intentionality is, something more than the simple orientation towards a goal. The idea underlying an intention is that of a *relation*. But this relation between me and the (mental) object given to me to perceive is not like that between two objects lying side by side on a table. One would like to say that it consists of a relation that 'actively relates itself'. This difference is absolutely crucial. There is a juxtaposition between these two objects on the table as soon as the two objects co-exist. On the other hand, the intentional relation is such that only one of its two terms exists: the perceiving subject, of course, with its mental states and all that is immanent in them. As for the other term of this relation, it only exists as the object of a *cognitive aspiration*: a sort of natural postulate (i.e. positing the substantiality of its object of interest) implicit in the mental activity of any person whose day-to-day life consists of dealing with things in the world.

Such an affirmation must certainly appear strange to someone who believes that this cognitive aspiration aims at the physical thing with which the hand or the mouth of the subject enters into contact. But if this physical contact does not always take place, if it can also take place in a non-intentional manner, if it can take place with regard to an object other than the one aimed at, what becomes evident is the following: *the intentional object is not the physical thing*. For example, in an act of perception, all the sensible qualities, the visual images, tactile impressions, etc., all the aspects the perceiving subject apprehends, pertain to the perceiving subject. This is not the case with regard to the table he perceives: the perceived object does not pertain to the perceiving subject. From this it follows that the subject is constantly in relation to something that is not a part of itself. In this relationship one of the terms actually exists while the other is, so to speak, only *virtual*. It is precisely this gap that the expression transcendental makes it possible for us at least to name.[12]

---

12 In the Kantian (static) version, philosophers used to talk about the permanence of the object through change as a condition of the possibility of our knowledge of a permanent thing: I can only perceive changes across the changing aspects of something permanent. Now, with Husserl, we are more inclined to talk in dynamic terms of positional acts. The term position is taken from Fichte, from whom Husserl learnt a great deal. More exactly, it is a matter of the positing of identity: I posit something as identical with itself and (to continue to talk in terms of acts) this something is envisaged through an act which links

Each time I see an object, I obviously only perceive one aspect of it, one side. Husserl talks of profiles: *Abschattungen*, adumbrations. I try to take in the object as a whole. But I am always restricted to partial views. But not in the sense of a cut-out; for these partial views lead me to expect more. They carry with them a sort of promise. The term he employs is presumption. What I see from this side I might take to be only a flat facade. But perhaps it is a three-dimensional object in relief or in depth. In his description of the development of perception Piaget talks of these 'pictures' or 'frames' ('tableaux') that the child perceives at first and which are not yet organized into a coherent whole.[13] Gibson, for his part, confronts the same problem by reformulating it in a Darwinian perspective. According to him, the appearance of the fovea in the course of evolution made it necessary for the brain to make do with a sequence of images released by ocular saccades; which means that the reconstruction of a unique world depends upon a perceptual binding holding between this succession of images.[14]

What is important is that these presumptions regarding the true nature of the perceived object can only be confirmed—failing which the identity of the object cannot be maintained—in subsequent acts (to talk in a rather simplistic manner). So each aspect exhibits a sort of 'pretension' (*protension*) emitted by the object to the extent that I follow it up through the course of its development, a pretension I am going to confirm or reject later, depending on circumstances. If I am caught up in an optical illusion, I will be deceived and so have to reject the presumption.

The contribution of the psycho-physiology of anticipation

In a preceding chapter, we gave numerous examples of anticipation. But the notion of perceptual momentum[15] gives us the chance of providing a nice

---

it up with other acts, notably those implied by the fact that, whenever I perceive something, it is as if (this is not just a metaphor) I sketched it out, drew up a plan of the object.

[13] J. Piaget and B. Inhelder (1948) *La représentation de l'espace chez l'enfant*, PUF, Paris.

[14] J.J. Gibson (1966) *The Senses Considered as Perceptual Systems*, Houghton Mifflin, Boston, MA.

[15] J.J. Freyd (1983) The mental representation of movement when static stimuli are viewed, *Perception Psychophys.* 33, 575–581; J.J. Freyd (1987) Dynamic mental representations, *Psychol. Rev.* 94, 427–438; J.J. Freyd (1992) Dynamic representations guiding adaptive behaviour, in F. Macar, V. Pouthas, and W.J. Friedman (eds), *Time, Action, and Cognition: Towards Bridging the Gap*, Dordrecht, Kluwer, pp. 309–323; J.J. Freyd (1993) Five hunches

illustration of the way in which the brain predicts the subsequent act. One shows a subject five successive photographs of a person in the course of throwing a ball or of jumping over an obstacle, after which one shows him a sixth photograph, which is sometimes the continuation of the preceding photos, sometimes the image of a different movement. The experiment shows that subjects can recognize—and this within very short reaction times—the last image when it is the prolongation of the preceding actions, whereas it takes them much longer when it is not.

Everything happens as if an anticipatory activity was written into the presentations of these successive outlines. This is what Husserl called 'the kinetic syntheses': an activity that is dynamic since it predicts a movement, and which is nevertheless extracted from this succession of static points of view, since we are only talking of photos. All of this indicates that the brain certainly does possess a propensity to prepare for what follows. Having identified the intention of a gesture in the course of being presented with the several initial stages of this gesture, he then goes on to construct the following stage. This concept of momentum has been the subject of a study employing magneto-encephalography.[16] A subject is shown the view of a lake he would have if he were seated at the bottom of the boat with a horizontal line representing the surface of the lake. The boat is progressively tilted in a series of images. By presenting these images an impression of momentum is engendered on the basis of the sensation of the body being tilted. It has been shown that there is an important difference in cerebral activity when a sixth image is presented,

about perceptual processes and dynamic representations, in D. Meyer and S. Kornblum (eds), *Attention and Performance XIV: Synergies in Experimental Psychology, Artificial Intelligence, and Cognitive Neuroscience*, MIT Press, Cambridge, MA, pp. 99–119; J.J. Freyd and R.A. Finke (1984) Representational momentum, *J. Exp. Psychol. Learning Memory Cognition* 10, 126–132; J.J. Freyd and R.A. Finke (1985) A velocity effect for representational momentum, *Bull. Psychonomic Soc.* 23, 443–446; J.J. Freyd and J.Q. Johnson (1987) Probing the time course of representational momentum, *J. Exp. Psychol. Learning Memory Cognition* 13, 259–269; J.J. Freyd and K.T. Jones (1994) Representational momentum for a spiral path, *J. Exp. Psychol. Learning Memory Cognition* 20, 968–976; J.J. Freyd, M.H. Kelly, and M.L. DeKay (1990) Representational momentum in memory for pitch, *J. Exp. Psychol. Learning Memory Cognition* 16, 1107–1117; J.J. Freyd and T.M. Pantzer (1995) Static patterns moving in the mind, in S.M. Smith, T.B. Ward, and R.A. Finke (eds), *The Creative Cognition Approach*, MIT Press, Cambridge, MA, pp. 181–204; J.J. Freyd, T.M. Pantzer, and J.L. Cheng (1988) Representing statics as forces in equilibrium, *J. Exp. Psychol. General* 117, 395–407.

[16] M.A. Amorim *et al.* (2000) Modulation of spatial orientation processing by mental imagery instructions: a MEG study of representational momentum, *J. Cog. Neurosci.* 12(4), 569–582.

depending on whether the latter is congruent with the different movements the boat has made previously or not.

The fringes of perception and the flux of consciousness

How did one come by the idea (especially Husserl) that perception had to be linked to anticipation? Two replies can be distinguished: an historical response and an epistemological response. Historically, this fundamental intuition of Husserl's can be assimilated to James' intuition concerning the 'fringes' or the overtones of the field of consciousness and the 'specious present' (a lapse of time more extended than the instant but which appears to the perceiving subject as the present). Basically, it is the same intuition with all three philosophers: James, Husserl, and not forgetting Bergson. This is what induced them to think of mental life in the very modern terms of a flux rather than of discrete mental states, and which sets them apart from the empirical tradition of Locke, Hume, and Berkeley who, starting from the fact (or the Newtonian prejudice) that things are always perfectly defined in themselves, could not imagine that their mental representations might not be equally well defined, and that the mind containing these representations might not be a collection of mental atoms.

Going back from these theoretical reconstructions of the mental to the lived experience of the mental, James draws our attention to our peculiar state of mind when someone says 'listen!' or when one has a word 'on the tip of one's tongue', when one has 'caught' what someone is trying to say, or when one is trying to say something one has not yet managed to say. In all these circumstances we experience an emptiness which is not for all that a pure and simple nothingness, since it already prefigures something, a thing which despite its absence is still sufficiently well circumscribed to make it possible for us to eliminate any other candidate. James insists on this: 'we have to admit that a good third of our psychic life is made up of these partial glimpses, fugitive but pre-emptory, founded in schemas of thought which are not yet articulated'.[17]

Husserl adds that this is the fate of each present in consciousness, not with a view to plunging mental life into vagueness and inarticulation but because it is important to extract, from the very heart of this experience, this dynamic

---

[17] W. James (1892) *The Principles of Psychology*, Henry Holt, New York, Chap. XI, The stream of consciousness, p.164. An assessment that for James only reaches the threshold of truth: 'Every definite image in the mind is steeped and dyed in the free water that flows round it. With it goes the sense of its relations, near and remote, the dying echo of whence it came to us, the dawning sense of whither it is to lead. The significance, the value, of the image is all in this halo or penumbra that surrounds and escorts it, etc.' (pp. 165–166).

a priori by virtue of which the later phases of psychic contents are already included in advance in those that preceded. This is in such a way that the order in which these phases of the flux of experience are connected is not simply the order of the causal succession of events but rather the order of the enduring experience in which each antecedent phase projects upon the following 'predictions' (more correctly *protentions*) which confer upon it a form. From an epistemological point of view, this need to look for the *a priori*, in the form of an act inserted into the flux, appears all the more pressing to Husserl for his being a logician and mathematician. For he was in a position to draw the comparison between the logico-mathematical ideal of a totally formal knowledge in which the content of knowledge can be given in a single, extra-temporal intuition and perceived objects which present themselves in a fundamentally temporal manner, even though they may also contain ideal or 'formal' aspects.

If all this is true, how can these formal aspects be manifest in something, namely the subject, who is essentially temporal? They are manifest through the actions of anticipation (with the broad definition we have given to the term action) accomplished by the perceiving subject. If the conceptual, ideal and formal (formative) dimensions of perception are to be grasped and understood, these acts will have to be recovered.

Husserl's theory of constitution: a tool for improving our understanding

Can Husserl's theory of constitution help us to understand the perceiving subject's ability to prefigure in advance what he is going to encounter in experience? To *constitute*: what does this mean in the end? It is certainly not a creation from the ground up. We do not have to suppose that the perceiving subject functions as a little creator God. To constitute means, quite simply, sense giving, or a weaker definition would be to be vitally interested in. It consists of making it be that the object is endowed with just such an interest for me. What is it then that enables things to be present to me as endowed with all sorts of interesting features? (Note that one can replace 'interesting' with 'intelligible'.)

A table, for example, exists for me with a meaning. In what sense? In the sense that, in addition to the fact that we have a series of presentations of it (objectives, points of view or adumbrations), we can lean on it, put documents on it that need to be read, put my cup on it so that I can drink from it. And across all these presentations an act is carried through that is not always evident but which can be brought out through reflection, that of positing it as being the same: 'it is the same table'. No one doubts that it is the perceiving subject who is responsible for the act that maintains it in being as the same. Psychologists talk of discovering invariants in the world. Just as one cannot simply have a series of presentations without doing anything, without carrying through a synthesis of unification, so one cannot simply undertake a series of analyses without doing anything. What interests the phenomenologist and the physiologist is the object *as perceived* in its natural element and bound up with acts of this kind.

One of us who is a physiologist still remembers the joy with which (around 1970) Batuev, a physiologist at Leningrad's Pavlov Institute, showed him the neuronal activity of the auditory system of an animal in his laboratory: these neurons responded vigorously to the natural meowing of a cat but were completely indifferent to any pure sound in the same wave frequency! The brain is definitely interested in meaningful events in the physical word belonging to its Umwelt.

The physiology of anticipation shows that an organism endowed with a brain (the supposed support of the 'mind') is not a simple processor (whether of data or computer programs) linking sensory inputs and motor outputs, and that everything inside is not to be regarded as the internal representation of things that pre-existed initially outside. For this organism behaves both practically and cognitively as an internal source of determination. It appears as if it were the origin of changes already set up within itself in an immanent fashion before they get expressed 'in the external world' (the internal simulation of action preceding movement). In parallel, it proves to be the source from which objective significations ('meaning of being') are attributed (immediately or pre-predicatively) to the 'external' objects of its intentional acts. These objective significations are also activated in an immanent manner 'before' being projected upon external objects, for instance, by modifications of the sensors through motor intentions, as shown by the experiments done by one of us.

In fact, constitution is not just the attribution of properties to a pre-constituted object but an originary constitution of the latter, and without which the latter could not support such properties: a pre-configuration of the analysis that the brain is going to make of the world and not just a mental representation, which always comes on the scene after the event. The decisive step in neurophysiology is therefore the transition from a bottom-up neurophysiology to a top-down neurophysiology, a *physiology of anticipation*.

Our view is that if one brings together two features exhibited by this physiology, the ability of sensors to be modified by top-down influences and the internal simulation of actions, one will get what Jean Petitot at one time called 'a naturalization of phenomenology',[18] except that phenomenology no longer has to be as disconnected from natural science as it used to be.

----

[18] At the time of the colloquium at Bordeaux on 19–21 October 1995, and which featured as the origin of the collective work, *Naturalizing Phenomenology* (J. Petitot *et al.* (eds) (1999) *Naturalizing Phenomenology: Issues in Contemporary Phenomenology and Cognitive*

Phenomenology and intuition

In line with its essentially intuitive approach to phenomena, phenomenology is known for having brought to our attention a quantity of concrete examples. Here is a list, composed on the basis of the published text of Husserl's 'Lectures on the Thing' of 1907, but which could easily be supplemented with reference to further unpublished material.

'I see a house.'
'I see the flight of a bird.'
'I see a leaf falling.'
'I hear the sound of a violin.'
'I hear children playing in the street.'
'I hear the buzzing of a bee.'
'I see and hear myself.'
'I see my hands.'
'I hear my words.'
'I hear the noise my body makes.'
'I see other persons: I see their gestures, their face, the expression of their face, the play of their physiognomy.'
'I don't have access to their psychic experience, but only to its outward expression.'

And so on and so forth. To what is Husserl trying to draw our attention? It is to the contexts in which experiences are lived out, just as they are apprehended from the point of view of the perceiving subject (in the language of recent psychology the talk is of an 'egocentric' point of view). And above all, by abstracting from whatever else one might know. In order to get to this fundamental level of phenomenological experience, the move consists of abstracting from all reported knowledge, from all those notions which we owe to the testimony of others, acquired knowledge, etc., which help us to interpret the brute, direct experience that we have. The goal of the phenomenologist is to get rid of every already constructed grid of interpretation (as far as lies within our power), of every schema that might presuppose knowledge acquired elsewhere, and to get back to this lived experience. Is this a form of subjectivism? No, rather a coming to terms with our actual subjective situation.

....

Science, Stanford University Press, Stanford, CA). Husserl's theory of constitution was taken to be something that demanded of the neurosciences no more than what they were already practising, or what was on their agenda for the next decades: namely, that all the cognitively relative values of our environment be considered as so many *autonomous* productions on the part of an activity capable of conferring (vital) value, which proceeds from the intimate and (intersubjectively) shared feeling we have of our actions and of our capacity for action in conjunction with the objects we assume as their goals, instruments, or obstacles to be overcome. In a word, for the living organism, autonomy is not the exception it was once taken to be, it has become the rule.

The invariant house

The house remains the same, whether it is seen from in front or from behind, from the interior or from the exterior. It is the house that remains the same, but only for me, of course. The ability to be astonished at the fact of having to admit this invariance of the object across its aspects is not (whatever they might say) a privilege reserved to the philosopher. The perceiving organism proves to be more than capable of apprehending, grasping, understanding (*Auffassen*) the identity, the invariance of a thing that is present in diverse ways depending on the different points of view adopted towards it.

Let us take an example. We know that the image of a face is broken up in the brain at the level of the visual cortex into networks which code separately the colour, the form, and the movement of components of the face. Then, along the so-called 'ventral' path, which joins the visual cortex to the temporal lobe, the image of the face is progressively reconstituted. But we do not know what it is that makes it possible for us to identify Peter's or Paul's face independently of the point of view.

But what is important from the point of view of the perceiver is that it is possible to distinguish what is given from what is understood. What is given is quite simply the front of the house. When the subject sees the facade he does not have to walk behind it to make sure it has a back. And if he does walk round to the back of the house, no doubt he still remembers the front of the house, although it is no longer given; not adequately given in any case, not given as such in experience. And this is why an organism capable of anticipating is also capable of being deceived, of entertaining anticipations which have to be rejected in the light of further experience, in the light of new profiles or appearances inconsistent with the anticipated profiles.

So these appearances have to be taken as facets, modes of presentation of an object, modes that support certain pretensions. When an object is present as a facade, this facade is not simply an image. It lays claim to being a house, one might say. It consists of a presentation that pretends to be more than what it gives itself out as being, since it not only has a front side but also a back side. And to discover, in trying to go around it, that the facade is only a decor or that it is the facade of a house other than the one thought one had identified previously is to suffer a sort of deception relative to an implicit anticipation.

So, what is to be found in experience are not just little images (or *petites perceptions*)[19] that are there once and for all. Rather, what is found is a sort of

---

[19] *Petites perceptions*: in the sense of Leibniz and Helmholtz, subliminal perceptions, that is, perceptions lying below the threshold of sensorial awareness but whose progressive accumulation does in the end give rise to a quite discernable difference. The existence of

arrow, a dynamic movement towards an object with regard to which we sense that it can present aspects other than those which it is presently presenting, with regard to which in fact we expect the imminent appearance of other aspects to complete the anticipations or the schema we have of it. There is at one and the same time the 'given' aspect, given immediately, given in full as a pure presence, and the 'understood' aspect which is not actually given but which will eventually come to be given if there are no corrections or revisions in the further course of experience. All of this is already contained in the perception, in the perceiving activity.

If this phenomenological description is carried over directly and without further qualification into neurophysiology, one might be tempted to say: 'My brain contains two, even three houses.' All of this agrees pretty well with a pluralist tendency in cognitive science, according to which it is very possible that there might be at one and the same time several representations of the same house in the brain, or to put it otherwise (in order to avoid the use of the word representation), several ways of processing the sensorial data or of anticipating events. One might then give Husserl credit for this discovery of the variety of simultaneous presentations of one and the same object (but we prefer not to go into questions of intellectual indebtedness).

If we walk around a house we see, in the first instance and in an 'egocentric' way, one house, then another, and somewhere in its neurons the brain has these differently ego-centred houses. At this point in the construction, they still remain different houses. Imagining a single house is not a simple process and sometimes we are unable to actually perform this work of unification. Likewise some patients are incapable of constructing a unique ('simultaneous') perception out of a group of objects that they perceive in sequence (a deficiency that goes by the name of *simultanagnosia*). Others get fixated on one unitary concept of the object (an allocentric mode of representation) and are incapable of noticing differences in objects. Moving on from a pathological to a pedagogical frame of reference it is worth noting that gifted children are immediately identifiable in a beginner's course on drawing from the fact that they draw spontaneously in perspective, with the object diminishing in size as a function of its distance from the viewer, while the rest only know how to compose a house, the abstract concept. The existence of such anomalies does not present a problem from the standpoint of a phenomenological description of normal experience.

---

such *petites perceptions* creates a link between the apparent discontinuity of conscious experience and the fundamental continuity of being. Their introduction renders obsolete the naïve dichotomy: conscious/unconscious.

The conditions under which, for us, normal subjects of perception, things take on a meaning can be, and are constantly, modified. These anomalies provide variational contributions to constitution (itself a variational process according to Husserl).[20] Or, to be more precise, the changing conditions of perception amount to so many contributing factors of constitution just as long as these contributions fail to get integrated into a new unity of meaning, dependent as they are upon distinct systems whose paths of connection have been undermined by pathology. This observation suggests the possibility of *an intentional psychopathology*,[21] a possibility already envisaged by Husserl who had become unsatisfied by the limits of the psychiatry of his day. Once this hypothesis of a plurality of systems underlying perception whenever a subject navigates in an environment has been evoked, what must not be overlooked is the natural connection between phenomenology and physiology, a connection that proceeds, once again, by way of anticipation.

Talk about representations results in our missing this essential component of experience, because when we talk of a representation we say, there is a representation in the retina, a representation in the lateral geniculate bodies of the thalamus, a representation located in V1, and so on. Each of these representations have their representational content (which is what makes them 'representations of …'): a content that is in principle entirely specifiable and whose decoding by the different programmes specialized in the cerebral processing of the optical signal in the visual pathways transmits all the information (and nothing but this information). There is no room for any reference towards a totality exceeding each particular represented content, such as the perceived house.

This dynamic activity on the part of the perceiving subject consists of a continually renewed anticipation, an anticipation that may prove fallacious in the further course of perception: anticipations can prove fallacious because we are not in the position of God. That is, we are not in an absolute but in a relative

----

[20] The idea of a variation implies that whatever is at time *t* exists as a variable; that is, it depends upon what has happened before *t* in a certain interval defined with reference not to a chronometric time but rather to a continuous series of sketches developed in the course of the visual exploration of a scene or of some thing (precisely 'a variety': *Mannigfaltigkeit*). Jean Petitot thinks that Husserl, the mathematician disciple of Weierstrass, had an implicit model in mind with integro-differential equations.

[21] Intentional psychopathology: a theory and practice of psychiatry putting into practice the Husserlian theory of intentionality with a view to understanding the treatment of psychic disturbances considered as vicissitudes of the noetico-noematic correlation, which does not always terminate in the constitution of the desired unitary object but is often exposed to the possibility of its diffraction (*Spaltung*). See L. Binswanger (1971) *Introduction à l'analyse existentielle*, Minuit, Paris.

situation, and so we are always laying claim to something more which might never be satisfied. Given the projective character of perception,[22] the perceiving subject is going to project upon the world its expectations, its desires. The latter are moreover developed in accordance with a schema by a group of neurons that are activated in our brain and so signify 'house', not for the brain but for the experience of the perceiving subject. Since this schema is projected upon the external world, its non-confirmation would give us the impression that there were two houses. Specialists in the field of neuroscience use cerebral imagery to try and decode the processes implicit in the multiplicity of possible points of view on one and the same house.[23] This work shows that particular regions: the *parahippocampus* and the *transverse occipital sulcus*, are involved when one presents a subject with video images taken by changing the point of view on the house and the subject does, nevertheless, succeed in recognizing the house. But of course we are still very far from being able to answer the questions posed above, and in particular that concerned with how the unity of the perception of *the* house is reconstructed on the basis of all these different views.

What the bat's brain has to say to the man's brain

One might object that what we have been saying is perhaps valid of a house that we perceive but cannot take account of the 'qualia' (purely subjective properties) of perception in so far as they are perceived by someone else, even a being with a mode of perception very different from our own. For example, how can we perceive the way in which a bat perceives the house?

It might not be altogether out of place to attempt to correct a tendency which is all too widespread, especially among Anglo-Saxon authors. In these circles, phenomenological description is habitually presented as a description of 'what difference it makes', 'what it looks like', to have this or that private experience when one is oneself the subject of such an experience. 'What it's like to be me?', or, as Thomas Nagel asks: 'What do things look like to a bat?'.[24] Since a bat possesses sensors specifically specialized in echolocation (localization of obstacles by radar), we, as humans, are quite incapable of grasping, relating, or explaining what the bat 'sees'. From this it seems to follow that there must be, objectively speaking, something like a bat's quite specific and

---

[22] See A. Berthoz (2000) *The Brain's Sense of Movement*, Harvard University Press, Cambridge, MA, p. 182.

[23] R.A. Epstein *et al.* (2005) Learning places from views: variation in scene processing as a function of experience and navigation ability, *J. Cog. Neurosci.* 17, 73–83.

[24] T. Nagel (1974) What is it like to be a bat? *Phil. Rev.* 83, 435–450.

different experience. Therefore those who want to reduce experience to what can be described in the kind of language humans use miss a part of what a broader conception of experience might have to offer. Such is the argument.

And from there, Dennett[25] has developed an argument which makes it easy to laugh at phenomenology: for once one is headed in this direction one can only waste one's time in a vain attempt at apprehending the inexpressible, employing, for the purpose, means which are—obviously—ill adapted, since the means for us humans to express facts are sentences or concepts. It is of course quite obvious that with a concept one cannot apprehend what is non-conceptual; with language one cannot apprehend what is inexpressible. By definition—so to speak, because even the notion of definition is itself a linguistic notion—the individuality of individual experience eludes all conceptual apprehension, conceptual apprehension being necessarily generic (or so Dennett argues, repeating Aristotle).

However, the target of this critique has little to do with what Husserl was trying to do: to interest us in the way in which things present themselves in their very phenomenality, rather than continuing to presuppose these things, in a paradoxical manner, as having always already been there, as being from the first decked out with all their phenomenal properties, even though, quite evidently, a state of original innocence has to be assumed with regard to all perceptual and cognitive activity. In other words, he wanted to warn us of the fact that, spontaneously, naïvely, we tend to attribute to things themselves properties which depend upon the act of perception. All of which assumes that we can place these things both inside and outside the conditions of any possible perception. We make of them something absolute even while pretending to take advantage of their relativity.

The objective point of view in all that?

A foreseeable criticism (one that has been a point of discussion between the two authors of this book) consists of saying that the neurosciences would gain nothing by taking seriously this phenomenological manoeuvre because it is archaic, one that reverses the course of evolution as well as of ontogenesis. In the end, it would amount to conferring an egocentric perspective upon the world, whereas Piaget has shown that what characterizes the development of the intelligence of the child is precisely its ability to get out, if not of lived experience itself (it would make no sense to talk of escaping from one's experience!), at least of any first-person description of the world, and so to gain

---

[25] D.C. Dennett (1991) *Consciousness Explained*, Little, Brown and Co., Boston, MA, pp. 43–65.

access to an allocentric perspective. If one concedes that, on the one hand, the evolution of animals has made it possible for them to develop a brain capable of manipulating abstractions by getting free of the perspective of the singular individual and, on the other, that the principle that ontogenesis reproduces phylogenesis is valid, that is to say, that the child does escape, little by little, from its local perspective as a perceiving organism by relying on the kind of presupposition in question, then the phenomenological manoeuvre could very well be described as archaic. For, in trying to get back to basics, it would be setting aside the power of mind to abstract itself from experience.

No interpretation should be dismissed in advance. Interpreting is an operation which consists of bringing the unknown back into the context of things known. An interpretation can favour, hinder, or hold up understanding. However, a psychological interpretation can be sketched out along the lines of the points we have made. The Husserlian theory of the constitution of the perceived thing on the basis of the kinaesthesia of the perceiving subject is nothing other than the child's conception of the world, characterized by Piaget as 'infantile realism' and 'egocentrism'.[26] Is such an interpretation going to help, hinder or block our understanding of this theory of constitution?

Let us get this straight: the theory of constitution is not trying to be a theory of the genesis of (adult) intelligence, an expression marred by mental reductionism. Nor is it a matter of trying to bring back the 'real' within the limits of the mental capacities of the individual. What the theory of constitution wants to explain is the way in which we gain access intellectually to an objective space, independent of us, intersubjectively comprehensible. This theory hopes to resolve the great question, which is not simply psychological but, before all else, epistemological, even ontological: how is it that a space which has nothing to do with the perceiving subject, which is structured differently from the visual field, a space in which objects owe us nothing, how is it that such a space comes to have a meaning for us? All we want to know is how we get to this point, how we fathom an enigma which does not appear as such to the greater part of mankind simply because they are caught up in it. A completely satisfying response would not mean abandoning objective science nor the cognitive science of perception but would make it possible for them to reach their goal.

---

[26] This description of the conception of the child as a 'realist' and as 'egocentric' is in fact contradictory: it is not possible to think that the real is both everything and the subject nothing and that the subject is everything, the real nothing! Later psychological literature criticized Piaget's doctrine of infantile realism (H.H. Wellman and D. Estes (1986) Early understanding of mental entities: a re-examination of childhood realism, *Child Dev.* 57, 910–923). On the other hand, the egocentric/allocentric opposition has been hardened by supposing a simple rocker switch where Piaget had presupposed a gradation with numerous intermediary stages.

The leading idea behind constitution is that it is possible to 'open up the perspective' of a subject closed in upon itself with a view to rejoining the objectivity of a spatial or temporal absolute. All of this presupposes that, from the start, lived experience enjoys a structure of a pre-systematic kind and that, for this reason, it should not be treated as a sort of inexpressible abyss. But this is precisely what is presupposed from the standpoint of 'everything depends upon structure'. There would then be the structure (the latter conceived along symbolic lines and so including language), and nothing underneath: no structuring of experience as such.[27]

As in Wittgenstein's *Tractatus logico-philosophicus*, it is the proposition, with its omnipotent logical structure, that accounts for the fact that there are objects in a world. It is the fact that we possess a language and that we can express ourselves through language by forming sentences that accounts for the fact that, in this world, we can identify something like an object, something like the bearer of a property, something like relations between objects.

By contrast, the idea behind a philosophy of experience, like that of Husserlian phenomenology, is that experience has to be structured in itself, and that it has to have contours which are not entirely dependent upon the fact that we possess a language. We do not want to claim that language plays no part in all this, nor do we want to deny that, within the limits of this dependence, there has to be an affinity between the contours of experience, its intimate structuring, and the way in which language, in particular in its metaphorical and so non-literal usage, predisposes us, invites us, and finally even obliges us to say the word. Certain linguists have adopted this path, a path equally remote from formal linguistics and from the physiology of lived experience.[28] They have said: if there is an affinity between experience and language why not plunge directly back into language ? Why put language between brackets as we seem to do, at least at first? The functional architecture

---

[27] On this subject it is worth bearing in mind Godelier's book on the enigma of the gift (M. Godelier (1996) *L'énigme du Don*, Seuil, Paris), a book in which one finds a severe criticism of the difficulties that Levi-Strauss' structuralism had created for the understanding of the mechanisms of the gift, and even for an interpretation of the work of Marcel Mauss.

[28] L. Talmy (2000) *Towards a Cognitive Semantics*, MIT Press, Cambridge, MA; L. Talmy (1985) Lexicalization patterns: semantic structure in lexical forms, in T. Shopen (ed.), *Language Typology and Syntactic Description. III. Grammatical Categories and the Lexicon*, Cambridge University Press, Cambridge, pp. 57–149; R. Langacker (1987–1991) *Foundations of Cognitive Grammar*, Stanford University Press, Stanford, CA; P. Cadiot and Y.-M. Visetti (2001) *Pour une théorie des formes sémantiques. Motifs, profils, thèmes*, Paris, PUF.

of the brain is only accessible through technology (cerebral imagery, etc.). Much easier than the latter for those of us who use language every day, should be its semantic analysis. Semantic analysis should therefore be treated as an analysis of experience. At any rate, the latter approach is not incompatible with our own attempt to gain direct access to the pre-configurations of lived experience steeped in our bodily being. And this, in as much as the 'motives', 'profiles', and 'themes' that ordinary language uses apparently draws solely from itself to make sense of things, in fact draws from a more deeply rooted constitution of the common life-world.

Chapter 6

A kinaesthetic theory of constitution

We are constantly kinaesthetic.

E. Husserl[1]

Having dealt with Husserl's kinaesthetic theory in the preceding chapter, we are now going to consider specific aspects of this theory, which should help us to reflect upon the foundations of a physiology of action. Physiology and modern psychology owe much to certain of Merleau-Ponty's writings[2]. By going back to his Husserlian sources we will perhaps be able to develop new hypotheses. Reconsidered from a physiological standpoint, Husserl's theory does indeed appear to have anticipated many of the recent discoveries on the functioning of the brain, from which one might be led to think that it can yield still more new ideas. The limited scope of this investigation does not require of us an exhaustive doctrinal exposition. In view of the fact that our attempt may appear trivial to the philosopher and abstruse to the physiologist or psychologist, we have tried, as far as possible, to define the 'technical' terms in such a way as to reassure the former with regard to the use we propose to make of them and enable the latter to derive valuable insights.

The eidetic: an antidote for an introspective biography

The phenomenological approach is especially attentive to the 'phenomena' by means of which things are present in the world. In other words, it apprehends things in their phenomenality by studying the way in which these things have

---

[1] E. Husserl, Manuscript transcription D 12 I, 5 September 1931, p. 17.

[2] Principally, *The Structure of Behaviour* (M. Merleau-Ponty (1942) *The Structure of Behaviour*, PUF, Paris) and *The Phenomenology of Perception* (M. Merleau-Ponty (1945) *Phénoménologie de la Perception*, Gallimard, Paris, trans. C. Smith (1962) *Phenomenology of Perception*, Routledge, London) but also, and more recently, his notes to lectures at the Collège de France: *La Nature* (M. Merleau-Ponty (1994) *La Nature*, Seuil, Paris.).

to present themselves to a living and perceiving being across presentations, *views*, and *points of view*. Its aim is therefore not to bring us back to a subjective and biographical interiority, which would not get us past the anecdotal level. Its aim is rather to carry us towards the things themselves, ordinary things, the things we call 'external', but by paying particular attention to the fact that these things are always *given* in a certain way. As explained in the preceding chapters, their 'mode of givenness' is always to someone who is somewhere, situated, and incarnate in a perceiving and acting body, someone who has intentions, desires, and beliefs.

To counterbalance the tendency to conceive of phenomenology as an invitation to turn inwards, to pay special attention to what goes on within us, and which might appear symmetrical with our familiar orientation outwards, an introspective observation of mental episodes supposed to be taking place inside each individual consciousness, a 'journey around my own room',[3] it is worth our while to introduce one of the most difficult notions from the point of view of any empirical (rather than theoretical)[4] study: the *eidetic*. The word is itself derived from the Greek *eidos*, meaning 'idea'—although *eidos* originally signified aspect, appearance—which obviously evokes Plato's theory of ideas, a theory we do not want to take on board. We should not underestimate the difficulty. Against a mentalist interpretation of phenomenology, what Husserl called 'psychologism', one could not insist more strongly upon its theoretical objectivity than by recognizing its eidetic character[5] as a discipline which, while basing its investigations upon lived experience, nevertheless still recognizes the role of processes of abstraction in perception and judgement. However, committing oneself to a thinking that rejoins experience offers no guarantee against falling back into verbal traps. With the word eidetic, we run the risk of being misunderstood. The very epitome of a rationalist metaphysics, it lies at the root of an unfortunate failure, in the past, to take the empirical sciences seriously.

----

[3] See X. de Maistre (1795/1984) *Voyage autour de ma chambre*, José Corti, Paris.

[4] See J. Petitot (1999) The eidetic morphology of perception, in J. Petitot *et al.* (eds), *Naturalizing Phenomenology: Issues in Contemporary Phenomenology and Cognitive Science*, Stanford University Press, Stanford, CA, Chap. 10, pp. 427–484.

[5] Phenomenology will never be able to come to terms with physiology and the neurosciences by allowing itself to be diluted into a vague introspective autobiography, nor yet by committing itself to any anti-logicist reaction, to the point of rejecting its eidetics, along with the logicism of the *Logical Researches*. Husserl's *Logical Researches* represented an approach to logic and mathematics along Fregean lines. That was the point of departure for phenomenology. Even though it retains the link with logicism and with an eidetics, it nevertheless goes beyond the latter to the extent that it is possible to save the notion of an eidetics even while abandoning the logicism. If phenomenology is ever to come to terms with the neurosciences it must remain what it is: an eidetic discipline.

It is not worth replying to this objection by trying to purge phenomenology of all suspicion of Platonic idealism. A better strategy consists simply of showing that idealism is not necessarily what one takes it to be when it is cast in the mould of an absurd opposition: an opposition between ideas separated from experience and an experience which, separated from ideas, ceases to possess any intelligible structure. As an eidetic analysis of lived experience, phenomenology teaches us to discover the *idealization* (no mere abstraction, since it is a creative act of the mind) at work at the level of the phenomenon. How? Every time that the very attempt to make use of our organs of perception (by relying in the first instance on our sensorial captors) plunges us into the flux of experience we recognize 'one and the same thing, something unique and identical' and so are brought to posit an ideality. To come to terms with the originality of the use made by the subject of this ideality, it is not enough to talk of abstraction. For this would be to neglect the projective aspect of the functioning of the brain, whose processes are responsible for the subject possessing this capacity. If there is a 'table' here, this table owes its unity to an act of the perceiving subject. It features as an object of perception, which only exists—and which only uphold itself in being—thanks to the constitutive (bodily as well as mental) operations that uphold it.[6]

Why do we bother to talk here of ideality? Because a unity, an identity, is not the kind of thing one can actually see with one's eyes or touch with one's hands. It belongs to the order of what can only be *understood*. But this *understanding* requires that we cross over from the actuality of the instantaneous and egocentric view one has of the thing to the dimension of potentiality; not any vague potentiality, but the potentiality of the indefinite series of other aspects that one could see by changing one's point of view (which implies de-centring), and for this very reason a potentiality anchored in what one sees; that is, a potentiality rooted in actuality.

In one sense one has done no more than say over again that the perceived is different from the felt. But, in another sense, this affirmation rejoins the objective of a workshop in the cognitive programme on 'abstraction'.[7] The neurophysiological foundations of perception contain mechanisms making it

---

[6] There is nothing particularly mystical or religious about the notion of ideality. Jean-Toussaint Desanti, a mathematical philosopher and disciple of Jean Cavaillès (and who was also a member of the governing body of the French Communist Party!) brings this out in his doctoral thesis on mathematical idealities: J.-T. Desanti (1968) *Les Idéalités mathématiques*, Seuil, Paris.

[7] The workshop on 'Abstraction', Collège de France, 7 December 2000, in the context of the Cognitique programme (ACI), funded by the French Ministry of Education and Research (1999–2003).

possible for us to 'construct abstractions'. For example, in the primary areas of the visual cortex, certain groups of neurons detect contours, others detect corners, whereas others again reconstruct 'contours that do not exist', as in the Kanizsa figures. So, the cognitive science community currently assumes that the brain's analysis of the world implies some sort of abstraction.[8] To be sure, one would feel more certain of remaining on strictly scientific ground if one restricted oneself to talking about 'levels of abstraction', as is the case with psychologists who work on perceptual 'constancies' and 'invariants'[9] without appearing to be aware of the seriousness of the contradiction implied by this departure from the dogma of empirical naturalism, according to which whatever exists has to be located either in the world or in the brain. Even on the phenomenal plane, that of lived experience, idealities are already operative, which means that this actuality is in fact infiltrated with the inactual.

And so, today, we are no longer obliged to uphold a dogma of this kind, one that would be opposed to the idea of forms as 'abstractions the brain constructs'. If this does not appear clear in all the variants of naturalism with which we are familiar, at least it is enough to satisfy the psychophysicists who work in close association with neurophysiologists, who themselves never stop discovering mechanisms of progressive abstraction, of simplification, of categorization, not to mention the hypotheses of symmetry and stationarity alluded to earlier.

When we are told that phenomenology helps us to discover the idealization (or abstraction or search for invariants) at work at the level of phenomena, the phenomenon as a domain of ideality could also become a source of perplexity for the physiologist. In fact, the one of us who is a physiologist suspects these 'idealities' of being nothing other than simplified procedures for categorizing the real and making it possible for a natural species like ourselves to rapidly identify those categories of object that are useful or harmful. Ideality would then figure as a single word to designate numerous processes of filtration and treatment of the real, thereby making it possible for us to grasp it by applying the repertory of our behaviour. Would we not be introducing the concept of something existing independent of the brain with the word idealization? Do we all really agree that by phenomenon is meant something that figures on the list in Chapter 5 of Husserl's examples, that is to say, this group of subjective experiences (upheld by the activity of the brain) that the subject has of the world and of its relations with this world ?

....

[8] See S. Zeki (1993) *A Vision of the Brain*, Blackwell, Oxford.

[9] Since the work of Gibson (referenced below), the development of these notions in psychology has been so considerable that the simple enumeration of the extant publications would defy the patience of the reader.

There is indeed a difficulty here. We are still talking of subjective experiences but having said that one has not said everything, because these subjective experiences are (without repeating ourselves) directed by an intentional arrow that points beyond the experiences themselves. They are not just experiences as belonging to a personal biography but experiences in so far as they are constitutive, to the extent that they orient the subject towards something other than themselves, and across which there emerges something that, this time, is not just a lived experience. This is what brings into play the notion of *phenomenon* (*phainomenon*, from *phainô*: meaning 'show', 'display', 'appear'): that something presents itself to someone, that the real, as independent as it is, is not absolutely independent, since it has to present itself.

This dual movement has not been adequately clarified in the phenomenology–physiology dialogue. First, the experience of sensation and the development of perception do, in fact, enable the world to emerge; that is, the world under different facets and as a function of given objectives.[10] But this emergence depends upon our intentions and the aims that we pursue. It is this double movement that we hope to clarify here. A movement that, on the one hand, enables a world to be constituted on the basis of interpretations that contain an element of abstraction and, on the other, specifies in advance what we want to perceive as a function of our aims. And both these notions belong together.

Kinaesthetic constitution according to Husserl

Let's first get straight about the etymology of the word kinaesthesia: *kinêsis* (movement) derived from *kineô* (to move) + *aisthêsis* (sensation, perception) derived from *aiô* (to hear, perceive). It is neither more nor less than a sensation of movement. In the theory of kinaesthetic constitution that interests us here, the term 'kinaesthesia', for want of anything better, is only employed to designate *both* the lived experience of gestures and postures, together with the orientation of the motor organs of perception *and* movement, even the acts used to simulate these movements from within. The experiences themselves (this cannot be sufficiently emphasized) are not sensations. Unfortunately, physiology is not at this time in possession of any way of understanding what an experience is. A similar difficulty can be seen in the field of the emotions with the notion of feeling, which is a complex combination of the perceived and the experienced.

In an attempt to make his description of the flux of experience more rational, Husserl envisaged the continuous succession of the aspects of a thing

---

10 A. Berthoz (2003) *La décision*, Odile Jacob, Paris, Chap. VII, pp. 177–198.

as forming 'a mathematical manifold (*Mannigfaltigkeit*) in the weak sense of that word.' He means by that the field of a kinaesthetic manifold of the adumbrations of the visual field which release as invariants approximately typical forms, an open field in opposition to the 'definite variety' of geometry, a science that determines all its possible objects *a priori* through a deduction from axioms.[11] The whole theory of the constitution of things for a subject rests upon the correspondence between two layers of proto-objects in which this manifold gets duplicated:

1 the *positing manifold* consists of the series of profiles appearing in the visual field, as examples of sensorial fields. (An impatient physiologist who wanted a direct transposition in terms of cerebral cartography would be inclined to talk of the several activities of the sensorial maps of the brain: visual cortex, somato-sensorial cortex, etc. But, of course, such a transposition is, at the very least, premature.)

2 the *motivating manifold* consists of internal goal-oriented activities linked to the kinaesthesia; for example, the experiences induced by eye movements in the course of exploring a scene. They are more evident in the case of the movement of limbs, since we feel inside ourselves the transition between the state of rest in the initial posture and the return to the state of rest at the end, passing across all the intermediary degrees of tension and relaxation. This complete series forms what Husserl calls a 'kinaesthetic unfolding'. The word motivating means here what initiates movement. This is the role played by kinaesthesia in perception.

Through the play of this positing and motivating manifold, a constituting character with regard to perceived things is conferred upon the perceptual activities of the subject. The kinaesthesia are in fact responsible for the fact that I do not get fixed indefinitely on one image when I perceive but constantly change aspects, passing from one initial and imperfect profile to another more satisfactory profile, and so on (unless, of course, deception transpires!).

With a view to clarifying these two concepts of a positing and a motivating manifold let us make a little detour across the work of the great physicist Ernst Mach, who had the intuition, just like Poincaré and Einstein, of the importance of subjective experience and of perception in the working out of the most advanced physical theories. Mach is known for his work on vection. Vection is the illusion we have of moving forward when, in a station where we are awaiting the departure of our own train, the train next to ours starts up,

----

[11] E. Husserl (1976) *Ideen zu einer Reinen Phänomenologie und Phänomenologischen Philosophie*, I, Hrsg. v. K. Schumann, Martinus Nijhoff, The Hague, §72, p. 150–152.

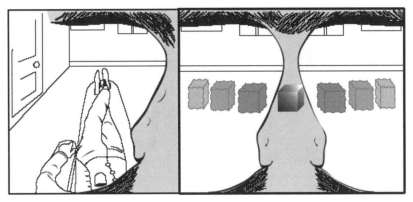

Fig. 1 Left: a reconstruction of E. Mach's monocular visual field. Right: an artist's image of the natural (binocular) visual field when presented with aspects of a three-dimensional object (a geometric solid) in the course of its visual exploration.

and we get the impression that it is ours that has started moving. Or again, while looking at a river from a bridge, we get the impression that it is the bridge that is moving forward. This illusion interested Mach for it illustrates the decision the brain has to take faced with a movement in the environment detected through vision: is it my body that moves or the world around me?[12]

Puzzled by this problem in kinaesthetics, and in order to get a better feeling for what he perceived of the world subjectively, Mach drew himself, stretched out on a sofa and looking at the room around him (Figure 1). The reader is invited to assess this image of the monocular visual field,[13] an image commented upon by its author in these terms: 'I was brought to do this drawing about seventeen years ago under rather amusing circumstances. A certain Mr L., now dead, endowed with so amiable a character that he was willingly forgiven for a good many eccentricities, forced me to read a book by Krause.[14] In this book one finds the following: 'Problem: carry out the self-intuition "I"—Solution: one simply carries it out.' So in order to get a humorous illustration of this philosophical *Much Ado about Nothing*, but also to show how

---

12 See E. Mach (1875/1967) *Grundlinien der Lehre von den Bewegungsempfindungen*, E.J. Bonset, Amsterdam.

13 E. Mach (1886) *Beiträge zur Analyse der Empfindungen*, Gustav Fischer, Iena, Fig. 1, p. 14.

14 The reference must be to the philosopher Karl Christian Friedrich Krause (1781–1832), the author of one of a number of systems of German idealism at the intersection of influences stemming from Kant, Fichte, Schelling, and Hegel: K.C.F. Krause (1904) *Sketch of a System of Philosophy (Entwurf des Systemes der Philosophie)*, Cnobloch, Iena/Leipzig.

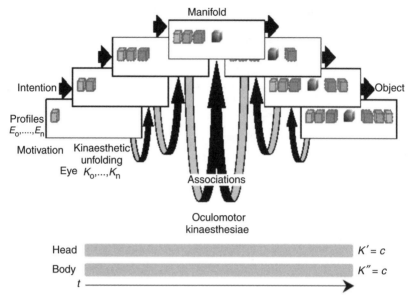

Fig. 2 Kinaesthetic constitution.

Profiles (E_0, ... , E_n): phenomena of the 'image' type are transitory appearances in the visual field, on which the visual presentation of an object of perception is based.

Manifold: a series of profiles, varying from the sub-optimal appearance from the side or from the periphery to the optimal, central appearance, whose regular unfolding from one instantaneous visual field to the other serves as the basis for the perceptual apprehension of the three-dimensional object.

Intention→Object: in one and the same intentional directedness of attention, the fact that the subject is constantly interested in obtaining a better presentation of the object means that this interest is renewed constantly once it has been aroused. This is represented graphically by a series of horizontal arrows connecting each instantaneous visual field with the immediately succeeding field. Motivation–Kinaesthetic unfolding (K_0, ... ,K_n): motor contingencies (varying from rest to maximum tension) to which modifications of the visual field are subjected through the shifting of the gaze with the renewal of the profiles (their passage across, or their deterioration from, the optimum). The 'elastic' vertical arrows linking each instantaneous visual field to the next evoke the motivating role of kinaesthesia (as inducing variation) as well as the need for the object to be in the central, optimal position as the target of motor activity. As viewers, we tend to keep coming back to the best distance, the best point of view.

Motivation–Associations: contingent synchronization between a series of profiles of the visual field and the unfolding of kinaesthetic sensations, a synchonization which obtains each time the gaze makes contact with a proto-object of interest. In so far as expectations are disappointed, due to the inability to integrate the profiles into the unity of the perceived object, the process is brought to an end.

Kinaesthesiae (K, K', K''): sensations of movement in the perceptual organs, sensations either actualized or only anticipated on the basis of motor intentions. We have only figuratively represented the kinaesthetic movements of the eyes (ocular motor K)

whereas the kinaesthesia of head movements (cephalomotor K') and body movements (somatomotor K'') are supposed to be constant in principle.

Time (t): the time of perceptual activities is a subjectively complex time that combines the specific temporality of the series of profiles in the visual field with the specific temporality of the unfolding of kinaesthesiae in the perceptual and motor organs. This is a constituting time by contrast with the ordinary concept of ('physical') time which, for its part, is a constituted time.

---

one actually carries out the self-intuition "I", I produced the drawing shown above.'[15]

This testimony shows how the physicist-philosopher went about grasping the properly subjective component of perception, in particular visual perception. But, of course, this picture does not contain the movement necessary for kinaesthesia. To explain Husserl's theory of kinaesthesia (for which he did not develop a schema, unlike the case of his theory of our experience of time)[16] we drew our inspiration from this drawing in which Mach has combined the (monocular) visual field and his own body (the theme of Chapter 7). We added the dimension of time (a subjective temporality, constituting, and not chronometric!) to bring to light the fact that our kinaesthetic perception unfolds at two synchronized levels: the level of the manifold aspects of the visual field and the level of the unfolding of the associated kinaesthesia. On the one hand, the continuously more satisfactory gradation of the perceiving subject's expectations moves from sub-optimal, lateral profiles to optimal frontal profiles through which the object is itself presented. On the other hand, the unfolding of the kinaesthetic series which runs alternatively from rest to tension, to maximum tension, to relaxation and so back to rest, in accordance with the progression in the efforts deployed in the 'motivation' of these same profiles.

In order to provide an informal presentation of the kinaesthetic theory (which we do not intend to state in the 'canonical' form of a list of axioms!) we are going to work with the schema developed above. The reader will be guided step by step in the interpretation of the latter through the commentary that is laid out in the legend to Figure 2.

Equipped with this schema, let us try to tackle the *positing* manifold. Husserl gives this name to what has been represented on the upper part of the schema with planes representing the sensorial fields of the motivating manifold laid

---

[15] K.C.F. Krause (1904) *Sketch of a System of Philosophy (Entwurf des Systemes der Philosophie)*, Cnobloch, Iena/Leipzig, note 9, p. 15.

[16] See E. Husserl (1966) *Zur Phänomenologie des inneren Zeitbewusstseins* (1893–1917), Husserliana X, Martinus Nijhoff, The Hague, pp. 93, 196, 199, 208, 210, 230, 235, 330–331, 365, 399, 412.

out horizontally along an axis represented by arrows. This axis represents the unfolding of time, not physical time but a subjective time[17] which encompasses the progressive enrichment of the perceiving subject's information relative to the exploration of its visual environment. From one moment to the next, the object is clarified, formed, stabilized so that its presentation becomes more adequate with regard to the expectations aroused by the previous profiles in the visual field. A first and imperfect impression arouses interest, the desire to know more: this means that a motivation has been associated with the profile in question, and which lead and guides the ocular kinaesthesia in the direction of an ever more satisfactory profile. The tempo of the scanning, the rate at which the sensorial field—here only the visual field—is explored and across which, or by means of which, we gain access to a field of objects (the notion of 'field' is used both for the constituting proto-space and the constituted objective space) makes available a series Husserl calls a 'field positing manifold', across which the subject becomes conscious of, conceives, or grasps one unique thing.

The arrow of the intentional orientation of visual perception towards 'the thing' is directed towards the (visually) perceived object by relying on the different and partial fields that it instantaneously connects, one with another. Each given field lets us understand that there is more to be seen from that side. Every other field draws us on towards yet another aspect and so on, and this in a dynamic relation of the completion of anticipations which continually incites us to look at this or that part of the visual field. *Little by little the object is marked out by successive profiles.* Thanks to an activity encompassing all the operations that contribute towards the clarification or the explanation of what is given by means of instantaneous fields, it becomes possible for us to grasp the object.

But all this is only made possible by the *experience of movement*. Such is the role of the *motivating manifold* (of movement, in particular ocular movement) in creating the *link between successive sensorial fields*. This necessary 'sticking back together' is according to Gibson the price that has, for example, to be paid by animals that have developed a fovea and a reduced visual field. They are restricted to having only a succession of views on the world, whereas

---

[17] We know that subjective time varies considerably as a function of action and context. For example, we always get the impression that the way back from a walk is faster than the way out: P. Fraisse (1984) Perception and estimation of time, *Annu. Rev. Psychol.* 35, 1–36; J.J. Gibson (1975) Events are perceivable but time is not, in J.T. Fraser and N. Lawrence (eds), *The Study of Time 2*, Springer, Berlin, pp. 295–301; I. Israël *et al.* (2004) Multifactorial interactions involved in linear self-transport distance estimate: a place for time, *Int. J. Psychophysiol.* 53, 21–28.

certain other animals (the pigeon, for example) have a panoramic view of the world. On Figure 2, the motivating manifold is reproduced by arrows beneath the visual fields, which represent the jump (or rather the effort experienced in making the jump) accomplished by making the movement from one perceptual field to another. The size of each arrow suggests the intensity of the effort accomplished in moving the perceptual organs with a view to passing from one field to another. With this diverse and flexible deformation of the arrows we wanted to convey the idea that, in the transition from one field to the following, the kinaesthetic tension was all the stronger in as much as the profile anticipated in the following field promised to be all the more adequate, with the result that the tempo of the kinaesthetic unfolding was all the more sustained. On the contrary, the tension subsided, and this tempo fell back, whenever the transition moved in the direction of an impoverishment of the profiles, as is the case when one looks towards the edges of the visual field or when a furtive object is outlined in too marginal a position.

Let us take as an example the movement of the eyes. In the course of a visual exploration, successive images of the world (positing manifold) are obtained by visual jumps called saccades.[18] The subject is made aware of each ocular movement by an intimate feeling of the corresponding movement (motivating manifold): an intimate feeling of moving our eyes to the right, to the left, of moving our eyes downwards, of turning our head, etc. At the level of the neuronal correlates, this is what the physiologists call the corollary discharge; that is, the information sent to the perceptual centres regarding the movement that the eye has just made.[19]

On this subject, Husserl has an interesting and insightful thesis to the effect that, regarded strictly from the standpoint of the initiation of movement, *motivation does not include intentionality*. At the same time, the intentionality that exclusively concerns the profiles is always deployed 'on the occasion of' a motivation. In other words, motivation plays a contextual role in the deployment of an intentionality; that is to say, a meaning directed towards something that has to be regarded as being, at first, empty of content, however specifically it may be determined with regard to its objective, and then maintained right through to saturation, its meaningful completion. New information arises

---

[18] See the summary on the control of occular saccades in A. Berthoz (2000) *The Brain's Sense of Movement*, Harvard University Press, Cambridge, MA and A. Berthoz (2003) *La décision*, Odile Jacob, Paris.

[19] E. von Holst and H. Mittelstædt (1950) Das Reafferenzprinzip. Wechselwirkung zwischen Zentralnervensystem und Peripherie, *Naturwissenschaften* 37, 464–476, trans. in C.R. Gallistel (1980) *The Organization of Action: A New Synthesis*, Lawrence Erlbaum, Hillsdale, NJ, Chap. 7, pp. 166–209.

only when I move my body. This is the point at which there arises a variation upon which the intention (which is not itself movement) can be grafted. This is a variation upon which this intention depends if it is to intervene, since it can only be realized through effective movement. This makes perfectly good sense even from the point of view of the motor function of the gaze, for example, because it is we who make our eyes move, even though these movements are not necessarily movements of such a kind that we can even claim that they are all intentionally directed.

It is not easy to grasp this link between intention and movement. In the 1950s and 1960s, and as a result of the work of Yarbus at Moscow,[20] great hopes were placed upon our being able to understand precisely what it was that the subject looked at by measuring the movements of his eyes. The ocular movements involved in the exploration of a visual scene can always be registered. And it will no doubt always be possible to discover regularities, preferred paths. Psychologists have therefore tried to relate the paths adopted by the gaze to the perception of the visual scene and so to find out what attracted the attention of the subject. Yarbus, for his part, had shown that the path pursued by the gaze of a subject differs as a function of his visual interrogation of the image, and in such a way that the series of ocular saccades directs his gaze towards different parts of the scene (here we can say that it is the series made up of the motivating manifold of the gaze movements that is intentionally directed by the positing manifold of the things in the course of their being constituted visually).

Over and beyond the fact that this analysis is extremely limited in what it reveals regarding perception, things do not always turn out this way, however. Sometimes the gaze bears upon an intermediary zone between several parts of the scene, a sort of centre of gravity relative to the different points of interest. This is the case with the gaze movements accomplished in the course of reading.[21] Sometimes the gaze simply wanders arbitrarily in search of samples, certain neuronal mechanisms making it impossible for the eye to get back to the point already explored the first time around (return inhibition).[22] As a result, the deployment of the details of this scene will not be reproduced in all their particular characteristics if one is restricted to filming these gaze movements.

---

[20] A.L. Yarbus (1967) *Eye Movements and Vision*, Plenum Press, New York.

[21] R.G. Reilly and J.K. O'Regan (1998) Eye movement control during reading: a simulation of some word-targeting strategies, *Vision Res.* 38(2), 303–317; J.K. O'Regan (1990) Eye movements and reading, *Rev. Oculomotor Res.* 4, 395–453.

[22] This return inhibition is a curious mechanism. When we survey a scene through a series of saccades we never end up looking at the point from which we started out.

Researchers of the Russian school following Yarbus were very disappointed to have to admit that the subject did not necessarily 'look' where his eye was oriented, and that the variations in the direction of gaze did not make it possible to predict the spot where his attention was directed. They even developed a hypothesis according to which we have 'a functional fovea', thanks to which we can pay attention to certain regions of the visual field without having to specifically direct our gaze towards that spot. Experimental evidence was obtained by Viviani, Berthoz, and Tracey about the properties of this functional fovea.[23] We also know today that the same eyes movements are implied during the saccade and during the attentional displacements, which are themselves intentional-attentional, as Husserl surmised in refusing to disassociate attention and intention in what he called 'intentional directedness'.[24] These attentional movements constitute a sort of *virtual kinaesthesia*, which complete the series of effective movements responsible for producing the sequence of sensorial fields. Over and beyond each profile actually given in an instantaneous field, this directedness points towards 'the thing in itself', relative to which presentation this profile only constitutes a transitory phase.

We have chosen to illustrate kinaesthetic constitution by restricting our analysis to the case of eye movements. But one could also take as our example the exploration of the environment by hearing, grasping, and even locomotion. Our schema of constitution can serve for the schematization of the memory of a journey, for example, if one considers that when we navigate in a town, with a view to registering the journey, the brain undertakes an engrammation of successive *views of the environment* (corresponding to the positing manifold), but also a series of associations (motivating manifold) between the movements of the subject as agent and the foregoing series of perceptions that are visual, acoustic, etc. This cognitive strategy for remembering journeys does not

----

[23] P. Viviani and A. Berthoz (1977) Voluntary deceleration and perceptual activity during oblique saccades, in R. Baker and A. Berthoz (eds), *Control of Gaze by Brain Stem Neurons*, Elsevier, Amsterdam, pp. 23–28; P. Viviani, A. Berthoz, and D. Tracey (1977) The curvature of oblique saccades, *Vision Res.* 17(5), 661–664.

[24] M. Corbetta *et al.* (2005) A functional MRI study of preparatory signals for spatial location and objects, *Neuropsychologia* 43(14), 2041–2056; J.M. Kincade *et al.* (2005) An event-related functional magnetic resonance imaging study of voluntary and stimulus-driven orienting of attention, *J. Neurosci.* 25(18), 4593–4604; S.V. Astafiev *et al.* (2004) Extrastriate body area in human occipital cortex responds to the performance of motor actions, *Nat. Neurosci.* 7(5), 542–548; S.V. Astafiev *et al.* (2003) Functional organization of human intraparietal and frontal cortex for attending, looking, and pointing, *J. Neurosci.* 23(11), 4689–4699; P. Holinger *et al.* (1999) Mental representations of movements. Brain potentials associated with imagination of eye movements, *Clin. Neurophysiol.* 110(5), 799–805.

necessarily have as its goal the construction of the representation of an object but is a good example of the way in which the kinaesthetic function plays a critical role. Experiments have shown that patients with hippocampal lesions can remember the list of landmarks they met during the journey but cannot remember well the association between their body movements ('turn left or right') and the landmark ('turn left at the fountain') and moreover they cannot remember well the sequence of these episodic events.[25] It is probable that animals transported passively are quite incapable of adopting this strategy (the spatial selectivity of their 'place neurons' is also very poor) since they have been unable to accomplish the movements normally associated with perception.[26]

But at best this would simply furnish us with a way of reconstructing our memory of a route in an egocentric fashion (that is, from the standpoint of a moving subject). The real question is to know how to move from this temporal succession to the ability to construct an objective, invariant, knowledge by, for example, drawing up a map of the town that makes it possible for us to take detours, to get back to the point of departure by another route.[27]

The eidetic: correlating the motivating with the expository manifold

Are we going to say, then, that to the two manifolds mentioned above a third component has now to be added, the *eidetic*, and this by supposing that, in addition to its series of images and sensations of movement, the brain also possesses a stock of *a priori* ideas concerning the world? This would be to misunderstand both the essence of these manifolds and that of the eidetic itself, and so to trivialize the whole theory of constitution. We would be falling back upon an ideology of mental representations in the brain, which would immediately relativize the contribution of both movement and kinaesthetic sensations to the constitution of the perceived thing. No, once a manifold of profiles has been put into operation and deployed in accordance with the

----

[25] S. Lambrey and A. Berthoz (2003) Combination of conflicting visual and non-visual information for estimating actively performed body turns in virtual reality, *Int. J. Psychophysiol.* 50(1–2), 101–115; S. Lambrey, I. Viaud-Delmon, and A. Berthoz (2002) Influence of a sensorimotor conflict on the memorization of a path travelled in virtual reality, *Cog. Brain Res.* 14(1), 177–186.

[26] See the work on spatial memory in navigation by A. Berthoz *et al.* already cited in Chapter 4, footnote 71.

[27] A. Berthoz (2001) Neural basis of spatial orientation and memory of routes: topokinetic memory or topokinesthesic memory, *Rev. Neurol.* 157(8–9:1), 779–789; D. Schmidt *et al.* (2007) Visuospatial working memory and changes of the point of view in 3D space. *Neuroimage* 36(3), 955–968.

tempo of a kinaesthetic unfolding belonging to a determinate kinaesthetic system, nothing more needs to be added to grasp the 'eidetic' structure of the thing in its identical self-sameness. *The eidetic is nothing more than the law of organization (or synchronization) of these two manifolds.* So a manifold is in fact the very opposite of a succession or non-structured collection, awaiting that complementary ingredient without which it would not acquire a form. A manifold only exists in so far as it is caught up in a dynamic through which the form of the perceived thing emerges (the 'popping out' phenomenon).

In other words, the eidetic operates as a spontaneous idealization in perception. To the extent that this eidetic structure is integrated into perception, the procedure of constitution effects what might be called an oblique displacement with regard to the line of ordinary time. But things don't just happen in the time of successive events (a subjective time, it should be remembered), for what also enters into play is the capacity of a subject to circulate freely in a field of transversal potentialities that are not actually realized in the sensorial present. This is what needs to be represented in the figure by blurring the contrasts and by smearing the images of objects into the instantaneous visual fields at the beginning and in the prolongation of their expository manifold. For the actual series always has a possible prolongation in the virtual, in a horizon of its alternative possibilities.

But of course, the schema of the figure—what makes it possible for us to interpret it in the sense of the memory of a route—remains linear and sequential, while the idealization or abstraction (construction of the map) is essentially parallel. This is much too sequential, and therefore also too egocentric, for it to be able to do justice to our capacity for idealization.

The mathematician Alain Connes testified to these capacities in the context of a lecture given at the Collège de France on his use of the mental imagery of a 'landscape' in geometry. A landscape unfolds all its planes at once, parallel to one another rather than one alongside one another in a sequence. So how does one get from the plan for a journey, from a series of events, to this sudden opening upon what is (and is only), properly speaking, a representation,[28] or even better an idea? The single plane of the printed page lends itself poorly to the evocation of the multi-dimensionality of the experience. And in fact our schema operates with a cut, a sample from the complete system of kinaesthetic constitution, a system that it is very difficult to illustrate in the space of a page since it implies the unfolding, in perspective, of all the possible lines

---

[28] A representation, in a strict, literal sense, which implies an extra mental object of conscious consideration, in contradistinction to the so-called 'representation' of the representational theories of mind, which is but a metaphorical extension of usage of the word in reference to any kind of mental activity whatsoever.

of association: not just the actual lines of association but also their prolongation in the dimension of the virtual. All this is in order to free up a place for habit, for our natural confidence in our ability to develop (our sense of know-how) other equally possible lines of association in place of those in which we happen to be engaged at the time.

What cannot be shown in this image is that, at the very same time that these successive profiles are accumulated (being integrated with each other in the course of their accumulation), a more fundamental mechanism is brought into play. The latter is not simply *the* allocentric representation, as if there were a simple juxtaposition of two modes of representation. For this is what makes it possible for the perceiving subject to objectify a perceived thing, an objectification that is only exceptionally the interior contemplation of a mental image: it can also be—and is more frequently—the positing of this thing (until physiology provides us with better explanations, words will continue to prove insufficient to describe this process) in the evidence of an optimal perception, its categorization by subsumption under a concept, the attribution to it of those properties belonging to it in the context of a judgment, its evaluation from an aesthetic point of view, etc.

So what has to be introduced is some indication of the fact that, at the same time that the brain takes into account this serial manifold of profiles unfolded successively across time, its capacity to analyse in parallel also has to be accounted for. In a word, these systems are activated in such a way that it becomes literally true to say (as do phenomenologists) of the perceiving subject (and of its constituting perceptual operations): it *spatializes*.

It is therefore up to the reader to imagine a construction in depth, relative to the plane of the page, and which is needed to do justice to the 'I can' of the own body. There is the 'I do', the 'I actualize', and, at the same time, an 'I could also actualize'. And that is what this cartographic ability, this unfolding of the line in space, depends upon. Husserl insisted on this: *we are constantly kinaesthetic*:

> 'I am at all times in one or another kinaesthetic stance; I am always in a certain posture and each posture belongs to one and the same total system of postures; I am always kinaesthetic in some way or other, at rest kinaesthetically, or in motion between one rest and another, between one stopping point and another.'[29]

These kinaesthesiae are distinct each from the other and are organized in complete circuits in which the above-mentioned phases alternate. At the same time, these kinaesthesiae give us the world; they are the circumstances in which the latter is present to a perceiving subject. Strictly speaking, the expository manifold, taken together with its motivating manifold, form a unique

---

[29] E. Husserl, D 12 I, (5 September 1931).

and integrated system which, in order to do justice to the objectification we talked about earlier, might be called the objectifying manifold. Introducing this terminological nuance attests to our determination to reconsider perception, a field of factual evidence, a robust if dispersed field, as the domain of an integrated constituting activity, and the perceived object as its product.

Sensori-motor contingencies and reduction of the degrees of freedom

Let's get quite clear about this: the manifold, whether positing or motivating, is not made up of mental representations, inside the subject, of physical things outside the subject. It consists of a series of profiles with their dynamic prolongations in the gestures they outline. There are no objects in space, only proto-objects in the course of being constituted through the inseparable interaction between a perceiver and its world. All the properties of things as they exist for the perceiver take on whatever reality they possess in this context. The equal power of these two types of manifold results from their close synchronization through 'associations' (a term as much Husserlian as it is Piagetian, as much Freudian as it is Watsonian, etc.) empirically instantiated in the course of the development and history of the individual.

These associations are created in the experience of the subject within the limits of the constraints imposed by our corporeal organization, in particular biomechanical constraints: the form of the orbits that delimit the visual field; the foveolar structure of the retina (the fovea upon which the image of its objects of interest has to be placed and maintained), the flexibility of its articulations, and even before that, the flexibility of the extra-ocular muscles; the elasticity of the muscles of the fingers, or, in symmetry with their elasticity, their biomechanical impedance (to what extent is the subject able to make use of these muscles in a movement, which itself varies with training, tiredness, age, and pathologies?). Upon these contingencies is grafted, reasonably enough, the recent theory developed by O'Regan and Noe,[30] who were also well aware of the role of regularities in the identification of invariants: as much as this can be credited to their theory without withdrawing the critique developed above (Chapter 2) concerning the sensori-motor approach.

---

[30] See J.K. O'Regan and A. Noe (2001) What it is like to see: a sensorimotor theory of perceptual experience, *Synthèse* 129, 79–103; J.K. O'Regan and A. Noe (2001) A sensorimotor account of vision and visual consciousness, *Behav. Brain Sci.* 24(5), 883–917; J.K. O'Regan and A. Noe (2001) Acting out our sensory experience, *Behav. Brain Sci.* 24(5), 955–975; J.K. O'Regan, E. Myin, and A. Noe (2005) Sensory consciousness explained (better) in terms of 'corporality' and 'alerting capacity', *Phenomenol. Cog. Sci.* 4(4), 369–387.

The fact that the organism is structured in this way both in its motor functioning (principally) and in the construction of perceptual invariants is taken directly into account in the functioning of the nervous system, and even in the anatomy of the body. To the extent that, in the course of evolution, organisms became more complex, solutions had to be found to reduce this complexity through what engineers call *reduction of the degrees of freedom*.[31] Our own body, with its multiple sense organs, assumes the form of a sensori-motor system which comprehends hundreds of degrees of freedom (reducible to the number of parameters to be controlled). However, for the living organism in its ecological context, the least action supposes complex operations which have to be realized in a very short space of time (capturing a prey or escaping from a predator is a matter of hundreds of milliseconds, while a squirrel's ability to leap from tree to tree calls for a fabulous mastery of precise movement, etc.). Given the brief lapse of time allowed by the action, the brain would be confronted with an insoluble problem if certain properties of the own body and of the nervous system, innate or acquired, did not help to simplify the task of motor control by subordinating it to one and the same motor command capable of controlling often complex movements.

To avoid repetition, let us just say that, in the course of evolution, numerous mechanisms have been put into place to simplify neuro-computation. For example, there exists a definite relation between the tangential speed of a finger used to draw a figure and the curvature of the line traced.[32] A simple movement can be induced by a single neuron in the motor cortex, even if it calls for several muscles, this thanks to the multiple projections of neurons toward groups of muscles that produce these elementary movements. A very close coordination between the movements of the arm and the forearm is obtained by mechanisms situated in the medulla, thanks to which the brain only has to control the global variables of the movement and not each muscle individually. Similar simplifications are to be found in the perceptual systems, like the similarity of the planes of space in which movement in the visual world is analysed by vision and the vestibular system.

All the same, this reduction in the numerical degrees of freedom that one discovers in the analysis of the motor and sensory systems is only interpreted today as a way of simplifying the neuro-computation. Otherwise life would simply be too complicated for the organism in its ecological context. If it had

---

[31] See on this subject: A. Berthoz (2000) *The Brain's Sense of Movement*, Harvard University Press, Cambridge, MA.

[32] H. Hicheur, S. Vieilledent, M.J. Richardson, T. Flash, and A. Berthoz (2005) Velocity and curvature in human locomotion along complex curved paths: a comparison with hand movements, *Exp. Brain Res.* 162(2), 145–154.

to run through all the calculations theoretically required for the effective realization of action, it would already have been devoured by the predator and this even before it arrived at a decision.

With regard to such an interpretation, an interpretation dependent upon the epistemological stance of the engineer or the evolutionary psychologist, the phenomenological approach could open up a way of getting beyond this undoubtedly trivial interpretation, and give us reasons for not being afraid to go this way, because a theory can be entirely true in an absolute sense even while remaining beneath the threshold of the truth in its formulation. Making no mention of the intentional dimension of the experience of the subject, an experience underpinned by these mechanisms, it amounts to an understatement. Or to put things otherwise, at its own level of course, which is that of an *a priori* analysis of the conditions of the possibility of perception and action for a subject, the kinaesthetic theory of constitution does no more than deploy what is itself the very object (regulative idea) of the cognitive neurosciences; that is to say, the anatomical, physiological, and behavioural foundations of our knowledge of the world (in the end, also the recognition of the other, without which this would not be a world in common; see Chapter 8).

An interesting research suggestion would consequently be to generalize the idea of the reduction of the degrees of freedom of the movements of the organism by looking for the physiological substrate of the intentional orientation of perception and of the gesture directed towards perceived things. The hypothesis here would be that simplifying principles would also be present in the neural processes aimed at projecting upon the world hypotheses and rules for the extraction of information relevant to or meaningful for the intended act. Going over these simplifying principles, one might then well ask why some principles have been chosen and not others. Is it simply because they were more effective on the biomechanical plane, concerned as it is with the adjustment of the actions of the organism to the laws of the physical world; is it because one of the functions of movement, as we saw earlier, is to perceive, in which case these solutions would have to be tied in to the *Umwelt* of each species; or is it because these solutions are dependent upon the neuronal organization itself?

We are well aware that the reader might have been left unsatisfied. We have promised a kinaesthetic theory of the constitution of the perceived thing, and, at this point, all that has been delivered is a theory of the oculo-motor and motor kinaesthesia involved in the visual constitution of the thing, more exactly its two-dimensional appearance. From another point of view, however, our programme is already too heavily loaded for us to get involved in this task and our purpose here is to lay foundations and offer a basis for debate. We are condemned to schematizing what we simply cannot explain in its entirety.

Schematizing the problem of reference frames and the multiplicity of spaces for action

Without sharing the diagrammatic optimism of the author of the *Tractatus Logico-philosophicus*, Wittgenstein, who held that the image sufficed in itself and that it was neither necessary nor even possible to say what has to be seen, we refer our reader to the following schemas. In three stages, these schemas will evoke by analogy the missing part of the scaffolding of a fully satisfactory kinaesthetic theory of constitution.

We shall first of all (in Figure 2) illustrate the correlation between the different kinaesthetic systems (oculo-motor, cephalic-motor, somato-motor, haptic). In addition, it is well known from neurology and from recent brain-imaging experiments that the brain uses separate mechanisms (or as we say today networks of areas) to deal not only with the different motor systems (there are for instance separate basal ganglia-thalamic-cortical loops for eye movements and limb movements) but also different spaces of action and perception. For instance, separate mechanisms are involved in body space, reaching space, distant space accessible only to locomotion, and environment space. A nice experiment with functional magnetic resonance imaging has shown that even when we have to point with a laser pointer to two targets respectively located 0.7 metres and 1.7 metres away separate networks of brain areas are involved.[33] These kinaesthetic spaces use a number of different reference frames, used in a very flexible manner by the brain.[34] They can be eye-centred, head-centred,[35] object-centred, or even environment-centred.[36]

---

[33] P.H. Weiss *et al.* (2000) Neural consequences of acting in near versus far space: a physiological basis for clinical dissociations, *Brain* 123(12), 2531–2541.

[34] A. Berthoz (1991) Reference frames for the perception and control of movement, in J. Paillard (ed.), *Brain and Space*, Oxford University Press, Oxford, pp. 81–111.

[35] J.R. Duhamel, F. Bremmer, S. BenHamed, and W. Graf (1997) Spatial invariance of visual receptive fields in parietal cortex neurons, *Nature* 389(6653), 845–848; Y.E. Cohen and R.A. Andersen (2002) A common reference frame for movement plans in the posterior parietal cortex, *Nat. Rev. Neurosci.* 3(7), 553–562; B. Stricanne, R.A. Andersen, and P. Mazzoni (1996) Eye-centered, head-centered, and intermediate coding of remembered sound locations in area LIP, *J. Neurophysiol.* 76(3), 2071–2076.

[36] G. Committeri *et al.* (2004) Reference frames for spatial cognition: different brain areas are involved in viewer-, object-, and landmark-centered judgments about object location, *J. Cog. Neurosci.* 16(9), 1517–1535; J. McIntyre, F. Stratta, and F. Lacquaniti (1997) Viewer-centered frame of reference for pointing to memorized targets in three-dimensional space, *J. Neurophysiol.* 78(3), 1601–1618; M. Carrozzo, J. McIntyre, M. Zago, and F. Lacquaniti (1999) Viewer-centered and body-centered frames of reference in direct visuomotor transformations, *Exp. Brain Res.* 129(2), 201–210.

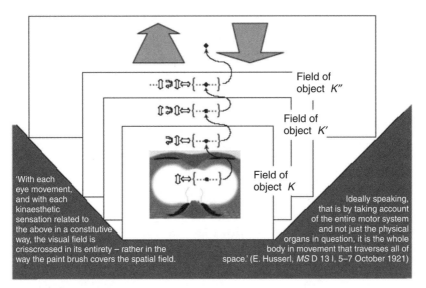

'With each eye movement, and with each kinaesthetic sensation related to the above in a constitutive way, the visual field is crisscrossed in its entirety – rather in the way the paint brush covers the spatial field.

Ideally speaking, that is by taking account of the entire motor system and not just the physical organs in question, it is the whole body in movement that traverses all of space.' (E. Husserl, *MS* D 13 I, 5–7 October 1921)

Fig. 3 Infinite constitution: the schema shown evokes the open character of complete kinaesthetic constitution with, in an order of ever-increasing complexity (suggested by a staging of the planes in perspective), the different fields of objects constituted thanks to the bringing into play of the different kinaesthetic systems developed by the body of the perceiving subject. The thick arrows refer back to the categories of possible movement in each kinaesthetic system; the full stops in brackets refer to the objects (or proto-things) at each level of complexity, established exclusively through the constitutive operations available to each kinaesthetic system; the S-shaped arrows refer to the constituted objects in a given field of objects to the relevant domain of kinaesthesia, in so far as the latter are associated with a field of objects of a higher order of complexity. These arrows are indicative of the initiation of a new kinaesthetic system in the process of constitution. The 'closed world', a constitutive product of each kinaesthetic system, is thereby opened up upon the infinite universe of classical science. This opening is inscribed in the perspective of just such a progressive mobilization of more and more complex constitutive operations, except that the idealization productive of an abstract space intervenes as the 'catastrophic' event which, while freeing this space for a new theoretical approach, conceals the underlying constitutive operations that have made this idealization possible in the first place (large, thick arrows on top of image).

Finally (Figure 3), it is time to move on to establish the continuity (or the interweaving) between the different kinaesthetic systems and the fields of objects constituted by the activation of each one of them. On the basis of a initial 'primary' field of objects (K) constituted thanks to shifts in gaze or saccades, an extension of K to the fields K', K'' … becomes possible. This extension is made up of objects the constitution of which calls upon the resources of ever more powerful kinaesthetic systems. At the horizon of this progression, and featuring as the *act* which carries this process to its logical conclusion, the idealization of the 'physical' world then makes its appearance. It makes its appearance on the basis of an experience of the perceived world, an appearance made possible by an action that the above-mentioned idealization reduces to the status of forgotten sedimentary layers of our familiar 'image of the world'.

Husserl also added that, even if the exploration of objects in the world is carried out with the eyes or the hands alone, it is the whole body that is involved in the process. He wrote: 'With each movement of the eyes and each kinaesthetic act operating within it in a constitutive manner, the visual field is shifted to and fro, as a whole, like the brush of the painter painting the spatial field. Ideally, and taking account of the complete motor system rather than the physical organs, the whole own body, while moving, explores infinite space.'[37]

The continuity of the common kinaesthetic operations of our everyday life, thus reformulated theoretically, is based upon the fact that the object (the proto-object) constituted by a primary kinaesthetic system (for example, the oculomotor system) is reproduced in constitutive operations of a second system (the cephalomotor system) which, in turn, promotes this object to a 'higher' level of constitution (the somatomotor system). And so it goes on in an unlimited extension of the practical intentional field inhabited by 'objects', better of objectivities that are ever richer in objective determinations. In this way the two-dimensional quasi-object of our example (what gets constituted through a purely visual constitution) gets re-constituted as three-dimensional, and it is this three-dimensional objectivity that becomes the material thing. In turn, the thing becomes the bearer of various practical values: for example, as a tool. And we should not forget that a symbolic praxis founded on the conventions peculiar to different human societies also gets grafted onto the kinaesthetic praxis, thereby giving rise to new fields of objectivities for an ever more extended kinaesthetic-symbolic constitution: works of art and other institutional values.

From the field to space

Our kinaesthetic theory of constitution says that objective space is the correlate of the totality of the body's motor activity; not just the movements actually carried out, but also those due to innate or acquired aptitudes, without overlooking the way in which their motor activity is enriched by our culture. This view of things rests on a critique of a naïve theory of perception

---

[37] E. Husserl, D 13 I, 5–7 October 1921.

in the empirical tradition of Locke, Berkeley, Hume, etc., a theory according to which perception is a sort of bombardment of our sensory receptors by elementary atoms of information, a cloud of incoming data which, as in modern formalist theories, would then later be structured by logical thought. Our critique, inspired by Husserl, assumes that the source of perception is not to be sought in such elementary data, such informational quanta but rather, and from the very outset, in *fields*. The spatiality of things in perceived space does not precede these things, as if it were an indifferent physical container; it enters into their very constitution from the outset. The thing is a concretion of the subjective process through which it is spatialized, a phenomenological thesis close to Gestalt theory.

For Husserl,[38] everything that reaches us from the external world presents itself to us in such a way that it is both the deployment of a form and the saturation of this form by content. This morphology is that of a field, a concept which, for him, is more fundamental than that of *space*. It is more fundamental—that is, more primitive—as are topological structures compared with those of Euclidian geometry.

Regarding these primary topological spaces, remember that all that is required is that they should possess certain very general properties: compactness, connectedness, the separability of their points by vicinities, etc. And that they should keep these properties despite certain deformations, provided alone that the latter are continuous and can accommodate stretching, bending, and folding; but not being torn apart or fused into a collage. In addition to these general properties, the figures of Euclidean geometry also have to be furnished with a more specific metric structure making possible a measurement of the distances between points and the angles between lines, the latter having an orientation defined in relation to the axes of some system of coordinates.

That being the case, no wonder that the child grasps first of all, as Piaget has shown,[39] the topological properties of objects and of space and only later their Euclidean properties! This means that it should be possible—this is the whole point of a theory of the transcendental constitution, more broadly, of a psychological genesis of space[40]—to get back to this more fundamental structure

---

38 See E. Husserl (1907) *Thing and Space. Lectures from 1907*, trans. R. Rojcewirz (ed.), Kluwer, Dordrecht, but also the manuscripts on the kinaesthetic theory as summarized by Jean-Luc Petit, a summary of which is downloadable from www.chez.com/jlpetit.

39 J. Piaget and B. Inhelder (1948) *La représentation de l'espace chez l'enfant*, Presses Universitaires de France, Paris.

40 Let us skip, for the time being, the difference between these two approaches, even if it is not that small!

and, from there, and proceeding in stages, to see how the perceiving subject can 'move from field space to ordinary space'. The kinaesthetic theory of the constitution of the meaning of being, of the 'spatial thing' on the basis of a series of field profiles and of kinaesthetic activations, gets quite close to a genetic psychology of the formation of the concept of space in the child.

At the very least it has to be said that these two approaches are not incompatible, even at the level of sensorial receptivity, a structuring capacity which is not just passive receptivity makes itself known. This corresponds to what in neurophysiology, for example, goes by the name of a *map*. That is, all the sensorial captors, or almost all of them, are organized with a topology, or rather a 'topy' (retino-topy, somato-topy, tono-topy), which in turn calls for a theory in itself, since it seems that the visual system, for example, analyses space according to a Riemanian[41] or affine and not Euclidean, geometry. Furthermore, this is probably a general property that also concerns motor control. Structural properties are already to be found in the analysis and even in the system responsible for the analysis.

We mentioned earlier[42] the spatial filterings and abstract constructions that are operative in the visual system right down to the lowest sensorial levels. Phenomenological analysis recommends that we take note of the crucial role played in perception by those mechanisms that pre-organize and pre-structure the apprehension of this data.

All the same, the *concept of a map is too poor* to do justice to what really happens in perceptual analysis. We now know that these somato-sensorial motor maps of the cerebral cortex can be very rapidly modified in the course of experience.[43] There is no such thing as a stable *homunculus*, as was supposed for some time. Even the hippocampus, the place in the brain where something like a 'spatial map' does get set up, can be modified by experience. The hippocampus of taxi drivers is different from that of the rest of us.[44] This very plasticity of the maps suggests that they have less to do with the representation

---

[41] Jean Petitot is working out the required geometry to describe the structure of the Husserlian field of perceptual constitution in terms of bi-dimensional, multi-layered Riemanian manifolds. He himself refers to J.J. Koenderinck (1984) The structure of images, *Biol. Cybernetics* 50, 363–370. See J. Petitot (1999) The eidetic morphology of perception, in J. Petitot *et al.* (eds), *Naturalizing Phenomenology: Issues in Contemporary Phenomenology and Cognitive Science*, Stanford University Press, Stanford, CA, Chap. 10, pp. 427–484.

[42] See Chapter 3 in this volume on the mechanisms of anticipation.

[43] See the bibliography of Michael Merzenich and his team, Chapter 4, footnote 65.

[44] E.A. Maguire *et al.* (2000) Navigation-related structural change in the hippocampi of taxi drivers, *Proc. Natl. Acad. Sci. USA* 97(9), 4414–4416.

of the anatomical body than with the material engrammation of the experience of the individual. So the lived flux, as that which expands (*Ausdehnung*, expansion, from *dehnen*, to expand), should not be fixed within rigid topographical frontiers. Rather, the persistent use made of the concept of *the map* is accompanied by a continual remodelling of the latter. It is now accepted that the geometry of maps is not necessarily Euclidean, despite the fact that Poincaré found the latter more practical! We have just appealed to the possibility that the visual system, as also perhaps the motor system, might turn out to be making use of principles arising from affine geometry.[45]

The importance of movements

Our *theory of constitution is also a radical motor theory* (as is, for example the pre-motor theory of attention developed by Rizzolatti and Gallese)[46] linking the emergence of perceived things with eye movements, but without attempting to reduce them to these ocular movements since, reduced in this way, these things would certainly no longer be the ordinary things with which we are familiar. They would not be things that resist, in particular, if only because the movements of our eyes are not enough to convince us that things cannot interpenetrate, slide into each other, or even telescope (like phantoms!). In this respect, it is the use of our hands that is most convincing (without forgetting the movement of our feet and of our entire body in so far as the latter is required to move up to and around and beyond things).

The importance of a radical motor theory of perception can be measured by the fact that it does not have to rely upon mental representation, as do most of the theories that present themselves as motor theories. Obviously, the word motor should not be reduced to the idea of muscles. This is why we prefer the term kinaesthesia and why we have given the name kinaesthetic memory to the memory of paths relying upon egocentric route mechanisms.[47] For the same reason it also becomes clear that the expression sensori-motor is not enough.

---

45 D.G. Liebermann *et al.* (2006) Intrinsic joint kinematic planning, *Exp. Brain Res.* 171(2), 139–173; T. Flash and B. Hochner (2005) Motor primitives in vertebrates and invertebrates, *Curr. Opin. Neurobiol.* 15(6), 660–666; O. Faugeras *et al.* (2004) Variational, geometric, and statistical methods for modeling brain anatomy and function, *Neuroimage* 23 (suppl. 1), S46–S55.

46 G. Rizzolatti and V. Gallese (1998) Mechanisms and theories of spatial neglect, in F. Boller and J. Grafman (eds), *Handbook of Neuropsychology*, vol. 1, Elsevier, Amsterdam, pp. 223–246.

47 See A. Berthoz *et al.* (2001) Bases neurales de l'orientation spatiale et de la mémoire des trajets: mémoire topographique ou mémoire topo-kinesthésique? *Revue neurologique* 157(8–9), 779–789.

Indeed, it would be better to say motor-sensorial in order to get closer to our idea that it is the intention to move that guides perception.

As Poincaré understood only too well, if fully spatial things *exist for us*, it is because we are capable of bringing into play (mentally anticipating) an entire series of movements, movements we become aware of through our kinaesthesiae at the very time that we carry them out. This is the basic principle underlying our analysis. We will already have accomplished a great deal by managing to establish as much as this at this point, and despite the on-going tendency of common sense (including the common sense of the scientific community) to presuppose things already existing 'out there' in physical space, with a view to introducing perception later on and so examining the activities of the perceiving subject in such a way as to render intelligible the internal representation of external objects.

But it is clear that the theory of constitution does not stop there. Between this principle and its final goal, the bringing to light of the subjective activities responsible for the constitution of *a world* endowed with meaning for those subject for whom this world is the domain of intervention and interaction, a great deal of empirical research is needed, research guided by the phenomenological description of lived experience.

Imagination: unfulfilled perception

In the schema of kinaesthetic constitution, and within each phase of a sequence of adumbrations, we now need to introduce the Husserlian concept of a superimposition (*Deckung*) of the actual series by all the alternative possible series. All that has been represented hitherto on Figure 2 has been the actual series leading from one adumbration to the next, because we placed ourselves in the best possible case, where the expectation is positively satisfied. We expect to see an object, the object presents itself, and we recognize it. But of course, the possibility of deception can never be excluded. Our expectations can be frustrated, even negated. If the unexpected is not to throw us into abysmal perplexity, it is because we know perfectly well that an expectation is not necessarily satisfied, and that it can always be revised, that we can always change our mind.

What now has to be introduced is the idea that in each of these successive phases of the process shown on Figure 2 there is a superimposition of states (an expression taken from quantum mechanics can be taken over here to advance the cause of phenomenology), by which we mean the unfolding of multiple expectations that are not necessarily compatible. At the level of the underlying neuronal systems, the neurosciences have shown that certain areas of the brain are particularly implied in this type of process, during a financial game for instance, and so intervene in the comparison between one expectation and the result obtained. This is the case with the anterior cingular cortex, an area of the frontal cortex at the interface between the part of the brain responsible for emotions and the attribution of value, the cognitive brain, and the brain responsible for action[48]

To clarify what we mean by superimposition let us take an example that goes back to Locke.[49] Imagine a ball turning around on itself. The subject viewing the ball expects that it remains smooth and uniform in its revolution but is not catastrophically surprised—because this remains in accord with his expectations—if, instead of the other side of the ball being of one uniform colour, there is a patch of a different colour. Moreover, this could also help to explain the fact that the patch is not spontaneously perceived as a hole in the ball but as a stain, an addition, or at least an interruption with regard to a basically uniform colour. For the subject implicitly maintains its initial expectation relative to the uniformity of the colouration and texture and simply *superimposes* upon it the unexpected event: a patch.

Or again, and this is perhaps a more meaningful case, suppose that the ball is actually dented in that part of its surface that is not initially visible. Well, as soon as the dented side is revealed, the dents as well as any other inequalities of its surface are integrated as if the latter fulfilled (in that sense of perceptual fulfilment studied in psychological literature with regard to examples like the Kanizsa triangle) an expectation proceeding from the subject, even though this was not his normal expectation in as much as the latter assumed that it would remain smooth over its entire surface.

Seen in this light, an ideally satisfactory schema for the constitution of an object should be capable of indicating that, in its intentional directedness, the first series of adumbrations, those that are effectively given to the perceiving subject in and through the sensing process, can always be continued by new series of adumbrations. In particular, those new series of adumbrations that are not given us through the channel of our sensory organs, but are given through 'imaginary variations' (a name presumably chosen by Husserl in tribute to Weierstrass, his mathematics professor at Berlin University, the famous 'lawmaker of analytical functions theory'). So, on top of the constantly changing aspects of a looming object in the visual field, we superimpose a new

[48] See P. Luu *et al.* (2000) Medial frontal cortex in action monitoring, *J. Neurosci.* 20, 464–469; B.J. Casey *et al.* (1997) A developmental functional MRI study of the prefrontal activation during performance of a go/no go task, *J. Cog. Neurosci.* 9, 835–847; H. Gemba *et al.* (1986) 'Error' potentials in limbic cortex (anterior cingulate area 24) of monkeys during motor learning, *Neurosci. Lett.* 70, 223–227.

[49] See J. Locke (1690/1961) *An Essay concerning Human Understanding* I., Everyman's Library, London.

layer of change, a change governed by our ability to move ourselves in non-sensory, virtual spaces.

The phases of the exploration of a landscape give different adumbrations and, in the transition from one to the other, variations arise: variations that are usually slight, with underlying constancies. This line of variation can of course be prolonged with, in the case of visual exploration at successive moments of lived time, sensory material for its content. But it can also take place, moreover continually does take place, in the absence of such a sensory material and so in an imaginative space where the object continues to be varied along the same line of variation. This is precisely what is meant by Shepard and Cooper's 'mental rotation',[50] what happens when the object itself rotates or when one changes one's point of view *vis-à-vis* the object (of course there are other mental movements aside from rotation). An imaginative and active, therefore not sensory, component is included in sensory perception itself.[51] Perception can simply ignore the variation (change blindness)[52] or remain open to it imaginatively.

....

[50] Mental rotation: the fact that in order to change the orientation of a mental image of an object the increased time required is as much as the angular disparity between two successive images is greater. See L.A. Cooper (1975) Mental rotation of random two-dimensional shapes, *Cog. Psychol.* 7, 20–43; L.A. Cooper and R.N. Shepard (1973) Chronometric studies of the rotation of mental Images, in W.G. Chase (ed.), *Visual Information Processing*, Academic Press, New York, pp. 75–176; R.N. Shepard and J. Metzler (1971) Mental rotation of three dimensional objects, *Science* 171, 701–703; J. Metzler and R.N. Shepard (1974) Transformational studies of the internal representation of three-dimensional objects, in R.L. Solso (ed.), *Theories of Cognitive Psychology: The Loyola Symposium*, Lawrence Erlbaum, Potomac, pp. 147–202.

[51] It would be interesting to develop the figure 2 further by taking the four last rectangles and finding a way to show two things. First, internalization, the fact that little by little we attain what is generally called 'representation' but which we prefer to call mental simulation or emulation. The word representation must not be employed too early since representation presupposes a detachment and an objectification of the constitutive sketches, whereas here we develop them from within. As soon as I form a representation, I am able to take account of it in and for itself, and it immediately becomes a new object, whose relation to the perceived object is eminently problematic. But even while immersed in experience we can still simulate objects mentally, a process of internalization that might be represented in the image, or simulated through a species of animation. On the subject of mental imagery, see S.M. Kosslyn (1996) *Image and Brain. The Resolution of the Imagery Debate*, MIT Press, Cambridge, MA.

[52] See: A. Berthoz (2003) *La décision*, Odile Jacob, Paris, p. 197; J.K. O'Regan and A. Noe (2001) What it is like to see: a sensorimotor theory of perceptual experience, *Behav. Brain Sci.* 24(5), 883–917; J.K. O'Regan et al. (1999) Change blindness as a result of mud-splashes, *Nature* 398(6722), 34; R. Reinsink et al. (1997) To see or not to see, the need for attention to perceive change in scenes, *Psychol. Sci.* 8(5), 368–373.

The range and variety of adumbrations, as we explained, are constitutive of the object. Thanks to them an object 'is given'. However, this variable material is made up of lived experiences that are 'fulfilled', for instance actually given sensations and images, but also of *empty perceptions*. When we explore a landscape, we restrict ourselves to taking samples. We do not bother to run through the continuous development of all the aspects of the landscape, nor to envisage all the parts of the surface of an object. We place our trust in the 'thing itself', or the perception through which it is given. Seeing a box, we assume that it has an inside, or rather, nobody is ready to suppose that it does not have one. A constant imaginative projection feeds the continuity of the intentional arrow as it goes through its adumbrations. There is therefore a continual interweaving of just such an imaginative activity with the sensing activity.

This is what can be read into Figure 2 from the fact that one does not see a continuous arrow filling out the still empty intention, the intention that has not yet been filled with the presence of the thing, with the object in its complete givenness. We preferred to suggest that each adumbration refers across itself to the next adumbration, and from within the same variety. Thus, the sketch of an object that is still far off, murky, unclear, difficult to discern, and whose details we still cannot make out, attracts us, guides us and refers us through itself toward a more precise view in which the aspect that interests us gets unfolded.

The intentionality that links up the adumbrations is therefore not a single arrow but a series made up as much of fragmented arrows as of adumbrations, arrows which never cease to project their several senses towards the unifying pole of the 'thing', and which, by the same token, trace out in advance the path of a single and complete intentional arrow. These referential arrows sit astride both the real and the virtual, what is effectively given and what is not given but only anticipated. It is this constant reference of one of the adumbrations towards the others which makes it possible for us to orient our mind towards the object directly in the present, which means that the *imaginary is also constantly present*, for there are always new gaps to fill.

A kinaesthetic theory of consciousness?

The problem of consciousness is nowadays a major preoccupation of neuroscience and of 'neuro-philosophers'. Although this question is not central to our purpose here we can offer some suggestions, and essentially this is that neither Husserl nor we ourselves (nor a number of many recent neurophysiological theories about consciousness) set out from anything like 'a consciousness in general', something that would float in a vacuum. Neither of us is interested in anything like *the* object, something that would confront this consciousness and that the latter would have to assimilate by interiorizing it, or which it would have to rejoin by somehow managing to get out of itself. This eidetics only concerns *conscious lived-experience*: an expression that almost has to be taken as a whole, and in which the term consciousness figures as a *syncategorematic* term (as medieval logicians used to say); that is, a term that is meaningless outside the context of the other terms with which it forms a *unity*.

To stay with perception, eidetic analysis has a programme, which consists of differentiating the complete system of structural regularities responsible for organizing the experience of a perceiving subject. To carry out this programme, no other consciousness is required than that immersed (like a fish in water!) in its own lived experience and which constantly lives through the very descriptive characteristics it describes. In as much as they are conscious, these lived experiences are not inert, like images, for example, but are dynamically oriented. They are not closed in upon themselves like mental objects ('pebbles in consciousness' as Sartre remarked ironically), but open to the things given by means of them across the relevant series of adumbrations. As a result, the priority accorded to *lived experience*, which itself lies at the root of any rigorously developed phenomenology of conscious processes, makes available to us an economical way of presenting this phenomenology, one that only makes use of those concepts that are strictly operational (naturalizable in neuroscience) in the analysis of the phenomena of perceptual experience.

What conscious experiences are implied by the event of perception? These are lived experience of the 'I can freely change what I am looking at' (an experience every perceiving subject will admit); such experiences as 'beyond the limit of a certain maximum of tension' (experienced by me), 'I can't turn my eyes further to the left, or to the right, or further upward, or downward', or again 'I always try to bring things into focus (*fovea*), where they are clear and distinct'. We are all familiar with experiences like those described in such expressions as: 'in being brought closer, things get detached from their background, while things that move away from me—or from which I move myself away—disappear into the horizon' (a paradigm of phenomenological description). Or again experiences like: 'I see the several aspects of the object in walking around it'. This implies that, in a certain sense, it assumes the plurality of its aspects and so becomes a voluminous object, a body in the geometrical sense, to the extent that I walk around it. For it is in this way I prove to myself that it really is an object and not just a facade. With experiences like those expressed by the words: 'I begin to feel the contours of the object when I pick it up and manipulate it', the tactile qualities of the object, its resistance to pressure, *its materiality*, begin to make themselves known, in as much as they resist and obstruct me.

In a word, we are talking about the totality of the forms of 'conscious apprehension' as and how they are apprehended in and through these experiences, in as much as the perceiving subject is constantly immersed in these experiences, and therefore in as much as they are not artificial or virtual mental states reconstructed in the representational space of a theoretical hypothesis. All these lived experiences assume the same form: 'I can do A', or 'I am doing A'. They are the explicit (and eventually the linguistic) expression of possible ways of employing our body. To clarify such experiences calls for a practical not a theoretical operation, an operation through which each subject can, by practising them himself, actually convince himself that he has them. Normally, these ways of using our body are available to us without our knowing about it (the *habitus* Pierre Bourdieu borrowed from Husserl). The sense in which we are prepared to call them conscious is rather that referred to above and not that in which they are taken (by the theoretician) to be 'conscious representations in our minds' without our actively contributing anything to them.

So what is consciousness, exactly? Consciousness, or conscious processes, at least for a theory that strives to be genuinely kinaesthetic along the lines of the model developed by the kinaesthetic theory of later Husserl, is the *totality of all those diverse modes in which the perceiving subject is able to make use of its body as the organ of its cognitive and practical intentions.*[53] But this is only— and this is the crucial point—to the extent that the bringing into play of these various ways of *using the body* contributes to the conscious perception of things. *Without the body in act nothing could be given to us to know.* Without our intervention as agents, the world would be devoid of objects. This is what has not been taken into account by those theoreticians of the mind who want nothing to do with consciousness, *in as much as it is actually lived*, and with the body, in as much as it is *the incarnation of consciousness.*

According to a recent theory developed by Dehaene and Changeux,[54] the appearance of consciousness is linked to the existence of a central network, a *global workspace* reuniting the different sensori-motor modules thanks to cortical neurons linking different parts of the cortex. By contrast, the theory developed by Llinas[55] sees the emergence of consciousness as being due to the activation, in parallel, of circuits linking the thalamus, the cortex, and the

---

[53] See the manuscript material devoted to the theory of kinaesthesia in the posthumous writings of Husserl, held in the Husserl Archives at Paris. A detailed résumé can be found on the personal website of Jean-Luc Petit (www.chez.com/jlpetit).

[54] See S. Dehaene *et al.* (1998) A neuronal model of a global workspace in effortful cognitive tasks, *Proc. Natl. Acad. Sci. USA* 95, 14529–14534.

[55] See R. Llinás (2001) *I of the Vortex*, MIT Press, Cambridge, MA.

basal ganglia. These two theories stand in a sort of perpendicular relation to each other. One emphasizes the cortico-cortical connections, the other, like Penfield earlier, the cortico-centrencephalic connections. But both of them share an advantage over other theoretical models in that they anchor the emergence of consciousness in perception–action processes. The future will determine which of them is right or whether they are in fact complementary.[56]

The problem with theories like these is that none of them takes account of what we have called the living of the experience, which does not mean that they cannot be brought to do so. Any and every theoretical model will eventually have to take account of the essential role played by structural regularities in the lived experience of a perceiving subject—a role which we, along with other phenomenologists, have already acknowledged, and which we hope to get others to appreciate more fully. Becoming conscious, or being conscious, has to be associated with the emergence of those invariants described by psychologists.

We propose that consciousness is part of the prediction mechanisms built up over the course of evolution. For example, we expect that a line figuring on an object gets prolonged, without deviating to the right or to the left, upwards or downwards. Let us suppose that we happen to realize that it is in fact prolonged in one uniform direction. This is however only one of several possibilities. *Being conscious of an object might depend upon our predicting the invariance of a property of the object, and to the eventuality of such a prediction being confirmed. It is at this crossroad between the hypotheses of the subject and what is contributed by its interaction with the world that consciousness arises.* But up until now, we have only mentioned one of the aspects of what should or could be called consciousness. 'All consciousness is consciousness of something'. This sentence taken from Husserl, has been repeated time and time again, often without much awareness of what it implies. In fact this formula imposes an extremely strong constraint upon the legitimate use of the word consciousness in phenomenology. Whoever makes use of it should always bear in mind that consciousness is not normally (what it does indeed become in the technical language of the theoreticians) an absolutely referential (or designative) term, a term that can be employed in discourse independently of any context, but must be used in such a way that a context is *always* presupposed, a context into which the subject is plunged, and this because it expresses a dimension of lived experience.

---

56 See also V.S. Ramachandran (1998) Consciousness and body image: lessons from phantom limbs, Capgras syndrome and pain asymbolia, *Phil. Trans. R. Soc. Lond. Ser. B Biol. Sci.* 353(1377), 1851–1859.

In this way, consciousness is bound up with each and every attentional operation. On the occasion of our becoming conscious of something, a quite peculiar phenomenon takes place, and which makes it possible for someone sitting in a room to be suddenly conscious of, for example, an ornament he never really saw five seconds earlier, even though he was looking at it. This phenomenon results from the fact that, all of a sudden, *we project the idea*—a pre-formed idea or *noema*—of a statue, dragged out of the recesses of our brain, from our memory, from our intentions, and that this guiding idea (this *noesis* with the *noema* belonging to it) encounters an object corresponding to it, and which is either 'similar or not similar'.

All that has now to be determined is why, all of a sudden, I project this idea. The structure of our lived experience, with its depth of memory, makes it possible for us to switch from an attitude in which we allow our glance to float without fixing upon any particular object because, precisely, at that very moment we are not envisaging any *noema*, to an attitude in which we get interested in an object, which thereby gets detached from its background. This background is commanded by the structure of a horizon, whose originally affective rather than cognitive character Husserl was more than ready to concede, since in order to come to terms with it he developed a theory of 'pulsional intentionality'.[57]

Physiologists and psychologists will be tempted to sum up what has just been said with the single expression, selective attention. Does this mean that consciousness is nothing other than what is called in psychology and neuro-physiology selective attention? Talk about attention explains nothing, gives us no hypotheses capable of coming to terms with the mechanisms making it possible for us to have this curious impression that the thing our attention is drawn to suddenly acquires a conscious value: 'This has become your object! The world has become your own!' For the brain has to contain mechanisms which account for the fact that, even without shifting one's eyes (motor theory of attention), even without looking in another direction, we can attend to this thing rather than another.[58]

On the other hand, the theory of intentionality, a theory designed to deploy an entire system of variations, of adumbrations, etc., tries to get us to understand not the underlying mechanisms (this is not its task) but the multiple and complementary activities demanded of a perceiving subject when he

---

[57] This at a time when psychoanalysis was far from being acceptable in university teaching! See N.-I. Lee (1993) *Edmund Husserls Phänomenologie der Instinkte*, Kluwer, Dordrecht.

[58] See the theory of attentional searchlight: F. Crick and C. Koch (1990) Some reflections on visual awareness, *Cold Spring Harbour Symp. Quant. Biol.* 55, 953–962.

becomes convinced that there is there in front of him not an illusion or a phantom but a truly real three-dimensional object.

A phenomenology in search of ontology?

But this is still not enough to show how we move from kinaesthetic sensations to things as real beings. We have to understand how we get from a motor theory of perception to an *ontology*, a theory of subsisting beings (*ontology*: from *on*: being, participle of the verb *einai*: to be; and *logos*: speech or theory). It is a matter of the first importance that there should be such a move, for without it our kinaesthetic theory of constitution would remain a constitutional theory without any constituted objects, a theory without anything to theorize about.

What is ontology? It is the theory of 'all that there is'. It is often held that phenomenology and ontology are opposed to each other. The former would be nothing more than the theory of *what appears*, the latter alone the theory of *what is*.

Since speaking subjects habitually employ a certain vocabulary in their discussions with each other, it has become usual to try to establish the universe of objects relating to their job or personal life or religious beliefs and ceremonies, that particular universe to which they are referring when they employ this vocabulary. For example, if we are employing the language of the furniture maker, the relevant vocabulary will include words like table, chair, dowel, and mortise. If, on the other hand, words like star, black hole, quasar, and telluric exoplanet are employed, we know we are in the realm of astronomy and will be referring to a universe of objects quite different from the first.

Certainly, possessing an ontology is something more than just using a dictionary, since it enables us to gain access to the referents of the words found in this dictionary and gives us the right to make up an inventory of available entities, of entities given in a correspondingly appropriate way. Having an ontology is a matter of having a system of *objects bearing properties* and which can be described simply because they find expression in a certain language.

In the same way, when the mathematician talks of Lie groups and already even when he talks in general of mathematical objects, he (unless he is a formal logician) certainly does not want to raise the question of whether his way of using words makes it possible for him to identify in the universe of objects something like a triangle, a circle, or a square. This is not his problem, so little so that each day he enriches his lexicon with new metaphors referring to still unnamed objects: a luxurious tropical forest from the standpoint of this amateur of desert landscapes, his colleague the logician! For his own part, the mathematician holds to the convention that if he gets involved in elementary geometry, from that moment on he will have his circles, his conic section, his cords, etc.

Similarly, a physiologist will discuss consciousness with words like neurons, glia, dopamine, synchrony, and oscillations. He will admit into his universe of discourse networks, connections, branchings, etc. The objects that appear in the world of the geometrician do not appear in the world of the physiologist and vice versa. Nobody will be bothered by this. However, in its being tightly linked to those who make use of each such type of discourse, this vernacular ontology cannot satisfy the one who asks: 'What is there, really?' without any further specification. This is the ontological question itself, once again.

The phenomenological theory of the intentionality of consciousness, a theory that tackles things themselves from the standpoint of what a perceiving consciousness knows about them, seeks to restore to perception that very ontological dimension it possesses naturally for the subject, a subject to which 'genuinely real' entities appear in a number of different ways, visually, through touch, haptically, to the extent that these same subjects move their eyes, touch with their hands, move their limbs.

To prevent any misunderstanding, it should be noted that there are *two ontologies*: the ordinary ontology that draws no conclusions because it is simply taken for granted that if we want to mean something by what we say we have to agree with our interlocutor regarding the domain of objects in question. This vernacular ontology comes to a dead end faced with the enormous question of determining how *there can be* objects for us independent of the fact that we do, or do not, have access to them. Beneath this shallow ontology we therefore have to bring to light a deep ontology. Husserl was perfectly well aware of this. 'This system of access to beings (brought about by kinaesthesia) does not provide us with access to something that might also be conceivable without any such access being possible.'[59]

Things constituted in and through our perceptive activity are such that the very idea of detaching them from our mode of access to them in such acts is quite simply unthinkable. For how could it possibly make sense to refer to things of such a kind that we could never have access to them?

To constitute is not to construct. Objective things are given to us in and through those series of acts described in the above chapters as objectifying acts, acts which are not appropriative, interiorizing, subjectifying, etc., but which bring about the very reverse of any such 'subjectification', and as a result of which the object fully exists for the one dealing with it. The mathematician, the traditional logician, for instance Frege,[60] wants to suppress this question

---

[59] E. Husserl, D 10 I, May 1932, p. 24.

[60] G. Frege (1884) *Die Grundlagen der Arithmetik. Eine logisch mathematische Untersuchung über den Begriff der Zahl*, Wilhelm Koebner, Breslau; G. Frege (1892) über Sinn und Bedeutung, *Zeitschrift f. Philosophie u. Philos. Kritik* 100, 25–50.

from the start with one crushing blow, a crushingly Platonic blow. It is simply decreed that one is not going to get involved with the question of how we gain access to numbers (in his case). One simply has to admit that as soon as one uses digits, algebraical letters, etc., the corresponding numbers exist. Otherwise we should be capitulating to psychologism, allowing the objects that interest the mathematician to be dissolved in the 'psychological wash-pot'.[61]

How do we understand that in and through certain modes of access Husserl calls 'modes of givenness', we are actively related to things which, we admit, are certainly not created by us? The question is too serious for our answer to be postponed. Let us try to determine straight away what Husserl meant by 'givenness'.

A plea for givenness

Why use the word, givenness? The justification of this term givenness (outside its usage by Husserl) is that it now becomes necessary to situate ourselves at a level that not only interests the physiologist but also the physicist and even the anthropologist, the level of a general (non-specific) ontology devoted to 'whatever is'. Givenness has to do with the way in which an object that exists in and for itself comes to be manifest for someone who gets to know it. Givenness also has to do with the organized totality of those constitutive operations thanks to which a subject is capable of giving itself an object. This terminology was introduced to resist the fixational temptations associated with the term sense data, which signifies that the object is simply what is there. However, a configuration in a visual field is not really data, far from it. For what are required so that it should exist are visual activities, the activity of gazing in order that some appearing thing acquire a stable form. So the word data is the end result of a process that has been brutally reified. The term givenness is more interesting on account of its progressive character (remember what was said earlier about the succession of intentional and perceptual apprehensions), this active disbursing of sense data across a certain duration in the life of the subject, all of which is evoked by this nominalization of an action word (to give; givenness). Something is given on the basis of nothing or, more exactly, on the basis of a sort of pre-phenomenal retention of what is not yet manifest. So givenness refers us back to an altogether more primary level. It is a matter of appreciating that objects, in so far as they support properties, even sense data, are not there from the first. They have to be elaborated. Terms like

---

[61] G. Frege (1894) Rezension von: E. G. Husserl Philosophie des Arithmetik I.', *Zeitschrift f. Philosophie u. Philos. Kritik* 100, 313–332.

elaborate, constitute, construct, and attribute designate this dynamic interaction between the subject and its world, a world which, for agents, is before all else their field of practical interaction. So these terms imply the same dynamic vocabulary.

Givenness saves us from a temptation inherent in transcendentalism: its excessive idealism. We are not talking about attributing to the subject the ability to create, from the ground up, an object that never existed before. What the subject contributes to the object is its *sense*. It has a sense for him, a sense that only emerges in relation to him, and this no matter what the nature of the object endowed with such a sense. Because any such object is the product of a living organism that has its habits, its desires, its needs, its filters, and its hypotheses on the world in which it lives, and so attributes properties *a priori* or at least seeks to find such properties in the external world. In fact, if there were nothing to support properties (substances), we would have no reason at all to attribute such properties. So there has to be something to which being green, being blue, being smooth, being hard, or being rough gets attributed.

The logical description of the world as it is rendered, in particular, by the advocates of analytical philosophy, assumes that there has always been an inventory of the world; that, quite simply, there has always been something: this, that, and the other thing. And that thanks to language we possess a repertory of attributions, of qualifying adjectives, of predicates, of functions, all of which become true by virtue of the fact that, here and there, the relevant things are to be found. All this works wonderfully well, except that it assumes the form of an *a posteriori* rational reconstruction of an experience often so ill-behaved as to refuse to conform to what is expected of it!

Chapter 7

The constitution of the own body

This is what distinguishes the body from all external things. On the one hand, the body of flesh and blood is also a thing, a physical thing like any other [...]. It is a thing among other things, having its changeable location amidst them [...]. On the other hand, this thing is precisely 'my own body' (*Leib*), what upholds my 'I'; the 'I' has sensations and these sensations are localized in the body, in part through thought, in part in a more immediately apparent way.

E. Husserl[1]

In this chapter we shall first explain why we have to ask the reader to consider in depth the problem of the body and more specifically our 'own body'.

From the description of lived experience to the constitution of its sense

A major difficulty for the working out of a theory of action consists of the fact that an essential part of the mechanism of control for movement and perception is completely inaccessible to consciousness. This is what explains, in part, the fact that one continues to recognize only five senses—vision, touch, smell, hearing, and taste—overlooking muscular and articular proprioception and the vestibulary system, which figure among the fundamental kinaesthetic senses; that is, that 'sense', or that 'knowledge', the body has of its own activity.[2]

---

[1] E. Husserl (1907) *Thing and Space. Lectures from 1907*, trans. R. Rojcewirz (ed.), Kluwer, Dordrecht.

[2] In the following list of publications, certain aspects of the role of the vestibular system will be found: A. Berthoz (1973) Contrôle vestibulaire des mouvements oculaires et des réactions d'équilibration, Doctoral Thesis, Faculté des Sciences, Paris; A. Berthoz (1978) Vision et système vestibulaire, *Encyclopaedia Universalis*, Paris, pp. 441–444; A. Berthoz

For we do 'know' where our hand is without having to watch it constantly and without having to be conscious of the fact that the 'sense of position' is given by specialized captors, and we do move our body without having to look around to know where it went. We take hold of a strawberry without crushing it and without even being aware that the 'sense of effort' is linked to particular captors and to a complex mechanism of integration that evaluates, predicts, and regulates the delicate force of our fingers. This ignorance of proprioception and the vestibulary system is also present in the oriental tradition. To be sure, Buddhists do identify six senses but the sixth is treated as the sense of consciousness.[3]

It is only when anomalies occur linked to cerebral lesions that can damage this fundamental structure and completely distort the experience that we become aware of the presence of the neuronal processing underlying our kinaesthesia. We can reach out for an object close at hand without having to fix it attentively in advance in order not to miss it, which again can happen when lesions disturb the nerve pathways commanding action or proprioception. We seize an object within reach without being obliged to target it carefully in order not to miss it. A ball thrown by someone is caught without it bouncing out from the palm of our hand, and this without our having to follow it attentively in its fall, something we can also do in the dark, provided

....

(1991) Reference frames for the perception and control of movement, in J. Paillard (ed.), *Brain and Space*, Oxford University Press, Oxford, pp. 81–111; A. Berthoz (1994) La Géométrie Euclidienne a-t-elle des fondements dans l'organisation des systèmes sensoriels et moteurs?, presented at 'Rationalité logique et intuition géométrique' held at the Ecole Normale Supérieure, Paris, 9–10 June 1994; A. Berthoz (1996) How does the cerebral cortex process and utilize vestibular signals, in R.W. Baloh and G.M. Halmagyi (ed.), *Disorders of the Vestibular System*, Oxford University Press, Oxford, pp. 113–125; A. Berthoz, W. Graf, and P.P. Vidal (1991) *The Head-Neck Sensorymotor System*, Oxford University Press, Oxford; A. Berthoz and G. Melvill Jones (eds) (1985) *Adaptive Mechanisms in Gaze Control. Reviews in Oculomotor Research*, Elsevier, Amsterdam; A. Berthoz, B. Pavard, and L. Young (1974) Rôle de la vision périphérique et interactions visuo-vestibulaire dans la perception exocentrique du mouvement linéaire chez l'homme, *C.R. Académie Sciences* 278, 1605–1608; A. Berthoz and D. Rousié (2001) Physiopathology of otolith-dependent vertigo. Contribution of the cerebral cortex and consequences of cranio-facial asymmetries, *Adv. Otorhinolaryngol.* 58, 48–67; A. Buizza *et al.* (1979) Otolothic acoustic interactions in the control of eye movement, *Exp. Brain Res.* 36, 509–522; I. Israël and A. Berthoz (1989) Contribution of the otoliths to the calculation of linear displacement, *J. Neurophysiol.* 62, 247–263; Y.P. Ivanenko *et al.* (1997) The contribution of otoliths and semicircular canals to the perception of two-dimensional passive whole-body motion in humans, *J. Physiol. (Lond.)* 502, 223–233.

[3] F.J. Varela, E. Thompson, and E. Rosch (1991) *The Embodied Mind: Cognitive Science and Human Experience*, MIT Press, Cambridge, MA.

that we know that the ball has been thrown. When we manipulate a small object between the thumb and index finger and apprehend it with precision we know automatically how to correlate and counterbalance the grip forces and the load forces exerted by our fingers on this object. This we can do without expending more energy than necessary and without letting it slip through our fingers by not trying hard enough, therefore with a margin of error well adapted to the circumstances of this action.

Moreover, if the object is unusually heavy or has an asymmetric mass, we are nevertheless immediately able to establish the balance of power needed to raise this object, without it overturning or falling. This is all part of our blind knowledge, of that implicit and immanent knowledge we all exercise in daily life. In a certain way, our hands know how to get around in surrounding space. Even in the dark we know whether what we are holding in both hands is a single object or two objects, and this only by virtue of the effort distributed between our haptic sense and the forces exerted on our hands by the object. In the same way, our hand immediately adjusts to a rigid surface along which we slide it, which makes it possible, for example, for us to find the keyhole of a door in the dark without too much difficulty, simply by sliding the key against the door.

Finally, we can follow a moving target with our finger, provided only that it moves in a predictable way. We can do this even in those phases of this periodic movement where we no longer see our finger, due to the fact that it is hidden behind a screen, or where the image of our finger is seen to deviate from its true trajectory, due to some laboratory device.

Another very important unconscious sensing process is performed by a brain structure called the superior colliculus. This contains a map of visual space connected to the retina. It controls eye and head movements but it is also involved in the rapid detection of moving objects. It participates in the anticipation of the trajectory of a moving object that we want to catch and plays an important role in 'blindsight'. In a previous book, we recorded the fact that so-called blind children could still play. Although they were incapable of reading letters, they could use their colliculus to catch moving objects: basket balls or ping pong balls. The neurophysiological properties of the neurons of the colliculus and their response to moving objects have been studied by Grantyn and Berthoz.[4]

In going over all these aspects of daily life we are not really going beyond a phenomenological description of experience in its structured character, an experience that is not indistinct but provided with its eidetic structure.

---

[4] A. Berthoz, A. Grantyn, and J. Droulez (1986) Some collicular efferent neurons code saccadic eye velocity, *Neurosci. Lett.* 23, 72(3), 289–294.

It is interesting to try and bring together what belongs to the order of a description of the lived experience of everyday life and which can be found in the writings of Merleau-Ponty, Sartre, Husserl, and others and what belongs to the objects of research of the neurophysiologist. The objects of one of the most sophisticated of contemporary sciences, the neurophysiology of motor activity—since each of the actions mentioned above are the object of research by teams comprising mathematicians, roboticists, imagery researchers, etc.— are nevertheless everyday gestures, belonging to the habitual repertory of the actions of any one of us. These aspects of the experience in question do not cease to be trivial just because researchers are interested in them, for they constitute a sort of mapping of all the moments, all the states making up the content of daily life; a repertory of actions which, in principle, can be extended indefinitely. The result is that we have to suppose that it can be progressively enriched and generalized to the point of recovering everything that makes up the experience of a life, the experience of an individual in its environment.

The step that now needs to be taken is the one that leads from a phenomenology of everyday life, just as it is lived out, to a much more ambitious theory, namely the theory of *the constitution of the meaning of the experienced world*. If we manage to draw up a repertory of those structural features which confer upon our lived experience its form—that is, its sense, for all lived experiences make sense to us—well, then we will be in a position to elucidate (without pretending to explain) why it is that, in the surrounding world of a perceiving subject, certain configurations of sensations get stabilized and appear as tables, and others get stabilized and appear as people, etc. In other words, everything that inhabits the world of an agent would emerge endowed with sense as a result of our identifying and distinguishing the different structural features that organize the experience.

In other words, regarding this experience one would now not only have a description without presuppositions, this description would be prolonged in a sort of genesis starting out from what confers sense upon experience, *the matrix of meaning* making up all the aspects of everyday life. From then on we should be in possession of a *constitutive* and not simply a descriptive, phenomenology. This is what it means to move from a description of experience to its constitution; that is to say, to an elucidation of what confers 'sense' upon this experience.

The senses of the word 'sense'

The true foundation of the work of the physiologist is the description of a repertory of behaviour covering the field of our interaction with the world. The familiar availability of this repertory of behaviour might give us the impression that we benefit from an intuition or knowledge of the external world that guides our acts, making it possible to accomplish them even when there are no sensorial inputs.

Is the physiologist prepared to introduce sense[5] into his description of action? And how should this term be understood? To answer this question it would be worth concentrating on one or other of the aspects where the passage from action to sense[6] becomes most evident. From a phenomenological point of view, the sense is 'that towards which I am intentionally oriented'. More exactly or more technically,[7] it forms the noematic correlate of a noetic act: the *noema* of a *noesis* (from the verb *noein*: to think).

Let us translate this into the slightly less exotic terms of signification. Signification is always arrived at across a reduction retaining only the biological aspect or the semantic aspect, or again the sociological aspect. By contrast, the *noema* is the signification taken in a sense that has not been reduced, the originary or proto-semantic signification (examples to follow hereafter). The legitimacy of such a notion makes it possible for us to talk of sense (or signification) with reference to those basic and constitutive acts on which the constitution of perceived things depends. These perceived things, just as soon as they are constituted in and through the acts of perceiving subjects, can eventually become the bearers of diverse significations: biological, semantic, and sociological. They are capable of eliciting our attention under one or other of these relations, as a function of our interests. In this way, any configuration of experience whatsoever, in so far as it is present as the goal of an intentionally directed act, would have a sense or be meaningful, or again, would make sense to us, in a given context of course.

In *The Brain's Sense of Movement*,[8] the ambivalence of the term sense was sufficiently underlined. The very title appeals to a play on words designed to

---

[5] An action and a description are necessarily endowed with sense. It does not follow from this that the sense the action has for the actor need feature as a theoretical object for the author of the description of this action. Nevertheless, this ought to be the case here, due to the perspective we have adopted, which implies a certain continuity between neurophysiology, even the biomechanics of movement, and the phenomenology of the experience of acting.

[6] The same holds as above: if the action has a sense, the transition in question does not have to apply.

[7] In the jargon of the philosopher, if you please. But we should not forget that a technical language is simply the language best adapted to the things it bears upon. There is no reason to deny philosophy a right that is regarded as perfectly legitimate in the sciences.

[8] See A. Berthoz (2000) *The Brain's Sense of Movement*, Harvard University Press, Cambridge, MA.

draw attention to the fact that the sense can be a sensorial captor, but also the directedness of a movement, or again the signification, the semantic character of a discourse. This title was chosen precisely to appeal to this three-fold meaning of the word sense, and this because a physiology of action needs to get beyond the traditional dichotomy: the physical (devoid of sense) and the semantic (endowed with sense). If you are suffering from Parkinsons's disease, your hand trembles. One has every reason to say that this movement is 'purely physical' since it expresses no particular intention to communicate on your part. If you hail a taxi, your hand moves again, but this time its movement has no other function than to express your intention to take a taxi. This time it functions as a sign, a physical movement bearing a certain semantic value (*semeion:* sign). In both cases there is a physical movement, to the extent that a body changes its location in space (translatory movement), but in the second case, this physical movement becomes something very mysterious since its physical aspect seems to disappear in favour of another, non-physical aspect, an aspect by virtue of which this movement could be inserted into a circuit of communication between humans. In effecting such a movement, I express something that someone else might possibly, though not necessarily, under-stand. The principal difficulty for the integration of sense[9] into the physiology of action is that one has to distinguish, and organize into a hierarchy, different levels in its mode of appearance.

Let us take as an example of a *first level* the notion of the identical object. If, with both eyes closed, we grab hold of a coffee cup with our thumb and index finger, we exert two kinds of pressure, a grasping pressure between the thumb and index finger and a lifting pressure with our whole arm. The highly predictable and anticipatory character of the regulation of these forces has been demonstrated in the laboratory, thanks to the manipulation of the con-ditions surrounding the prehension of a small object between the thumb and the index finger. Depending on whether the surface is rugged or slippery or whether the fingers are or are not anaesthetized the prehension will vary in effectiveness. The grasping force is a reflex released by the sensation of slip-ping; the lifting force brings into play a voluntary intention: the two forces work together to make the adjustments needed to accommodate the variable conditions of action. This is what has been discovered.[10]

---

[9] Same remark: unless, of course, the physiology of action is reduced to a simple biome-chanics of movement.

[10] G. Westling and R.S. Johansson (1984) Factors influencing the force control during pre-cision grip, *Exp. Brain Res.* 53(2), 277–284; and also, by the same team: G. Westling and R.S. Johansson (1987) Signals in tactile afferents from the fingers eliciting adaptive motor responses during precision grip, *Exp. Brain Res.* 66, 141–154; and A.M. Gordon et al. (1991) The integration of haptically acquired size information in the programming

But if one takes note of what the subject perceives of the identity of the object while lifting it one might be inclined to think that this identity is only possible if the efforts deployed by him are *concordant* (Husserl's expression). And one might be surprised to find that their concordance, or coherence as we would also say, requires that the *grasping force and the lifting force should be first de-correlated, and then re-correlated*. For the subjective experience of the agent, just as long as there is de-correlation, there are two objects or at any rate not one; so there is ambiguity. But as soon as a perfect correlation has been obtained, all of a sudden the object becomes for him self-identical: it has been 'identified'. On this basis, does it not make sense to say that what has been disclosed thereby is a tactilo-kinaesthetic foundation for the object's *sense* of being identical? No doubt the identity of the object does not depend exclusively upon the effectiveness with which it is grasped but, for all that, it certainly does owe a great deal to the latter. Here we are already obliged to recognize a minimal meaning of the word sense.

However important this correlation might be, the correlation that has to be established between different data captured by our sense organs somewhere in our cognitive circuits for it to be possible for us to identify an object as unique, such a correlation is not yet what grants full and complete signification to the object. At least, it does not suffice to determine whether this signification is already what any signification in general must be: 'for someone and in relation to something and to someone else.' Perhaps it is nothing more than the persisting trace of a physical-semantic dualism. But it is difficult to imagine how we can account for the emergence of something non-physical (because endowed with sense) by simply heaping physical conditions upon physical conditions.[11]

A *second level* at which sense makes its appearance can also be envisaged. It results from the variety of uses of an object taken to be unique (identified). Let's go back to the example of a cup used to drink coffee. A child who turned the cup upside-down could sit her doll on top of it. From that moment on, it becomes a miniature stool. Filled with water, a small fish could swim in it, and so it becomes an aquarium. This availability of objects, or tools, to be

of precision grip, *Exp. Brain Res.* 83, 483–488. The neuronal correlates of this dynamic adjustment of (peripheral) tactile kinaesthesia and the (internal) motor kinaesthesia in manual prehension have been more exhaustively examined by cellular recordings of the somato-sensory cortex in the monkey. I. Salimi et al. (1999) Neuronal activity in somatosensory cortex of monkeys using a precision grip. I. Receptive fields and discharge patterns, II. Responses to object texture and weights, III. Responses to altered friction perturbations, *J. Neurophysiol.* 81, 825–857.

[11] We cannot pretend here to have solved the 'quarrel of universals' as so beautifully described in the book by Alain de Libera: A. de Libera (1996) *La Querelle des Universaux de Platon à la fin du Moyen-Age*, Seuil, Paris.

assigned to different uses has been at the basis of the theories of Vygotski.[12] It is pretty obvious that the convergence or the coherence of the sensory data received as a result of actions like prehension is not sufficient to enable this coherence to achieve the status of a sense. There is a gulf due to a certain idea of signification as belonging to a higher level.

These two examples lead us to a fundamental notion: that of *levels of sense*. The different ways we use a cup (which confer upon it as many different senses)[13] could not subsist in my mind if the cup did not have a certain identity that can be, but is not necessarily, founded in its permanence. Permanence is too strong a condition for an identity that has to be sufficiently flexible to live through the series of variations or adumbrations (see Chapter 6). We know how important for the child is that stage in its development where it acquires the idea of the permanence (not to be confounded with identity) of the object. All cognitive operations directed towards objects depend upon this.[14] If, without our knowing why and especially without our being surprised by it, the object were to suddenly disappear, we could make no use of it. So is it not obvious that being a permanent object functions as an underlying signification (a substrate) upon which others can be constructed, in particular, values possessing practical significance?

Between the physiology of action and a trivial physiology of movement there is therefore *a radical difference*. The establishing of that correlation, or coherence, which gives us the object, *the very first level described above for the coffee cup, imputes this achievement to movement, while the second level is obliged to attribute it to action*. If this correlation is carried through in an *act* (endowed with intentional structure), it implies, by anticipation, a subjective relation, that is a relation established between, on the one hand, a perceiving subject, the I (we might also call this relation 'egocentric')[15] embodied in its

---

12 Lev Semionovitch Vygotski, soviet psychologist and educational theorist.

13 Wittgenstein summed up the pragmatic conception of meaning implied by this attempt to take into account the diversity of contexts in which language is actually employed with his famous expression: meaning is use.

14 We are not going to try to reproduce the very considerable body of literature on the child's acquisition of the permanence of the object. A summary of such work can be found in many recent contributions to child psychology.

15 Egocentric is a term derived from psychological rather than phenomenological literature, even though what it designates is the agent's ego, and even if it describes egological lived experience from the standpoint of its 'centrality': the here and now of the living present.

own body and, on the other, the object; not just the ready-made object of common sense but the object considered in the most primordial strata of its constitution for a subject.

But this relation between the perceiving subject and the object constituted in this way *is only possible if the perceiving subject is itself constituted and so endowed with a certain permanence.* We have seen in the preceding chapter that this is possible thanks to kinaesthesia. A part of the constitution of sense (or a level of the multi-layered sense of being of the perceived thing) is therefore bound up with the possibility of constructing[16] a perceiving body which is, at one and the same time, both in the world and a perceiving subject. This is why a physiology of action has to resolve the problem of the constitution of an 'I', of the unity of an own body as a centre of possible relations. In Husserl's own words: 'To *the sense* of our perception of the things there belongs the spatial position of the object in relation to the spatially located I centre, which is that centre from which all spatial orientations unfold, from which things are displayed (that is, as always co-apprehended in and through their appearances).'[17]

This is the reason why we have decided to devote this chapter to the own body and to its coherence.

Internal model and body schema

The idea that the brain disposes of a mechanism for the identification of the own body is not new. Already, at the start of the twentieth century, neurologists worked out the notion of the body schema.[18] They also distinguished it from another mechanism enabling the brain to have an image of the body.[19] Recently, the question of the existence of such a schema, already confirmed by the experience of the phantom limb with persons whose limbs have been amputated, has been renewed by the discovery of areas of the brain, situated in

---

[16] Berthoz (*The Brain's Sense of Movement*) holds that with the autistic child the difficulty of communicating is not so much a linguistic difficulty as a difficulty stemming from the fact that the child has not succeeded in constructing a unified perception of its own body. Even though this expression suggests the utilization of materials and a technique of construction, it is clear that what is at stake can only be lived experience and a living creature's sense of its own existence.

[17] E. Husserl (1907) *Thing and Space. Lectures from 1907*, trans. R. Rojcewirz (ed.), Kluwer, Dordrecht.

[18] H. Head and G. Holmes (1911/1912) Sensory disturbances from cerebral lesions, *Brain* 34, 102–254.

[19] H. De Preester and V. Knockaert (eds) (2005) *Body Image and Body Schema*, John Benjamins, Amsterdam.

the parieto-temporal lobe, whose electrical stimulation provokes out-of-the-body illusions or bodily duplication illusions.[20]

More and more inclined towards the hypothesis that, in the course of evolution, brain structures have been evolved making it possible to constitute, from within, a 'virtual body', modern physiology stood in need of a concept to characterize the corresponding mechanism. Having already discarded the notion of a schema, they borrowed from the roboticists that of the *internal model*. This notion of an internal model has already been referred to in earlier works.[21] In fact, faced with the exceptional richness of the repertory of actions but also their apparently 'automatic' (as Janet called it)[22] character—that is, their ability to anticipate and the role of kinaesthesia—the physiology of action posits the existence of networks of neurons in the brain enabling it to simulate or emulate properties of the body or of the external physical world. The construction of these 'internal models' might be innate. But they might also be constituted by the activity itself, through play, experience, learning during onto-genesis or even, later on, by training for a job.

The idea of an internal model was first formulated in the 1950s, and in relation to the cooperation of different sources of information in the perception of movement. As was noted above, the brain can perceive movement thanks to a combination of visual, proprioceptive, and vestibulary information. Engineers like L. Stark and L. Young at the Massachusetts Institute of Technology,[23] working on the perception and control of movement, developed the hypothesis that the contribution of the brain was not limited to processing or combining these informations but that there existed, in the neuronal circuits, a system similar to one with which the roboticists of that day were familiar: *a Kalman filter*.[24] Any system equipped with such a filter possesses the property of being able to predict the future state of its sensorial captors.

....

[20] P. Kahane, D. Hoffmann, L. Minotti, and A. Berthoz (2003) Reappraisal of the human vestibular cortex by cortical electrical stimulation study, *Ann. Neurol.* 54(5), 615–624; O. Blanke *et al.* (2002) Stimulating illusory own body perception, *Nature* 419(6904), 269–270.

[21] A. Berthoz (2003) *La décision*, Odile Jacob, Paris and J.-L. Petit (éd.) (2003) Repenser le corps, l'action et la cognition avec les neurosciences, *Intellectica* 1–2, no. 36–37.

[22] P. Janet (1889/2005) *L'automatisme Psychologique. Essai de psychologie expérimentale sur les formes inférieures de l'activité humaine*, L'Harmattan, Paris.

[23] L. Young (1984) Perception of the body in space, in *Handbook of Physiology. The Nervous System. Sensory Processes*, vol. III, American Physiological Society, Bethesda, MD, pp. 1023–1066.

[24] Kalman filter: a mathematical operator endowed with predictive properties that is still used in robotics, for example.

According to the models developed at that time, the perception of movement resulted from a comparison between the predictions of the Kalman filter and the real states of the captors. This notion was remarkable because it supposed that the brain, on the basis of previous experience, contributes to the evaluation of movement by making such a prediction. Perception stopped being the simple taking notice of an actually effective state and became instead the true constitution of a state that was only probable. Recently, it has even been suggested that the central analysers that process visual and vestibulary information possess *a priori* knowledge, an internal model of the force of gravity, one that is taken into account in situations where the brain has to evaluate the orientation of the head.[25] In a sense the recent developments of the use of Bayesian modelling of these processes (see below) are but the continuation of the search for an optimal model with predictive properties.

Let us take an example to illustrate what is called today an internal model. When we grasp the cup of coffee, our brain emits a motor command that coordinates the muscles of the arm, of the eyes, etc. This coordination is in part the work of the cerebellum. Physiologists and roboticists came up with the idea that neuronal networks in the cerebellum possess properties such that, if a copy of the motor command is transmitted to this structure, signals emanate from these networks making it possible to pre-view what movement will effectively be executed by this arm, even before it is carried out. This is possible thanks to the fact that the networks of the cerebellum transform the motor signals, filter them, as would be done by a real arm possessing a mass, an elasticity, and even a particular geometry. In other words, these networks are internal models of the arm. Similar mechanisms have been supposed hypothetically at the level of the spinal chord, which might also contain networks of neurons making it possible for it to simulate the mechanical properties of the limbs.[26]

These different internal models can be learnt simultaneously and without mutual interference or alternatively they may be hierarchically organized at several levels, with sometimes quite high levels of generalization. We need to know, for example, whether the internal model is valid for both hands—for there are internal models for both hands—or whether there are models

---

[25] L.H. Zupan and D.M. Merfeld (2005) An internal model of head kinematics predicts the influence of head orientation on reflexive eye movements, *J. Neural Eng.* 2(3), 180–197; D.M. Merfeld, L. Zupan, and R.J. Peterka (1999) Humans use internal models to estimate gravity and linear acceleration, *Nature* 398(6728), 615–618.

[26] E. Bizzi, A. D'Avella, P. Saltiel, and M. Tresch (2002) Modular organization of spinal motor systems, *Neuroscientist* 8(5), 437–442.

specific to each effector organ and non-transferable.[27] It has been found necessary to accept a differentiation into levels, a differentiation which is initially anatomical and conceived in a phylogenetic perspective.

Certain of these models are present at a 'low level', for example, those located in the medulla. The most spectacular example is furnished by the frog, where the medulla has been sectioned in such a way that the brain is disconnected. Russian researchers (their study was reproduced by Bizzi and coworkers)[28] have shown that the medulla, isolated in this way, is capable of guiding the paw of the frog towards a point on its skin that is scratched. This presupposes the existence in its medulla of certain primitives (a term from robotics) possessing the same mechanical properties as the limbs. Other internal models are supposed to be of a higher level:[29] for instance, in the cerebellum, the basal ganglia, or even the parietal cortex where it is generally admitted that the cerebral substrate of the body schema is located.[30]

At the present time, it is assumed that the internal models simulate a variety of properties: geometric properties, like limb shape, form, or posture, cinematic properties, like the length of the muscles, the angles of the articulations, dynamic properties like the inertia of the arm, the muscular forces themselves, the torques to which the articulations are subjected, or even what is called *impedance*, not an electrical but a biomechanical impedance; that is, the ability of the hand to absorb the impact of forces, a property close to elasticity.

In the same way, it is supposed that there might be internal models for proprioceptive sensibility, for cutaneous external sensibility, etc. In addition to these internal models of the own body, there might also be internal models for extra-corporeal space, notably for the object in so far as it features as the goal of action or a tool to be manipulated, for there certainly is a 'tacit knowledge'

----

[27] D.M. Wolpert, Z. Ghahramani, and M.I. Jordan (1995) An internal model for sensorimotor integration, *Science* 269, 1880–1882; D.M. Wolpert, C.R. Miall, and M. Kawato (1998) Internal models in the cerebellum, *Trends Cog. Sci.* 2(9), 338–347; D.M. Wolpert and Z. Ghahramani (2000) Computational principles of movement neurosciences, *Nat. Neurosci.* 3, 1212–1217.

[28] E. Bizzi, A. D'Avella, P. Saltiel, and M. Tresch (2002) Modular organization of spinal motor systems, *Neuroscientist* 8(5), 437–442.

[29] K.V. Baev (1997) Highest level of automatisms in the nervous system: a theory of functional principles underlying the highest forms of brain function, *Prog. Neurobiol.* 51(2), 129–166.

[30] See A. Berthoz (2003) *La décision*, Odile Jacob, Paris, pp. 129–131, 134–135, 151–152, and 167–168. For an epistemological discussion of internal models, see J.-L. Petit (éd.) (2003) Repenser le corps, l'action et la cognition avec les neurosciences, *Intellectica* 1–2, no. 36–37, p. 30–36; Section 2, pp. 127–180.

of the properties of the tool or the instrument, for example with craftsmen or musicians, a knowing how to manipulate adapted to the mechanical or physical properties of the object in question, or the kind of instrument employed. Finally, an internal model is needed for surrounding space, with its geometry and even its gravitational effects on the fall of a body one wants to catch. Berthoz' team has, for instance, shown that the brain has some internal processes akin to Newton's laws which allow it to predict the impact force of a falling object.[31]

The importance of internal models derives from the functions attributed to them. Let us look at a few examples. First we will look at that the model enabling us to anticipate the consequences of our actions. The internal simulation via a model of the previewed action makes it possible to correct the action before its execution, or almost at the same time as it is actually carried out. It is a question of gaining time but also of increasing the precision with which the action is controlled. When Europeans wanted to construct the Airbus A380, this giant of the air, an important part of the behaviour of the plane could be entirely simulated (or emulated) even before the plane took flight. Models of the plane and of its environment were used to this effect. The same sort of thing arises with internal models of the arm: they make it possible for us to anticipate the consequences of a gesture before it is executed, or even during its execution.

This action, guided or modified in this way by an internal model, is no longer 'stimulus-bound' (to use the expression employed by Chomsky[32] to refer to a stimulus which would be nothing more than the trigger for an automatic outcome), as if this action did no more than follow a predetermined programme subject to corrections at intermittent points in the trajectory. These corrections have to be introduced whenever there is too great a difference between the effect relayed back through the captors and the effect estimated in advance on the basis of the internal model. The brain then only has to update certain parameters of this internal model without having to change it for another model. So it abandons one predetermined mode of motor control (which by analogy with the programming of computers is called a default mode) to pass over to one or other of the available strategies in a list of alternatives.

---

[31] J. McIntyre *et al.* (2001) Does the brain model Newton's laws? *Nat. Neurosci.* 4(7), 693–694; M. Zago and F. Lacquaniti (2005) Visual perception and interception of falling objects: a review of evidence for an internal model of gravity, *J. Neural. Eng.* 2(3), S198–S208; I. Indovina *et al.* (2005) Representation of visual gravitational motion in the human vestibular cortex, *Science* 308(5720), 416–419.

[32] N. Chomsky, (1966) *Cartesian Linguistics*, Harper & Row, New York, p. 9.

So the brain would not just be working to determine the desired movement alone, it would be processing *the motor error*, the difference between the position desired but not realized, of the arms or the hands and the future position corresponding to the goal, were the action ever to be realized. Henceforward, by coding the movement in terms of difference vectors rather than the absolute position hoped for, the brain's biological machinery would be concerned with relative values (differences between what is wanted and what is obtained) and not just with absolute values.

Sherrington and his successors were only interested in action as a (more or less complex)[33] reflex. The alternative conception has the additional, and by no means trivial, advantage that once installed through some learning procedure, the internal model can be modified by intention and memory, etc; not to mention the possibility of choosing the most effective and the most flexible strategy. For example, let us suppose that, with his eyes closed, and employing only his hand, the reader wants to explore the edge of a table to find out its form.[34] He will only make use of haptic perception. In this situation the brain has two possible strategies: the first consists of permanently pressing the table to obtain a continuous control of the force applied; the second of making an *a priori* internal model of its form and simply verifying that the force perceived conforms to the hypothesis formulated.

In the 1980s another hypothesis was formulated by Gurfinkel and Levick.[35] Posture would not be controlled 'bottom-up', and by way of a local control of the stiffness of the muscles, but 'top-down' and by way of a global simulation of the effect (to get the body to lean) envisaged on the schema of the body. An overall effect which would then later be analysed out into local mechanisms at the segmentary level, just like the boss of a major industrial enterprise who gives overall instructions to be followed by different specialized services, or like an admiral commanding the overall strategy of the fleet, while leaving to each commander on board the leeway to adapt the instructions to his particular case. The internal model is therefore important in that it makes it

---

[33] C.S. Sherrington (1906) *The Integrative Action of the Nervous System*, Yale University Press, New Haven, CT.

[34] J. McIntyre, E.V. Gurfinkel, M. Lipshits, J. Droulez, and V.S. Gurfinkel (1995) Measurements of human force control during a constrained arm motion using a force actuated joystick, *J. Neurophysiol.* 73, 1201–1222; D. Toffin, J. McIntyre, J. Droulez, A. Kemeny, and A. Berthoz (2003) Perception and reproduction of force direction in the horizontal plane, *J. Neurophysiol.* 90, 3040–3053.

[35] V. Gurfinkel and Y.S. Levick (1991) Perceptual and automatic aspects of the postural body scheme, in J. Paillard (ed.), *Brain and Space*, Oxford University Press, Oxford, pp. 147–162.

possible to integrate the goal and the global intention of the gesture or the action, and moreover to move from the global to the local.[36]

Inverse models and Aristotle

The term inverse model was also borrowed from the roboticists to designate the internal models with regard to which the motor information is 'rehearsed'. This inverse analysis, which is then later reversed, finds a curious precedent in Aristotle's theory of deliberation in the *Nichomachean* and the *Eudemian Ethics*.[37] This theory has been taken up again by way of a philological examination of texts and the application of the instruments of modern logic, and now takes up an entire section of the theory of action in analytical philosophy.[38]

Practical reasoning proceeds in the following way: 'I want this' is the first proposition, then 'I can only get this by employing that means' is the second proposition, and the conclusion is an action (not its description) that takes the following form: 'I employ this means to obtain that end'. The classical example seems almost puerile (a misleading impression!). 'I am cold; I won't stop being cold until I construct a house; I construct a house in order to stop being cold.' In what sense is this a deliberation if this logical succession of propositions leaves no room, at least apparently, for choice? It is because it represents formally a series of steps made up of plausible considerations (whether consisting of wishes or judgements) taken into account by the agent, and whose conclusion is no longer a logical proposition following from other propositions, but an action. An action which can always be justified rationally (by a retrospective reconstruction of the practical reasoning involved) with reference to the steps that led up to it, which can eventually find expression in terms of propositions of the kind mentioned above, in particular when one reflects on what one has done.

---

[36] Let us remember that the body in question is the acting body or embodied action, and not the body as an object in physical space.

[37] Aristotle, *Nichomachean Ethics*, trsl. H. Rackham, Harvard Univ. Pr., 1975; *Eudemian Ethics*, trsl. H. Rackham, Harvard Univ. Pr. 1981.

[38] See G.E.M. Anscombe (1965) Thought and action in Aristotle: what is practical truth? in *Collected Philosophical Papers of G.E.M. Anscombe. Vol I, From Parmenides to Wittgenstein*, Basil Blackwell, Oxford, 1981, pp. 66–77; D. Davidson (1980) How is weakness of the will possible? *in Essays on Actions and Events*, Oxford University Press, Oxford, pp. 21–42; D. Charles (1984) *Aristotle's Philosophy of Action*, Duckworth, London; C. Natali (1989) *La saggezza di Aristotele*, Bibliopolis, Naples; J.-L. Petit (1991) *L'Action dans la Philosophie analytique*, PUF, Paris; R. Ogien (1993) *La faiblesse de la volonté*, PUF, Paris; C. Natali (2004) *L'action efficace. Études sur la philosophie de l'action d'Aristote*, Peeters, Louvain-la-Neuve.

The very possibility of this kind of deliberation depends on the fact that we have the choice of means. The goal, on the other hand, has certainly to be determined beforehand. But we are unsure as to whether the means are appropriate to attain it. And the passage from the premises to the conclusion of a syllogism of this kind is not made by the application of a rule drawn from syllogistic theory but by the agent's decision to adopt one of the means to the exclusion of the others. No one, to the best of our knowledge, has yet drawn attention to the fact that this analysis of actions in terms of an inverse model (later reversed) only applies quantitative measures to Aristotle's theory of deliberation. In so doing it makes it possible to bridge the gulf between the physiology of action and decision theories in the field of economics, the latter representing the more direct heirs of peripatetic rationalism. All this is despite the reluctance of the authors of these highly sophisticated theories to acknowledge their indebtedness to such Aristotelian 'trivialities'.[39]

Sense and internal models of the body

The problem that arises here is that the concept of an internal model designates a wide range of very different mechanisms. The term is therefore ambiguous and needs to be made more precise. Worse, in the classical conception of the body schema and of internal models, *no room was left for the attribution of a 'sense'*. In this interface between physiology and phenomenology the critical question becomes that of determining whether it might not be possible to undertake a critical analysis of the notion of an internal model which would, at one and the same time, both do justice to its fruitfulness and make it possible for us to develop this concept in such a way as to introduce a sense component, as defined above. This is the question that will be examined in the following sections.

First of all, let us get back to standard epistemology. From the point of view of positivist epistemology (whose standpoint it is not our intention to criticize) of the kind found in the classical history of science and of technology, one might think that the concept of an internal model, first developed in robotics, had simply been transferred from one discipline to another. This sort of exchange of concepts between disciplines and their re-employment in a new context is current practice, and, in addition, one that is recognized and considered legitimate by epistemologists. In particular, those interested in the

---

[39] See the critique of these theories developed by A. Berthoz (2003) *La décision*, Odile Jacob, Paris, Chap. I, pp. 19–41.

contribution made by the imagination in science have seen in this procedure a good example of imaginative cross-fertilization, the end result of which is that researchers are put on the track of new ideas and new approaches.[40] And this procedure is all the more legitimate in the case of the cognitive neurosciences in that these disciplines are essentially inter-disciplinary. The reciprocal recognition of the perhaps irreducible diversity of the methods employed is essential to their successful development, for here we are talking about disciplines where it is both possible and necessary to import and export; that is, to exchange concepts.

Whereas the modern formulation of the concept of an internal model lends itself well to quantification, this was not the case with the concept of the *body schema* (which is different from the body image)[41] employed by neurologists at the beginning of the twentieth century. In so far as the analysis is taken in this direction, it can be shown that a *mechanical model* can be developed from neuronal internal models. This is what has been done by, for example, McIntyre and others,[42] when they conceived of a system of springs adequate to account for the biomechanical impedance of the hand. The paradigm case is the model of the oscillator (a small mass attached to a spring). It has rendered good and faithful service in physics to explain gravitational attraction, the laws of electricity and of electromagnetism, etc. These mechanical models can be treated as analogues for the motor processes that interest us; that is, anticipatory processes.[43] With regard to those mechanisms that are materially realizable, there exist—one can draw up an inventory of such possibilities—equations to

40 M. Black (1962) *Models and Metaphors*, Cornell University Press, Ithaca, NY; M. Hesse (1966) *Models and Analogies in Science*, University of Notre Dame Press, Paris; P. Ricœur (1975) *The Rule of Metaphor*, trans. R. Czerny, University of Toronto Press, Toronto.

41 See S. Gallagher (1986) Body image and body schema: a conceptual clarification, *J. Mind Behav.* 7, 541–554.

42 J. McIntyre *et al.* (1995) Measurements of human force control during a constrained arm motion using a force actuated joystick, *J. Neurophysiol.* 73, 1201–1222; D. Toffin *et al.* (2003) Perception and reproduction of force direction in the horizontal plane, *J. Neurophysiol.* 90, 3040–3053.

43 D.G. Liebermann, A. Biess, J. Friedman, C.C. Gielen, and T. Flash (2006) Intrinsic joint kinematic planning. I: Reassessing the Listing's law constraint in the control of three-dimensional arm movements, *Exp. Brain Res.* 171, 139–154; H. Hicheur, S. Vieilledent, M.J. Richardson, T. Flash, and A. Berthoz (2005) Velocity and curvature in human locomotion along complex curved paths: a comparison with hand movements, *Exp. Brain Res.*, 162(2), 145–154; R. Sosnik, B. Hauptmann, A. Karni, and T. Flash (2004) When practice leads to co-articulation: the evolution of geometrically defined movement primitives, *Exp. Brain Res.* 156(4), 422–438.

describe them mathematically. Jordan,[44] Kuo,[45] and Wolpert[46] have already attempted to carry through this programme by making an exhaustive review of the mathematical and technological apparatus needed to render these internal models operative. All of this seems true, at least in the sense that it cannot be attacked from a technical point of view. For all that, it still stands in need of philosophical interpretation.

The crippling formalism of internal models

However valuable it might be to provide a mathematical formulation for the technical performance of the concept of an internal model, the outcome is still not altogether satisfactory.[47] The internal model makes it possible to employ mathematical concepts familiar to engineers, like the *Kalman filter*,[48] or like another concept one encounters in the literature, the *Smith predictor*.[49] But each type of model can only account for a part of the functioning. In the end, it amounts to no more than a magnificent working hypothesis.

To illustrate the limitation mentioned above, one could do no better than to turn to Wolpert and his collaborators and their series of studies devoted to the modelling of the functioning of the cerebellum. If we compare the studies by Wolpert and colleagues from 1995 and 1998 (cited above), we can note the progress made in their thinking. For first of all they proposed an internal model with two components: (1) a *forward model* of the dynamic of the arm whose function it was to estimate the position of the arm in the course of movement, and (2) a retroactive model of proprioception, plus (3) a Kalman filter to ensure the weighting of the two models, the forward and the retroactive model. This theoretical structure is well constructed from the mathematical standpoint.

....

[44] M.I. Jordan (1995) Computational motor control, in M.S. Gazzaniga (ed.), *The Cognitive Neurosciences*, MIT Press, Cambridge, MA, pp. 597–609.

[45] A.D. Kuo *et al.* (1998) Effect of altered sensory conditions on multivariate descriptions of human postural sway, *Exp. Brain Res.* 122, 185–195.

[46] D.M. Wolpert, Z. Ghahramani, and M.I. Jordan (1995) An internal model for sensori-motor integration, *Science* 269, 1880–1882; D.M. Wolpert, C.R. Miall, and M. Kawato (1998) Internal models in the cerebellum, *Trends Cog. Sci.* 2(9), 338–347; D.M. Wolpert and Z. Ghahramani (2000) Computational principles of movement neurosciences, *Nat. Neurosci.* 3, 1212–1217.

[47] An objection of the same type is to be found today in another field, linguistics, where the renewed interest in the contextual use of verbal forms renders unacceptable the abstract character of Chomsky's grammars, in so far as they represent mathematical models of the linguistic competence of a speaker.

[48] See above definition.

[49] O.J.M. Smith (1959) A controller to overcome dead time, *ISA J.* 6(2), 28–33.

But if one enquiries into the physiological evidence supportive of the application of the hypothesis to the functioning of the brain one becomes aware of the distance that still separates the model from the reality. For example, experimentation shows that subjects moving their arm in the dark tend initially to overestimate the force they have to exert with their arm and along with it the distance this arm has to cover; then, later on, they tend to get back to an estimate closer to their actual performance.

This is the empirical evidence. How is it accounted for? It is with a model in which the parameters of the Kalman filter have been chosen in such a way as to always prefer the motor-based estimate of the forward model, in the first instance. In the second instance, it will always prefer the sensory-based estimate of the retroactive model. The estimates of the (simulated) trajectory of the hand governed by an internal model whose parameters have been adjusted in such a way as to provoke this seesaw effect prove capable of simulating successfully the initial increase of the bias in the estimate of the subjects, but this falls short of offering a physiological explanation, since no hypothesis has been advanced capable of founding 'in nature' just such an adjustment of the parameters.

In a theoretical model developed by Wolpert, Miall, and Kawato,[50] inspired in the first instance by models of Slotine and colleagues,[51] each subordinate module branches out into direct 'predictor' models and inverse 'controller' models, these paired models competing with each other for the final control of the movement. Supervising the smooth running of the whole, an 'assessor' internal model is assigned to estimate and to weigh that share of the responsibility for this motor control which has to be attributed to each of these modules as a function of variations in the context.

What this theoretical model has to account for is the following: (1) the apparatus has to acquire its internal models 'of the world and the body' on the basis of a state of 'original innocence'; (2) the environment in which action takes place is unknown in advance, so the internal models in question have to make it possible to divide the environment up into a series of contexts which can be mastered one by one; (3) and finally, in order to ensure the constant effectiveness of action, the internal model has to select the control module adapted to the actual context.

If the objective is to simulate the autonomy of the agent with reference to external reality by making possible a purely internal control of behaviour, this objective is still far from having been attained. In fact, however, the actual

50 D.M. Wolpert, R.C. Miall, and M. Kawato (1998) Internal models in the cerebellum, *Trends Cog. Sci.* 2(9), 344.

51 S. Hanneton, A. Berthoz, J. Droulez, and J.J. Slotine (1997) Does the brain use sliding variables for the control of movements? *Biol. Cybernetics* 77(6), 381–393.

'objectively true' state of affairs seems to be surreptitiously reintroduced at several levels. Knowledge of this state of affairs is required for the definition of motor error; without it no comparison can be made in the learning process and in the attempt to estimate the share of the responsibility to be attributed to each module in the control of movement.

All the same, this modelling procedure does carry with it a physiological validity, since it seems capable of taking account of certain aspects of motor control. The problem of the control of posture and of movement can be described, in fact, by a hierarchic ordering of levels where each centre (spinal chord–cerebellum–basal ganglia–cortex) contains an internal model of the immediately subordinated centre, and in such a way that the subordinated centre does not exert its control directly over the limb that carries out the movement but only on an internal model which simulates its properties, a simulation that takes place at an ever more global level in proportion as one climbs the hierarchical ladder of these centres, right up to the level of the most global internal model, which is the schema of the acting body. The univocity of this hierarchy and the unity of the body schema presupposed by it still need to be discussed. We will get back to this later.

In any case, this principle of the 'replacement of empirical reality' by internal models is precious for our thesis because it leads us back to the threshold of our theory of constitution. For the latter also assumes that empirical reality is not the point of departure but the outcome of a formative process brought into play by the organism that interacts with it.

Nevertheless, there remains a real danger of excessive formalism in the working out of the physiology of internal models of movement, still highly cybernetic in conception. This danger is accentuated by the fact that its functional schematization relies upon concepts of feedback and feed-forward: (1) motor command, (2) engendering synergies predicting the desired state of the body, (3) proprioceptive afference, (4) a comparison between predictions of the initiation of movement and the effectuation of such movements triggering the error signal, and (5) error correction.

The Bayesian probabilistic approach

In the end, what makes the internal model plausible from a biological standpoint is that it makes it possible to manipulate a predictive tool, and in this it rejoins the phenomenological analysis of the anticipatory character of perception and of the constitution of the object. Hitherto concepts of internal models were largely borrowed from robotic engineering. But over the last fifty years we have seen the development of another formalist and computational approach proceeding from the specialists of the probability calculus. For in fact to predict is to attribute a certain probability to an event in an uncertain world. Moreover, the probability that an event occurs is itself linked to the actual state of a system, to an experience of its past states and to a certain evaluation of the variables which are likely to be important in the future. This combination of a present state, past experiences, and the prediction of the future, a combination one also finds in the thinking of Husserl with his correlative notions of retention/protention, lends itself to a Bayesian analysis.

The difficulty of prediction follows from the inevitable imperfection of the internal models. Those who uphold the subjective probabilist approach seek to make allowances for this imperfection, for this lack of knowledge that an agent necessarily has regarding himself, the world, and the consequences of his own actions. Probability is an excellent tool for quantifying this lack of knowledge. For the probabilist approach is an extension of classical logic, in that it makes it possible to attribute to each state, to each event, to each prediction, a probability value, a value calculated according to rigorous rules and founded on a precise expression of the agent's lack of knowledge.

What is new by comparison with other models is not just the combination of present state, past experiences, and future prediction; rather it consists of the most rigorous possible evaluation of the knowledge (certainty or uncertainty) one has of the present state, of the incidence of past experience, and of the future consequences of our actions. This evaluation arises as the result of two quite simple rules, as follows.

1   The probability of the conjunction of two variables A and B is equal to the product of the probability of the first variable and the conditional probability of the second variable relative to the first: $P(A\ B) = P(A) \cdot P(B \mid A)$. We owe this rule to the Reverend Thomas Bayes from which the Bayesian model derives its name.

2   The probability of a variable is the sum, over all the possible states, of the second variable, of the conjoined probability: $P(A) =$ sum over B of $P(A\ B)$. This rule, called the marginalization rule, is just as important as Bayes' rule.

In spite of their apparent simplicity, probabilistic models have given spectacular results in neuroscience and in experimental psychology, for they make it possible, with a minimum number of hypotheses and parameters, to account for a wide variety of experimental results.[52] These models also complement

---

[52]   J. Laurens and J. Droulez (2007) Bayesian processing of vestibular information, *Biol. Cybernetics* 96(4), 389–404; M.O. Ernst and M.S. Banks (2002) Humans integrate visual and haptic information in a statistically optimal fashion, *Nature* 415(6870), 429–433; S. Deneve, J.R. Duhamel, and A. Pouget (2007) Optimal sensorimotor integration in

and complete older models: the Kalman filter turning out to be but a particular case of the Bayesian model applicable under certain restrictive conditions.

The advantage of this kind of modelling seems to be that it makes it possible to choose variables that 'make sense' to a subject rather than just the classical variables of movement, space, and energy. In this way, qualitative aspects of the selection of an action can be taken into account. But we are still very far from having developed this formalism to the point of being able to attribute a sense to a decision-making process. And besides, it has been some time since the psychologist D. Kahneman, today a Nobel Prize winner in economics, warned economists against treating man as a Bayesian calculator.[53] We are therefore faced with a paradox: neuroscientists model the brain using a rule invented by the Reverend Bayes at a time when some economists seem to doubt its relevance for human decision-making!

The most important task today is to confirm the physiological relevance of the use of internal models in the cognitive sciences. And this task cannot be limited to a few technical adjustments, such as looking for more powerful concepts, or devising modelization 'expedients' on the basis of procedures relevant to organisms.

Internal models and phenomenology: emulate versus simulate

Could phenomenology contribute to the development of the present conception of internal models? The hypothesis concerning the existence of internal models in the cerebral mechanisms has contributed to a better understanding of certain capacities for *simulation* but not for the *emulation* of the environment and of the *body in act*. Simulation and emulation: the first is just a copy of a collection of states; the second, an internal creation, an invention. Whereas simulation can, at the limit, be tied down to flight and computer simulation, emulation, in our view, can only be tied down to lived experience. When we emulate an action from within, we live it, a dimension that the model-makers seem not to have broached. We put ourselves into it 'in flesh

recurrent cortical networks: a neural implementation of Kalman filters, *J. Neurosci.* 27(21), 5744–5756; W.J. Ma, J.M. Beck, P.E. Latham, and A. Pouget (2006) Bayesian inference with probabilistic population codes, *Nat. Neurosci.* 9(11), 1432–1438; D.C. Knill and A. Pouget (2004) The Bayesian brain: the role of uncertainty in neural coding and computation, *Trends Neurosci.* 27(12), 712–719.

53 D. Kahneman and A. Tversky (1973) On the psychology of prediction, *Psychol. Rev.* 80, 4, 237–251; D. Kahneman and A. Tversky (eds) (2000) *Choices, Values and Frames,* Cambridge University Press, Cambridge.

and blood' as Husserl describes it, all the more so as emulation makes further use of and, at the same time, gives new meaning to something it owes a lot to: inter-personal empathy.[54]

The most familiar settings for empathy are to be found in 'team spirit' on the football field, in the classroom, at the work post in the factory, or in armies on campaign. However, it is our view (we are not going to try and support this view here) that simulation/emulation can not be reduced to any of the alternative proposal with which one is familiar under this name in the literature: flight simulation for pilots, the simulation of a living organism by robots, the simulation of a physical process by mathematical models, the theory of simulation as opposed to the theory of the theory of mind in philosophy of mind (Alvin Goldman),[55] etc. What leaves us unsatisfied from a phenomenological point of view is that one keeps falling back on automatic and objective mechanisms whose functioning can never really be properly 'internal'; that is to say lived out from within, because it is only observed from without.

Representing processes pertaining to living beings through objective mechanisms whose functioning cannot fail to miss the specificity of interior experience remains a permanent danger—a danger to which even phenomenology is exposed—and this no matter how satisfying such a procedure of representation might be from the standpoint of accommodating certain rational requirements. In an important manuscript from 1931, Husserl undertakes a scrupulous description of the dynamic of kinaesthesia, tracing this dynamic right back to instinctual impulses, in the phenomenon of the orientation of vision and the projection of the hands in the direction of an object of interest: specifically, for the newborn baby, the mother's breast, just as soon as it distinguishes itself from the indifferent background of experience. After a few pages, haunted by a doubt, Husserl asks himself the question: 'can one adopt this description? For all of this can *take place* without my being attracted to it or turning away from it in aversion',[56] and in so doing gives evidence of his proverbial intellectual honesty.

To avoid this outcome, a *theory of simulation has to be developed that makes the agent alone responsible for the act of simulating the action he is about to perform.* 'The act,' Husserl insists, 'is in the: "I am doing," "I am still active" throughout the entire time period in which the act is carried out, and it is

---

[54] See Chapter 8 on conjoint constitution.

[55] A.I. Goldman (1993) The psychology of folk psychology, *Behav. Brain Sci.* 16, 15–28; A.I. Goldman (1992) In defense of the simulation theory, in Mental simulation: Philosophical and Psychological Essays, *Mind Language* 7, 104–119.

[56] E. Husserl, *MS* C 16 I (end 1931), p. 18.

I who make this act happen.'[57] Along the same lines, Varela[58] has argued for a pragmatic approach to the mind and to its relations with the world. He introduced into cognitive science the concept of *enaction*, a cross for him between phenomenology and the Buddhist tradition. His idea is that Western philosophy and physiology are weighed down by a dichotomy between the human mind and the world. Rejoining Merleau-Ponty and the phenomenologists in their critique of the notion of representation, he claims that Buddhism, not as a religion but as a reflection on the relation between mind and world, discovered something that has eluded Western thought.[59] What he uncovered was the *lack of any justification ('groundlessness') for the idea that one could separate the perceived world and the perceiving subject*. This in turn implies that the notion of representation has to be abandoned.

He also develops a thorough critique of Husserl who, following Hubert Dreyfus,[60] he interprets as the promoter of a purely theoretical approach to cognition, which he attacks. But he also criticizes Husserl as a thinker who failed to recognize what seems to him to be 'a fundamental fact': *that the ego, the perceiving I, does not exist as a unity*. For his part, Varela gives great weight to a contradiction between the shattering and fragmentation of the perceiving I, going as far as the absence (according to his Buddhist beliefs) of a unique ego, on the one hand, and, on the other, the intimate feeling we have regarding the unity of our existence as agent, the intimate feeling of the permanence of our identity as body-object, etc.

Delving into the unpublished manuscript material has given us the right to reject this allegation in what concerns Husserl by affirming the following: whatever may be the case regarding the identity of the I and the world, the kind of Buddhist belief that no one could possibly expect to find in the thinking

---

57 E. Husserl, *MC* B III 9 (October–December 1931), The problem of the act, p. 19.

58 F.J. Varela, E. Thompson, and E. Rosch (1991) *The Embodied Mind: Cognitive Science and Human Experience*, MIT Press, Cambridge, MA.

59 Without making an exception of Husserl, and this despite the importance he accords to Merleau-Ponty, who continued the line of thinking developed by late Husserl, but with the exception, curiously, of certain specialists in the field of artificial intelligence, like Minsky, whom he cites frequently (F.J. Varela, E. Thompson, and E. Rosch (1991) *The Embodied Mind: Cognitive Science and Human Experience*, MIT Press, Cambridge, MA, p. 153–158, 178–180, 184–185, 198–199).

60 H. Dreyfus regards Husserl as responsible for the ambiguous model of cognition derived from artificial intelligence: cognition conceived as being oriented towards an ideal object (*noema*) reducible to a 'mental representation' or to a 'system of computational rules' capable of being adequately expressed in 'a symbolic description': H. Dreyfus (1972/1979) *What Computers can't do: The Limits of Artificial Intelligence*, Harper & Row, New York; H. Dreyfus (1982) Husserl's perceptual noema, in H. Dreyfus and H. Hall (eds), *Husserl, Intentionality, and Cognitive Science*, MIT Press, Cambridge, MA.

of this representative of the transcendental philosophical tradition, the tension (if not the contradiction) between a shattered I and a unified I was so little overlooked by Husserl that it undoubtedly became an existential drama haunting his later thinking.

'What are the kinaesthesiae themselves and what relation do they have with the acts of the I that accompanies them; the I which is directed through them and across them to …? Perhaps this very attempt to talk about acts directing kinaesthesia is already misguided?[61] [...] Are kinaesthesiae really something I-like? But then, what does the subjectivity in question here mean?[62] [...] What is the particular affinity between this kinaesthetic process and the I in its activity? [...] Is the I itself anything at all outside of its concrete acts in the concretion of actual life?[63] [...] But then what are we to make of pure subjectivity, the identical I of affection, of real acts, of feelings? [...] The same world for me—the same I. What kind of identity are we talking about? *How could constitution possibly be multifarious?*'[64]

However unfounded Varela's critique may be, it should not be neglected, if only on account of the influence his thinking has had and the impact it has been able to make in the cognitive sciences, thereby contributing to the re-orientation to which we hope our manifesto modestly contributes. To be in a position to decide about this, not on the basis of what is imputed to Husserl and to phenomenology but by taking account of what is at issue here, we are now going to introduce the typically Husserlian concept of the 'own body'.

The absence of the own body in the philosophical tradition

This is the moment at which we are obliged to beg the reader not to lose sight of the fact that the expression 'own body' (in French *corps propre*, in German *Leib*) means something completely different from the expression body.

---

61 E. Husserl, *MS* D 10 IV (June 1932), Difficulties with kinaesthesia, p. 9.

62 E. Husserl, *MS* D 10 IV (June 1932), Difficulties with kinaesthesia, p. 11.

63 'What is the specific affinity between this kinaesthetic process and the I in its activity? [...] But is the I something over and above its concrete acts enacted in the concreteness of life, and is a concrete act thinkable otherwise than as a process through which something runs off, something that could just as well run off from the self itself, inactively, or again, as a nodal point which runs off in an immediately active way and which is even immediately activable. But this is an originary property, therefore not one which can be immediately activated on one occasion and not on another. In the same way that the I is awake, therefore active as awake, it is always already in its activations. Before all else, it is active in its immediately active processes.' (E. Husserl, *MS* D 10 IV (June 1932), Difficulties with kinaesthesia, pp. 13–14).

64 E. Husserl, *MS* D 10 IV (June 1932), Difficulties with kinaesthesia, p. 18 (our emphasis).

Otherwise, he will only see in what follows a grotesque mistake, which scholarly memories going back to his final school year might oblige him to contest.

In the grand classical rationalist tradition going back to Descartes and Kant, the question of the own body hardly ever arises. With Descartes, this question is pushed to the side as not being either a genuinely philosophical or a genuinely scientific question. The own body was a matter of brute experience. What we are is a physical body, a thing that we are despite, and alongside, the fact that we are also a mind, which becomes clear to us through reflection. We are a body, but about our being a body science can say nothing, even though it furnishes us with a theory of bodies in general. Why? Because this science only takes account of the body in so far as it occupies space and, in measuring it, describes the space it occupies in terms of geometry and mechanics, disciplines that ignore sensorial qualities as something belonging to the subjectivity of experience. Do we really have to insist upon this? The *Treatise on the Passions of the Soul*, based entirely upon the mechanical metaphor of the automat commanded by a system of bellows pushing 'animal spirits' into the 'tiny vessels' of the nerves and muscles, is poles away from any thinking about the own body.[65]

With Kant, the difficulty surrounding the own body is to be located elsewhere. For he drew a sharp distinction between external experience, the experience of objects of perception, and internal experience which was, for him, the experience of a succession, in time, of psychic contents, mental states, states of consciousness, and sensations. Lived experience was uniquely located in the category of temporality. But it seemed to him so difficult to think this temporal succession that he felt obliged to borrow from space (and despite the external character of the experience we have of it) the idea of the line to represent, however imperfectly, the passage of time.

In other words, the own body has always been broken up, split between a totally temporalized psychic interiority and an exteriority which also includes our body, but only as some kind of an object. The body, as mine, still did not exist in philosophy, except perhaps in the work of Spinoza (it was Damasio whose book on Spinoza brought this to the attention of the public).[66]

This being the situation in the philosophy of the body, it would have taken a bid for power, or at least a great deal of inventiveness among several thinkers

---

[65] See R. Descartes (1649/1953) Les Passions de l'âme, in *Œuvres et Lettres*, Gallimard, Paris, p. 695–802.

[66] A. Damasio (2003) *Looking for Spinoza: Joy, Sorrow, and the Feeling Brain*, Harcourt, Orlando, FL.

in revolt against the dis-embodied intellectualism of classical philosophy (Maine de Biran, Nietzsche, Bergson, and others, all of whom were to some extent preceded by Fichte) to bring into being a thinking about the own body.[67] But in spite of our readiness today to recognize in Spinoza,[68] for example, a precursor, it is only with Husserl that we find someone capable of undertaking a systematic rehabilitation of the own body as the primordial operator in the constitution of the world, of the meaning of the being of things. This does not in any way detract from the accomplishment of Merleau-Ponty, who was the one who did most to develop this notion in our language. We also find in Varela a reflection on 'the embodiment' of the mind.[69] Rather, however, than first placing ourselves on the plane of the mental to look afterwards for a way of incarnating the mental we will try to think of the own body directly.

Husserl was the first to conceive of the own body as the primordial operator in the constitution of the perceived world, of the meaning of the being of things.[70] He was the first to systematically develop the idea that only by living our experience of having a body (across the kinaesthesia furnished by the organs of perception and movement) does it become possible to confer upon these things and this world, originally, the meaning of being that they later come to have for us, we who interact with them through perception and action.

---

[67] The physiologist might object to this: 'Has no place really been allotted to the body in all of Western philosophy? What of Spinoza, Jean Nicod and John Searle and Canguilhem and Bachelard? And what of Eastern philosophy, the Japanese and the Chinese and Buddhism?' We could also point to Cassirer and such British philosophers as Alexander Bain, a Scotch philosopher, rather than letting it be thought that Husserl alone 'had all the right answers'. This changes nothing as regards the fact that it is to him that we owe the systematic conception of a programme of investigation to be undertaken in relation to the own body and at the interface of the cognitive sciences and of phenomenological philosophy.

[68] A. Damasio (2003) *Looking for Spinoza: Joy, Sorrow, and the Feeling Brain*, Harcourt, Orlando, FL.

[69] F.J. Varela, E. Thompson, and E. Rosch (1991) *The Embodied Mind: Cognitive Science and Human Experience*, MIT Press, Cambridge, MA.

[70] E. Husserl (1989) *La Terre ne se meut pas*, Minuit, Paris; E. Husserl (1952) Ideen zu einer reinen phänomenologie und Phänomenologischen Philosophie. II. Phänomenologische Untersuchungen zur Konstitution, Hrsg. v. M. Biemel, Martinus Nijhoff, The Hague; E. Husserl (1973) *Zur Phänomenologie der Intersubjektivität*, I–III, Hrsg. v. I. Kern, Martinus Nijhoff, The Hague; E. Husserl, *MS* BIII 9 (October–December 1931) Das Aktproblem; C16 I (end of 1931) to VII (May 1933); D10 I (May 1932) to IV (June 1932); D 11 (1931), D 12 II–VI, D 13 I–IV; BI 9 I–VII, etc.

The own body

The body I am is the body in which feeling, perceiving, and knowing prevails. Prevails translates into English the German verb *waltet* which means to be active in one's body, act in and through it or, if you want, to occupy it effectively. In any case, we use prevails in the sense of being there. In what concerns the physical things of perception we have shown (in Chapter 6) how it is that by going back to the acts of the agent that constitutes their sense, the possibility arises of these things acquiring a sense for him.

If one wants to create a place for the own body in phenomenology, it has to be thought of as having the meaning of being precisely that body where I prevail. To say of a certain body that it is an own body is not to attribute to it a property among others, like size, whiteness, or weight. To say of a certain body that it is an 'own body' is already to attribute to it a possessive pronoun: as if one were to say 'here is my body' and, in a quite different context, '*Ecce homo*'. This is the body in which I experience my states, my sensations, including those that are traditionally thought of as 'external', despite the fact that, as kinaesthetic sensations, they are, and can only be, internal; that is, proprioceptions for the physiologist and psychic interiorities for the phenomenologist. In a word, this *body possesses a sense*, and this sense has to be understood in a dynamic manner, by trying to recover the operations to which it owes this sense.

Here we find ourselves in an extremely tense situation whose description takes on the troublesome form of a tautology, that of having to designate, in the perceiving subject who has the experience of being a body, the constituting operations which have made it possible for this body to acquire the sense of being precisely what it is, an own body. The paradox consists of the fact that the body, as the unity of its organs, does not precede but rather, in the order of constitution, follows upon the constitution of the organs of which it is composed. Clearly, I must first have hands, feet, eyes, etc., and use them practically in my relations with things, in order to be able to acquire the sense of being that body whose organs are its parts.[71] As a descriptive problematic, the situation is much tighter than in the case of the perception of an external object, of something that is not me, and on which I only take up a point of view. Does the

---

[71] E. Husserl, *MS* D 10 III (June 1932), p. 36: 'Genetically, and in and of itself, the own body is not constituted ontically prior to the constitution of its moving and changing parts, nor to the practical mastery, by the Ego, of the course of their changes. The constitution of the members of the own body, as physical contents appearing in the visual field precedes that of the unity of the body; in their reciprocal constitution they get unified as 'organs' of one and the same body.'

phenomenological method make it possible for us to constitute coherently not just the objects of perception but also the body itself, as the product of the constituting operations of the subject?

An acceptable response to this question will have to come to terms with acts which are (1) meaning-giving, (2) the acts of the perceiving subject itself, and (3) the same acts as those brought into play in order to confer a sense upon surrounding objects. We have to be very attentive to the constraints that weigh upon this description, because it will be our respect for these constraints that confers rigour upon the phenomenological method.

However, if I want to constitute the body, that is, give the body a sense in the same way that I confer a sense upon surrounding objects when I perceive them, we come up against an obstacle. For to confer a sense upon the own body I have to rigorously apply the same operators that I applied in the case of objects. In advance, I have to suppose that the object remains the same through the different aspects of it that I catch when I go around it, when I pick it up, a variety of aspects that I have to pull together as a whole, etc., all of which I do as a matter of course. So I have to be able (as explained for all other objects in Chapter 6) to deploy in perspective a series of adumbrations of this own body, reunite the relevant series of adumbrations, and thread them all together as one unitary series through which the thing gets posited as being itself single and identical.

Why can't this be done? Because none of these attempts at a description, at meaning-giving, succeeds in the case of my own body, on account of the fact that, in this case precisely, *I am inside it*. What is it then that distinguishes the body in so special a way? First of all, the body is 'always here'. By contrast, external things are there, or rather can only become things for me to the extent that those that are here can be placed over there. Their different appearances when they are here and when they are there do not stand in the way of my recognizing them to be the 'same things'. The immanental relation in which I stand with respect to my own body makes it impossible for me to take up such a point of view on it. Indeed, this is what is meant by immanence: *the fact of being one with my body entails the impossibility of taking up with respect to myself an other point of view, with a view to developing adumbrations of myself*.[72] But in the absence of this power of adumbrating, of forming pre-objective manifolds that can be both differentiated and integrated in the course of experience in the way that is typical for things (Chapter 6), things could not exist for the perceiving subject that I am, and so not with respect

---

[72] See the drawing in Figure 1 (p. 147), after the one by E. Mach himself, done shortly after a cerebral attack that left him hemiphlegic.

to my own self, to the thing that I also am. Once again I have to combine in a certain regulated way the relevant visual and kinaesthetic information in order to be able to perceive this body as belonging to me.

This difficulty can be taken up another way: it has been noted that certain patients do not recognize their body as belonging to them, or attribute to someone else the possession of their arm, for example. Somato-agnosies vary widely, and somato-paraphrenia is one of the examples of this inability to recognize a part of the body as one's own. Schizophrenic patients have difficulty in attributing movements of parts of their body to themselves, a disturbance known as agentivity, a deficit probably due to the lack of linkage (corollary discharge) between areas of the brain producing the movement and those perceiving it.[73] Identifying one's body as one's own is an actively cerebral, and therefore vulnerable, process.

Perhaps this obstacle is not insurmountable. But it does nevertheless remain an obstacle for the standard phenomenological method, which consists of varying the perspective, identifying the differences that result therefrom, and projecting that arrow of intentionality which maintains the pole of identity of the thing. A way of understanding this contrast between the manner in which we confer a sense upon our body and the manner in which we confer a sense upon other objects is to draw attention to the fact that the objects of perceptions are all of a certain type, always the same. *Grosso modo*, the object of perception can be manipulated, detached from its context as an object upon which I can always focus at will while ignoring the surrounding world. This is evidently not the case with the own body.[74]

---

[73] See C.D. Frith (1992) *The Cognitive Neuropsychology of Schizophrenia*, Lawrence Erlbaum, Hove; C.D. Frith *et al.* (1991) Willed action and the prefrontal cortex in man: a study with PET, *Proc. R. Soc. Lond. Ser. B Biol. Sci.* 244, 241–501; E. Daprati *et al.* (1997) Looking for the agent. An investigation into consciousness of action and self consciousness in schizophrenic patients, *Cognition* 65, 71–86; M. Jeannerod (2002) *La nature de l'esprit*, Odile Jacob, Paris, Chap. X, pp. 169–185.

[74] If this type of object closes off the domain of the theory of perceptual constitution and in such a way that it would make no sense to even want to confer a sense upon something through perceptual acts which could not be brought under it, then it follows necessarily that the own body cannot be constituted. Its meaning of being does not proceed from our acts or, if ever it does, we wouldn't know what to say about it. This would invalidate the procedure of constitution, since the latter consists in nothing other than the re-effectuation, here and now, of all the sedimented layers of the meaning of the constituted being in question through sequences of acts which I am actually capable of producing, I the perceiving subject. The own body does not emerge out of a constitution of this kind because it can only be present as the environment of each perceived thing, never as a thing which would in turn have to be situated in an environment providing it

But we cannot stop there and simply refuse to accord any meaning of being to the own body. This would be to recreate a metaphysical dualism between a world reduced to its physical being and a disembodied constituting subject, and so would be contrary to the intention of phenomenology (similar in this respect to that of physiology) which is to recover, in the 'lower' levels of kinaesthetic experience, the evidence of a subjective activity that the intellectualist tradition reserved exclusively for the higher spheres of pure thought.

The neurosciences can help us in this progressive excavation of lived experience. For the brain has developed mechanisms to resolve this difficulty regarding the appropriation by the subject of that body which is its 'own'. If one looks in a multi-panelled mirror one can get, simultaneously, different views of one's body. This is exactly what happens towards the age of one when the child identifies its image in the mirror. It acquires a view on its body that is taken from an 'other' point of view and identifies itself as being who it is thanks to this experience of the free availability of this double point of view. This is on condition, of course, that it does not see itself in duplicate.[75]

Unity of the body schema or multiplicity of body schemas?

But the idea of a body schema[76] (which must not be naïvely assimilated to the philosophical concept of the own body)[77] is, apparently, about to be broken up to give way to a multiplicity of perceptions of the body. So perhaps we shall

---

with a background. A radical impossibility: the fact of my own immanence *vis-à-vis* my body excludes the very possibility of taking up perspectival views on it, views which I would only be able to assume if I could get away from it. And this in turn would immediately exclude the possibility of giving a meaning to my body as the intentional pole of unity: the only possible way in which meaning-giving can arise.

75 See the chapter from A. Berthoz on the double in A. Berthoz (2003) *La décision*, Odile Jacob, Paris. The question of the early recognition, by the child, of the image of its own body in the mirror, as a basis for the consciousness of self, has been raised elsewhere: P. Rochat (2003) Five levels of self-awareness as they unfold early in life, *Consciousness Cog.* 12, 717–731; P. Rochat (1998) Self-perception and action in infancy, *Exp. Brain Res.* 123, 202–109.

76 H. Head and G. Holmes (1911) Sensory disturbances from cerebral lesions, *Brain* 34, 102–254.

77 The suggestion made by Merleau-Ponty in his *Phenomenology of Perception* (M. Merleau-Ponty (1945) *Phénoménologie de la Perception*, Gallimard, Paris, trans. C. Smith (1962) *Phenomenology of Perception*, Routledge, London) under the influence of Goldstein's observations (which have become controversial since) on the patient Schneider, should be resisted.

never be in a position either to reproduce (in a mental representation) or to 'have' (the order is important here) this 'object', the own body, with the result that we shall only ever have an imperfect and partial perception of any unity comparable with that we can have of external objects. The reader need only practise a little introspection[78] to discover that all he effectively has is successive perceptions of parts of his body. (The difficulty here is that our awareness of the lived body is mostly unconscious while the experience of our bodily parts is more or less conscious.)

In order to truly understand the lived experience of what the own body is and to bring to light the extraordinary assemblage represented by the multiplicity of body schemas, perhaps it will prove necessary to set aside, or at least to suspend, for the moment, this concept of unity. All this is so that we can bring it back again later, so to speak, and so be in a position to do something with it. For it is easy to be misled by the notion of the unity of our body, a concept that does exist in the language, but which does not perhaps correspond with anything to be found in our perception. Perhaps we have simply imposed this notion upon the body. To be in a position to deal with this question concerning the plurality and the unity of the body schema and of the meaning that it confers upon our body, it is important to recognize that this unity is not given from the outset but that it is 'constructed', as they say, or even better, constituted.

The proof is that, in the centres of the brain that deal with the body, one finds neurons that encode movements in very different frames of reference. In the superior colliculus, which coordinates the movements of the head and the eyes, the neurons work in the space of the retina (retinotopic coding); in the putamen, which handles the limbs, the neurons encode in the space of the limbs; in the hippocampus, the place neurons, which encode the place of the body in a room, work in allocentric coordinates linked to the environment. The rule is then, diversity and not unity. So where is the own body? We find ourselves referred back here to Varela's critique, cited above, and the idea that there is *no central ego* (even though the latter idea is not logically implied by that of the own body).[79] Might not the I and

---

[78] Introspection is often (wrongly) confused with phenomenological description, that is, with an eidetic description where the experience of the individual person is simply treated as an exemplary instance for free variation with a view to extracting intuitively grasped invariants.

[79] See the passage from Husserl partially cited above: 'What are kinaesthesia in themselves, and what relation do they bear to acts of the Ego by which they are accompanied; that Ego which is directed towards them as they run off; Could it be that this talk of 'acts directing kinaesthesia' is misleading? (p. 9). But surely the expression "I move (my leg)",

the Self[80] be nothing more than instantaneous successions of the flux of co-occurrences?[81]

But just as the physiology of the perception of colours, which showed that *the* colour does not exist in itself but that the latter is rather a flexible and fluctuating construction of the brain, did not result in the abolition of the notion of the 'true colour' of the object; in the same way, a physiology of the perception of the own body will not result in an abolition of the certainty that we have of inhabiting 'our body'. And this is so even if it turns out that nothing like a 'virtual', an 'own', or a 'unique' body is anywhere to be found, a certainty shattered by our observation of pathological cases. Perhaps this certainty we have regarding the fact that we seem to inhabit a body comes to us from the observation of the bodies of others and from the fact that we 'construct' (interpret) the body of the other as an object (or that we look at our body as though it were an object in the mirror). Perhaps it even depends upon the context of the surrounding culture: the idea that we are individuals no doubt has something to do with the system of exchange and of wage labour.[82] Everyone owns at least his body, except of course in systems of slavery and of serfdom (where we encounter barbaric practices such as mutilations, dismembering, and quartering).

All the same, in this feeling of certainty we have regarding our ability to act we find implied a 'certain sense' of the unity of our body. We could not act if

....

"I avoid the insect bite by moving my leg", etc., should be understood quite differently from the expression "I feel", in relation to the sensorial data furnished by the bite, or a sensation of movement, like that of a fly running along my naked foot? Could it be that kinaesthetic sensations also pertain to the Ego? But then what are we to say about this subjectivity (p. 11)? And what of the purely subjective, of the identical 'I' of affection, of acts, of feelings? [...] The same world for me – the same 'I': what kind of identity are we talking about? Surely there are many kinds of constitution? (p. 18)' (D10 IV (June 1932) Difficulties connected with kinaesthesia). Ignorance of texts such as these leads to summary judgements on Husserl's dogmatism regarding the subject!

[80] Ego, Self, own: the amalgamation of heterogeneous concepts such as these, habitually employed in everyday discourse, makes the task of criticizing phenomenology relatively easy. Armed with a critique based on amalgamations such as these, we are today faced with a 'neuroscience of the Self' which would like to throw out the results of centuries of reflective philosophy.

[81] F.J. Varela, E. Thompson, and E. Rosch (1991) *The Embodied Mind: Cognitive Science and Human Experience*, MIT Press, Cambridge, MA.

[82] See the discussion of the role of money in the dissolution of primitive communities into individual proprietors of their own labour force, one of K. Marx' favourite themes (K. Marx, *Grundrisse der Kritik der Politischen Okonomie*, Dietz, Berlin, 1974), in J.-L. Petit (1980) *Du travail vivant au système des actions*, Seuil, Paris.

we were multiple and if, what is more, we were persuaded of the fact of being so. One of us[83] proposed the idea that autistic children suffer from a deficit in the constitution of the unity of the own body and that it is this shattered perception of themselves that prevents them from establishing a relation with others. Without an own body—Husserl reminds those who get excessively enthusiastic about the empathic fusion of consciousnesses of precisely this—there is no social communication.[84] Pathological deficiencies in the sense of what it means to be an I can even lead the agent to commit criminal acts; for example (to take an example offered by Hegel), confronted with an arsonist who says that it wasn't he who set light to the house, and eventually to the entire town, but his hand, one should not rule out the possibility that he might be sincere (in cases of multiple personality), contrary to what is suggested by the purely institutional and legal conception of the origin of responsibility defended by Hegel himself.[85]

That there might be a unity of the own body despite the multiplicity of referential frameworks, of selections between captors, internal simulations of different parts of our body, remains a central problem that has to be tackled in the contemporary physiology of action. Whether one is talking about *coherence*[86] or *binding*,[87] what has to be understood is effectively the linkage between the incomplete perspectives we have of our body, and which are sequentially ordered in time. So how do we come by the idea of the permanence of the body?

---

[83] See A. Berthoz (2000) *The Brain's Sense of Movement*, Harvard University Press, Cambridge, MA.

[84] E. Husserl (1973) *Zur Phänomenologie der Intersubjektivität*, I, p. 70: 'The aesthesiological-kinaesthetic layer of constitution makes of the body (*Leibkörper*) an own body (*Leib*), a sensorial field and an organ of the Ego. And in such a way that the subject can express itself through this body, have corporeal expressions that serve to express its states of mind. [...] If it is true that one can separate the bodily (aesthesiological) and the mental (spiritual), the first is primordial (*das Primäre*) for empathy (*Einfühlung*). It is absurd to connect the whole problem of empathy with purely expressive movements, corporeal expression of the mind, as one ordinarily does, and as Lipps himself also did in his research, however valuable that research might have been. Grasping the 'expressivity' of acts and mental states depends on a prior grasp of the body (*Leib*) as own body (*Leib*).'

[85] G.W.F. Hegel (1996) *Philosophy of Right*, trans. S.W. Dyde, Prometheus Books, Amherst, NY.

[86] A. Berthoz (2000) *The Brain's Sense of Movement*, Harvard University Press, Cambridge, MA, Chap. 3.

[87] W. Singer (1990) Search for coherence: a basic principle of cortical selforganization, *Concepts Neurosci*. I, 1–26.

The unity of the own body: from multi-sensorial integration to the act

This question is not perhaps as overtly thematized in Husserl's unpublished manuscripts, but it is to be found there all the same. And in this sense, that, in order to understand the specific constitution of the own body across its kinaesthetic adumbrations, a change of category proves necessary; that is, by no longer considering the own body solely as the result of what is called today 'a multi-sensorial integration', but by crossing over to the category of action, in order the better to understand its sense. Because the own body as a thing having its own meaning of being is after all something practical, caught up at each instant in an intentional act.

Later on, it might turn out that the body also proves to be an aesthetic thing, an object of theoretical enquiry, or whatever you want. But in the first instance it has to be taken as something practical. What confers upon our body, the body we inhabit as agents (even if it is absurd to ask who this 'inhabitant' is), what confers a sense upon the body for us, is the fact that it is the original location of our intervention in the surrounding world through our actions; in a word, it is itself made up of our actions. So what we have to do is extract from what we know about our body, either conceptually or through lived experience, an operator capable of accounting for the synthesis it represents as a principle of unification or of coherence as between the different insights we have into our own body from within. This idea conceals an intuition which needs to be developed physiologically.

What it is to act?

From the standpoint of the operator responsible for pulling together the internal aspects of the body, we now need to ask what it is to act. To act is to grasp things and to appropriate these things by making use of them as a function of our intentions. To act therefore presupposes that there is a world already constituted for us, a world of things which already enjoy a certain stability, a certain permanence in so far as they are arrayed around 'me'. This in turn presupposes the prior constitution of these things.

The analyses developed by Husserl in his *Thing and Space*,[88] will make it possible for us to come to terms with these presuppositions (by identifying important structures of lived experience concealed beneath an appearance of triviality). In particular, by recognizing that anything close at hand can

[88] E. Husserl (1907) *Thing and Space. Lectures from 1907*, trans. R. Rojcewirz (ed.), Kluwer, Dordrecht.

become further off and that what is further off can be brought close at hand, without the unity of the thing being in any way altered. Rather the contrary, its different appearances are for me, essentially, occasions for bringing into play my perceptual ability to posit the existence of just such a unity. To be able to act is to exercise a power to deploy in perspective, and on the basis of my self, appearances of surrounding things. And this, not just in the two dimensions of the visual field but equally in the third dimension brought to such things by our eye movements, the movements of our hands, the movements required to walk around objects, etc. (see Chapter 6). It is a combination of movements that gives us the visual image of the third dimension. This is the point at which *Thing and Space* stops being of help to us, since the programme is limited to the visual and kinaesthetic (oculomotor) constitution of perceived things as things existing in the physical world.

Husserl does not try to hide the difficulty. In his last lecture, devoted to the constitution of the external body as a moving body, the final step in the constitution of the thing, he declares:

> In general, we have not taken into consideration the own body which is, nevertheless, even if only partially, also a thing that appears, and this even if we abstract from the problems we have just pointed out. We talked as though the I were a mind equipped with eyes, a disembodied mind which for all that, received just the same series of appearance of things as we do, together with the same group of kinaesthetic sensations.[89]

This is not the place to undertake a systematic presentation of the problem, like that undertaken in the *Lectures from 1907*, for example. Instead, we will look for guidance in the labyrinth of unpublished manuscripts on the constitution of the own body, properly so called. A fruitful way of approaching the problem is through certain later attempts at a phenomenology of the instrument, stemming from the 1930s.[90] The ability to act also includes the possibility of extracting one thing from that system through which it is given, the system of orientations. They are hereby presented as being close at hand or far off, to the right or to the left, etc. We can tear things away from this system through which they spontaneously present themselves to us and divest them of their external properties, with a view to tying them in to the own body. This moment of linkage with external things which, in the first instance, seemed to be things whose disclosure remained independent of the own body, is the decisive moment for action.

----

[89] E. Husserl (1907) *Thing and Space. Lectures from 1907*, trans. R. Rojcewirz (ed.), Kluwer, Dordrecht, §83, p. 329.

[90] E. Husserl, *MS* C16 V (September 1931); D10 I (1932) to III (June 1932).

In this way we can selectively associate a thing with the source point; that is, the place where the perceiving subject is itself situated. We find here two aspects, two presuppositions of action, which are also two factors in the constitution of the own body:

1 the fact that there are things whose mode of presentation depends both upon my own accompanying movements and upon my compensating for their own movements, an argument used by Poincaré, to keep their unity: visual constitution;

2 a fact that no longer depends upon the above-mentioned visual constitution; that is, upon the eyes and the organs supporting the eyes, but rather upon my ability to grasp with the hands, a new, *haptic* power.

How does this haptic constitution of my own body proceed? By taking hold of, a taking hold through which we appropriate a thing as the extension of a motor organ. This act of taking hold manifests itself, literally, whenever we manipulate a tool. In an analogical manner, it is operative whenever we put on our clothing and wear it, whenever we make use of a piece of furniture (the artisan at his bench), whenever we get into a car and transform it into a vehicle.[91] In every such instance it is a matter of a linkage that gets set up with the own body and which depends upon a handling operation. This is what can be extracted from the notion of action by going back to its corporeal roots.

The own body is what takes hold of

Husserl supposes that the own body is the result of a double constitution: (1) the constitution of things that are principally visual and (2) a new constitution with reference to a repertory of constitutive resources (adumbrations and kinaesthesiae) already involved in the procedure of constitution at this same visual stage. This new constitution is typically haptic; that is, tied to the ability we enjoy to take hold of, grasp.[92] Showing a notable premonition of the scientific knowledge which would have made it possible for him to recognize the existence of muscular and articulatory proprioceptors, Husserl insisted upon the tactile aspect of the haptic sense. But it is evident that he had in view

---

91 One finds fragments of a phenomenology of changing appearances (points of view, if you prefer) through the very fact of participating in the movement of a car in *Thing and Space* and of a plane (or a spaceship) in E. Husserl (1989) *La Terre ne se meut pas*, Minuit, Paris.

92 This is what Merleau-Ponty had in mind in his formula: 'Vision is touching with the eyes.' But the theme goes back further. Maine de Biran has this to say: 'We do not see as though we were not already accustomed to touching, and we do not touch as though we had never seen.' (Maine de Biran (1987) *Mémoires sur l'influence de l'habitude*, Vrin, Paris, p. 185).

this haptic sense, whose power is precisely to combine a variety of perceptions, forces, cutaneous pressures, limb displacements, etc. Examples: we pick up a tool. We wear a piece of clothing. For even wearing is a kind of taking hold of. We make use of tables and chairs in our daily environment, beginning with our room. We 'run around in a car'. We 'make use of a vehicle'. We travel 'by plane'. All of this results from a description of the totality of things taken from the point of view of the use we are able to make of them. What is interesting is to re-define the very reality of objects as a function of their possibility of being linked to the own body, and in this way, as a function of their being granted a sense by an agent acting on the basis of his body and exerting his haptic power, his hold over.

In fact, constitution is ordinarily just as much haptic as it is visual, vestibular, acoustic, or olfactory, because perception is basically multi-modal, the dominant senses at any one moment being those that are most relevant to the action in hand, together with its consequences. What modern physiology brings us, and what was already anticipated by Husserl's in his analysis, is the idea that, in perception (not distinct in this respect from action), the brain selects sensors as a function of action, of memory, and of its intentions. This projective and anticipatory character of perception is actually one of the most promising axes of the physiology of perception and action.

Prehension, appropriation, 'approprioception'

Another consequence of these thoughts that deserves to be developed is that it requires us to rethink the problem of the relation between the senses. The multi-sensorial aspect of perception has to be reconsidered. For example, we often consider that vision gives us information about the external world while the haptic sense is linked to the own body, to the skeleton, to the skin, etc. Husserl had the extraordinarily insightful idea that vision too is internal perception of the own body. This is what David Lee rediscovered when he described the 'proprioceptive function of vision'.[93] There is no dichotomy between the two forms of perception. Even if one of them should be treated as a camera, both are cameras of a kind, since each in its own way invokes a sense of depth and distance, so they should not be disassociated. According to the traditional dichotomy, there is proprioception and exteroception: vision is both an exteroceptor and a proprioceptor and that the haptic sense can be both a proprioceptor and an exteroceptor is illustrated by the dual perception

---

[93] D.N. Lee and J.R. Lishman (1974) Visual proprioceptive control of standing in human infants, *Perception Psychophys.* 15, 529–532.

of the two hands when they touch each other. As exteroception, vision is what tells us about the world out there. The haptic sense is the sense that informs us about what is to hand. But there is more to it than that, for cooperation between vision and the haptic sense is essential for two functions:

1 to complete the description of the properties (appearances) of the object in order to constitute it as an object in the world. This is the trivial sense given to it by contemporary physiology;

2 to enable our consciousness of the own body to emerge. In a more general way, multi-sensorial interaction does not just complete the description of the world, it appropriates it. So it should be called (let us risk the barbarism): 'approprioception'.

Force-feedback

This interweaving of the perception of self, of the own body, and the object is well illustrated with the modern notion of the *force-feedback*.[94] Let us invite the reader to take hold of the stem of his glasses (apologies to those who don't wear any) while keeping his or her eyes closed. By agitating your glasses you are able to figure out a good many properties of these glasses, their flexibility and even their geometry, for example. This is possible thanks to what has been called force-feedback; that is, the *force exerted by the glasses on your fingers*, and not simply the force that you exert on the frame of your glasses. An apparatus, the joystick with force-feedback, makes it possible to study this remarkable property. It is made up of a handle equipped with little motors. The subject is presented with the image of an object on a screen, a cup of coffee for example, and a cursor. Whenever the cursor makes contact with the image of the edge of the cup, the little motor of the handle is activated and produces on the finger the same force as that which would be produced by the edge of the cup when it resists the finger. However extraordinary it might appear, it turns out that this return of effort immediately creates the illusion of really touching the cup, as if the cup was at the end of the finger which, in fact, is only touching the joystick. This is no longer just a matter of prolonging the body by means of a tool, as in the Iriki experiences, to which we will come back later, but of an object perceived across a computer simulation, and which suddenly becomes real, due to

---

94 Compare to Maine de Biran: 'Resistance is met with and is constantly reproduced whenever we touch and even, though more obscurely, in what we see, in every step we take, in every movement we make in the external world.' (Maine de Biran (1803) Mémoires sur l'influence de l'habitude sur la faculté de penser, Presses Universitaires de France, Paris, 1954, p. 246).

the haptic sense. It is haptic virtual reality. In the laboratory of the one of us who is a physiologist, and following the suggestion of V. Gurfinkel, a force-feedback system was designed which flew on the Russian space station MIR under the name of ROBOTOP. Today videogames, surgical robotised systems, teleoperation systems, and even virtual museums are equipped with this.[95]

In contemporary scientific literature, there is much talk of the 'virtual reality' aspect of the perceived object. The cup has been objectified and so becomes real, even though it does not exist. But there is another aspect that has not been duly noted, and which the notion of the constitution of the own body requires that we investigate. For this example shows that over and beyond simply becoming conscious of my finger, all of a sudden, I actually touch the cup. *My own body is constituted in and through this feedback of force at the same time, and in proportion, as the virtual object becomes real.*

Husserl's basic intuition is quite clear on this point. He was so well aware of the importance of 'I am taking hold of something' that he talks about it as a violent disturbance that takes away from the thing its visual properties. But this intuition is not enough in itself. What we now have to do is embark upon an empirical study of the process, and this will require that we look for a method capable of integrating experience, and our sense of lived experience, into science.

The own body as the transformer of the subjective into the objective

For Husserl, we have first of all the system of orientations in the first-person perspective. The own body is the point source, the zero point on the basis of which directional perspectives are unfolded. It is the centre of an entire spectrum of possible directions of attention. But in addition to this original role of directed activity, of perspectives on the object that we call 'egocentric', the own body has a second property. It also captures in a certain way the objects it manipulates, and assimilates them to parts of itself. It can therefore also be seen as a sort of compass tracing out the sphere of belonging of the ego, and thanks to which I can say of all the things to which I have direct access that they are 'ready to hand'. Among these directly accessible things we find,

---

95 The first handle with a return of effort linked to a visual stimulator to study its role in the perception of objects was put together in the cellars of the Institut des Cordeliers in Paris by A. Berthoz' laboratory, in cooperation with Victor and Eugenio Gurfinkel from the University of Moscow, and was developed for experiences in space by the CNES and the Matra company under the name ROBOTOP then COGNILAB. This apparatus was installed on the Russian space station MIR.

of course, my body, but also all those objects I make use of regularly, which are more or less directly associated with me.

What then is the relation between these two sets of things? A direct link, as powerful as it is contingent, is created whenever I take hold of an object and displace it, and this by virtue of the fact that it now becomes a part of my body, in a certain sense, at least as long as I keep hold of it.

The constitution of the own body has a fundamental property, namely this, *that although it remains invariant it can be modified as a function of the action in progress.* An example is given by the temporary extensions of the body implied by the use of tools of all kinds, and in all sorts of circumstance. In his later manuscripts, Husserl insists upon the special status to be attributed to the act of taking hold of an object in the external world, and so making of it a prolongation of the own body (not, for all that, an outgrowth of this body since, as an inert object, this extension cannot be animated kinaesthetically). This act assumes a foundational value both for the sense of the experience of the own body and, in reverse, for the practical constitution of the world.

The own body functions as a transformer of the subjective into the objective, and reciprocally. I get into my car. The car becomes an extension of myself. I get out, and the car becomes an external object once again. The own body, this curious object, can, at any moment, take advantage of its special status to assimilate to itself an object in the external world, and thus confer upon this relation between the subject and the world the quasi-epistemological status of knowledge through action and knowledge through praxis.

This is an entirely new idea in physiology: *where no one has ever before talked of a change in the status of the object starting from the moment when it is linked to the body.* 'Linked': that could be taken to refer to the desk where I work, to the clothes I wear, or, in general, to any extension of the body in the context of a practical activity in which the body is involved. For the latter is caught up in the agent's sphere of belonging. In this frame of reference, what is it then that confers a sense, a biological sense, upon the tool? It is the fact that it has become a 'non-kinaesthetic extension of the own-body',[96] as Husserl puts it.

....

96 E. Husserl, *MS* D10 I (May 1932): 'Non corporeal things picked out by the place zero do not yield kinaesthetic sensations like limbs, but they participate in such sensations when they are linked to a member (p. 20)'; 'The object grasped in the hand immediately loses its ability to appear at rest or in motion like an external object; it becomes, so to speak, a part of the own body, with the exception of kinaesthesia, which are missing [...]. It is precisely this inversion that obviously lies at the root of the possibility of any apperception of the body as own body (p. 58)'. D12 I (5 September 1931): 'Even if haptic touching is not yet practical, like pure vision, it has the property of being able to change into pressing, striking, sliding, etc., to the extent that the appropriate pressure is applied.

Obviously, the tool is not invested with kinaesthetic sensations like an organ of the body, but it participates in the system of the body, which is itself constituted kinaesthetically. And this to the extent that the tool is integrated in a transaction at the interface of two systems: the system of the *objectifying perspectives of perception* and that of the *ownness sphere of the body*. The tool is in truth only one of the aspects of a phenomenological structure of experience referring back to a functional structure of the brain, a structure whose functioning we have only just begun to investigate.

In fact this phenomenology of the body, prolonged through the tool, has been quite recently put on the track of its neural correlates thanks to the work of Atsushi Iriki and his team at the Tokyo University of Medicine.[97] They studied the visuo-tactile neurons corresponding to the region of the hand. A monkey carrying implanted electrodes was trained to retrieve food pellets with a rake. The size of the visuo-tactile receptor field for the recorded neurons was measured at three stages of the experiment: before the use of the rake, during, and after. To obtain an evaluation of the visual receptor field of these neurons, a map was drawn up of the activations obtained when, in the immediate environment of the monkey, a food pellet was dragged within its reach.

What was discovered was an extension, in the axis of the rake, of the visual receptor field of the visuo-tactile neurons whenever the monkey used the rake or, in the words (audacious for physiologists) of the authors, 'whenever he intended to make use of it'. This receptor field returns to its previous configuration just as soon as the monkey stops using the rake, even if he is still holding it in his hand. The phenomenologist would say that the probable substrate of the kinaesthesia of the hand gets transformed in such a way as to incorporate the instrument employed in the action in progress. Ovid, with his *Metamorphoses*, turns out then to have been less of a poet and mythologist than a physiologist!

This observation bore on the 'distal' neurons of the hand, but an analogous observation has been made on the 'proximal' neurons of the shoulder, where a similar structure has been found. The authors were not unaware of what

....

By an appropriate coordination of the fingers employed to touch something from several sides, this touching can also change into handling, carrying, etc. From pure touching in which the image of the *res extensa* is constituted haptically [...] a world emerges in which we can intervene by acting, by moving what is at rest, by carrying through changes which were going to happen anyway and, in this way, subjectivizing what, in a certain sense, is simply there, in itself, in external things by including such things within the frame of our own body (p. 34).'

[97] A. Iriki *et al.* (1996) Coding of modified body schema during tool use by macaque post-central neurones, *NeuroReport* 7, 2325–2330.

appears to us to be a direct validation of phenomenological description, even though they remained within the modest frame of an experimental report, since they made an explicit reference to Merleau-Ponty in their article of 1996. However, this extension does not coincide with eye movements. To prove it, the eye movements were also recorded and the action potentials released by the presentation of food were superimposed upon eye movements recorded while looking. And here we see clearly the disjunction of the two. It now becomes clear that we have a modification in the inner sense of the own body in action, whose obvious 'cause' (a causality as inextricably motivational as it is inductive) is the intentional use made of the rake.[98]

Corollary discharge: anticipation and identification of the own body

At this point we want to advance a new thesis concerning the interpretation of the corollary discharge. For this could play as crucial a role in the constitution of the own body as it has been suspected to play a central role in agentivity, the perception that we are the agents of our actions, as mentioned above. Let us recall what is at issue. When the brain commands a movement of the eye or hand, it directs an efferent copy or corollary discharge at numerous centres other than the motor organs. The reader could get an idea of this by pressing on one eye, from the side, while keeping the other closed. He will see the world move. This manœuvre produces a very slight displacement of the visual world on the retina, which is interpreted by the brain not as a movement of the eye but as a movement of the external world. On the other hand, when the eye makes a simple saccade, one that also induces a visual movement, we do not perceive any displacement of the world. This is due to the corollary discharge which informs the areas of the brain implied in the perception of voluntary displacement and produces this remarkable perceptual stabilization.

Our body is animated from within by a spontaneous motor activity, an activity that can be summed up in a happy formula drawn from Husserl when

---

[98] The further work of the same team, however ingenious the protocol might have been, is not so interesting to the phenomenologist. From an ecological viewpoint, their intervention consisted of teaching the use of the rake to a macaque, a species that does not spontaneously use tools. However inoffensive this might appear, they have gone on from there to try and make use of technological means much further removed from the normal conditions of action. In order to be able to control and manipulate arbitrarily the body schema of the monkey in relation to its real anatomy, they taught it to recognize and to direct the image of its hand reconstituted on a computer screen (A. Iriki *et al.* (2001) Self-images in the video monitor coded by monkey intraparietal neurons, *Neurosci. Res.* 40, 163–173).

he said: 'at the same time that we see things in movement in the space outside us, we set this activity up from inside of ourselves'.[99] Let us ask ourselves whether this proposition does not match, to some degree at least, what is meant by corollary discharge or copy of the motor command. This idea has been discussed for some twenty or thirty years thanks to von Holst and Mittelstædt.[100] Baker, Berthoz and colleagues were among the first to show that such a discharge was present in the vestibular nucleus for eye movements, and it is now well documented at the neurophysiological level by the identification of multiple re-entry paths sending copies to different levels of the central nervous system, and so informing the perceptual systems of the agent's movements and intentions to move.[101]

But is there more to it than this? What might be interesting is this something more. Can we find in the phenomenology of the own body an idea that might make it possible to develop the concept of corollary discharge? Physiologists have suggested several uses for this efferent copy of motor orders: to gain time in the treatment of proprioceptive or exteroceptive information concerning the movement in progress (feed-forward function); to provide the feedback information in the slave systems of motor control (automatic systems whose later actions are subordinated to the result of their own previous actions); to update the sensorial maps in a dynamic fashion (Droulez and Berthoz' model);[102] to modify the coordinates in the parietal cortex by furnishing the regions that encode the visual targets in retinal coordinates with information relative to the movement of the eye expressed as a function of cephalic coordinates, etc.

Although von Holst and Mittelstædt saw the importance of the corollary discharge in the processes of motor control, it is doubtful whether they ever really imagined that it might be a fundamental mechanism in the constitution of the own body, even though their criticism of the kind of reductionism to elementary external causes, basic to reflexology, and their research into the foundations of the autonomy of the organism in the endogenous activity of

---

99 E. Husserl, *MS* D10 I (May 1932), p. 8.

100 E. von Holst and H. Mittelstædt (1950) Das Reafferenzprinzip. Wechselwirkung zwischen Zentralnervensystem und Peripherie, *Naturwissenschaften* 37, 464–476.

101 R. Baker, A. Berthoz, and J. Delgado-Garcia (1977) Monosynaptic excitation of trochlear motoneurons following electrical stimulation of the prepositus hypoglossi nucleus, *Brain Res.* 121(1), 157–161; A. Grantyn, A. Berthoz, and R. Baker (1977) Excitatory effect of the superior colliculus on the motor neurons of extra-ocular muscles of cats, *C.R. Acad. Sci. Hebd. Seances Acad. Sci. D.* 284(12), 1087–1089.

102 J. Droulez and A. Berthoz (1991) The concept of dynamic memory in sensorimotor control, in D.R. Humphrey and H.J. Freund (eds), *Motor Control: Concepts and Issues*, John Wiley, Chichester, pp. 137–161.

the brain, already oriented their thinking in the direction of a recognition of the truly autonomous power of the human agent to 'make sense' with its body.[103] Our hypothesis is that what this corollary discharge is the cerebral correlate of is not simply the intimate knowledge we have of the motor orders we emit, but also *the extent to which our motor intentions are impregnated with our experience of inhabiting an own body, an experience that extends to a continual re-modelling of its geometry as a function of its movement.* These motor intentions participate in the animation of this continuous and closed surface that I discover I have when I see myself from all sides.

One might wonder how we can pretend to have overcome dualism even while continuing to employ the terminology of 'inhabiting' which seems to presuppose it, at least for the English-speaking reader. 'Inhabit' translates poorly the German verb *wohnen*, which appeals to a specific characteristic of the being a human being, thereby exposing our use of the term to a confusion of a certain mode of being with the occupation of a building, a council house for example! In fact this terminology is so little stained with dualism that it is regularly used by both the highly Cartesian Husserl and the highly anti-Cartesian Heidegger.[104]

Might not an analysis conducted in Hussserl's terms make it possible to bring us this something more? A way to do this is perhaps opened up by the above-mentioned interpretation of the corollary discharge as that spontaneous activity that we bring into play from within at the same time that we see external things in movement, things that we intend eventually to capture. The 'something more' would then be this idea of objectification. The copy of the action produced by the body is not just a perceptual stabilization, it would then also be necessary to make of the own body an object like any other object. But—*horribile dictu*—'an object lived from within'.[105]

....

103   E. von Holst and H. Mittelstædt (1950) Das Reafferenzprinzip. Wechselwirkung zwischen Zentralnervensystem und Peripherie, *Naturwissenschaften* 37, 476: 'If the eye is effectively incapable of distinguishing between its own movement and that of the environment, the animal – which after all does possess a central nervous system consisting in something more than connections between receptors and muscles – is perfectly capable of drawing the distinction between the two. Thanks to the principle of reafference, *he is able to recognize the constancy of his own objective environment.*'

104   See his lecture at Darmstadt on the 5 August 1951: Building, Dwelling, Thinking, in *M. Heidegger: Poetry, Language, Thought*, trans. A. Hofstadter (2001), Harper & Row, New York.

105   In case the reader might be ready to abandon the very idea of the object (as he has been invited to do by Varela and the entire Buddhist tradition) and to replace the latter with another concept, that of the 'abject'. In that case, the corollary discharge would make of the own body an 'abject'.

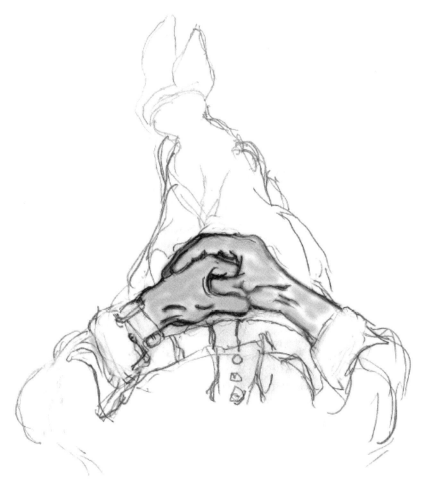

Fig. 4 The hand touching and touched

Everyone is familiar with the peculiar experience that arises when one touches one hand with the other. What happens is this curious ambiguity consisting in one of the hands being perceived as actively touching while the other is perceived as passively touched (Figure 4). This is a situation that can be inverted at will. The dialogue established between phenomenology and physiology makes it possible for us to discover that, just as in the experience of the hand touching and touched, at the very moment I grab hold of a cup of coffee in front of me, and as soon as I touch it, I appropriate it and assimilate it to the own body, even while letting it assume the status of an object existing outside of me. This condition is, however, an absolutely general constraint of any kind of instrumental action: nothing can be done without it.

The idea at the bottom of all this is that whenever I grab hold of a tool and make of it the prolongation of my body, the mechanism I bring into play contributes essentially to my sense of having a body. But at the same time, let us remember that it also contributes to my body keeping its status as an object. The objectifying dimension of perception—too easily forgotten in the present day fashion of the 'embodiment' of perception in cognitive science literature—depends upon this double contribution. It is a dimension as essential as that which shoves the object away from me, because this object will not be indefinitely associated with my own body. I can always get rid of it. In the same way, the touched hand remains external, becomes an object for me. When it is a matter of the two hands of the same body, the situation is paradoxical.

Such is the enigma of the own body for those who remain captivated by the Greek tradition, assimilating contemplation and theoretical consideration. The vast world is composed of objects possessing a continuous surface, closed in on themselves. I too am an object possessing a continuous surface, closed in on myself. Moreover, I 'inhabit' my body in no more particular a way than I 'inhabit' the cup. Thus we have a dual status of being at one and the same time both an external object and an 'object' animated from within. The own body is the locus of this double belonging.

The reader informed of the classical work of Frith, Jeannerod, and others[106] and of their common hypothesis concerning the aetiology of the influence syndrome of schizophrenics—which they envisaged as a disturbance of agentivity, of the self-attribution of action—might perhaps find the analyses developed above a trifle naïve. Jeannerod's 'pragmatic' theory of action is indeed a classic of physiological literature. But let us take a look at the place these authors accord to kinaesthesia. This would not be a fruitless task, if only because our manifesto is intended to bring to light differences of opinion and so to provoke argument. Frith, for his part, does not try to conceal the fact that he takes kinaesthesia to be of small importance. He takes their role to be solely palliative. In other words, it is only when 'it doesn't work' (his own words)[107] that kinaesthesia has a role to play, a role which, for this reason,

[106] C.D. Frith (1992) *The Cognitive Neuropsychology of Schizophrenia*, Lawrence Erlbaum, Hove; C.D. Frith *et al.* (1991) Willed action and the prefrontal cortex in man: a study with PET, *Proc. R. Soc. Lond. Ser. B Biol. Sci.* 244, 241–501; E. Daprati *et al.* (1997) Looking for the agent. An investigation into consciousness of action and self consciousness in schizophrenic patients, *Cognition* 65, 71–86; M. Jeannerod (2002) *La nature de l'esprit*, Odile Jacob, Paris, Chap. X, pp. 169–185.

[107] An expression in line with his de-connexion theory of schizophrenia he voiced in his conference at Berthoz Seminar, Collège de France.

is solely palliative. They feature, so to speak, as evidence for the failure of self-attribution. So, contrary to what Husserl thought, they are not constituting.

Furthermore,—and here we diverge radically from the whole mental representation school of physiology—the structure of lived experience brought to light in phenomenology with the help of the concept of the own body is not a structure of judgement, nor of what makes up the content of judgement, the mental representation. It is rooted at a much deeper level of the incarnation of the living being. However, all the experimental protocols conceived in this representational frame of reference in order to bring out the failure *of judgement* on the part of the agent in his attempt to attribute to himself the perceived effects of his action (visual effects in the deflection of a line traced with reference to a predetermined trajectory; tactile effects resulting from his tickling himself or being tickled by a robot) never get beyond *judgement*. Worse, the judgement in question is verbal, reflective, and *a posteriori*: impossible on such a basis to capture the pre-reflexive, preverbal feeling of our immanence in an acting body.

To be persuaded of this, it is enough to pay attention to a circumstance that has remained unchanged since the pioneer experiments both of Held and Freedman (1963) on the manual control of a trace across a prism[108] and of Nielsen (1963) on the illusion of attributing to oneself the hand (that of the experimenter seen in a mirror) seen tracing a line that deviates from the rectilinear.[109] The instructions bear always, and exclusively, upon the act of judging whether the result of the action conforms with what the agent really wanted, and this on the basis of a mental representation formed after the fact. For example, in the illusion of a loss of control of the tracing hand seen in the mirror (when the image of the hand of the experimenter is substituted for that of the subject) the subject is asked to judge whether or not the movement of his hand tracing the line was in response to his conscious intention that it should be perfectly rectilinear.

....

[108] R. Held and S.J. Freedman (1963) Plasticity in human sensorimotor control: studies of disordered motor-sensory feedback raise questions about man's coordination in outer space, *Science* 142(3591), 455–462.

[109] T.I. Nielsen (1963) Volition: A new experimental approach, *Scand. J. Psychol.* 4, 225–230. See also recent work on the same paradigm: A. Posada, N. Franck, S. Augier, N. Georgieff, and M. Jeannerod (2007) Altered processing of sensorimotor feedback in schizophrenia, *C.R. Biol.* 330(5), 382–388; C. Farrer *et al.* (2004) Neural correlates of action attribution in schizophrenia, *Psychiatry Res.* 131(1), 31–44; N. Franck *et al.* (2001) Defective recognition of one's own actions in patients with schizophrenia, *Am. J. Psychiatry* 158(3), 454–459; N. Georgieff and M. Jeannerod (1998) Beyond consciousness of external reality: a 'who' system for consciousness of action and self-consciousness, *Conscious Cogn.* 7(3), 465–477.

'We choose who we will be the next moment'

The attribution of a meaning of being to our own body depends essentially upon kinaesthesia. Husserl distinguishes two categories of kinaesthesia. First, *objectifying kinaesthesia* (KO). These objectifying kinaesthesiae function in the perceptual mode. Their function is simply to objectify the thing that the touched hand has become. These are not, as Husserl reminds us, 'the kind of kinaesthesia that bring our two hands together in accordance with one's desire'.[110] For there is another contribution made by kinaesthesia, a contribution which, this time, goes back up to the source of our motor intentions and which Husserl calls 'motor kinaesthesia' (KM), and this with a view to distinguishing them from the objectifying kinaesthesia. However, we do also feel the motor kinaesthesiae that invade the touching hand. So, in addition to the feeling of being acted upon, we have to recognize *a feeling underlying action*. In this way, a doubly kinaesthetic contribution is brought to the theory of constitution. In order to account for the way in which our feeling of being a body arises, we have to bring into play both groups of kinaesthesia, KO and KM. And if we can play with our different organs in such a way as to evoke this reciprocal touching/touched relation, it is simply because of the contingent, dual way in which the sensori-motor functions of our body have been set up: the touched hand can arbitrarily turn into the touching hand, the touching hand, into the touched hand. Each in turn can be animated by motor kinaesthesia or uphold objectifying kinaesthesia.

We now need to examine the relation between this dichotomy and experiments done on monkeys, which show a great difference in the activation of the neurons of the superior temporal suleus, depending on whether its arm is touched by a stick or whether it touches its own arm.[111] The neurons of the somato-sensory cortex also exhibit different activities under these two conditions.[112] In other words, the brain 'thinks' that when it touches an object it makes use of sensorial information to characterize the object, and that this has nothing to do with the structures responsible for constructing the own body. On the other hand, when one is passively caressed, then the cerebral activity is principally devoted to the constitution of the own body. With humans this

---

[110]   E. Husserl, *MS* D 10 III (June 1932), p. 41.

[111]   D.I. Perrett and A.J. Mistlin (1990) Visual and somatosensory processing in the macaque temporal cortex: the role of 'expectation', *Exp. Brain Res.* 82, 437–450.

[112]   M.A. Nicolelis (2005) Computing with thalamocortical ensembles during different behavioral states, *J. Physiol.* 566(1), 37–47; A.A. Ghazanfar and M.A. Nicolelis (1997) Non linear processing of tactile information in the thalamocortical loop, *J. Neurophysiol.* 78(1), 506–510; M.A. Nicolelis (1996) Beyond maps: a dynamic view of the somatosensory system, *Braz. J. Med. Biol. Res.* 29(4), 401–412.

fundamental difference between touching oneself and being touched is brought to light through the tickling experience. We can't tickle ourselves! Different regions of the brain are activated when we touch ourselves, which fails to produce the tickling sensation, and when we are tickled by others, which does indeed produce the laughing reaction![113]

In fact at least three kinaesthetic functions need to be distinguished: *objectifying kinaesthesia* for *external objects (KO), objectifying kinaesthesia for the own body* (KOCP) and which constitutes it as an object in the world, and *motor kinaesthesia* (KM) which informs the agent about its wanting to move and its intention to do so.

How is it then that we come by this feeling that there is a body we inhabit? We came by it because, with our two hands, which are organs of action, we are able to operate haptic links with objects—such as a hammer—which thereby become extensions of the own body and which are arbitrarily substitutable each for the other by virtue of the fact that they have been taken from my environment. Constitution, the attribution of the meaning of being to our own body when we are an agent is linked to the fact that there are motor orders, and also to the fact that there are objectifying kinaesthesiae (visual, tactile, proprioceptive afferences). But that is not all. The most important thing is that there is in addition *an interaction* and a *continual co-evolution between the somato-motor and somato-sensory topographical maps* which make up, together, the system of re-afferences (a constant returning upon themselves of these afferences) to which we referred under the name motor kinaesthesia. So what has just been said about the hands could be taken up again with respect to other parts of the body.

Of course, the notion of 'maps' has to be taken with a pinch of salt, however commonplace its use might have become with the specialists of cortical cartography.[114] Taken just as it arises through the topographical readings obtained in the anatomical or physiological study of the monkey, this notion certainly does not include what features, in our view, as the neural substrate of the constitution of the own body: the possibility of *simulating action without*

---

[113] S.J. Blakemore (2003) Deluding the motor system, *Consciousness Cog.* 12, 647–655; S.J. Blakemore, J. Smith, R. Steel, C.E. Johnstone, and C.D. Frith (2000) The perception of self-produced stimuli in patients with auditory hallucinations and passivity experiences: evidence for a breakdown in self-monitoring, *Psychol. Med.* 30(5), 1131–1139.

[114] C. Xerri (2003) Plasticité des représentations somesthésiques et illusions perceptives: le paradoxe du membre fantôme, in J.-L. Petit (éd.), Repenser le corps, l'action et la cognition avec les neurosciences, *Intellectica* 36–37, 67–87; C. Xerri *et al.* (1999) Representational plasticity in cortical area 3b paralleling tactual-motor skill acquisition in adult monkeys, *Cerebral Cortex* 9, 264–276.

moving the body, a possibility brought to light through the illusion of the phantom limb with amputees or brain-lesioned persons.[115]

The constitution of the own body cannot be reduced to a re-shuffling of the pack! This is why the notion of maps has to be understood in an extended sense, following the example of Gerald Edelman[116] who, without entirely rejecting maps (indispensable after all to the modelling process) nevertheless proposed to envisage them as emerging out of dynamic processes implying entire networks of structures. In the course of ontogenesis and indeed throughout the entire length of individual experience, one process (re-entrance) ensures the selection and the correlating of groupings of cells functionally associated through perceptual activities, even though these groupings are situated in different anatomical and cerebral regions. This process establishes reciprocal links between the maps at the root of the perceptual categorization of the environment.[117]

So we have to assume an integrated system of somato-sensory and somato-motor maps which constantly modify each other, a system brought into play whenever I take hold of an object independent of me, thereby making of it a prolongation of my body. It is across this prolongation of my body that I acquire the sense of being my own body. This continual adaptability of the neuronal schemas of the body is doubtless required in order that this kind of functioning should be possible. Michael Merzenich, to whom we owe the discovery of the exceptional plasticity of the sensory cortical maps, writes as follows:

> To a large extent we choose what we will experience, then we choose the details that we will pay attention to, then we choose how we will react based on our expectations, plans and feelings, and then we choose what we will do as a result. This element of choice, and the relational nature of awareness in general, have almost never been considered in neurophysiological experiments. We realize now that experience coupled with attention leads to physical change in the structure and future functioning of the nervous system. This leaves us with a clear physiological fact, a fact that is really just a mechanistic confirmation of what we already know experimentally: moment by moment we choose and sculpt how our ever-changing minds will work, we choose

---

115 A. Berthoz (2003) *La décision*, Odile Jacob, Paris, pp. 165–166.

116 G. M. Edelman and G. Tononi (2000) *Comment la matière devient conscience*, Odile Jacob, Paris.

117 G. M. Edelman (1989) *The Remembered Present. A Biological Theory of Consciousness*, Basic Books, New York, Fig. 3.1, p. 45. Other mechanisms have also be taken into account, like those on which Rodolfo Llinás has laid stress, and which emphasize a continuous oscillatory flux in the loops linking the thalamus to the cortex across the basal ganglia (R. Llinás (2001) *I of the Vortex*, MIT Press, Cambridge, MA).

who we will be the next moment in a very real sense, and these choices are left embossed in physical form on our material selves.[118]

The plasticity of the somatotopy of the secondary sensory brain areas has to be recognized.[119] This plasticity is modulated by the experience of the subject throughout the entire course of his life and largely controlled by his motor activity through the use he makes of his own body and other things. Hence the hypothesis that appears revolutionary when set against the localizationalist and clinical tradition since Gall and Broca and the cartography of the homunculi of the cerebral cortex (Penfield and Rasmussen): body maps are never fixed and final. They are not there to reproduce the independent and already constituted form of the physical body in accordance with invariable laws displayed across an inert screen. For the form of the physical body is not ready-made, and so the cerebral cortex cannot passively register its projection. There has to be a continuous and epigenetic co-evolution of the body in action and the active brain, whose very activity implies a reciprocally structuring influence as between the sensorial and motor quasi-maps, which are interwoven and functionally interdependent. This transition from a static topographical conception of the body–brain relation to a pragmatic (actional) conception spells the end of the dualist ideology of representation derived from the theory of mind adopted by the cognitive sciences.

To go from there to declaring that this development prepares the way for a philosophy of action more in accord with the contemporary neurosciences than is the academic discipline that has grown up under this name involves a step we are not going to take. All we are trying to do here is get ourselves out of the clutches of an opposition that must remain paradoxical in contemporary neurophysiology, an opposition arising from the concept of the homunculus, which tended to get us to think of the organization of 'cerebral representation' and, more particularly, the cortical representation of the body, as fixed (the end result of development in the course of childhood), on the one hand and, on the other, recent results bearing on cerebral plasticity in the adult; for instance, the ability of the brain to reconfigure itself after the amputation of limbs.

To get out of this opposition, we are going to propose the idea that this image or, since we can hardly talk of image here, this apparent fixity or rigidity

....

[118] M.M. Merzenich and R.C. deCharms (1995) Neural representations, experience, and change, in R. Llinás and P. Churchland (eds), *Mind and Brain*, MIT Press, Cambridge, MA, p. 76.

[119] M.M. Merzenich *et al.* (1983) Topographic reorganization of somatosensory cortical areas 3b and 1 in adult monkeys following restricted deafferentation, *Neuroscience* 8, 33–55; M.M. Merzenich *et al.* (1984) Somatosensory cortical map changes following digit amputation in adult monkeys, *J. Comp. Neurol.* 224, 591–605.

of cortical representation, would be nothing more than a kind of photographic snapshot extracted from a permanently dynamic process, which is that of the constitution of the self, which, or so we think, is due to mechanisms bearing upon the identification of the own body, linked in large part to the exploration of one hand touching another.

More about will

Of course, we have to make sure that our KO/KM distinction does not overlap, quite simply, with that which holds between the two concepts: sensorial input and efferent copy. What seems new to us is precisely this: that the duality and the complementarity of these two mechanisms is essential for our body to be experienced as belonging to us. Experimental data confirm this impression that we are on the right track. Two complementary discoveries, that (1) intention is 'motor cognition'[120] and (2) of the 'sense of action',[121] have made a decisive contribution to the constitution of the own body. In other words, *action is promoted to the rank of an entirely separate sense*, an original source of knowledge by comparison with exteroception or proprioception. And this knowledge is not the representation of a pre-constituted object but contributes *not just to the recognition of the object by the agent but also to the recognition of the agent by itself.*

The first point (1) was established by Patrick Haggard, who brought back into service the protocol of a chronometry of the will thought up by Benjamin Libet. Some explanation is needed here for the benefit of the reader. Libet himself presented his result as proof of the delay of the formation of a conscious intention to act in relation to the cerebral activity preparatory to action. But, one weakness of his protocol was its inability to justify the attribution specifically to a *voluntary intention* of 'the event' (phase of the preparatory motor potential) corresponding to the 'judgement W' (will) of the subject. For Libet, this intention was apparently reducible to any previous event whatsoever in a temporal succession of two events: 'an experienced desire or a desire that precedes action'.[122] But, should we really disqualify in this manner as an illusion, or a retrospective interpretation, the conscious experience we actually live through of the intentional relation (conceived in the mind of the agent)

---

[120] P. Haggard (2005) Conscious intention and motor cognition, *Trends Cog. Sci.* 9(6), 290–295.

[121] E. Van den Bos and M. Jeannerod (2002) Sense of body and sense of action both contribute to self-recognition, *Cognition* 85, 177–187.

[122] B. Libet (1982) Readiness potentials preceding unrestricted 'spontaneous' *vs.* Pre-planned voluntary acts, *Electroencephalography Clin. Neurophysiol.* 54, 333.

with the external event? The question was to determine the empirical status of the experience consisting of intending to do something one does voluntarily (the 'intentional arrow' of the phenomenologists) by associating it with a specifically chronometric effect.

This is exactly what was found. The effect in question is a contraction of the interval of time estimated between the action (to press a button) and the consequence of this action (the beep), a contraction that can be verified whenever the agent is itself the cause of this action. On the other hand, an expansion of the same interval of estimated time occurs whenever this agent is no longer itself the cause of the sound signal. For the phenomenologist, this means that the intentional orientation of the action towards something willed has entered a phase susceptible to empirical investigation, with all due respects to Husserl, who understood that there really was something such as the *noema* of action!

But could this action, which now has to be recognized as a form of cognition because it 'has an object' just like perception has one, still be the purely receptive and representative cognition of a pre-constituted thing, and this in accordance with the standard model? No: the act of aiming to do something one intends to do, knowing full well[123] what it is that one is doing, this act does not perhaps change anything in the physical world. For all that it still contributes to the constitution of the agent's own body.

This is what has been shown by Marc Jeannerod with Nielsen's classical paradigm for the study of illusions in the attribution of intentions.[124] Motivated no doubt by the desire to underscore the unconscious character of the mechanisms that account for the preparation of action as the auto-attribution of 'agentivity' to the agent by itself, in his earlier work Jeannerod tended to limit the role of conscious willing to the anomalies of motor control. Now he was forced to admit that the 'sense of action' had acquired the status of something still needing explanation. Self-recognition (which he takes to depend upon a *representation of the body* while we make it depend upon a *bodily experience*) rests *identically* upon the congruence of the visual and kinaesthetic signals and upon the concordance between the intentions of the agent and the corporeal effects of its actions, whenever he is their author.

Here again one finds an intentional relation between the conceived intention and the objective consequences of the action effectively produced by the agent.

---

123 It is the incorrigibility of our knowledge of intentions whose impossibility has been shown up by analytical philosophers of action using logical arguments: any claim to knowledge must normally be corrigible!

124 T.I. Nielsen (1963) Volition: A new experimental approach, *Scand. J. Psychol.* 4, 225–230.

This relation is indispensable for the constituting role of the action with respect to the own body. In fact, as soon as the subject sees the (gloved) hand in the mirror raising its thumb when it was his own motor intention to raise his index finger, he refuses to recognize this hand as his own. But in the absence of movement, recognition proves more difficult.

The operations involved in the transcendental constitution of the sense of being a body would indeed prove to be a piece of vainglorious conjuring if they were not rooted in our corporeal organization and if they did not bring this organization into play, perhaps in a more eminent manner than ordinary activity. This rootedness in the body is required of any theory of the incarnation of meaning that wants to take up its stand in the wake of lived experience and not in that of the arbitrary conventions of language. The act of conferring a meaning upon one's own body is grounded in the fact that it prolongs, and so makes explicit, the sketch of a corporeal movement founded in the kinaesthetic system, and not in any pre-existing, and so almost axiomatically accepted, convention that wants to determine in advance the meaning that has to be conferred upon the own body, and in so doing makes of it just one representation among many others.

The neurophysiological work of constituting what is called the body schema could very well not be due entirely to mechanisms of the touching/touched type; that is, the exploration of the own body by itself, even if the bringing to light of the singularity of the own body owes a great deal to the philosophically happy choice of this paradigmatic example. In fact, phenomenological description grasps the own body as an acting body, a continually busy body, continually at work at some task. And this is what is meant by the German verb *hantieren*, which French phenomenologists, following Merleau-Ponty, have rather poetically (and misguidedly) translated as 'our body haunts the world'. From the physiological point of view, the constitution of the own body as acting body also, and necessarily, brings into play mechanisms set up to explore the external world.

No doubt Merleau-Ponty was more spontaneously attached to this fluid circularity that envelopes the subject and the world in the constitution of the own body than Husserl ever was.[125] For Husserl set out from a Cartesian position (whose merely provisional and strategic character he slowly and laboriously uncovered), and so from a position he was eventually prepared to give up,[126] but not before having proved to his own satisfaction that it was untenable.

....

[125]   M. Merleau-Ponty (1942/2002) *La structure du comportement*, PUF, Paris; M. Merleau-Ponty (1964) *Le visible et l'invisible*, Gallimard, Paris.

[126]   E. Husserl (1960) *Cartesian Meditations*, trans. D. Cairns, Martinus Nijhof, The Hague.

The represented and the lived body

The fact that the own body draws its sense of being a body for us from the actions that we are only able to accomplish by bringing into play its practical powers implies that the own body is not enclosed within itself as by a frontier, as is the physical body in the way we ordinarily think of it. It is a lived and not simply a perceived (in the sense of represented) body. The flexibility of the perception of the lived body is such that, in illnesses such as anorexia, certain persons (women especially) can have the impression that their body is enormous even when they are quite slim and, on the other hand, persons afflicted with elephantiasis can have the impression that the size of their body is normal.

The diversity of the temporal flux of our intentions is such that there is a constant renewal of the sense and meaning of our own body. And as long as we are active, the work will not be finished! However, all of this requires an integrated articulation of the own body, a harmonious synergy as between the different organs, beginning with the two hands.

But motor error, and the difference between the information supplied by different senses, also has a part to play. Jacques Droulez insists on this: coherence is important but the ability to 'de-cohere' is no less important for the organism.[127] Sometimes one only becomes aware of the existence of the body through vertigo. One of our colleagues who paid little attention to the vestibular system (like most of us moreover, since the work it does and the contribution it makes remain largely unconscious) went through an episode of vertigo stemming from the vestibular system. Known as benign paroxystic vertigo, this condition hits us in the morning when we wake up. Little fragments of our otoliths, which migrate during sleep to the ampulla of the semicircular canal, provoke, when we stand up in the morning, a powerful illusion of rotation. The victim of this condition told us that he had suddenly become fully conscious of this function. Vertigo yields a sensation, an astonishing perception of which we are now fully conscious. It brings the existence of our own body to full conscious awareness.

In the same way, Husserl's robust idea of 'harmony' (his expression for today's physiology coherence) was that harmony is always aimed at and that, although it is never wholly achieved, it is constantly sought as a response to a

---

[127] J. Droulez and C. Darlot (1989) The geometry and dynamics implicit in the coherence constants in 3D sensorimotor coordination, in M. Jeannerod (ed.), *Attention and Performance III*, Laurence Erlbaum, Hillsdale, NJ, pp. 495–526.

variety of dissonances.[128] The vital issue is that of not stumbling upon a catastrophic dissonance. For a radical discongruity in the sensorial information available to the perceiving subject—and to the practical intentions of the agent—might bring with it the destruction of the own body and its environment, not to mention the collapse of the life-world.[129]

---

[128] E. Husserl (1907) *Thing and Space. Lectures from 1907*, trans. R. Rojcewirz (ed.), Kluwer, Dordrecht: 'It belongs to the general essence of conflict, of being otherwise, that it should presuppose a foundation of agreement.' This foundation becomes the horizon of an infinite quest in the later manuscripts where constitution, after being static, becomes dynamic. E. Husserl, *MS* B III 9 (October–December 1931), Das Aktproblem: 'each "creative" real doing serves a universal goal of life centred on the Ego: will to unity, to harmony of being as something that has constantly to be re-established by correction.'

[129] Something that often does transpire in disturbances like spatial anxiety and agoraphobia, but also in such psychiatric afflictions as anorexia, autism, etc. See I. Viaud Delmon *et al.* (1999) Anxiety and integration of visual vestibular information studied with virtual reality, *Biol. Psychiatry* 47, 112–118; I. Viaud-Delmon, A. Berthoz, and R. Jouvent (2002) Multisensory integration for spatial orientation in trait anxiety subjects: absence of visual dependence, *Eur. J. Psychiatry* 17(4), 194–199; I. Viaud-Delmon *et al.* (2000) Adaptation as a sensorial profile in trait anxiety: a study with virtual reality, *J. Anxiety. Disord.* 14(6), 583–601. Physiology and phenomenology both share a certain commitment in favour of the anomalies of constituting the world of living that sets them apart from physics, to the extent that the (classical) physicist, who considers things independently of our access to them, dreams of an exclusively normal system of experience. Never having had any reason to relate sensorial qualities to the corporeal conditions (normal or abnormal) of the subject of experience, this physicist, Husserl observes, 'has nothing to offer the physiologist' (E. Husserl, D 13 XV (1910–1918), p. 33). On the importance of anomalies for the constitution of the world of normality, see J.-L. Petit (1996) *Solipsisme et Intersubjectivité. Quinze leçons sur Husserl et Wittgenstein*, Cerf, Paris, pp. 23–72.

Chapter 8

A key to intersubjectivity: conjoint constitution

This chapter deals with the question of our relations with others:[1] intersubjectivity. For a century or so, physiology has mostly been a physiology of the perceiving and acting subject. Philosophers might call it a solipsistic physiology. During the same period, social psychology[2] has kept declining (at least in France). Today we note a tremendous growth in the evidence bearing on the perception and observation of the other, the neural bases of emotions, etc.: the solipsistic brain has given way to the social brain. The new fast-growing interest in so-called neuro-economy[3] and the development of experiments in cerebral imagery bearing on empathy and the perception of emotions in the other attest to all this.[4] This is the context in which we are now going to present some theoretical ideas for a physiology that is not just subjective but *intersubjective*.

....

[1] Alain Berthoz made this subject the object of several of his lecture courses at the College de France in 2004 and 2005. See the résumés in the *Annals of the Collège de France* and in A. Berthoz (2004) *La décision*, Odile Jacob, Paris and A. Berthoz and G. Jorland (eds) (2004) *L'Empathie*, Odile Jacob, Paris.

[2] See D.T. Gilbert, S.T. Fiske, and G. Lindzey (eds) (1998) *The Handbook of Social Psychology*, Oxford University Press, Oxford.

[3] See references cited above.

[4] On emotion neuroscience see A. Damasio (1994) *Descartes' Error: Emotion, Reason, And the Brain*, Harper Collins, New York; J. LeDoux (1998) *The Emotional Brain: The Mysterious Underpinnings of Emotional Life*, Simon & Schuster, New York; J. Panksepp (1998) *Affective Neuroscience: The Foundations of Human and Animal Emotions*, Oxford University Press, Oxford. On the neuroscience of empathy: P.L. Jackson, A.N. Meltzoff, and J. Decéty (2005) How do we perceive the pain of others? A window into the neural processes involved in empathy, *NeuroImage* 24, 771–779; T. Singer *et al.* (2004) Empathy for pain involves the affective but not sensory components of pain, *Science* 303, 1157–1162; K.R. Leslie, S.H. Johnson-Frey, and S.T. Grafton (2004) Functional imaging of face and hand imitation: towards a motor theory of empathy, *NeuroImage* 21, 601–607; S.D. Preston and F.B.M. de Waal (2002) Empathy: its ultimate and proximate bases, *Behav. Brain Sci.* 25, 1–72.

Of course, we cannot hope to do more than sketch out this huge programme, a programme that has already been dealt with in other works.[5] It is still too early to think in terms of a synthesis on this subject, but workshops are already examining it from different points of view.[6]

We began this book by raising the question of how we succeed in giving meaning to the idea of a world exterior to us. Then we went on to consider how, within the frame of this world, we come to make sense of our own presence in it, to make sense of our being a body. Finally, the third panel in the triptych will deal with the question how we are able to encounter, that is to say, give meaning to, the existence of subjects other than ourselves, other animated own bodies similar to us.

The neurosciences of today have brought to light a radical difference in the way the brain deals with inanimate bodies and living bodies, those of animals or humans. For example, faces or living bodies are processed in the fusiform gyrus, whereas places and objects in the surrounding world (buildings, landscapes) rely upon the parahippocampus.[7] Through the examination of agnosias and designation disturbances, neuropsychology has shown significant dissociations between the identification of parts of the body and of objects, including those one carries on one's body, like spectacles.[8] Finally, different areas of the brain are activated when one asks a subject to identify an artificial hand (that of a robot) and a natural hand.[9]

Contact with someone else also entails completely different activities from those solicited by an object. For example, it is now well established that eye contact with another person activates the amygdala in a quite spectacular way, the amygdala being a basic brain centre for emotion and the evaluation of emotional value of facial expressions by the limbic system. A particular structure of the parietal cortex, the extrastriate body area,[10] is implied in a quite specific

---

5   A. Berthoz *et al.* (eds) (2003) *L'Autisme*, Odile Jacob, Paris; A. Berthoz and G. Jorland (eds) (2004) *L'Empathie*, Odile Jacob, Paris.

6   Scientific animation workshops of the Réseau des Sciences Cognitives d'Ile de-France: 'Systèmes résonnants, empathie, intersubjectivité', 31 March 2005, ENS, and 6 June 2005, Collège de France (a summary of the arguments is available at www.risc.cnrs.fr/pdf/Syst_resonnants.pdf).

7   E.A. Maguire *et al.* (2001) Distinct neural systems for the encoding and recognition of topography and faces, *Neuroimage* 13(4), 743–750.

8   See the chapter on designation by A.-C. Bachoud-Lévi in A. Berthoz and G. Jorland (eds) (2004) *L'Empathie*, Odile Jacob, Paris, pp. 89–119.

9   Y.F. Tai *et al.* (2004) The human premotor cortex is 'mirror' only for biological actions, *Curr. Biol.* 14(2), 117–120.

10 See the literature on the extrastriate somatotopic areas: P.L. Jackson *et al.* (2006) Neural circuits involved in imitation and perspective-taking, *Neuroimage* 31(1), 429–439;

manner in the processing of the movements and expressions of the body. The processing of the bodily expression of emotions also relies upon quite specific networks.[11] The brain is obviously built with many interacting and specialized networks involved in different aspects of cognitive and social abilities.

Husserl's fundamental hypothesis is that the *recognition of the other as another own body is rooted in the structure of kinaesthesia, the primary constitutional operator. The experience of the 'own body' gives meaning to the world, to oneself and to the other.* To be in a position to evaluate both the novelty and the limits of this conception, we shall have to look at different facets of this relation and analyse the mental processes accompanying the fact of observing an action without doing it, of acting without observing oneself acting, of understanding, of imitating or learning how to perform an action for oneself, or again, understanding such an action by relying on nothing other than our own ability to act. For the world is peopled with agents and not simply with objects.

In the systematic exposition of his kinaesthetic theory (at work in the constitution of the spatial thing) in *Ding und Raum*, Husserl adopted a simplifying abstraction which consisted of not taking account of the existence of the other, and so not taking into account the influence that the existence of the other might have on the perceiving subject and on the procedure of constitution. Although he was well aware of the importance of the factors he had not accounted for, he intended to leave the intervention of this further dimension of intersubjectivity for a later and more complex stage in the analysis. An arbitrary procedure certainly, and one which earned him the pitiless criticism of Heidegger, who accused his master of a Cartesianism for which intersubjectivity represented nothing more than a plastering over of defects in the analysis of the solitary subject. Hence his so-called 'Cartesian solipsism' (from *solus* and *ipse*: the self, all alone).

But Heidegger's objection is quite unfair because, for Husserl, the meaning of our actions is spontaneously intersubjective.[12] By intersubjective we do not mean something that goes on between two persons, each of which remains

R.F. Schwarzlose *et al.* (2005) Separate face and body selectivity on the fusiform gyrus, *J. Neurosci.*, 25(47), 11055–11059; S.V. Astafiev *et al.* (2004) Extrastriate body area in human occipital cortex responds to the performance of motor actions, *Nat. Neurosci.* 7(5), 542–548; B.M. de Jong *et al.* (2002) Brain activation related to the representations of external space and body scheme in visuomotor control, *Neuroimage* 14(5), 1128–1135.

[11] J. Grèzes and B. De Gelder (2005) Contagion motrice et émotionnelle in *A. Berthoz et al.* (eds) *L'Autisme. De la recherche à la pratique*, Odile Jacob, Paris, pp. 295–319.

[12] See E. Husserl (1960) *Cartesian Meditations*, trans. D. Cairns, Martinus Nijhoff, The Hague, Part V and also E. Husserl (1973) *Zur Phänomenologie der Intersubjektivität*, Husserliana XIII, XIV, XV, I. Kern (ed.), Martinus Nijhoff, The Hague.

isolated in his own perceiving ego, his 'solipsistic' I: 'I all alone, his Majesty the subject constituting the world'.[13] The idea here is that we escape from the solitude of being a perceiving subject just as soon as we gain an intimate feeling, through our own kinaesthesia, for the very actions we are in the course of performing. And this because these actions intervene in a world to whose constitution they contribute and because this world cannot take on its full meaning save as a world for others as well as myself. Only so can there be a direct relation between the kinaesthesia of the perceiver and the kinaesthesia of the agent. This is why the baby, very early, reproduces the facial expressions of its mother, a reproduction that is not simply 'emotional contagion' but shows that perceiving the action of the other is intersubjective from the very beginning.

Theories of simulation: can they account for intersubjectivity?

The literature in philosophy and the cognitive sciences includes a theory of simulation which, rightly or wrongly, has been presented as a substitute solution for the theory of the theory,[14] which provided, at the time, a conceptual framework for psychological research into the relation to the other.[15]

Its authors—principally the American philosophers Alvin Goldman[16] and Robert Gordon[17]—hoped to avoid intellectualism (if not solipsism, which didn't bother them much) in the conceptualization of the cognitive

----

[13] The position to which Descartes was driven back to by the application of his own method, once he had insisted upon the calling into question of all beliefs, since the belief that persons other than oneself exist forms a part of such a totality.

[14] D. Premack and G. Woodruff (1978) Does the chimpanzee have a 'theory of mind'? *Behav. Brain Sci.* 1(4), 515–526; A.M. Leslie (1987) Pretence and representation: the origins of 'theory of mind', *Psychol. Rev.* 94, 412–426; H. Wellman (1990) *The Child's Theory of Mind*, MIT Press, Cambridge, MA; J. Perner (1991) *Understanding the Representational Mind*, MIT Press, Cambridge, MA; S.P. Stich and S. Nichols (1995) Folk psychology, simulation or tacit theory? in M. Davies and T. Stone (eds), *Folk Psychology*, Blackwell, Oxford, pp. 235–255.

[15] For a discussion of these theories see also F.J. Varela, E. Thompson, and E. Rosch (1991) *The Embodied Mind: Cognitive Science and Human Experience*, MIT Press, Cambridge, MA.

[16] A.I. Goldman (1993) The psychology of folk psychology, *Behav. Brain Sci.* 16, 15–28; A.I. Goldman (1992) In defense of the simulation theory, *Mind & Language* 7(1–2), 104–119.

[17] R.M. Gordon (1992) The simulation theory: objections and misconceptions, *Mind & Language* 7, 1–2, 104–119; R.M. Gordon (1995) Folk psychology as simulation, 1, 158–171.

foundations of the relation to the other.[18] They hoped to get there by opting for a conceptualization based upon the commitment[19] of each cognitive subject in the relation to be conceptualized. If I want to understand this relation I have to resist the temptation to abstract myself from it and, on the contrary, take advantage of the fact that I am involved in it. So it was a matter of looking for a mode of conceptualization that implied commitment, even the self-commitment of the agent. In sum, in all its relations with the other the cognitive subject is always supposed to be more or less preoccupied with the quest for an explanation of the behaviour—they themselves used the term 'action' in spite of the difference between behaviour and action—of a certain physical system, with a view to predicting its further outcome, the physical system in question being, it goes without saying, that of the other (physical reductionism).

Efforts were then made to account for the development of our relations with others under the general head of theories of simulation. We can't do more than offer an unavoidably distorted summary, for numerous highly elaborate and interesting versions of these attempts were made.[20] Starting with the attribution to the system under consideration of internal states (a mind), the process continued by attributing to these internal states a causal influence over the movements of the same system and finished up by subsuming (subordinating) these states and movements under covering laws associating these internal mental (psychic) states with the external physical movements of the behaviour. These are the presuppositions of the theory of simulation. In this context, it would be enough to 'put oneself in the place of the other'. Taking up the point of view of the other was supposed to offer a practically valuable cognitive strategy, since it would make predictions possible, but with the further advantage of a computational (and representational) economy. We will come back to this later.

A theory of this kind could be said to have lightened the load by comparison with any 'heavier' theory; that is, a theory calling for more principles of explanation. To understand what the other is going to do, I would only need to

---

[18] In witness to such intellectualism: 'We believe that cognitive development in young children is like theoretical changes in science' (A.N. Meltzoff (1999) Origins of the theory of mind, cognition and communication, *J. Communication Disorder* 32, 253).

[19] The reader may have recognized the Sartrian expression: 'engagement', not however employed in its political sense.

[20] See the classical references in texts already cited by Goldman, Gordon, Stich, and Nichols, and for the recent renewal of the theory of simulation in relation to mirror neurons, see V. Gallese and A.I. Goldman (1998) Mirror neurons and the simulation theory of mind-reading, *Trends Cog. Sci.* 12, 493–501.

make use of my own theory of mind, a theory I am supposed to have developed with regard to my own self in the course of my own ontogenetic formation and through appropriate learning procedures. The very same theory I normally make use of to plan my own actions, make my own choices, is simply projected by me upon the other. In other words, I make use of the computational and representational resources of my own organism to understand and attribute equivalent resources to the other.

It is obvious that a proposal of this kind has been worked out within a solipsist horizon, if only because everything happens within the mind of one and the same rational individual. After all, the other could be nothing more than a roughly resembling dummy, a simple screen for the fictive projection of the self, seeing that it is enough to substitute the other for the self as the basic reference of the word 'I'. When I say 'I', I normally refer to myself. But in certain special circumstances, for example when I think about what the other is going to do, or when I am dreaming or when I imagine someone else's life story, I put the other in the place of my 'I'.

Computational cognition and solipsism

To put together a coherent perception of one's own body and of one's own self is certainly necessary if one is going to interact with others. But if I am absolutely convinced that everything that happens around me remains just so many different ways in which I enter into relation with myself, talk to myself, represent something to myself, explain myself to myself, predict the future on the basis of what I myself experience, etc.,[21] I am quite simply incapable of entering into a genuine relation with others. The relation to the other simply cannot penetrate an intellectual life purged of anything that might call into question the sovereignty of my intellect. The other has become an element in a spectacle in which I no longer participate. This is perhaps what happens with autistic children, all the more so since they seem not to be able to constitute a coherent perception of their own body.[22]

So the question is, can the psychological and neurological foundations of the relation to the other be adequately conceptualized in terms of a theory of internal representations and of computations performed upon representations regarded as contained in an essentially solipsistic mind-brain? Let us at least give our reasons for thinking that the reply cannot be entirely positive.

---

[21] All of which is expressed in psychology by the term egocentric.

[22] This idea was put forward in A. Berthoz (1997) *Le sens du mouvement*, Odile Jacob, Paris, p. 103 and taken up again later by U. Frith under the name of central coherence theory.

Let us take as our example a classical theory. In *Mental Models*, Johnson-Laird[23] constructs a computational theory of mental calculation, a performance of natural thinking whose specificity he tries to retrieve in its difference from its construal through the use of logical formalism.[24] His hypothesis is that, in daily life, rather than getting caught up in any explicit reasoning process relying upon logical criteria of correctness, we manipulate the equivalents—the mental models—of propositions in a syllogistic reasoning. He suggests that we succeed in this manner in making the same calculations as machines or as the logician manipulating his abstract symbols, and with the same results. We find a similar procedure with certain 'representational' theories that start out from the assumption that the mind is a computer, that the mind calculates, except that what is calculated is not just numbers but symbols and the truth values of propositions or even narrative structures. On this basis they think they are capable of attacking a problem like the difference between mental calculation and theoretical calculation, the logical calculus.

One might also try to work out a computational—but not exclusively logical or formal—theory of the relation with the other by basing this relation on the fact that it is certainly constrained by rules, and that following these rules is an equivalent of the kind of calculations performed by the brain-computer. In fact the human species possesses, in its genetic heritage, genes which enable the brain of the individual to develop particular capacities commanding an entire repertory of comportments.

Of course, capacities such as these are not specific to 'relations with others', still less to intersubjectivity. For alongside the genes which, in the newborn baby, determine in advance the characteristics of its mother, of the form and texture of the breast that is going to supply it with milk, we also find those, for example, that release fear when confronted with a spider. The ethologists Lorenz[25] and Tinbergen[26] have shown with their *filial imprinting* that an animal can be brought to follow an object in movement just as long as it replaces its mother at a precise moment in its development, known as the critical period.[27] In addition to ethologists, developmental psychologists and

---

[23] P.N. Johnson-Laird (1983) *Mental Models. Towards a Cognitive Science of Language, Inference, and Consciousness*, Cambridge University Press, Cambridge.

[24] On this subject, see the commentaries in A. Berthoz (2004) *La décision*, Odile Jacob, Paris, pp. 30–33.

[25] K. Lorenz (1943) Die angeborenen Formen möglicher Erfahrung, *Zeitschrift für Tierpsychologie*.

[26] N. Tinbergen (1979) *Social Behavior in Animals*, Methuen, London, 1953.

[27] In biology the name critical period is given to those moments in the development in the course of which a sensorial system or a comportment is specifically brought into play.

psychiatrists have taken account of the fact that the brain contains innate mechanisms bearing on the recognition of the other. For both of these authors (neither of whom, it is true, thought of the development of the individual as a matter of computation!), the brain could not be solipsistically conceived since it participates in a relation to a world (*Umwelt*) with which this individual remains in constant interaction.

From now on, it becomes reasonable to add to the processes which, in the first instance, are employed to 'model the other and the world'—the internal models of the physical world and of the body which formed the topics of Chapters 6 and 7—further processes which, in addition, contain mechanisms bearing on the relation with the other. So it is that one finds oneself in possession of a theoretical model capable of satisfying both requirements. All the same, it is clear that these operators remain, at bottom, turned inward on themselves, to the extent that they apply the operations their programmes make possible to the information circulating in their circuits. But in another sense, one can think of them—even if only metaphorically (and this is the whole question)—as open to the external world. But let us be clear about one thing. It is not our intention to underestimate the fundamental importance of the contribution made by mathematics or logical formalism in the simulation of the functioning of the brain.

Several mathematicians of high standing, such as Daniel Bennequin and Jean-Jacques Slotine, are presently working as full-time members of the laboratory of that one of us who is a physiologist, and Jean Christophe Yoccoz, Professor at the Collège de France and holder of the Field medal, actively participates in seminars and debates bearing on models in physiology just as, at one time, in Moscow, the great mathematician Gelfand participated in the work of the little group of physiologists who revolutionized our understanding of motor mechanisms. We ourselves are associated with groups of modellers and work within the frame of major European programmes in neurorobotics, an entirely new frontier.[28]

. . . .

If at this precise moment the conditions are not right for the functioning of the system, a lasting deficit ensues. This is the case with vision but also with more complex comportments like filiation. What has to be stressed is that action is fundamental for the determination of this process, as has been shown by the classic studies of Held and Hein on vision. Two baby kittens played on a roundabout: one walked, pulling the other in a basket. The kitten transported passively developed a deficit in its visual system. The same holds of the system of place neurons in the hippocampus which can only become operatively selective if the animal is active (P.D. Martin and A. Berthoz (2002) Development of spatial firing in the hippocampus of young rats, *Hippocampus*,12, 4, 465–480).

[28] Like for example the European programme 'Neurobotics' directed by roboticist Paolo Dario, and in which ten robotic laboratories and six neuroscientific laboratories collaborate.

But it has to be admitted that we are now up against what looks like a really difficult question: how to open up this machine, a machine naturally inclined to shut down upon itself and which does not in fact have an external world in the sense in which it is perfectly reasonable to say of a subject or an organism that it interacts with such a world? As a matter of fact, and to get back to our brain–computer metaphor: a computer doesn't have an environment. Which means no 'world', no 'environment' (*Umwelt*), no 'own body', and so no 'other'. All the elements needed for a phenomenology of experience are lacking, not incidentally, but as a matter of principle.

One solution, perhaps (this eventuality should not be discarded), is that we construct computers designed especially to do just this, but which will only increase the difficulties, unless we restrict ourselves to models designed to imitate only the most trivial aspects of behaviour! For example, if I want to construct—and this is what roboticists are doing today[29]—a machine that is sensitive to the 'anger of the other' or that detects 'the aggressive character of the other', I can remain within the frame of a quite simple computational function by placing a module[30] behind the camera which recognizes forms and detects, for example, the characteristic traits of the face our fellow humans make when confronted with danger. This is no doubt about the way the amygdala[31] functions in our brain. But we will still not have got much further in the perceptual modelling of faces than this particular mode (an aptitude selectively developed or learned, or so we are told, by those 'physionomists' who specialize in watching the faces of customers who come into casinos).

....

[29] The roboticist A. Takanishi, of the University of Waseda in Tokyo, constructs humanoid robots that express emotions and are capable of interacting with humans.

[30] Clearly this type of functioning does exist in the brain. The toad, for example, disposes of two neuronal analysers which make it possible for it to distinguish between an earthworm it would like to capture (the corresponding module identifies a long form which moves in the direction of its length) and a predator like a bird of prey (detected by means of a module that identifies a large form whose surface is expanding).

[31] The amygdala is a structure of brain that receives visual information, among other things, and that contributes to the identification of what rewards or punishes, the danger or pleasure that a given form can procure. Its role was discovered by neurologists (Klüver and Bucy), who showed that monkeys whose amygdala had been severed were no longer afraid of a snake placed in their cage. The neurophysiologist Ledoux showed how the amygdala could release a rapid fear reaction as a result of visual forms proper to each species. Since then, brain imagery has been used to show that the amygdala is implied in most of the very rapid processes of emotional identification, visual contact and other aspects of social interaction. It is involved in rapid and stable 'short circuits' devoted to the release of protective reactions, for example. This rapid pathway is completed by 'long circuits' making it possible to analyse environmental stimuli at greater length, compare them with what is retained in memory and make inferential judgements about such stimuli.

This problem is serious even if it is not insoluble *a priori*. Roboticists are very interested in this question since they have to get groups of robots to work together, in playing football just as much as engaging in deep-sea exploration. The challenge is formidable. Should robots be constructed to imitate life forms? A lively debate separates those who, following the pioneer efforts of roboticists at the Massachusetts of Institute of Technology in the USA, are trying to develop biomimetic robotics and those who refuse to admit the interest in developing such an approach, and who go so far as to criticize the craving for publicity exhibited by the latter. The spectrum of possible options still remains wide open. One might mention the Animat approach resolutely committed to the development of biomimetic robots.[32] In order not to lose sight of the link with a phenomenology of the own body (Chapter 7), we should also take account of a school of autonomous and interactionist robotics—the embodied-embedded robotics of Andy Clark[33] to cite only one example—a school adamantly opposed in its theoretical orientation to Turing robotics derived from Turing machines.[34]

All the same, in view of the fact that this approach to the relation with the other does remain computational, one has the right to doubt whether it can ever enable us to understand what is essential to this relation, and so will only serve to conceal from view the underlying biological mechanisms and, in particular, leave entirely unsolved the problem of the attribution of meaning to the actions of the other.[35] So we now need to look into other theories capable of opening up more fruitful approaches.

Knowledge of the other without inference?

Representational theories, but also simulation theories, start out from the common assumption that an inference is a necessary condition for the

---

[32] M.A. Amorim *et al.* (2000) Modulation of spatial orientation processing by mental imagery instructions: a MEG study of representational momentum, *J. Cog. Neurosci.* 12(4), 569–582. On this subject it is worth consulting the symposia organised by J.A. Meyer under the heading *Animat: From Animals to Animats*, III, MIT Press, Cambridge, MA, 1994.

[33] A. Clarke (1997) *Being There: Putting Brain, Body, and World Together Again*, MIT Press, Cambridge, MA.

[34] A.M. Turing (1950) Computing machinery and intelligence, *Mind* 59, 433–460.

[35] In the book by Varela *et al.* (F.J. Varela, E. Thompson, and E. Rosch (1991) *The Embodied Mind: Cognitive Science and Human Experience*, MIT Press, Cambridge, MA, p. 63 and on) will be found an in-depth critique of computational approaches, including those that use neuronal networks.

recognition of the other. However, the observations of primate researchers at the beginning of the twentieth century (Kœhler), of psychologists of emotion (Zajonc),[36] and also more recent observations in neurophysiology[37] suggest an alternative type of function that would not make use of mechanisms of the inferential kind. Zajonc wrote that 'feeling and preference do not stand in need of inference.' What are the observations in question? Without pretending to be original, we would like to remind our readers of facts that are often overlooked, before appealing to recent experimental results.

To start with, there are facts familiar to observers that they have only failed to take note of thanks to an intellectualism pushed to the limit in the field of cognition. This is, without talking about the extension of this field to what does not on the surface appear to belong to it, but which is included in it nevertheless, like *qualia*, the *sui generis* qualities of lived experience or again the emotions, with regard to which we also have a neo-behaviourist and a computational theory.[38]

First of all, the existence of non-inferential mechanisms in what we call today motor or emotional contagion[39] and which we hesitate, of course, to label as 'low-level' mechanisms, is evident in everyday life. For example, seeing someone yawn makes us want to yawn. In a lecture hall, if an attentively followed speaker yawns, after a few minutes, nearly half of the spectators will have yawned. We don't really need a theory of mind to understand a performance of this kind! Obviously, one could always say that a theory of mind was implied. The newborn baby sticks out its tongue at whoever sticks out his or her tongue at it.[40] At the level of emotions, we mentioned above the role of the amygdala in quick and automatic emotional reactions.

We find the same kind of thing with imitation which, to a considerable degree, is also non-inferential. All the same, it is clear today that *imitation* should not be confused with *emotional contagion*. Wolfgang Kœhler's observations,

---

[36] R.B. Zajonc (1980) Feeling and thinking: preference needs no inferences, *Am. Psychol.* 35(2), 151–175.

[37] Because they stress the role of structures belonging to the 'emotional brain' (amygdala, orbito-frontal cortex, pole of the anterior cingular cortex), structures not directly implied in cognitive activities.

[38] E.T. Rolls (1999) *The Brain and Emotion*, Oxford University Press, Oxford.

[39] J. Grèzes and B. De Gelder (2005) Contagion motrice et contagion émotionnelle, A. Berthoz *et al.* (eds), *Autisme, cerveau et développement: de la recherche à la pratique*, Odile Jacob, Paris, pp. 295–319.

[40] A.N. Meltzoff and M.K. Moore (1977) Imitation of facial and manual gestures by human neonates, *Science* 198, 75–78.

at his primate laboratory in Tenerife, have been illustrated with the photograph of a monkey in the course of mimicking the solution, as if to help his fellow monkey in its effort to grab a banana suspended in the roof of the cage by standing on boxes piled unsteadily on top of one another.[41] An anthropomorphic prejudice cannot be attributed to a camera. And yet we have the image. We see with our own eyes something like an act of manual apprehension transferred from the spectator monkey to the acting monkey, thanks to a direct identification. In the face of this evidence the debate about the attribution to the monkey of a theory of mind seems strangely speculative.

All the same, the mechanism of imitation is unquestionably of another order altogether from that of simple motor contagion. For example, in order to imitate, a monkey has to have developed *conjoint attention*;[42] that is to say, the capacity to observe an object or a person by simply following the other's gaze. A child of less than one year still has not developed this capacity. In fact, conjoint attention presupposes the development of areas of our brain, which are susceptible to complex processing procedures. Processing relations between the self and the other is much more complex than simple contagion.

A recent event has thrown light on the neuronal foundations of imitation and on our understanding of the other's actions: the discovery by Giacomo Rizzolatti, and his team, of *mirror neurons*. We have already mentioned this, but we now need to come back to it again, if only because an entire literature has been developed working on the assumption that mirror neurons, or systems of such neurons, lie at the root of intersubjectivity. This discovery had nothing to do with any enterprise aiming at a neuronal implementation of the *theory of the mind* of the other. They were not in the least concerned with any theory of mind. Nor were they trying to deal with classical mental states, such as beliefs and desires, since their work bore on the neuronal bases of manual actions which, at the time, they preferred to talk of as 'motor events',[43] rarely as actions.

This was the start of a hunch about the existence of a non-inferential mechanism designed to set up in resonance repertoires of action (Rizzolatti talks of 'vocabularies') through the observation of the actions of the other; hence the idea of mirroring. The story is pretty well known. What has not been

[41] W. Koehler (1917/1927) *L'intelligence des singes supérieurs*, Paris, Alcan.

[42] N.J. Emery (2000) The eyes have it: the neuro-ethology, function and evolution of social gaze, *Neurosci. Biobehav. Rev.* 24(6), 581–604; N.J. Emery (1997) Gaze following and joint attention in rhesus monkeys (*Macacca mulatta*), *J. Comp. Psychol.* 111(3), 286–293.

[43] G. di Pellegrino *et al.* (1992) Understanding motor events: a neurophysiological study, *Exp. Brain Res.* 91, 176–180.

noticed is that even Rizzolatti himself still does not attribute to these mirror neurons the function of furnishing either the substrates for, or the neural correlates of, a theory of mind, not even a theory of mental states. Very quickly, others have stepped in where he feared to tread. Jean Decéty, for example, has suggested that imitation with the baby 'who sticks out his tongue at whoever sticks his tongue out at it' is the missing link between mirror neurons and a theory of mind.[44]

The existence of a mirror system in humans has been confirmed, first by using transcranial stimulation,[45] then thanks to several series of experiments with cerebral imagery.[46] What we have become accustomed to calling the mirror system in fact covers several cerebral areas in the form of a network, bearing on quite specific parts of the pre-motor dorsal and parietal cortex and the upper temporal sulcus. According to the research protocols employed, these areas are differently described: sometimes as coding the repertory of the actions of the individual, sometimes as a network underlying motor imitation and learning, sometimes as the neural foundations of empathy, verbal communication, and culture. Whatever the description, this network (assuming that it does possess the unity of a network) is probably one of the most fundamental mechanisms making it possible for us to comprehend ('prehend' at the same time, and with) the other.[47]

....

[44] A.N. Meltzoff and J. Decéty (2003) What imitation tells us about social cognition: a rapprochement between developmental psychology and cognitive science, in C. Frith and D. Wolpert (eds), *The Neuroscience of Social Interaction*, Oxford University Press, Oxford, pp. 109–130.

[45] L. Fadiga *et al.* (1995) Motor facilitation during action observation: a magnetic stimulation study, *J. Neurophysiol.* 73(6), 2608–2611. With the help of transcranium magnetic stimulation (TMS) these authors have shown that, in the subject before whom an actor executes manual movements, enhanced muscular potentials are evoked in the right hand when one stimulates his Broca's area.

[46] G. Rizzolatti *et al.* (1996) Localization of grasp representations in humans by PET: 1. Observation versus execution, *Exp. Brain Res.* 111, 246–252; S.T. Grafton *et al.* (1996) Localization of grasp representations in humans by PET: 2. Observation compared with imagination, *Exp. Brain Res.* 112, 103–111; J. Grèzes *et al.* (1998) Top-down effect of strategy in the perception of human biological motion: a PET investigation, *Cog. Neuropsychol.* 15, 553–582.

[47] A point on the history of science: in 1995, Jean-Luc Petit organized a workshop at the University of the Human Sciences in Strasburg and at the Biomedical Institute of the Cordeliers in Paris (at a moment when the country was paralysed by a lorry strike and by student demonstrations). G. Rizzolatti was invited to this workshop on the empathic effect of actions and intersubjectivity between species. This was precisely the year when, in an e-mail message issuing the invitations for this workshop, the suggestion was

Having said this, we now need to qualify our assertion and so avoid any uncritical extrapolation from the monkey's gesture in taking a seed and putting it in his mouth to the totality of our relations with others. Even the proposition advanced by Michael Arbib and Rizzolatti, concerning the possibility of a direct relation between the mirror system and the appearance of language, due to the proximity of the pre-motor area containing the mirror neurons[48] and the Broca's area, is the subject of an intense debate.

It has been shown recently that the areas of the pre-motor cortex involved in the mirror system are probably not exactly the same as those involved in language. Evidence for a connection between action and language is as follows: on hearing phrases bearing on manual actions (or actions done with the feet) but not phrases using abstract concepts, magnetic stimulation (TMS) of the cortical areas of the hand (or feet) induces a modulation of the motor potentials evoked in the muscles of the hand (or feet);[49] or again, the Broca's area is activated by observation of the silent speech of a human subject as also by the observation of lip-smacking, a form of communication specific to the monkey;[50] or yet again, when the motor areas are stimulated by TMS, more intense motor potentials are evoked in a subject on hearing words containing consonants (r, f) than on hearing pseudo-words containing the same phonemes or bi-tonal sounds with the same phonetic profile;[51] yet another example, language areas (left lower frontal and upper temporal gyrus) are activated in the same way by hearing spoken words and by deaf and dumb subjects seeing the signals that make up their language (the American Sign

....

mooted (by J.-L. Petit) that mirror neurons might be the neuronal substrate of intersubjectivity. This suggestion was taken up and exploited by others quite outside the phenomenological context in which it had been developed, and an entire literature on 'brain and intersubjectivity' emerged without reference to Husserl. But it is worth remembering that these things had been said by someone else earlier, and that, in any case, too much should not be made of this claim. For intersubjectivity, the very foundation of the social link, cannot be reduced to empathy, still less to a resonance between the Broca's areas of the brains of an observer and an actor.

48 See G. Rizzolatti and M.A. Arbib (1998) Language within our grasp, *Trends Neurosci.* 21(5), 188–194; M. Makuuchi (2005) Is Broca's area crucial for imitation? *Cerebral Cortex* 15(5), 563–570; I. Stamenov and V. Gallese (2002) *Mirror Neurons and the Evolution of Brain and Language*, John Benjamins, Amsterdam.

49 G. Buccino *et al.* (2005) Listening to action-related sentences modulates the activity of the motor system: a combined TMS and behavioral study, *Cog. Brain Res.* 24, 355–363.

50 G. Buccino *et al.* (2004) Neural circuits involved in the recognition of actions performed by non conspecifics: an fMRI study, *J. Cog. Neurosci.* 16, 114–126.

51 L. Fadiga *et al.* (2002) Speech listening specifically modulates the excitability of tongue muscles: a TMS study, *Eur. J. Neurosci.* 15, 399–402.

Language in the USA and the Langue des Signes Québécoises (LSQ: Québec Sign Language) in Québec),[52] etc.

It should be added that this mechanism is certainly not the only one to function in the resonant mode. For example, another network relatively distinct from the first is implied in the perception and the observation of the other's emotions,[53] and these two networks no doubt do interact with each other, as well as with yet other networks in the emotional life of the individual.

Let us not reject inferences altogether

All the same, we should not forget that even if the brain makes use of mechanisms for knowing which are direct, and so in a certain sense non-inferential, with a view to grasping the real and interacting with the world, this does not mean that more abstract computational, or logical, or mathematical mechanisms do not also exist, made possible in humans thanks to the development of the prefrontal cortex and to a cultural heritage.

We have to assume that networks of different cerebral areas might be implied in more complex aspects of the relation with the other, and at a higher level. We are talking here about a hierarchy, or of a heterarchy,[54] of mechanisms that have made their appearance in the course of evolution, and have become accessible through learning procedures. Dehaene and Changeux have, for example, proposed models for conscious processes and high-level cognitive processes developed along the lines of Norman and Shallice's theory of the supervisor.[55] The idea of a hierarchy of mechanisms has recently been modelled by Etienne Koechlin, who attributes a hierarchically ordered role to different

[52] L.A. Petitto *et al.* (2000) Speech-like cerebral activity in profoundly deaf people processing signed languages: implications for the neural basis of human language, *Proc. Natl. Acad. Sci. USA* 97(25), 13961–13966.

[53] R. Adolphs (2002) Neural systems for recognizing emotion, *Curr. Opin. Neurobiol.* 11(2), 169–177; C. Keysers *et al.* (2004) A touching sight: SII/PV activation during the observation and experience of touch, *Neuron* 42(2), 335–346; B. Wicker *et al.* (2003) Both of us disgusted in my insula: the common neural basis of seeing and feeling disgust, *Neuron* 40(3), 655–664; J. Grèzes and B. De Gelder (2005) Contagion motrice et contagion émotionnelle, in A. Berthoz *et al.* (eds), *Autisme, cerveau et développement: de la recherche à la pratique*, Odile Jacob, Paris, pp. 295–319.

[54] This concept of heterarchy is discussed in A. Berthoz (2004) *La décision*, Odile Jacob, Paris.

[55] D.A. Norman and T. Shallice (1986) Attention and action: willed and automatic control of behavior, in R. Davidson *et al.* (eds), *Consciousness and Selfregulation*, IV, Plenum, New York, pp. 1–18; S. Dehaene and J.-P. Changeux (1997) A hierarchical neuronal network for planning behavior, *Proc. Natl. Acad. Sci. USA* 94, 13293–13298 (two crucial

areas of the brain to account for such functions as placing in context, and remembering, as well as the defining of goals and sub-goals to initiate, control, and guide the perception–action cycle.[56] As with all the major mental faculties, what is in the beginning treated as a single faculty operating by itself turns out to be made up of a plurality of mechanisms running parallel to each other or contained within each other. We have already made this point. Initially the talk was of memory as such, and in fact there are several mechanisms involved in remembering; of attention as such, and there are numerous attentional mechanisms; of emotion as such, and there are numerous different mechanisms for diverse types of emotions.

So, in the course of carrying through the critique we want to make of any approach that assimilates the brain to an inferential machine, whether formal or computational, we have to be careful not to deny the power of these computational approaches. How to understand what the other understands? What has to be interiorized? A philosopher (Richard Avenarius)[57] who insisted that this is just what one should not do employed the term 'introject'. So how does one introject a theory, an epistemology, into the other?

Empathy

If we want to discuss our interactions with others and the possibility, mentioned above, of a co-constitution of the world, it is impossible to avoid evoking the notion of empathy. We can offer no more than a few insights here. Anyone interested in this subject can refer to the recent work in neuropsychology and the philosophy of psychology, as well as to the contributions assembled in the collection edited by Alain Berthoz and Gérard Jorland.[58]

Empathy can be traced back to the German *Einfühlung*,[59] composed of the verb *fühlen*: to feel (the substantive *Fühlen* also designates the sensorial organs

....

texts, one on the pre-frontal, the other on consciousness). Other models have been proposed but it should be noted that at this time none of them actually addresses the specific problem of the relation with the other.

[56] E. Koechlin *et al.* (2003) The architecture of cognitive control in the human prefrontal cortex, *Science* 302(5648), 1181–1185.

[57] R. Avenarius (1891) *Der Menschliche Weltbegriff*, O.R. Reisland, Leipzig.

[58] On the history of the concept of empathy, it is worth reading the chapter by G. Jorland in *L'Empathie* (G. Jorland (2004) L'empathie, histoire d'un concept, in A. Berthoz and G. Jorland (eds), *L'Empathie*, Odile Jacob, Paris, pp. 19–49, as well as G. Jorland and B. Thirioux (2008) Note sur l'origine de l'empathie, *Revue de Métaphysique et de Morale* 2, 269–280, and B. Thirioux, G. Jorland, M. Bret, M.-H. Tramus, and A. Berthoz (2008) Direct perspective taking within self-other interaction (in press).

[59] See J.-L. Petit (1996) *Solipsisme et intersubjectivité*, Cerf, Paris.

of an insect, its antennae) and the locative prefix: *ein*. What is pretty clearly indicated by this use of language is the fact of feeling oneself into something in some way or other (well or badly, easily or not, freely or under constraint), in other words, feeling this way through the contemplation of something in which one has become absorbed. This concept was introduced formally into psychological literature by the philosopher Theodor Lipps (1851-1914), who was professor at the University of Munich from 1894 to 1914. His theory of *Einfühlung* was first presented in 1903, in an article of the review: *Archiv für die gesamte Psychologie w*ith the title: *Einfühlung, innere Nachahmung, und Organenempfindung, which* means: 'empathy, interior imitation and organ sensation' more than it does 'organic sensation', for it is a matter of the organ in movement.[60]

This theory has in the past been presented as lying at the root of the idea that empathy is the psychological principle essential to the perception of the other. But the translation of *Einfühlung* by empathy, which can be traced back to Edward Titchener's *Experimental Psychology of Thought Processes* of 1909, implies at the very least a change of category, even if it cannot be written off as a flagrant mistranslation. In fact, *Einfühlung* did not bear directly upon the perception of the other but rather upon aesthetic pleasure, a pleasure whose object might be another person and more particularly the expressive gestures of some other person, all of whose movements could moreover be treated as expressive gestures (which is highly debatable). But the object of this pleasure could also be a thing, another living being, or some feature of a landscape.

However, there is a fundamental difference between intersubjectivity and *Einfühlung*.[61] *Einfühlung*, intropathy or projection of the self upon the other, is certainly not all that intersubjectivity amounts to. Determining whether the first is a part of the second is a question in itself. In any case, intersubjectivity, or the relation to other, is a much vaster and richer structure than empathy. With the disappearance of Marxist sociology and its dogmatic objectivation of 'collective entities', it no longer appears shocking to want to make of intersubjectivity the foundation of the social link (it is what we are doing here) and the condition of the possibility of all those institutions that uphold human culture. On the other hand, even if one does stick an empathic mechanism into the brain, one will still not have taken a step in the direction of uncovering a

---

60 He developed it further the same year in the second section of his longer work: T. Lipps, *Grundlegung der Ästhetik* (1903), Leopold Voss, Hambarg/Leipzig.

61 J.-L. Petit insists on this in *Solipsisme et Intersubjectivité* (J.-L. Petit (1996) *Solipsisme et Intersubjectivité*, Cerf, Paris) as well as in the chapter in *L'Empathie* (J.-L. Petit (2004) Empathie et intersubjectivité, in A. Berthoz and G. Jorland (eds), *L'Empathie*, Odile Jacob, Paris, pp. 123–147).

correlate for the 'social act'; that is, an act that calls for a plurality of agents (and not a quasi-act that only looks as though it appeals to a plurality of agents because it remains strictly private, as is the fact of watching someone do something).[62]

Above all, it seems to us that the current theories of empathy do not propose a mechanism capable of explaining the recognition of the existence of the other as an other self. Let us not exclude the possibility that it does make sense to postulate the existence of such a mechanism, as long as this recognition depends (we will come back to this later) upon the personal history of each individual. In any case, even before we can feel the emotions of the other, even, following Gérard Jorland, putting oneself in the place of the other without necessarily experiencing its emotions, it seems clear that the other will first have to be perceived as an other and not as an object, as an other living being endowed with the same capacities and dispositions as one's own self. The own world, our *Umwelt*, has to be a shared world.[63]

Mirror neurons, or mechanisms for the coupling of repertoires of action, should then be regarded as the precursors of what? No doubt, of an immediately sympathetic (or antipathetic) relation, but certainly not of intersubjectivity. To support this thesis, let us take the question up again at the most fundamental level and on the basis of a motor theory of perception. We know that Husserl's phenomenological programme of transcendental constitution is founded on the possibility of constituting the world on the basis of the motor or kinaesthetic intervention of the subject in this world. To stick to the most primitive conditions of constitution in so far as it is founded in kinaesthesia, subjectivity is, in the end, nothing other than the position adopted by that agent whose acts make this constitution possible. It turns out that the notion of agentivity has recently acquired a neurophysiological content with the idea that, when a movement (or an action) is prepared, the structures

---

[62] See J.-L. Petit (2005, 2006) Les systèmes résonnants: bases neurales de cognition sociale? *Psychiatrie Sciences Humaines Neurosciences*, 1st part III, 15, 240–247; 2nd part IV, 16, 16–22.

[63] This is the leading theme of the lectures on Husserl by Petit to be found in J.-L. Petit (1996) *Solipsisme et Intersubjectivité*, Cerf, Paris: ' "I am with others in a common world": an evidence that is not "normally" called in question […] – even though it can be […] in the case of madness, of racism and of xenophobia […] Outside these examples, it is not – happily – taken for granted that others appear as vermin to be eliminated, or as elements in the world's furniture which have to be noticed merely in order not to bump into them. The thing is not inconceivable in itself but it is – precisely – only conceivable in very special contexts such as these (indoctrination, intense emotional state, acute social crisis, etc.)' (pp. 7–8).

that induce such a movement trigger off corollary discharges that inform other structures implied in perception. These signals, stemming from the motor and pre-motor regions of the frontal area, induce a characteristic inhibition of the activity of the post-central somato-aesthetic areas (rolandic cortex). Cerebral imagery brings this to light through a comparison with the activation of the same regions due to the tactile cutaneous stimulation (passive) of different parts of the body. This inhibitory activity informs the brain as to whether the tactile sensorial data accompanying the movement is due to an initiative of the agent itself rather than to external forces. It is also, no doubt, responsible for the fact that we cannot tickle ourselves. It has also been suggested that lesions in these parallel anticipatory paths are responsible for diverse pathologies in which patients fail to recognize the action they themselves have brought about, as in the case of schizophrenia.[64]

Other as co-constituting

What does genuine intersubjectivity[65] truly consist of? It consists, for a given subject, of being able to recognize the other as having itself and, on the basis of its kinaesthesia (as defined by us), this power of constituting the world in the same way that he constitutes it for himself. This is so much so that one could ground the relation with the other not on empathy in general but, more precisely, upon empathy with the actions of the other. When we see someone acting, we are not just the visual witnesses of the movements of another body. In truth, what we see is someone actively structuring his world, and this because we ourselves are already capable of structuring our own world through such acts. We find here a deep-rooted identification of subjectivities linked to their identically constitutive roles. On this basis, we may find a way to describe the relation with the other, both physiologically and psychologically, which will overcome some of the inadequacies surrounding an explanation grounded in mirror neurons and empathy.

Intersubjectivity would then be that act through which I recognize the other as capable of (which also implies: free not to do so) constituting with us a common world. And from there, it becomes easy for us to understand a capacity that plays a major role in child psychology, that of being able to change

---

64 C.D. Frith (1996) *Neuropsychologie cognitive de la schizophrénie*, PUF, Paris; M. Jeannerod (2002) *La nature de l'esprit*, Odile Jacob, Paris.

65 The entire literature in cognitive science devoted to the topic of *intersubjectivity* (with the exception of a few rare phenomenological authors like, for example, Shaun Gallagher) rests on a confusion between intersubjectivity and empathy, going so far as to include, over and beyond empathy, any gregarious tendency whatsoever.

one's point of view and so to 'put oneself in the place of the other'. Provisionally, we shall once again fall back on this popular expression, meaning by it not, as one is often inclined to believe, taking up the spatial position of the other, but rather: looking at the world from the other's point of view. But in re-using this expression in this way, we must not allow ourselves to be taken in by it. For we need to make it mean more than it initially, and ordinarily, does actually say. This is not just the fact of imagining the world as it is seen by the other—a condition which already implicitly presupposes intersubjectivity (sedimented in a pre-linguistic layer of experience, according to Husserl)—but rather the fact of the world being re-activated in a conjoint *act*. In a word, this amounts to recognizing the other as co-constituting.

This is the working hypothesis we want to derive from our examination of Husserl and his phenomenological approach. For the moment it remains purely theoretical and so will have to be confirmed by empirical experimentation. A prejudice in favour of simple causal explanations might lead us to think that it is because we have the ability to change our point of view, and so to put ourselves in the place of the other and see the world from over there, that we can recognize the other as possessing this quite particular status of being a subject in the world, a subject also capable of constituting the world for itself.[66] But think about this. At the level of the constitution of meaning, the relation is the very reverse. It is not because I am able to place myself in the position of the other and so see the world (a world already there and so already constituted) as the other sees it that there is in this world someone other than me. On the contrary, if I am ever to be able to think of the world as already constituted, it is only because it has already been constituted by another subject who co-constitutes it along with me. It is constituted, let us add, by an other who is, initially, precisely not one among other constituted objects (constituted by a solitary subject) in the world but an other altogether, another man or woman, completely different from myself but already equipped with the afferent transcendental prerogatives belonging to a co-constituting subject.

It is this recognition of the other as co-constituting that makes it possible for me, thereafter (in a logical not a temporal order), to put myself in the place of this other; that is, if one wants to allow into scientific discourse expressions drawn from common sense.

---

[66] See the chapter by A. Berthoz in *L'Empathie*: A. Berthoz (2004) Physiologie du change-ment de point de vue, in A. Berthoz and G. Jorland (eds), *L'Empathie*, Odile Jacob, Paris, pp. 251–275.

Conjoint action and conjoint attention

Now we are reaching the really interesting and novel part of our exposition, the part that deals with *shared constitution*, an action with two actors, a *conjoint* action. At last we have an expression anyone can understand. But who can make sense of an expression which, for all that, still remains fashionable in theory of mind, the expression 'shared representation'? In whose mind or brain are we going to place such a representation? Intersubjectivity ('first philosophy' as Husserl calls it) consists of sharing with the other the constitution of the world, even while maintaining the unity of this world.[67]

We think that the behaviour known as conjoint attention, a behaviour which does not appear until the age of one, does, as we have already indicated, provide us with a possible key to this co-constitution of the world.[68]

To be sure, this has to be the same world, the same *Umwelt*, without which the relation with the other would split apart into a multitude of incommensurable solipsistic worlds which would, at the same time, destroy each other. This destruction is precisely what follows from the thesis of subjective relativism,[69] to which any conception of mental life as inclusion, reception, or construction of representations in a mind or brain (taken in isolation) is condemned. And it is considerations such as these that carry us to the heart of Husserl's theory of intersubjective constitution and, in so doing, take us closer rather than further away from the centres of interest of those physiologists who, in raising the problem of the coherence of an agent's experience, will find in the above a motive for extending it to two (or more) agents. The world needs to be coherent for at least two agents because its constitution has been brought about (and never ceases to be brought about) by several agents.

To sum up, *intersubjectivity* is not just simply a matter of establishing a computational correspondence, of having an internal model of what the other

---

67 Without overlooking the fact that the constitution of a common world cannot be reduced to the synchronization of the respective actions of two agents in a shared task, we would like to mention some recent research by G. Knoblich and his team on the paradigm of 'shared representations' that we have been criticizing: N. Sebanz *et al.* (2006) Joint action: bodies and minds moving together, *Trends Cog. Sci.* 10(2), 70–76; N. Sebanz *et al.* (2005) How two share a task: co-representing stimulus-response mappings, *J. Exp. Psychol. Hum. Perception Performance* 31(6), 1234–1246.

68 For conjoint attention see the bibliography above.

69 This thesis can be traced back to Protagoras ('Man the measure of all things') and which haunts modern anthropology: the incommensurability of worlds is to be found in the linguist B.L. Worf's (1956) *Language, Thought and Reality: Selected writings of Benjamin Lee Worf*, J.B. Carroll (ed.), MIT Press, Cambridge, MA.

is thinking. Nor is it just a matter of establishing resonant mechanisms, representations, or what have you, of the other. It is a matter of *taking part in a conjoint action through which there arises a unique world which is, at the same time, a world for several agents.*

In an earlier work,[70] we insisted on the fact that communication between persons is only possible on the basis of a prior construction of the unity of the own body, and a coherence as between different perceptual and motor systems. This theory of coherence now finds a new extension. For in order to construct a common world, it is necessary, first of all, that each agent should have resolved for itself the problem of coherence; but it is also necessary that the mechanisms essential to the construction of such a common world, through conjoint action, should be operative. This means that, in the case of autism, it is not enough to stop at the theory of central coherence. A new theory of co-coherence has to be set up. The observations of Jacqueline Nadel, at the Salpêtrière Hospital, on imitation in children, takes on a capital importance in the light of this idea.[71] If two children playing together are so inclined to imitate each other, it is because they are learning to co-constitute the world through a shared action, the first and most fundamental of the ways in which we become capable of interacting with the other. The extraordinary filmed recordings made by Jacqueline Nadel of her own interaction with autistic children show that the establishment of communication with them sometimes passes via a shared action within a certain physical proximity, a shared gesture and so 'shared kinaesthesia', in the deeper sense of this word, and so not a shared representation or anything implying a theory of the mind.

Recognizing and respecting the other as partner

The phenomenological philosopher is tempted at this point to bring recent discoveries in the neurosciences into closer relation with Husserl's transcendental theory of constitution, understood from the standpoint of the different levels we have sought to distinguish, together with their different perspectives and possible extensions. This approach differs radically from all other methods,

----

[70] See A. Berthoz (2000) *The Brain's Sense of Movement*, Harvard University Press, Cambridge, MA.

[71] J. Nadel (2006) Does imitation matter to children with autism? in S. Rogers and J. Williams (eds), *Imitation and the Social Mind*, The Guilford Press, New York, pp. 118–137; J. Nadel and N. Aouka (2006) Imitation: some cues for intervention approaches in autistic spectrum disorders, in T. Charman and W. Stone (eds), *Social and Communicative Development in Autism Spectrum Disorders*, The Guilford Press, New York, pp. 219–235.

whether logical, psychological, or epistemological, in that it is not limited to analysing objectified totalities out into their constitutive elements with a view to developing, later, a procedure for their logical reconstruction. By going back to an absolutely minimal and so indispensable foundation, we hope to get at operations that are not simply abstract logical operations but acts effectively and concretely realizable by the living, acting, and perceiving subjects that we are inasmuch as we live out our lives in the flux of one and the same lived experience.

This foundation, it will be remembered, is made up solely of adumbrations drawn from the visual or tactile fields, etc., across which phantoms (or pre-percepts) of objects of perception are profiled, along with the kinaesthetic sensations and motor kinaesthesia which, between them, serve to place in perspective and to objectify these phantom objects. And so we were drawn to distinguish between objectifying kinaesthesia responsible for structuring the collections of adumbrations that Husserl calls 'positing' (because the object given through them is placed in perspective) and motor or motivating kinaesthesia, thanks to which the subject experiences itself continually as the source of motor initiatives in its own exploratory or manipulatory development. These kinaesthesiae are themselves responsible for continuous and regular variation in the adumbrations. This variability has to be understood as extending to all the dimensions of the perceptual experience of an agent in the course not only of its visual, but also its tactile and its haptic exploration of the surrounding world.

Given the above, if there is for us something like 'the person of the other' over and above 'this assemblage of flesh and bone', which is the body of the other (Descartes)—in other words, if for us it is meaningful to talk of the other, if, in this sense, there is an other—and if its recognition is not just a concession to the pressures of the social environment, nor reducible solely and exclusively to an ethical problem, given all that, then it is through the contribution made by the other to the process of the transcendental constitution of anything and everything that exists for us that the validity of this assumption (of the existence of the other) is put to the test. Either there is a constitutional partner, or there is nothing at all, hence the temptation to ask whether the reflections contained in this book might not throw light on the mysteries surrounding the negation of the other by fanatics of varying kinds. But we have to be careful not to fall into a *petitio principii* nor yet take refuge in the lofty heights of edification! For I cannot admit and so respect the other if, at the same time, I do not admit that (at the transcendental level) he or she is my 'equal'. That a company director treats his secretary or his cleaner as his equal is something no one is likely to believe. For all that, this does not prevent him from treating them as persons! From time immemorial, we have always wanted to recognize the other as an equal, over and above all the divisions imposed by life in society. It is this profound equality that finds expression in religions, in the statutes of a republic, and in the Declaration of the Universal Rights of Man.

The difficulty is the following: can I accept something like a shared constitution, 'I', the transcendental ego who, since Descartes, remains the epistemic subject of science? Is it even conceivable to push things as far as this ultimate humiliation for the ego, that of discovering that constitution—its very own act— is essentially co-constitution? And so to have to give up my dream of egoistic omnipotence. This is certainly the reason why Husserl tells us that 'intersubjectivity is first in itself' (by comparison with the subjectivity of the ego). Even though he has been accused of putting the subject at the root of everything, his message is that *I am only a subject because there is intersubjectivity.*[72]

To establish the above thesis, Husserl begins by reinstating the Cartesian (therefore solipsist) position. Inevitably (but this inevitability is an ordeal that has to be suffered!) he comes up against the limits of solipsism: the cogito. From there he goes on to secure, not without a struggle, the means to get past this enclosure within the cogito.[73]

Husserl is living witness to the following existential drama: constitution is also, is even first and foremost, an operation that the subject has to carry through concretely. It is not just a conceptual connection, a stylistic literary effect, even less a game played out on paper with written symbols, just as meditation, with Descartes, is also a task to which one has to apply oneself personally. This is the stem upon which we graft our proposal to the effect that there must be biological correlates for the procedure of constitution. Constituting something is a matter of working on and with oneself, struggling against—and finally overcoming— the inertia of one's own system. And the energy expended has to be drawn from one's own resources. This task brings into play structures, which have to be materially inscribed somewhere in the brain of the one engaged in it.

This is why this duplicated constitution, this intersubjective co-constitution, has to be a surpassing of limits, those limits set to any constitution, which would

---

[72] E. Husserl (1973) *Zur Phänomenologie der Intersubjektivität*, I–III, Hrsg. v. I. Kern, Martinus Nijhoff, The Hague; see the commentary in J.-L. Petit (1996) *Solipsisme et Intersubjectivité*, Cerf, Paris.

[73] See his lectures at the Sorbonne of 23–25 February 1922, and especially the fifth and last, which forms the basis of a later presentation at Strasbourg which, by virtue of its length and difficulty, creates difficulties for the entire work: E. Husserl (1960) *Cartesian Meditations*, trans. Dorion Cairns, Martinus Nijhoff, The Hague.

remain purely solipsistic. For some, getting out of solipsism is like dunces 'playing hookie'. They have not understood the drama, the antagonism, the ordeal involved in constitution. Constitution attests to the need not only to attain, but also to relive an ontological foundation, the ultimate ground on the basis of which alone the being of each and every thing in the experienced world can be constructed.

This foundation, which is at first necessarily subjective, still proves to be superficial and so has to be replaced by a still more fundamental intersubjective foundation, a substitution of foundations rendered possible by the discovery that *Einfühlung* is rooted in kinaesthesia which, at the same time, opens up our subjective experience on the other. Even though grounded in the intimate feeling I have for my own movements, *Einfühlung* makes it possible for me to rejoin the other. This immediate accessibility to the other comes not through his or her movements, nor yet through my subjective sensations of his or her movements, still less any 'representation of the goal being pursued'; rather it comes to me across the movements of the other in so far as they are co-constitutive of the meaning of the world. Kinaesthesia then turns out to be my only way of getting out of solipsism. This is the experiential basis upon which the connection between the phenomenology of intersubjectivity and the neurosciences rests.

Constitution by 'co-action'

There are those who, either because of their ignorance of the unpublished manuscripts or on account of their resistance to the transcendental theory of intersubjective constitution, accuse Husserl of having missed the solution to a difficult problem: the paradoxical absence of any unity to the 'I' or 'self' of the perceiving subject, an absence suggested by modern physiology or even by certain Eastern or Western techniques of introspection. That consciousness should lack such a unity matters less when the constituting role of the subject is transferred to kinaesthesia in conjoint action and, by means of the latter, to a constituting intersubjectivity more fundamental than this subject itself. In response to their suspicion regarding the dogma of the unity of transcendental consciousness with Husserl, our response is that this suspicion echoes Husserl's own puzzlement about such unity:

> What is the status of this pure subjectivity, of the identical I of affection [the fact of being affected by a sensorial stimulus], of acts and of feelings? [...] The same world for me – the same I. What kind of identity are we talking about? How could constitution possibly be multifarious?[74]

---

74 See E. Husserl, MS D10 IV (June 1932), Schwierigkeiten der Kinästhese, p. 18.

We have seen that there is no such thing as one unique corporeal schema but rather a multiplicity of internal models (Chapter 7). If it turns out to be the case that the corporeal schema has much to do with the consciousness of self, the inevitable conclusion has to be drawn: that this consciousness of self lacks any such unity. We need to get back to David Hume or, for the lovers of literature, to this rapid succession of states magnificently described by James Joyce in Blum's monologues in *Ulysses*. This vertiginous linkage has been recovered at the neuronal level by Llinás in his *I of the Vortex*.[75] So we should be talking about conscious processes in the plural, which is, moreover, what we have always been doing. It is quite unnecessary to look for a philosophical foil to defend an untruth contrary to evidence so elementary that the scientist can congratulate himself on the fact that his science does not get too far away from common sense.

The same question is taken up by Varela in the chapter on 'The self at the centre of the storm' in *The Embodied Mind*.[76] After having described the succession of states of consciousness making up the 'self', he claims that Kant tried to resolve the problem of the unity of consciousness by creating a 'transcendental ego-self', a notion that can be brought into relation with that of a 'supervisor' in Shallice's sense,[77] and which is more familiar to psychologists. Varela, reinterpreting in his own way, and in a Buddhist perspective,[78] Kant's transcendental consciousness (without reference to his predecessor Schopenhauer) criticizes a conception he is too quick to attribute to Kant and in accordance with which this ego is disconnected from the flux of instantaneous states of consciousness he characterizes as 'impermanent'. The 'self' is in fact for him a transitory 'transcendental state' renewed from time to time by sensible experience. Regarding the question whether Kant really missed this impermanence, it is enough to refer the reader to what we have already said on the subject of his choice of the schema of a line for the representation of subjective time.

---

[75] R.R. Llinás (2001) *I of the Vortex*, MIT press.

[76] F.J. Varela, E. Thompson, and E. Rosch (1991) *The Embodied Mind: Cognitive Science and Human Experience*, MIT Press, Cambridge, MA, p. 59 and on.

[77] Supervisor: attentional system hierarchically dominating a memory system containing the behavioural schemas of the organism. This system activates the schemas relevant to the action underway and inhibits all others. Notice that this hypothesis concerns the motor organization alone and so not the unity of consciousness.

[78] He goes on to be more specific: the tradition emanating from a part of the collections of Buddhist canonical texts, namely the *Abhidharma*, which should not be confused with the *Vinaya*, on the one hand, or with the *Sutras*, on the other.

For us, the constitution (not the 'creation') of this subjective unity of conscious processes has its foundation in action, an action that unites the diversity of processes in question around its own intentionality (strictly speaking, around the practical noetico-noematic polarity).

'Like anything else,' Husserl notes, 'acts also get temporalized. The I that focuses upon the temporal dimension of an act is directed towards a persisting objective unity that is constantly being overlaid with variations derived from the on-going flux of retentional intentionality. An apprehension which, in flowing off (apprehending-retaining), constitutes the actual unity of its result: the "this", this being.'[79]

In the same way, only shared action can unite two subjectivities in one and the same flux of constituting interactions. The co-constitution of the world presupposes not just Varela's 'enaction' but also 'co-action'. We cannot understand the other except by being a 'co-agent' along with him.

The ontogenesis of intersubjectivity and the parable of the outstretched arms

Typical of the genesis of intersubjectivity through kinaesthesia are postures induced by tenderness and which we shall call 'the parable of the outstretched arms' whose unfolding has been filmed by Ajurriaguera[80] and that Van Gogh has so beautifully represented in his painting of the child, the mother, and the gardener. We are talking about these extraordinary sequences of gestures in which mother and child hold their arms out towards each, one after the other, whenever they are at a certain distance from each other.

This all happens around the first year when the child begins to walk, a period when the recently deceased Jean-Denis Degos told us that designation begins and, on the basis of the latter, objectivation.[81] For hours the child can move from its mother to someone else. He always comes back to his mother with his arms outstretched. There is a reciprocal exchange, which ends with a hug, symbolized so magnificently by a statue of Canova (an adult version of the same gesture). Ajurriaguerra grasped intuitively the fundamental—because it

[79] E. Husserl, *MS* BIII9 (October–December 1931), *Das Aktproblem*, p. 86.

[80] In his lecture at the College de France on 'The Corporeal Expression of Emotions', given on 30 January 2002, A. Berthoz chose to show Ajurriaguerra's films on postures of tenderness.

[81] See the chapter by A.C. Bachoud-Levy and J. D. Degos in *L'Empathie* (A.C. Bachoud-Levy and J. D. Degos (2004) Désignation et rapport à autrui, in A. Berthoz and G. Jorland (eds), *L'Empathie*, Odile Jacob, Paris, pp. 89–119).

was constitutive—character of the gesture in establishing, maintaining, and renewing the mother–child relation, and of the unity of the two, which is more than just a sharing: a symbiosis between the child and its mother that lasts throughout its first year. It is a great and universal human affair immortalized in painting by Van Gogh in his *Mother, Child and the Gardener*, and by Picasso, Chagall, and others.

Relating this observation to the philosophical tradition, one might say that the meaning, including the biological meaning, of these gestures, these movements, so also these kinaesthetic sensations, is that they carry us back to a stage prior to individuation. They revive a layer in our sense of ourselves which is pre-individual. Kinaesthesiae have this characteristic of being constitutive because they are individuating.

The sense I have of inhabiting my body intimately, of investing my body with my efforts and my motor intentions in each and every one of my actions, and already even in my postures, is a sense which 'individuates' me, which makes me aware (not without effort, that is, without working at it) that I am an 'individual'. This is what throws light upon these comings and goings of the child who leaves its mother's arms only to come back to them again. He or she takes possession of a personal structure, actively individuates itself. Let us go a little further and venture the suggestion that this acquisition of autonomy is gained by the fact that the child does not simply go towards its mother but alternatively towards its mother, and then towards someone else. The child leaves its mother who, until then was its sole port of call. The intentionality of its act to 'go towards' breaks up in two directions. This presupposes, first of all, an inhibition of the attraction to the mother (inhibit and inhibit yet again, in order to evolve!). Our intuition is that neuronal inhibition certainly has a role to play in the process whereby the child wins its autonomy over fusion (Max Scheler's *Einsfühlung*, criticized by Husserl). For in order to gain the world of the other, it is certainly necessary to suppress, to inhibit, a part at least of our own world.

But above all, the child cannot go towards the other unless it has already drawn the conclusion that it is itself an individual, alone in the world, so that it can choose, change its point of reference. For being itself means no longer perceiving the world from the point of view of the mother. This also presupposes a radical change of point of view, of referential. This is a curious movement that supposes that one must first get away from the other (the mother) in order, thereafter, to be able to be reunited with the other. In Freud, there is, perhaps, too much talk of the mother; but in Piaget, too little.

To sum up: taking the trouble to analyse Husserl's project in some detail—if only to take it in the direction of its naturalization through the neurosciences—means that we shall have to rebuild our psychology of the relation to the other. In order to do this, we have to find an explanation capable of rendering intelligible this apparently direct apprehension of the other. Having said that, we need to take a step back, by showing that, in fact, one can never have a truly direct apprehension of the other, because a part of his experience necessarily remains inaccessible to us, in as much as it takes the form of a perception grounded in an own body. Hence the paradox: on the one hand, we have to get rid of any representational theory, to construct a theory of direct perception; but at the same time, there can be no direct perception since the other cannot be perceived completely.

What we would like to call 'ap-presentation' preserves this twilight zone. The fact that I certainly cannot apprehend the other teaches me that I really have to do with an other, and not to an object I have myself constituted, with the result that one is constantly expecting something new. To take up references which are perhaps more familiar, Husserl makes use of William James' theory of the fringes of consciousness,[82] a theory that is applicable primarily to physical objects. He uses the notion of the 'margin'—'penumbra'—of the field of perception to introduce us to this particular dimension of our perception of the other. For the other is never given to us frontally, only laterally.

But this lateral presentation is not the same as that which prevails with regard to the non-present sides of a physical thing. The other is given to us in such a way that we get to know him or her better and better as a result of our meetings. Just as we get to know an object better by walking around it and getting to know its other sides, so we get to know the other better (without ever knowing him or her completely) to the extent that we spend more and more of our time with him or her; in other words, to the extent that we see the other from other points of view, in other contexts. What is also true is that this ever-deepening understanding of the other is also developed further when we, so to speak, 'historicize' the point of view of the other. And it was precisely this historical dimension to our perception of the other that Dilthey (and the entire hermeneutical theory following from him)[83] helped us to understand.

From the neurophysiological point of view too, this help us to make progress, even if it only offers us a rather shady image: the word adumbrations (*Abschattungen*) already implies a penumbra. This helps us to understand why looking for a 'grandfather neuron', that is, a neuron containing the concept of the other, is absurd. No matter how hard we search we will never find in the brain anything but neurons that can be activated in relation with our

[82] W. James (1890) *The Principles of Psychology*, Holt, New York.

[83] P. Ricoeur (1985) *Time and Narrative III*, trans. K. McLaughlin and D. Pellauer (1988), University of Chicago Press, Chicago, IL.

perception of the other only to the extent that they are themselves recruited in the course of an active exploration of the other. And to grasp this difference we need to understand the following: an exploration cannot be reduced to the brief lapse of time needed to take in the visual scene with our eyes. If this exploration is to be of such a kind that it actually makes possible access to the other, it is essential that it should be prolonged over time into the history of an interpersonal relation.

This is as much as to say that we could never find in Alain Berthoz' head a Jean-Luc Petit neuron, nor in the head of Jean-Luc Petit, an Alain Berthoz neuron. Nevertheless, this does not mean that, on the basis of certain features of Jean-Luc Petit (or of Alain Berthoz) that have been committed to memory, his way of thinking, his way of expressing himself, his facial expressions, and so on, we cannot reconstitute, in our experience at a given moment, something that has already acquired a familiar identity. In support of this idea we need to remind ourselves of Penfield's experiments in subjecting his patients to an electrical stimulation of the brain. The stimulation of the temporal lobe induced 'memories of past experiences' which were genuine reconstructions of episodes actually lived through.

A similar suggestion, one that discounts the possibility of an Epinal imagery theory claiming that we have mental representations of each other, nevertheless opens the way, or so we think, to a new theory of the dynamic of lived experience preserving what is essential in our capacity to identify the other. For this is what is really important. We simply do not live in a confused and on-going flux of sensations (Hume) nor yet in a ready-made and definitive categorization (we won't quote anyone here!) which would make it impossible for us to obtain access to the other, and would only serve as the basis for his or her exclusion. Even if we are now walking into a fog, let us decide to continue walking, we will get there all the same, using such clues as enable us to determine where we are. (A group of artists from Marseilles who constructed installations intended to make their spectators live in environments where their sensible body is pushed to its perceptual limits called their group Clear Fog.)

So the foundation of the relation with the other and of empathy is the possibility of co-constituting a world with the other. For that, it is necessary that the subject should already have constituted its world, that this world should not simply be possible, but also perceptually coherent and kinaesthetically practicable, and that there should already be for him an own body that he perceives as an object in the world: in other words that he (the agent) should have gone beyond the stage of an undifferentiated experience and that he should have become an 'individual'. What we are claiming is that kinaesthesiae play an essential role in the process through which the world is co-constituted by myself and the other. For they allow for the fact that the necessary transformations of this world should be done in a conjoint fashion. As a metaphor for this ontological (ontogenetic) condition of intersubjectivity in action, we would like to remind our readers of the importance of dance movements in the establishment of a body 'common' to all the dancers in a ballet troupe.

Analysis of the Condottiere

At the Louvre, the reader will find among other portraits stemming from the Renaissance, that of the Condottiere, one of those mercenary captains who recruited armies to defend (or pillage) towns like Florence, in particular. This picture is attributed to the painter of the Renaissance, Antonello da Messina, and is supposed to represent the Duke of Bari, Sforza Maria Sforza. Theodor Lipps offers us a way of understanding the fascination this picture evokes in us. More precisely, he underlines the fact that we understand the pride this individual exudes directly, and without having to appeal to any hypothesis and, in particular, without relying upon any theory of mind rooted in analogical inference, the main target of his criticism.

What is meant by the expression analogical inference? Normally, an inference is not analogical but syllogistic. The conclusion is extracted mechanically from the propositions posited as premises. Analogical inference rests upon an analogy, a creative act of the imagination. I know how things go on in others by basing my conclusions upon a transfer, to the other, of something like (the analogy) what I know goes on in me. But since the other is someone different from myself, there is always some risk of error in this transfer, and it is this that makes it impossible to confer upon this inference any demonstrative (apodictic) validity. But it is still a mode of reasoning even though it might not be logically rigorous. If there are other persons for me, this is supposed to be the conclusion of a piece of reasoning (at least according to the theorists of the philosophy of mind). *Einfühlung*, on the other hand, dispenses altogether with any appeal to reasoning. I perceive the other person, the other living being, in short the other, directly. This perception is a direct apprehension. Merleau-Ponty talked of the object being at the end of one's gaze, the object in question here being, of course, the other. What now leaps to mind is the astonishing correlation between the theories the phenomenology of *Einfühlung* sought to refute at the beginning of the last century and the theories currently doing the rounds: theory of mind and so on.

We simply do not need to say: the condottiere here expresses the same things I would have expressed had I been in his shoes. We grasp his pride directly, as a psychic quality. Indeed, what strikes us when we look at this portrait is that the painter has underlined the musculature of the cheek. And in particular one or two muscles. From there, the reader might say to himself: 'I, when I give expression to pride or determination, I too have this contraction of the mouth, which is just the sort of way one forms one's face when one wants to exhibit determination. What strikes me is that when I look at this cheek, by a sort of mirror effect I am empathically affected by a tendency to do likewise.'

Indeed, the reader would be quite right to pay particular attention to the anatomical details of the expression. This is what makes Darwin's *Expression of Emotions* so up to date, he, whose inquiring mind extended to the work of an impressive number of authors, philosophers like H. Spencer[84] and A. Bain;[85] anatomists like Duchenne de Boulogne,[86] P. Gratiolet,[87] and C. Bell,[88] without forgetting Lavater's controversial (not so for Darwin) *Physiognomy*,[89] nor overlooking either the painter Le Brun's *Lectures*[90] or Lessing's observations on the *Laokoön*.[91]

Could one object to Lipps' analysis on the grounds that what this face evokes is not some ephemeral psychic effect of pride? That what it produces in me is, on the contrary, an emotional contagion—like William James' emotional reverberation[92]—an imitation of the face that gives me the impression that I am proud. We know that looking at a smiling face (activating the zygomatic muscles) induces a contraction of the same muscles in the observer. Then we should have to say that I find myself expressing the same thing 'by contagion', and that it is this that induces in me the same feeling. Every one of us can in fact carry through the same experiment. It is enough to adopt a posture or a facial expression of sadness or joy, or even of anger, to experience the corresponding emotion.

Nevertheless, when one analyses a portrait, as the professional physiologist is able to do, accustomed as he is to moving from the sort of aesthetic

84   H. Spencer (1855) *The Principles of Psychology*, Longman, London.

85   A. Bain (1855) *The Senses and the Intellect*, Parker, London; A. Bain (1859) *Emotions and the Will*, Parker, London.

86   Duchenne de Boulogne (1862) *Mécanisme de la physionomie humaine*, Editions de la Maison des Sciences de l'Homme, Paris.

87   P. Gratiolet (1865) *De la physionomie et des mouvements d'expression* J. Etzel, Paris.

88   C. Bell (1806) *The Anatomy and Philosophy of Expression*, J. Johnson, London.

89   J.C. Lavater (1775–1778) *Physiognomische Fragmente zur Beförderung der Menschenkennntniss und Menschenliebe I-IV*, Winterthur, Leipzig.

90   C. Le Brun (1667) *Conférences sur l'expression des différents caractères des passions*, Paris.

91   G.E. Lessing (1766) *Laokoön: oder über die Grenzen der Malerei und Poesie*, Berlin.

92   W. James (1884) What is an emotion? *Mind* 9, 188–205.

contemplation that induces fusion to that sort of withdrawal from the object under consideration that goes along with the investigation of certain aspects of the musculature of the face (whose names he is of course familiar with), what can easily pass unnoticed is the change in attitude. One has taken leave of the attitude characteristic of aesthetic contemplation, an attitude that is 'in resonance' with its subject, with a view to adopting a reflective attitude, which is obviously secondary.

Ledoux, using the example of fear, ventured the hypothesis that two different mechanisms were needed to account for this duality of postures. When we catch sight of a viper, the image of the viper is very rapidly processed by the amygdala (in less than one-tenth of a second), which in turn induces a feeling of fear. But a second mechanism running parallel to the first is also released. More slowly than the first, it brings the image of the snake to the visual cortex and then, from there, to the temporal lobe where the identity of the snake is established, and where its characteristics (for example the fact that its head is or is not triangular) are compared with the memory of different sorts of snake stored somewhere in the brain. And this is how we are brought to realize that the snake is not a viper but an inoffensive grass snake. Our fear is inhibited, and we may even set about capturing the snake! However, it has to be admitted that the debate concerning the relative primacy of the affect[93] or of cognition[94] remains open, and the future may very well show that the functioning of the brain is so very flexible and so dependent upon learning and context, on intention and attention, that both hypotheses may turn out to be true in different circumstances.

The acrobat

After this first group of examples, we can move over to the paradigmatic case of *Einfühlung*: that of the acrobat. This has just recently been the subject of a first collaborative study between physiologists and artists, and which makes use of brain imagery,[95] while a second study devoted to the symmetries to be found in empathy is under way.[96]

---

[93] R.B. Zajonc (1984) On the primacy of affect, *Am. Psychol.* 39(2), 117–123.

[94] R.S. Lazarus (1984) On the primacy of cognition, *Am. Psychol.* 39(2), 124–129.

[95] M. Bret, M.-H. Tramus, and A. Berthoz (2005) Interacting with an intelligent dancing figure: artistic experiments at the crossroads between art and cognitive science, *Leonardo* 38(1), 46–53. M. Bret and M.H. Tramus gave a conference at the seminary of the 2001–2002 course of A. Berthoz at the Collège de France on 'Perception and Emotions' (30 January 2002).

[96] Thesis submitted by Bérangère Thirioux and directed by G. Jorland and A. Berthoz.

The example of the acrobat appears in Lipps' *Grundlegung der Ästhetik*.[97]
While we are following the audacious and perilous movements of the acrobat
on his wire, we feel incipient impulses relating to movements that are not, however, the movements of our own limbs. Watching from the immobile security
of our chairs, we not only follow the movements of the acrobat but also experience these movements in him through identification with him. We put
ourselves in his position, feel ourselves acting through watching his actions.
Through him, we live out his willed activity. And this activity is lived out in the
drama of his performance. Was it appropriate to use the word drama? In this
case, certainly, for it reminds us of the danger to which the artist is exposed in
each of his manoeuvres on the wire as he strives to keep his balance.

But Lipps was not satisfied with this 'subjective' description, that is to say, a
description developed exclusively from the point of view of the subject itself.
For he also proposed the following, a thesis that interests any neurophysiologist interested in anticipation. 'There exists a psychic, or central [or as he says
himself elsewhere, a 'biological'] connection, an original connection that can
be explained no farther, between the optical perception of the movements of
the other and incipient impulses in the direction of the appropriately corresponding movements.'[98]

The example is obviously well chosen. For it highlights the frontier between a
banal theory of internal simulation, a theory that isolates the mental operations
in relation to what happens externally, and a theory that takes account of what
actually happens when, while looking at someone else, we have the feeling of
doing something in him, with him. This is what strikes us when we look at the
acrobat (a computerized replica) constructed by our colleagues at Paris VIII
University, what must have struck Lipps himself, and which strikes everyone else,
notably Gibson[99] when he developed his theory of 'direct' perception. We actually get the impression of being over there, up there. And this brings out the
limits of any theory of simulation. For what is simulated necessarily remains
located in the brain. Simulation does not give us the feeling of being over there.

The results of researchers like Jean Decéty or Julie Grèzes[100] on the observation of movements interpreted in the light of the theory of mental

[97] T. Lipps (1903) *Grundlegung der Ästhetik*, Leopold Voss, Hamburg & Leipzig,
pp. 114–124.

[98] T. Lipps (1903) *Grundlegung der Ästhetik*, Leopold Voss, Hamburg & Leipzig, p. 117.

[99] J.J. Gibson (1966) *The Senses Considered as Perceptual Systems*, Houghton Mifflin,
Boston, MA.

[100] J. Decéty and J. Grèzes (1999) Neural mechanisms subserving the perception of human
actions, *Trends Cog. Sci.* 3, 172–178; J. Decéty (1998) The perception of actions: its putative

simulation,[101] on the one hand, and the internal model[102] theories and the mirror system, on the other, make it possible for us today to see that our brain disposes of mechanisms that set up a little 'tight rope walker in our head'. But is this enough? If we really think through the message conveyed to us by Lipps, we see that his intuition—a third option perhaps—is that we are able to go further than simply simulating mentally the replica of a tight rope walker, that we really are capable of projecting ourselves upon the world. Because we have this ability to be elsewhere than in our own body, to feel something other than our own muscles, we really do succeed in escaping from ourselves, a little like the double,[103] the *Doppelgänger*, and the heautoscopy.[104] This brings out the limits of the theory of simulation, which is restricted to saying: we are going to imagine the movements that are made by others, re-live in ourselves the movements made by players in a game of football. There is something more to it than this: something almost magical.

Transforming things in other minds

Let us see if we can recreate intellectually this possibility of going further than the possibility of re-playing our movements internally, as athletes do in their own mental training. For this construction of the internal equivalent still derives from representation. We are still in a reflective position, that of a spectator with regard to oneself, whereas in *Einfühlung* we forget ourselves altogether. We are projected out into the world, and this is the mystery whose foundations we now have to understand, which has to be elucidated through a neurobiology quite different from that available to us today.

Everything hangs in the balance. If we are wrong, the representationalist we have been criticizing will turn out to have been right. If there is no way of capturing alien intentions! We are each of us locked up in our own brain and—hypocritical anti-dualist protestations to the contrary—Descartes

effect on neural plasticity, in J. Grafman and Y. Christen (eds) *Neuronal Plasticity: Building a Bridge from the Laboratory to the Clinic*, Springer, Berlin. pp. 109–130; J. Decéty *et al.* (1997) Brain activity during observation of actions. Influence of action content and subject's strategy, *Brain* 120, 1763–1777; J. Decéty (1996) Neural representations for action, *Rev. Neurosci.* 7, 285–297.

101   V. Gallese and A.I. Goldman (1998) Mirror neurons and the simulation theory of mind-reading, *Trends Cog. Sci.* 12, 493–501.

102   See the bibliography on internal models in Chapters 5 and 6.

103   A. Berthoz (2004) *La décision*, Odile Jacob, Paris, Chap. VI, pp. 143–151, 168–171.

104   A. Berthoz (2004) *La décision*, Odile Jacob, Paris, pp. 147–148.

was right. We are all solipsists. But we are not obliged to assume this position. For what is in question in *Einfühlung* is more than just an apprehension of something. It is our projection out into the world.

Lipps based this freedom to get out of ourselves on the hypothesis of a first level of integration or self-activation, on the basis of which lived experience would be attributed either to my body or to that of the other. For I live the experience of this body (which is mine) here, and not that of that body there. But remember our thoughts on the own body in Chapter 7. The internal loops are animated by an activity that is not restricted *a priori* to my own body. This would also help to explain why it is that, in dream, one can dream of being oneself, or someone else, or even to be somewhere else. All of this assumes that the contact with the own body has disappeared. And in particular the control over our own movements, which has been effectively blocked.

There are other interesting examples. A tree: whatever can be said about it poetically taps into a range of expressions referring to our bodily experience. What is a tree for us? It is what stretches out its arms just as we stretch out our arms, what grabs the ground with its roots just as we grab hold of something with our hands. The light dawns. We project dynamics. And more than just dynamics, we project efforts that are directed, tendencies to move towards a goal. And this simply by relating to that space 'external to ourselves' which just happens to be occupied by the tree. And without which the tree could not be the being that it effectively is for us.

And because there is a direct connection between the sense of our own worth and a determinate posture, we read an intrinsic sense of worth into art-works or into natural configurations that do not possess any such worth 'by nature'. Another important observation is that our ability to co-constitute the world along with the other—that is, with other living beings—is not simply a competence but a natural propensity which can lead us to transform the world, in order precisely to find in it the equivalent of ourselves!

It leads to this odd behaviour, so strange if one thinks about it, and yet so familiar, which is to transform things into animals or into persons. Listen to a pipe smoker taking about his favourite pipe. It is as if he shared his life with it. It is the same thing with cars. We have all heard people at dusk exclaiming in the presence of a rock: 'It's an elephant' or 'it's a dog or a wolf'. Refusing to admit that bodies in the world are inanimate, we project life upon them, along with the capacity for self-activation. By conferring upon them an animate status, we give them a sense for ourselves. All that is required is that they should have a certain form, enough to start us speculating. In Japanese and Chinese geomancy (the art of installing a building), mountains are dragons: 'the dragon of the North'. Properties of an animate body are attributed to the natural environment. They come alive because we see them in the light of a collection of regularities pertaining to the acting bodies that we are. However, saying that *Einfühlung* is this activity of attributing to the world properties drawn from ourselves is dangerous, if only because attribution stems from judgement, from predication. No, decidedly, we should not be talking about attribution but about living. Living in. Absorption in an experience. Absorption, experience … You see that in order to give expression to all this, we are obliged to rehabilitate a romantic vocabulary: becoming 'absorbed in', 'released into', 'lost in', or 'fulfilled through'; being 'solicited by'; to be in an 'elective affinity with …'. In that it frees us from fixation, a dynamic terminology of this kind is certainly a fluid terminology.[105] One sees the risks one is running. At the same time, we should not expect this kind of intuition to lend itself to conceptual precision.

---

[105] What does not fluctuate is the concept with its terrible *Fregean frontier*, a frontier thus named after the logician G. Frege, who bluntly emphasized the requirements of 'strict delimitation' (*scharfe Begrenzung*), as the condition of the possibility of an expression having meaning. Meaning being taken in the strong sense of reference to an object (for proper names) or to a truth (for sentences). See G. Frege (1892) über Sinn und Bedeutung, *Zeitschrift für Philosophie und Philosophische Kritik* 100, 25–50.

Index